# A History of
# European Housing
# in Australia

This collection of essays is the first systematic attempt to explain the social, administrative, technical and cultural history of 'European' housing in Australia. Written by a collaborative team of scholars from a wide range of disciplines, it explains how Australian housing has evolved from the ideas brought by the first settlers, and what makes Australian housing distinctive in social terms. This book covers a broad range of topics including the ways in which houses reflect social values and aspirations, the relationship between houses and gardens, the home as a site of domestic production and consumption, and an exploration of how housing provides the basis for developing a sense of community. The book will be invaluable for students of urban affairs and those engaged in housing and the design professions, as well as policy-makers and analysts in the public and private sectors.

**Patrick Troy** specialises in urban research at the Australian National University. Previously he has worked as an engineer, town planner, urban researcher and public servant. He is the author and editor of thirteen books on various aspects of Australian urban development, including *Australian Cities* (Cambridge University Press, 1995).

**Dedication**

This book is dedicated to Rita Coles, who in her professionalism, commitment, integrity, generosity and good humour exemplifies all that that is good in research into urban issues in Australia.

# A History of
# European Housing
# in Australia

Edited by
## Patrick Troy
Australian National University

CAMBRIDGE
UNIVERSITY PRESS

PUBLISHED BY THE PRESS SYNDICATE OF THE UNIVERSITY OF CAMBRIDGE
The Pitt Building, Trumpington Street, Cambridge, United Kingdom

CAMBRIDGE UNIVERSITY PRESS
The Edinburgh Building, Cambridge CB2 2RU, UK
40 West 20th Street, New York, NY 10011–4211, USA
10 Stamford Road, Oakleigh, VIC 3166, Australia
Ruiz de Alarcón 13, 28014 Madrid, Spain
Dock House, The Waterfront, Cape Town 8001, South Africa

http://www.cambridge.org

First published 2000

Printed in Australia by Brown Prior Anderson

*Typeface* (New Baskerville) 10.5/12 pt.   *System* QuarkXPress®   [PH]

A catalogue record for this book is available from the British Library

*National Library of Australia Cataloguing in Publication data*
A history of European housing in Australia.
Includes index.
ISBN 0 521 77195 1 hardback
ISBN 0 521 77733 X paperback
1. Architecture and society – Australia – History.
2. Architecture, Domestic – Australia – History. 3.
Europeans – Australia. 4. Architecture, Colonial – Australia.
I. Troy, Patrick N. (Patrick Nicol).
728.0994

ISBN 0 521 77195 1 hardback
ISBN 0 521 77733 X paperback

Contents

FIGURES

PLATES

TABLES

In 1965 the Research School of Social Sciences created the Urban Research Unit to undertake studies of urban Australia. The unit underwent several transformations, first into the Urban Research Program, and finally into the Urban and Environmental Program. Throughout its thirty-five years the unit/program focused on research into urbanisation, planning, the urban environment and infrastructure investment. A major theme was to try to develop a debate about the Australian city and how urban Australia lived. A question in all its work was 'Why?' This meant that we had to ask why Australians were housed the way they were; and why Australian cities took the form they had.

One of the features of debates over public policy in Australia is that too frequently they ignore the history of the issues or phenomena being considered. Nowhere is this more evident than in relation to housing. The unit had conducted a large amount of research into housing, issues and the history of specific aspects of housing, but it suffered for want of a good general understanding of the housing history of the nation. The Urban Research Program resolved to remedy that deficiency and accordingly embarked on a major project to chart the history of the way Australians were housed. This meant that we had to explore the housing histories of the invaders as well as that of the original occupants. This large undertaking was the object of a collaborative effort of scholars from across the nation. Peter Read edited *Settlement: A History of Indigenous Housing in Australia* (AIATSIS). This volume on the history of European housing is the companion book to that enterprise.

The closure by the Research School of Social Sciences of the Urban and Environmental Program marks the further withdrawal by that school from an interest in multi-disciplinary scholarship on Australian society. The closure means that this book is the last product of that school's muti-disciplinary essay into urban research. The role the Urban and Environmental Program and its predecessors played in trying to co-operatively, collaboratively develop debates in which scholars from different regions and disciplinary perspectives could contribute to the elucidation and better understanding of Australian urban issue, which this book exemplifies, is now at an end.

When it commenced its research, the Urban Research Unit faced a situation where there were few texts by Australians about Australian cities and their peculiarities and problems. We now face a situation where there is a substantial body of published scholarship on them. We can claim that the range of interests and diversity of perspectives in this book fits well in that tradition and, indeed, may been seen as an apposite point at which to take a pause. The Research School of Social Sciences may never resume an organised or systematic muti-disciplinary interest in urban and environmental issues but we may be sure that, so long as Australia remains an urban nation, urban and environmental concerns will remain at the centre of political, social and economic life in Australia. By attempting this first study of the development of European housing in Australia, we hope we are setting the framework for the next phase in the development of our understanding of what gives Australian cities their distinctiveness; it may help us understand what we want to preserve, and why. We hope that the book stimulates research and helps develop better, more informed policy about housing in Australia. We also hope that its publication will mark a renaissance of a national interest in multi-disciplinary research into urban and environmental issues.

Patrick Troy

This book is the product of a large collaborative exercise which ran over a long xi period. The authors are individually and collectively indebted to two anonymous reviewers, together with the comments made by Max Neutze, Tim Bonyhady and Peter Self. My colleague Nicholas Brown not only wrote a chapter but generously and importantly helped keep the whole project on an even keel at times when it seemed it would founder. Phillipa McGuinness, Peter Debus, Paul Watt and Janet Mackenzie all gave support, encouragement and criticisms in appropriate proportions and for which I am grateful. Coralie Cullen and Christine Cannon both made significant contributions to the production of the book, and Libby Conrick rose to the challenge to produce an index when all seemed impossible. But the greatest debt is owed to Rita Coles who, through the dramatically changing fortunes of the Urban and Environmental Program and the destabilising, diverting energies of some of the more primitive minds in the Australian National University managed to keep track of everyone and everything while maintaining her sanity and grace.

**Conversions**

LENGTH

1 inch = 25.4 mm
1 foot = 30.5 cm
1 yard = 0.9 m
1 mile = 1.6 km

MASS

1 pound = 454 g
1 ton = 1.02 t

AREA

1 acre = 0.4 ha

VOLUME

1 cubic yard = 0.7 $m^3$

CURRENCY

There were 12 pennies (d) in one shilling (s), and 20 shillings in one pound (£). When Australia converted to decimal currency in 1966, $2 were equal to £1.

**Blair Badcock** is a Reader in Geography at the University of Adelaide with teaching and research interests in urban and housing studies.

**Nicholas Brown** is a Research Fellow in the Urban and Environmental Program, Australian National University, completing a biography of R. I. Downing and working on a social and environmental history of south-eastern New South Wales.

**Graeme Davison** is Professor of History at Monash University. He is the author of *The Rise and Fall of Marvellous Melbourne* (1978), and *The Unforgiving Minute* (1994), and co-editor of *The Oxford Companion to Australian History* (1998).

**Tony Dingle** is Associate Professor, Department of Economics, Monash University. His research interests are in urban and environmental history.

**Robert Freestone** is Associate Professor, Faculty of the Built Environment, University of New South Wales.

**Lionel Frost** is a Senior Lecturer in the School of Business, La Trobe University.

**Alastair Greig** is a Senior Lecturer in the Department of Sociology, The Faculties, Australian National University, and author of *The Stuff Dreams Are Made Of: Housing Provision in Australia, 1945–1960* (1995).

**Graham Holland** is an Honorary Associate in the Faculty of Architecture at the University of Sydney, where he taught construction for many years. His major research interest has been the production of housing and particularly the activities of owner-builders. He is working on a history of owner-building in Australia from 1945 to 1960.

In 1987, **Katie Holmes** co-ordinated a local history project on Carlton, Victoria, which produced a series of booklets: 'Among the Terraces'. She now lectures in women's studies and history at La Trobe University.

**Chris Kynaston** is Lecturer in Sociology at the McAuley Campus of the Australian Catholic University and currently undertaking a project on women's role in sourcing of household income in Australia and Britain.

**Miles Lewis**, Architectural historian, Reader in Architecture at the University of Melbourne, Vice-President of the Comité International d'Architecture Vernaculaire, Fellow of the Australian Academy of Humanities.

**Clem Lloyd**, Foundation Professor, Graduate School of Journalism, University of Wollongong.

xiv   **Susan Marsden** has written several commissioned histories and heritage studies relating to Australian housing. She is presently National Conservation Manager at the Australian Council of National Trusts and a Visiting Fellow at the Urban and Environmental Program, Australian National University.

**David Merrett** works in the Department of Management at the University of Melbourne where he is an Associate Professor. He has published widely on Australian financial institutions and once dabbled in urban history.

**Glenn Mitchell** is a lecturer in science and technology studies and communication and cultural studies at the University of Wollongong. His research interests include history of medicine, biotechnology and environmental history.

**Patrick Mullins** is Reader in Sociology at the University of Queensland and currently involved in an Australian-South Korean collaborative project on consumerism and sustainable development.

**Mark Peel** works in the School of Historical and Gender Studies at Monash University.

**Patrick Troy**, AO, Professor and Head of the Urban and Environmental Program, Australian National University.

**Kimberley Webber** is the senior curator of social history at Sydney's Powerhouse Museum. She has developed a wide range of exhibitions on topics as diverse as Arnott's biscuits, postwar migration to New South Wales and the development of the film *Strictly Ballroom*. In 1996 she completed her doctorate on the introduction of technology into the Australian home, *Romancing the Machine*.

# Introduction

## HOUSE AND HOME

*Patrick Troy*

In the two centuries since invasion, European Australians have built cities with a distinctive form of housing. The colonists stepped ashore with a set of inherited regulations and construction processes, and clear ideas of what constituted a house. They were immediately frustrated by the shortage of familiar, traditional materials and of skilled labour to build houses to meet their ambitions. They early endured all manner of privations as they sought to re-create in this alien climate and environment the comforts of home as they had known them. They also faced a situation where the availability of land and the disposition of activities was quite unlike anything any of them had experienced. Initially, the design and form of housing was heavily influenced by the composition of households, responsibilities and behaviour of household members, the prevailing social values, behaviour, attitudes to and aesthetic values of, the institutional context, technological development and practices of the northern European colonists—specifically those from England, Scotland, Wales and Ireland.

We have had many splendid histories of the early years of colonisation and of individual houses and architectural styles. There has, however, been little scholarship directed to an understanding of the social history of Australian housing—that is, the full and complete range of intersections between the house as built form and home, and the material, technological, economic, regional and cultural contexts which surround it. This volume is part of a project designed to focus attention on the Australian house as a home in the hope that it leads to a better understanding of why 'the Australian house' is distinctive and, by extension, how Australian cities developed their form.

A history of Australian housing which did not embrace the history of the accommodation of its indigenous people would be incomplete and misleading. Another book, *Settlement*, dealing with the housing of indigenous Australians, edited by Peter Read, has been published as the first part of the project.

The two books in this project are each the product of a collaborative enterprise. Each is the outcome of a series of exchanges and workshops involving the contributors and a large number of critics. Each has the strengths and weaknesses of such co-operative, iterative processes undertaken by independent scholars across the nation. These books do not claim an exhaustive coverage, but they do present diverse and fresh perspectives which, in opening a kind of conversation, might stimulate further thinking about the homes Australians have made.

There are some obvious areas which are not addressed here, both because a complete treatment of the topic is beyond the compass of one book, but also because the focus is on tracing the Australian house and home as both the stereotype and the dominant and distinctive form: the free-standing, family-defined residential unit, primarily in an urban or suburban environment. This book makes only passing reference to multi-unit dwellings or flats, not because they are not important forms of accommodation but because this form has only become significant in relatively recent times.

In place of an all-inclusive ambition, the essays in this book have concentrated instead on refining a selection of issues, including:

- the socio-spatial arrangement of houses
- the materials of which houses were built
- the mode of construction and technological evolution of houses
- how houses reflect the social values and aspirations of their owners (a majority of them have been occupied by their owners)
- the relationship of houses to their gardens, and their importance as sites of domestic production as well as consumption
- the services that houses need to be part of or connected to the city
- the way houses were paid for and how their ownership signified an illusion of egalitarianism
- houses as the shell for the development of a sense of community, of neighbouring, but simultaneously affording the privacy households seek.

The issues of the politics of housing and housing policy are only briefly touched on. We would be disingenuous, however, if, as a collaborative group of scholars, we did not acknowledge our belief, hope and ambition, that a better understanding of our housing history would ultimately be reflected in better housing policy. This is the cornerstone belief of all scholars who think that, once they have satisfied their curiosity and first known the nature of things, their work might not only entertain but also inform those who wish to change the world for the better.

The book does not set out to provide a chronological account of the Australian house, although the themes selected deal chronologically with the major issues and periods of stress and consolidation. Some periods appear to be covered more fully than others and, of course, there are significant overlaps. The explanation for this is that we have selected themes and periods which typify the historical trajectory of housing in Australia. The rate of progress or development in any field of activity is not uniform. The rate and direction of

2

development or evolution of houses is particularly uneven, depending as it does on the changes in the availability of materials, on technological advancement, on changes in household composition and behaviour, and on changes in attitudes and expectations. Against these fluctuating dynamics and influences, the durability of houses means that over their long lives they are used by different households in different ways. A house which is perceived to provide ideal accommodation in one period is seen to be inadequate or unfashionable in another. That is, a house may be structurally unchanged from the time it was built and have undergone few modifications, but its history will be different according to who took shelter in it and made themselves comfortable. The relationship between the relative durability of the 'house' and the layered history of 'home' is at the core of this book, one of the central themes running through all the chapters.

The introductory context reminds us of the prehistory of the Australian house. In Chapter 1 Graeme Davison explores the preference for single-family houses but also discusses the kinds of housing the colonists from different regions of Britain sought in Australia. This account of the demand for single-family owner-occupied houses covers a later period, but it gibes well with the earliest initiatives of Governor Phillip who sought to ensure that the form of housing in the new colony was one house on an allotment of 60 feet frontage and 150 feet deep. Phillip's initiative set the tone for what became characteristic of the style of housing and the form of Australian urban development.

In Chapter 2 Susan Marsden offers an exploration of the regulatory framework imported in the baggage of Governor Phillip, along with his prefabricated house, and applied throughout the colony. The discussion sketches the different evolution of building regulations over the next century and a half in the states. This evolution covered the progressive introduction of regulations covering fire, safety, health and amenity that influenced the form and design of housing. Many of the regulations were based on 'scientific' theories such as the miasmatic theory of disease transmission. The book concludes with Patrick Troy's discussion of the evolution over the last half century of a set of uniform building regulations applying throughout Australia and indicates the way in which the new regulatory regime will affect the future development of housing. That is, the history recounted here records the history of the institutions which affect the style of houses as much as that of the houses themselves and the way they become homes.

Within this institutional framework, Chapters 3–5 by Miles Lewis, Tony Dingle and Glenn Mitchell explore the ways in which the colonists made do, how they used local materials and adapted the building conventions and techniques they imported from England, how they used new materials and new construction techniques, the way they were forced to build their own houses and how this became an option for households of small means. Owner-built housing in Australia became the ultimate expression of 'if you want something done cheaply and properly (but not quickly), do it yourself'. These chapters discuss the extent to which housing constructed by its occupants has, from the

3

outset, been the domestic creation of national capital, literally creating the hearth and the wealth of the nation. Whether or not housing was paid for by the sweat equity of its owner-builders, the story of how we paid for it and what measures governments take to facilitate house construction and home ownership remain a topic of social and political discussion.

In Chapters 6 and 7 by Kimberley Webber and Nicholas Brown the book progresses through a discussion of the transformation of houses, including the differentiation and arrangement of rooms, the development and equipment of the kitchen. Chapters 8–10 by Robert Freestone, Patrick Mullins and Chris Kynaston, and Katie Holmes go on to discuss how people made themselves comfortable and consider the house in its garden, including the house and garden itself as an important site of domestic production as well as characteristic of the form of urban Australia. A house cannot exist as an island: in order to function it must be connected to the range of urban services available in the city. Lionel Frost and Graham Holland in Chapters 11 and 12 explore those connections and also the 'connections' houses make with their environment or the way people take environmental factors into account in building and using their houses.

4          Home ownership in Australia has always been at a high level—higher than in comparable developed countries. Chapter 14 by David Merrett explains how we paid for our houses. The ownership of homes of reasonable quality has almost been enshrined as a right of citizenship. Blair Badcock in Chapter 15 helps us understand how home ownership helps define and give apparent substance to the myth of the egalitarian nature of Australian society. No history of housing would be complete without consideration of those who fail to find accommodation in the conventional sense. These are the people who are homeless, who for some period of their life find they cannot cope. Chapter 17 by Clem Lloyd discusses how their needs for shelter are met as a measure of the way Australian society subscribes to humanitarian ideals.

The story of housing is, in part, one of adaptation to changed circumstances, but it is also one of the ways in which Australians chose to reflect their wealth and self-image. The famous Federation House can be seen as local expression of national sentiment at the time of the founding of the nation. The style was and is highly regarded for its aesthetic values, but in many cases it is a style which produced houses with rooms which were poorly lit. We can only speculate whether similar national sentiment will result in a Republican House, and if it does what it will be like and how much notice its builders take of the environment. Will it be a postmodern pastiche? Do we see its forerunners in the housing on the Gold Coast or the large peripheral estates of suburban Australia? Will it be energy-efficient? How would we know?

It is a commonplace that houses reflect the aesthetic and other values of their occupants. Alastair Greig in Chapter 13 explores the changes in house style at different times as reflections of the fads and fashions of society at those times. This story also recognises that a house is not a home and a community is more than a collection of dwellings. Mark Peel in Chapter 16 tells the story of the desire for, and expression of, community and neighbourliness as an integral part of the Australian dream.

A study of our houses and the way we make homes of them is a study of the structure and nature of Australian society and the way we project ourselves to the world: it goes to the heart of notions of citizenship. We have, since invasion, improved our structures and their durability.

For more than a decade political leaders have been trying to change the form of Australian housing (and of Australian cities). Residents have been remarkably resistant to those changes. This book will help those trying to understand the historical origins and cultural strength of that resistance.

# Colonial Origins of the
# Australian Home

## Chapter 1

*Graeme Davison*

6    Few words in the lexicon of colonialism are more resonant than the word 'home'. Home—often spelt with a capital H—denoted the lands from which the colonists had come. 'Almost everybody in this land calls Great Britain *home*', noted James Backhouse in 1839, and a century later the usage was still common. Home, however, also had a more immediate reference point in the dwellings which successive generations of immigrants built in Australia. 'They call houses homes in Australia', an observant English visitor noticed in 1937, emphasising the large emotional investment Australians made in their dwellings.[1] Home was thus both an idea and a place, an object of affection located far away, in the homeland from which most colonials had come, and near at hand, in the houses which they had built in the new country. These new homes were shaped by pressures of both emulation and avoidance: a desire, on the one hand, to reproduce loved and familiar styles and patterns of life; and, on the other, to escape the crowding and poverty of houses which were no longer home-like. A history of Australian housing may properly begin by exploring this formative relationship between homeland dreams and the character of the colonial house.

    Like echoes of a past life, the homeland experiences of Australia's immigrants continued to shape the society they created on the other side of the world. They carried with them notions of property, family and independence which they had learned in the land of their birth. The architectural forms in which these aspirations were expressed in Australia may have been different—as different as weatherboard bungalows from thatched cottages—but the aspirations themselves were largely those instilled by their forebears. Because the past life of the immigrant is largely hidden, like the submerged seven-eighths of an iceberg, its influence often escapes the colonial historian. The materials to reconstruct the process of acculturation to the new land are hard to come by. Often we can reconstruct it only conjecturally, by matching the demographic and social traits of the group from which the immigrants were drawn, the cultural characteristics of the home society, and the characteristics of the new.

From the 1820s wealthy Australian colonists had begun to emulate the architectural fashions of their English counterparts, notably the romantic Gothic or Italianate villa popularised by John Claudius Loudon and his *Suburban Gardener and Villa Companion*.[2] Even into the twentieth century the style of the Australian house continued to emulate the villa ideal. But style, in the scholarly sense, may have been a less powerful influence on the character of the Australian house than the popular customs and beliefs about home and homeliness which the colonists brought with them. We need to rewrite the history of Australian housing from the inside out: beginning, not with architectural styles, or the technologies of construction, but with the underlying convictions about domestic life which shaped people's ideas of home.

The founders of urban Australia, from the convict era to World War II, were mainly drawn, not from the villa-owning classes, but from those mobile sections of the British working class that had contributed most to the urbanisation of Britain itself. The decision to seek a new life in Australia was often the last step in a journey that had already led the emigrant, by stages, from a village or provincial home to London, Liverpool or Glasgow. The homes these emigrants created in the new land were based on those essentially British ideals which the cities of the homeland had nurtured, but which they denied to the majority of their inhabitants.

Australia, to use the language of Louis Hartz, was a 'fragment society'. A distinctive part of the Old World had been transplanted to a new and more hospitable environment, where its inner potential could unfold without the inhibitions and conflicts that had curbed its growth at home. The character of the 'fragment' was defined, not only by the historical moment of its plantation (the United States in the late eighteenth century, Australia during the first half of the nineteenth), but by the distinctive social and geographical origins of the immigrants who implanted it. In his essay on Australia in Hartz's *The Founding of New Societies*, Richard Rosecrance identified the immigrant parents of modern Australia as 'a homogeneous group of city folk of humble economic and social origins' who had been drawn especially from among the '"residue" who could not go to North America'.[3]

Although it is indeed instructive to compare the characteristics of the emigrants who voyaged to the antipodes with the exodus to North America, it is not entirely accurate to regard them as being defined by their *inability* to join the larger transAtlantic migration. In some periods, it would almost be more accurate to regard the North American emigrants as those who were unable to get to Australia. In the early 1850s, when the gold rushes made Australia briefly the main destination for British emigrants, a government official noted that 'In the last two years there has sprung up a spontaneous emigration of the labouring classes to Australia, but they are by no means the poorest labouring class,

7

like those who go to America, as is evident from the mere fact that they pay a considerable sum for their passage.'[4] Throughout much of the nineteenth century, in fact, it cost about four times as much, and took three times as long, to get to Australia as it did to get to the United States. In order to recruit sufficient labour, and to compete with the nearer attractions of North America, the Australian colonial governments were obliged to offer assisted passages to the great majority of newcomers.

The broad effect of these arrangements was to compress the stratum of British and Irish society from which the Australian immigrants were recruited. Although Australia attracted relatively few of the skilled industrial workers whose labour was in high demand in the United States, the emigration agents who scrutinised applicants for assisted passages effectively excluded the most illiterate and unskilled of the working classes. Unskilled Australian immigrants were most likely to describe themselves as 'agricultural labourers'; and North Americans simply as 'labourers'; but since agricultural labour was what the Australian Emigration Commissioners sought, applicants for assisted passages probably described themselves as such, whatever their occupational experience. 'Many of them I believe have come out under false representations; they have got recommendations as farm servants, and have been shipped as such, but they do not prove to be of that class when they come here; they come chiefly from towns as mechanics or labourers', a Sydney street missionary believed.[5] So far as one can judge from these defective occupational returns, unskilled labourers formed a smaller proportion of the Australian than the American outflow, and were relatively least prominent during the booms of the 1850s and the 1880s, when the cities grew most rapidly.[6]

## England

Emigration to Australian cities in the nineteenth century was dominated by three broad streams from England, Scotland and Ireland. The largest came from London itself or originated in southern England and came by way of London. Emigration statistics do not enable us to establish precisely the regional origins of the Australian inflow, much less the urban component of it, but there are many less formal evidences of its strength. The English-born were the largest component of the mid-nineteenth-century Australian elite, and more than half of these were from London or southern England.[7] About half the English exodus to Australia seems to have originated in London, or originated in the south-eastern counties of England, and migrated, often in stages, to London before embarking for the colonies.[8] The emigrants seem to have been drawn from that mobile, ambitious but 'uneasy' stratum of the British working class which congregated, so far as we can locate it precisely, in zones of insecure craft or semi-skilled labour on the inner perimeter of London and other large towns. Many belonged to the groups described by Charles Booth, in his famous survey of London and its poor, as Classes D and

E, the earners of small but relatively regular wages. 'There are some of them', Booth noted, 'who, when wages are near the lower figure, or the families are large, are not lifted above the line of poverty; but few of them are *very poor*, and the bulk of this large section can, and do, lead independent lives, and possess fairly comfortable homes.'[9] Poor but not destitute, unskilled but not unresourceful, they had much to gain, and little to lose, by leaving the country that gave them birth. Few seem to have improved their prospects since arriving in the metropolis and some had fallen down the social scale.[10] It is reasonable to suggest, with Douglas Pike, that their decision to emigrate was precipitated by 'unsatisfactory urban experience'.[11] We may picture them as mobile, marginal individuals, carrying folk memories of a departed age of rural independence, and living within sight, but not yet within reach, of the suburbs emerging on the fringes of the metropolis.

London exerted a strong influence upon the way in which Australians thought about home. Consider, for example, the evidence of Australian place names. Australia's capital cities have many suburbs named after the capital's leafy satellites—Richmond, Paddington, Kensington, Camberwell and Ascot—but very few after the more densely settled neighbourhoods from which the immigrants had probably come—Stepney, Whitechapel, Clerkenwell and Bethnal Green. Their eyes, and ideals, were already trained on the rural hinterland rather than the city itself. The row-house, often modelled on the London terrace, would become an important feature of the colonial city, though less so as the century unfolded.

The political dreams of mid-nineteenth-century workingmen of almost all political persuasions incorporated the idea of small-scale, usually rural, land ownership. In a world where property conferred political rights, and aristocratic privilege was inseparable from the aristocratic monopoly of land, it was natural for reformers, both radical and liberal, to see the redistribution of property and the widening of political rights as inseparably bound. As early as the late eighteenth century working men in northern towns like Leeds had formed building clubs, pooling their savings and drawing lots for the privilege of taking the first loan, as a means of securing their own freehold cottages.[12] In 1842 the fiery Chartist leader Fergus O'Connor argued that, instead of relying on middle-class benevolence to achieve the franchise, working men might achieve it themselves by joining together in a freehold land scheme that would enable them to qualify for the forty-shilling franchise.[13] As an Irishman, O'Connor had an instinctive sympathy with ideas of peasant ownership. 'Whether we look at ancient or modern nations, we find that general contentment and competence has ever been the concomitant of small proprietorship, and that pauperism and all its accompanying evils has followed the monopolising of the soil by a few', asserted O'Connor's *National Instructor* in 1851. The Chartist Land Plan promoted by O'Connor in the late 1840s—which produced several experimental village communities, one at Watford on the outskirts of London—was one flawed attempt to put this ideal into practice. O'Connor saw small-scale landownership as an antidote to the ills of industrialism. If the land were redistributed, and aristocratic pleasure grounds turned over to 'spade-culture', there would be no further talk of pauperism or surplus population, for the increased productivity of the soil would be enough to support everyone. 'Home-colonisation', as such schemes were called, was sometimes presented as an alternative to foreign emigration.[14] It was a flawed alternative, said some critics, arguing that the only real prospect of freehold ownership for most British working men was in the colonies. 'It is there only that the bulk of our people can hope to exchange for the uncertainty of subsistence in the land of their birth, a probable means of gathering together a freehold land and a patrimony for their children', declared the London *Builder*, dismissing the land societies as a creation of 'designing men' more concerned for their own benefit than their shareholders'.[15]

O'Connor's dream of creating a modern peasantry was doomed, not only by his own deeply flawed leadership, and the economic and social crisis of the late 1840s that all but destroyed the Chartist movement, but by its own internal contradictions. By the early 1850s only one or two of the string of rural villages O'Connor had planted across southern England, survived. But the ideal of small-scale landownership did not die, although it may have taken on a more privatised and pragmatic character. By 1853 new freehold land societies were springing up along the London fringe at Putney, Ealing, Wandsworth and Wood Green. Rather than O'Connor's romantic, backward-looking, communal ideals, the land and building societies harnessed the more limited and prudential aspirations of an independent, self-improving lower-middle and working class. Their aim was 'to facilitate the acquisition of freehold land, and the erection of houses thereon,—and to enable such of its members as are eligible, to obtain the county franchise,—and to afford all of them a secure and profitable investment for money'. It was an ideal of economic and political independence which was increasingly linked, in the minds of its supporters, with the sanctuary of the detached suburban house.[16] 'Why should not the labouring man endeavour, in the intervals of relaxation from toil, to get away from the noise, and smoke, and dirt of of a dingy town, and to breathe the purer atmosphere of the suburbs?', a 'Labouring Man' from Bradford asked readers of the *Builder*.

In his popular tract *Happy Homes and How to Get Them* (1866), the Free Church clergyman and housing reformer James Begg set out the moral and political rationale of the building society movement. He drew strongly on the moral inheritance of the Evangelical revival, with its exaltation of the ideal of Home ('The idea of Home, with all its delightful associations, its concentrated power and far-reaching influences, is as certainly of Divine origin as the existence of man himself'), as well as the anti-aristocratic and self-improving ideals of mid-Victorian liberalism. Home ownership was both a blow for individual self-improvement ('The very struggle to rise in the world by the acquistion of property, in which working men are thus called to engage, is a thoroughly wholesome one') and a blow against class division. It endorsed the acquisition of property, but it also challenged aristocratic power.

It will be found that wherever you have a few persons possessing the great mass of the houses in which others reside, you have a society divided into two great classes—a class of capitalists, and a class who may virtually be called serfs; and so long as the mass of the people live in houses belonging to other men, so long will you look in vain for that spirit of universal independence which it is so desirable to cherish on the part of the mass of the community. If you have men living in their own houses, you will have independent men, but if you have a multitude of them living in the houses of other people, you will find that there exists a comparatively degraded population, because this kind of poverty and serfdom will be found to go hand in hand.[17]

To understand the contemporary resonance of the idea of 'independence' and its linkage to the idea of home ownership, we must appreciate the multiple forms of dependence which it promised to overcome. Begg enumerated four great benefits of home ownership.

First, it gave working men security in their old age and a legacy to their widows and children. In an era before state pensions, old age and death were a frightening prospect and a scarcely brighter reality. To be able to leave a secure home to one's kin was to confer not just a financial bonus but, in all probability, a ticket out of the poorhouse. Second, under the county franchise, house ownership conferred the right to vote; it made a man a citizen. To be a freeholder, to have a 'stake in the country' was the traditional basis of membership in the political nation. It was not until the *Second Reform Act* of 1867 that male English householders were granted the suffrage. The Australian colonies would grant the suffrage to all adult males by the mid-1850s, but voting for municipal councils and for the colonial upper houses was limited by a property qualification until the mid-twentieth century. Third, ownership increased the owner's social status and self-respect; or, to put it the other way about, it lessened the obligation of deference. And, finally, by encouraging thrift and frugality, ownership was an 'incentive to rectitude of conduct and formation of correct habits'. To the early Victorians, who looked upon vice as a form of enslavement, the virtues encouraged by the process of obtaining a house were almost as important as the economic, social and political benefits.

Not everyone, not even every working man, supported the idea of working-class home ownership. Owning or buying a house was both a benefit and a burden. In London, where casual and seasonal employment was more the rule than the exception, being tied to the one house could handicap the householder in his search for work. 'If a man follows an occupation the locus of which changes from time to time, it is a very convenient thing indeed for him to be able to live near his work. If he was the owner of his house he would be to a certain extent tied to the one locality, and that might be very inconvenient.'[18] The more secure a man's employment, the more likely that he would want, and could afford, a house of his own. 'Those who are in constant work turn their thoughts to the acquisition of a house in which to live, and are more thrifty than the wandering workman, who takes his tools on his back, and lives first in one place and then in another', the MP for Woolwich, in south London, observed. Renting rather than buying was a matter of necessity rather than preference, he thought. 'They have to follow their work, of course, in a great many cases, but it is not by any desire on their part.'[19]

Whether they wanted to be owners or not, the stark reality was that only a tiny minority of English city-dwellers managed to attain ownership. The best estimates suggest that no more than 10 per cent of dwellings in English cities were owner-occupied, and that in the larger cities like London and Birmingham the proportion was even smaller, as low as 1 or 2 per cent.[20] From the 1840s onwards ideals of petty proprietorship had a stronger hold on the British working-class imagination than romantic ideas of suburban retreat. A home of one's own, however humble, was more attractive than rose gardens and Gothic architecture. But the gap between ideal and reality was also larger. Emigration promised to close that gap, but it arguably did even more to advance the prospect of home ownership than the suburban way of life.

From the gold rushes of the 1850s to World War II and beyond, the home and garden ideal was a favourite theme of Australian immigration agents and pamphleteers. 'What can I gain by going to Victoria?', asked James Ballantyne, anticipating the question of his working-class readers. 'He will be able, whether by economy or saving, or through the help of one of the numerous building societies, to secure a comfortable freehold for himself and thus possess what every Englishman glories in—a house which will be *his castle.*'[21] Almost a century later, the yearning for home ownership was just as strong among British working-class emigrants. A survey of British emigrants to Australia in 1959 found that over 90 per cent of couples aspired to become home owners, even though fewer than one-third had been owners in their homeland.[22]

Immigrant letters often testified to the newcomers' ambition to acquire their own homes and to their success in achieving it, using language that emphasised their aspirations to 'independence' and 'respectability'. 'I am determined to buy a piece of land shortly and I intend joining the building society', a newly arrived carpenter wrote to his wife from Melbourne in 1850. 'I will Endeavour to purchase about an Acre of Land on one of the Townships so that it will at all times be your Own and a home as long as you live', promised another.[23] The suburbs created by the working-class immigrants of the 1850s were very different from the bourgeois utopias of contemporary London or, indeed, from the first villa suburbs of Sydney and Hobart. The free, skilled immigrants of the 1850s, often imbued by Chartist ideals of small proprietorship and respectability, and lured by the prospect of rapid social mobility, had given the once-aristocratic suburban idea a radical democratic twist. In terms of health and beauty, and perhaps of social amenity as well, the Australian frontier suburb may have represented no great improvement upon the cities of the old country; but in the eyes of its immigrant inhabitants, fleeing the oppression of landlords and craving homes of their own, it was a kind of paradise.

The suburbs created by the newcomers were as much a filling out of respectable British working-class ideals as a filtering down of middle-class ones.

**Plate 1.1** Central Brunswick, Melbourne, corner Sydney Road and Albert Street looking south, 1866. (La Trobe Picture Collection, State Library of Victoria)

While offering a new sense of privacy and proprietorship, they were also a characteristic product of British working-class traditions of self-help and co-operation. Charles Booth had described the middle stratum of the London working class, from which so many Australian urban immigrants had been recruited, as 'the recognized field of all forms of cooperation and combination'.[24] Friendly societies and building societies enabled working people to utilise their collective means to enhance their individual security and prosperity. To immigrants, no longer able to rely on the informal help of kin and neighbours, the friendly society was an indispensable source of assistance in times of sickness or bereavement. 'In combinations like these there was much greater security in moving from place to place', noted an official of the Rechabites, a temperance friendly society.[25] Building societies flourished, especially among the working classes of the industrial north and midlands. 'The great bulk of them are composed of working men, and they are the most popular institutions we have in the town', boasted the official of a Birmingham society.[26] In London their clientele had gradually widened and by the 1870s was said to comprise 'the lower and middle classes'.[27]

As popular as the institutions of co-operative thrift were in the land of their birth, they flourished even more luxuriantly in the lands to which they were transplanted. The first Australian societies continued to stress the link between property ownership and political rights. 'Where freeholds are obtained, political rights go with them, and therefore when we look upon the free and open field that now lies before these societies in this colony, compared with those of our fatherland, we may reasonably expect results of tenfold advantage', a Melbourne building society official predicted in 1850. Once manhood suffrage had been attained in the mid-1850s, the formal link between home ownership and the vote was weakened, yet home ownership was still believed to make a man a better citizen. By giving him an interest in the state, building societies were bulwarks against the 'Levellers, Socialists and Red Republicans' who might seek to overthrow it.[28] Building societies enjoyed such a vogue during the 1850s and 1860s that towards the end of the decade, as the flow of immigrants abated, there were fears that the market had been saturated. 'The establishment of building societies is one of the most valuable of the cooperative institutions that we possess; but is it not possible that the institution may be worked to death?', asked the Melbourne *Building Times* in 1869.[29] In 1874, when there were 9.3 building society members per thousand in England and Wales, there were 25.1 per thousand in Victoria. Over the following two decades, the English ratio rose steadily and by the end of the century approximately equalled the Victorian ratio.[30] By then, however, the contribution of the movement to the Australian urban landscape was so obvious that an English visitor could claim, with pardonable exaggeration, that the Melbourne working classes were 'the absolute owners of the suburbs'.[31]

In some parts of Britain the home ownership ideal was reinforced by more traditional housing practices. A large source of English immigrants to Australia was the south-west, where the tin mines of Cornwall contributed strongly to the expansion of the Australian mining frontier.[32] Of the settlers of the 1850s, who did so much to democratise the suburban idea, many were goldminers from the tin-mining districts of West Cornwall, a region where traditions of owner-occupation and owner-building were strong. Thanks to the traditional tribute system, under which groups of workers leased a mine in return for a proportion of the metal they mined, many Cornish villagers were able to accumulate enough capital for their own cottages situated on small farm allotments. A parliamentary inquiry into town allotments observed 'a strong and *bona fide* desire on the part of the working population to acquire the freehold' in the mining villages of Cornwall.[33] On the Australian goldfields, these traditions were reinforced by the privilege, conferred by the miner's right, for the miner to erect a dwelling on his own plot of land. Weston Bate, the historian of goldrush Ballarat, notes that almost 90 per cent of miners in plebeian East Ballarat owned their own homes in 1870. As the goldfields declined, and their children made their way down to the great metropolis, it was natural, however, that they should retain their parents' aspiration for cottage homes of their own. As John Lack shows in his fine history of Footscray, many of the exodus from the central goldfields made their way back to the western suburbs of Melbourne, where levels of owner-occupation were among the highest in the metropolis.[34]

## Scotland

We may think of the relationship between migration and urban growth as a response to two reciprocal movements: one was centripetal, drawing young migrants from the declining British and Irish countryside to the growing cities; the other was centrifugal, pushing the growing urban populations outward, either to the suburbs or abroad.[35] The pressures of population growth varied from region to region throughout the British Isles, but the cityward movement was more than a simple reflex of rural decline. Nowhere were the forces of urbanisation nor the pressures for emigration stronger than in Scotland. From the ninth most urbanised country in Europe in 1750, it rose to become second only to England and Wales in 1850. Some of the pressure was generated as Highland landlords turned over their estates to large-scale grazing, forcing their tenants to seek refuge in the cities or abroad. But for every Highland crofter driven from the land, there were many more Lowland farmers and labourers lured by the booming textile factories of Glasgow, Dundee and Aberdeen, the shipbuilding yards of the lower Clyde and the banking, government and educational establishments of Edinburgh.[36]

15

From the late eighteenth century to World War II, Scottish cities remained the most densely populated and poorly housed in Britain. Most Scottish town-dwellers lived in tenements, three- or four-storey buildings divided horizontally and vertically into separate flats or 'houses' which were entered from a common stair. The tenement dwellings of the Edinburgh middle class were often palatial; but the typical working-class flat had only one or two rooms, and no tap, sink or water-closet of its own. Families slept four or five to a room, often in bed-closets recessed into the walls. As late as 1901 more than two-thirds of families in Glasgow lived in dwellings of only one or two rooms. 'I have seen human degradation in some of its worst phases, both in England and abroad', said one observer in the 1840s, 'but I can advisedly say that I did not believe until I visited the wynds of Glasgow that so large an amount of filth, crime and misery existed in one spot in any civilised country.'[37]

These conditions were in part a consequence of the traditional structure of the Scottish urban land market, which differed from the English in several important respects. Land was not let to builders or speculators in the English manner, on say a 99-year lease with fluctuating rents, but transferred in exchange for a feu or annual payment which did not vary throughout the term of the agreement. The owner's interest was therefore in maximising his own future income by in turn placing such conditions on the development of the allotment as would maximise the development of the land. Building solidly and densely, rather than cheaply and sparsely, was the Scottish style.

Scottish landlords also traditionally enjoyed great authority over their tenants: they demanded an annual rent paid in advance and had wide powers to evict for non-payment. Owner-occupation was virtually unknown in Scotland. Poor housing was also in part a reflection of the Scottish wages and living standards, which remained well below the English average throughout the century.[38]

But if working-class Scots lived cramped lives, it was not because they were indifferent to the appeal of domestic privacy. In a cold climate, tenements were simply cheaper and easier to heat than detached houses, while gardens were unusable through much of the year. But if Scots tolerated higher-density housing than the English, they decidedly preferred row-houses with their own front doors to tenements with a common stair. 'We find that the common stair has an immense drawback because if there be a bad tenant upon the staircase, that bad tenant spoils the comfort of the whole of the people; and, moreover, it is often difficult to fix down the responsibility upon a single individual, if a stair is not well-kept, or any discomfort arises.'[39] We have little direct evidence of Scottish housing preferences until the mid-twentieth century. In 1942 when the Department of Health asked Scots what kind of housing they wanted after the war, many found it difficult, after such a long history of deprivation and disappointment, to define their ideal house except in negative terms. 'Any house in which we have a door of our own', was a typical remark. 'Any house with a bathroom' or 'Anywhere where we do not have to go up more than three flights of stairs' were others.[40] A few years later, a sociologist found that most Glaswegians aspired to a house with its own front door, and if possible a bungalow, that is, 'a house as unlike a tenement flat as possible'.[41]

Long before Glaswegians could formulate their housing ideal, many of their uncles and aunts had sought relief from the congestion of the city by moving halfway across the world to the less congested cities of Australia. More than half of Scotland's natural increase in the later nineteenth century was lost to foreign emigration, giving it a rate of emigration second in Europe only to Ireland. Scots favoured Australia as a destination more than either the English or the Irish but within Australia they were more likely than other immigrant groups to settle outside the metropolis, many of them as pastoralists in such areas as Victoria's Western District or in the New England region of New South Wales. At the end of the gold rushes, the Scots of Melbourne and Sydney clustered mainly in the inner city, especially in the waterfront areas of South Melbourne, West Melbourne, Williamstown, Balmain and Glebe, the centres of ship-repairing, engineering, and flour-milling, the traditional industries of urban Scotland in which many of them were employed. In 1861, their residence pattern was less dispersed than the English-born (over 80 per cent dwelling in the inner ring, compared with 77 per cent Irish and 70 per cent English). A Scottish immigrant, Maggie Brown, who settled in Fitzroy in the early 1850s, compared her house, one of a pair of 'verandahed cottages', with her mother's house back in Scotland.

> We have a front door with a knocker on it, and about two yards of a wooden walk in front covered with a verandah to keep off the rain or heat and between that and the street a plot of grass grows, so that we can have wallflowers or any other flowers, and round that a nice white railing and a neat little gate to ourselves. I can tell you it looks very nobby.

The cottage was a modest one, even by Australian standards. What made it seem so 'nobby' (elegant, fit for a nob) to a Scottish tenement-dweller was the opportunity for individual self-expression and identification created by a front door and front gate of one's own.[42]

## Ireland

Although many English and Scottish emigrants had been born in the countryside, they usually came by way of London or Liverpool and had often felt the tug of the metropolis for years. Irish emigrants, who comprised about a quarter of the Australian inflow, were, by comparison, the most rural and traditional in origins and outlook. They usually came straight from the farm, where the letters of relatives already in Australia or the pamphlet of an itinerant emigration agent had reached them, and they set out on the long voyage, with many a backward glance and many a bitter tear, but with scarcely more than a few days' rest in Cork or Liverpool to familiarise them with the bustling urban world they were about to enter. They often saw themselves as exiles, continuing to look backward wistfully to the Home they had left, only slowly reinvesting their emotions in the new homes they recreated in the towns and cities of the New World. Their conceptions of home were a step removed from the English and Scottish (and largely Protestant) notion of the home as a private refuge of the nuclear family. For Irishmen and women, David Fitzpatrick writes, 'Home was not only a symbol of shelter and comfort, but also a scene of sociability, matchmaking and breeding.'[43]

Australia's Irish immigrants knew little of the heart-breaking poverty among the boatloads of hungry, landless labourers who fled the Great Famine to the United States in the 1840s. They were generally the younger sons and daughters of farmers who sought, we may conjecture, an opportunity to acquire abroad the modest freeholds that agricultural improvement and a galloping birth-rate had denied them at home. The long journey to Australia, writes David Fitzpatrick in a penetrating study of the sources of Irish emigration, was 'both feasible and tempting to those economic outcasts whom "modernization" had left with cash but without a life-line'.[44] As countrymen and women, Irish immigrants had a natural tendency to settle in the countryside, often rather precariously, as small-scale agriculturalists. 'I generally find the Irish more disposed to go in the country than the Scotch or English', the proprietor of a Sydney servant registry testified in 1859.[45]

17

Many Irishmen and women doubtless emigrated with the hope of recreating in the new land the farms and homesteads they had lost in the old. Some became tenant farmers, free selectors or even squatters, but many others ventured no further than the coastal cities, or, if they did, soon returned there. The men often clustered in the densest inner-city neighbourhoods near the waterfront and railway yards, in places like Darlinghurst and West Melbourne, where they earned their living as labourers, carters and navvies. Like their countrymen who migrated to English and American cities, they occupied the lowest rung on the occupational ladder and some of the most crowded and dilapidated housing. In Liverpool and Manchester, some streets and neighbourhoods were more than three-quarters Irish, but even in the most Irish ward of Melbourne the Irish were outnumbered by the English.[46] In 1887 the Irish-Australian journalist J. F. Hogan strongly repudiated the suggestion of the visiting English novelist Anthony Trollope that there was 'an Irish quarter' in Melbourne.

> There is no such thing as a distinctive Irish quarter in Melbourne, known and recognised by that contemptuous term. Irishmen and their families are to be found in all parts of the city and suburbs, and everywhere they form a peaceable, orderly, and industrious element in the general population, not a 'residuum of poverty and filth', as Mr. Anthony Trollope insinuates . . . Of course, [he conceded], some suburbs will be more representatively Irish than others. For instance, North and West Melbourne, from their general proximity to the central terminus of the Victorian railway system, where many hundreds of Irishmen are regularly employed as porters, guards, pointsmen, engine-drivers, etc., have necessarily a larger Celtic population than South or East Melbourne.[47]

While the waterfront and railway yards were the single largest centre of Irish employment and residence, the poorer sections of the rural–urban fringe, where suburban shanty towns merged into market gardens and agistment paddocks, also offered an avenue for the employment of traditional Irish skills in horticulture and horsemanship. Furthermore, Irish male immigrants were far outnumbered by Irish females, mainly single women, many of whom were dispersed into the suburbs where they worked as domestic servants in middle-class households and often eventually married non-Irish husbands. In 1861 Irish females outnumbered Irish males by two to one in middle-class St Kilda, while in plebeian West Melbourne the ratio was roughly one to one. The Irishtowns which grew up in Australian cities in the 1850s were seldom as miserable or as segregated as those of contemporary British or American cities. But here, as in the United States, Irish city-dwellers often gravitated to occupations, such as labouring and carting, which utilised their peasant skills, and to outlying neighbourhoods where they could plant a few potatoes and continue to keep horses, pigs and other livestock.[48] Even Melbourne's most densely populated and most Irish locality, Hotham (North Melbourne), had more pigs and poultry per acre than any other part of the metropolis. Self-styled Irishtowns emerged on the south-west fringes of Sydney near Camperdown and Randwick, at South Richmond and Preston on the poorer fringes of Melbourne, and in Lower North Adelaide, the plebeian annex of South Australia's first suburb.[49] By convention, these settlements became known as 'suburbs', but they embodied very different notions of property and rural seclusion from the romantic villa suburbs on the other side of town.

The spectre of outright hunger had largely receded well before the peak of Irish emigration to Australia in the 1850s and 1860s. It was the insecurity and dependence, and the uncertain future of tenant farming and labouring, that Irish emigrants to Australia mainly sought to escape. Most farmers held their land on yearly tenancies, and although their tenure was more secure in practice than the legal terms implied, the fear of eviction was never far from their minds. Labourers were even less secure, holding their cottages usually on sub-tenancies that could be revoked at the landlord's will. 'Independence'—a word as charged with meaning for Irish labourers as for self-improving English artisans—meant, above all, freedom from the landlord and the threat of eviction. 'This is the place where a man makes all for himself independent of any master for at once you purchase land here you have it forever without taxes or any other Cess', Michael Hogan wrote to his brother from a freehold cottage in South Melbourne in 1856. It was a country 'where we can enjoy ourselves with the best of every thing independent of a landlord or the Galling Yoke of oppression', he continued.[50] Michael O'Neill, a Brisbane land agent, promised to make 'everyman his own landlord', confiding to his customers that, as an Irishman, he was opposed to the locking up of land for improvement.[51] In 1887 Phillip Mahony wrote to his brother Lawrence in County Cork from his new home in Footscray, a bleak industrial suburb on the western fringes of Melbourne. He recalled with sadness the conversations his family had enjoyed in 'that grand Old Homestead' in Ireland, but believed it would be a 'consolation for you all to know that they are all happy out here away from perhaps tyranical landlords & Irish Baillifs'.[52] By the time these words were written, the yoke of oppression had begun to be lifted from the shoulders of the Irish farmer; but the memory of past injustices remained strong in the mind of Irish immigrants, and perhaps grew stronger the more they prospered in urban Australia.

19

## Conclusion

The desire for domestic privacy might be answered in several ways: some householders looked simply for a single-family dwelling, even if the house itself was in a poor and crowded neighbourhood. Some placed a higher value on the home's environs: they wanted a detached house with its own front door and its own front garden and backyard. Others cared less about the physical state of the house and more about who owned it. A crowded hovel would do, so long as there was no rent to pay and no landlord who could turn them out. Different sections of the working class and different regional and ethnic groups probably valued these elements in different ways. Middle-class English emigrants, and working-class ones too to some degree, seem to have placed a high value on external space; in Australian cities they quickly became the most suburbanised section of the immigrant population. Scots seem to have placed a high value upon family privacy and private ownership, but a lower one upon the detached house and garden. The Irish, on the other hand, while craving a bit of land on which to keep a pig or goat, cared less either about ownership or domestic privacy; they were more likely than either of the other groups to share their house with another family or with extended kin.

In 1858 the economist, Stanley Jevons, then working as an assay officer at the Sydney Mint, made a pioneering social survey of the town. His eye fell particularly on an immense stretch of new wooden cottages to the south of the city in the neighbourhood of Redfern. 'This sudden appearance of a whole suburban district is what can only be seen in a new and highly progressive country and in modern times', he observed.

20

> But nowhere, perhaps, except in Australia could be seen collections of
> such hastily erected frail and small habitations, devoid of every pretence to
> ornament, and in many cases belonging to, and built by, those who inhabit
> them. Almost every labourer and mechanic here has his own residence on
> freehold or leasehold land, and unpretending as it is to any conveniences or
> beauties, it yet satisfies him better than the brick-built, closely-packed, and
> rented houses of English towns.[53]

The homes which these displaced urbanites built in Australia were cut-price bastard versions of the romantic ideal. England—or more precisely London—was its primary point of reference, but Cornish, North Country, Scottish and Irish experiences and ideals also came into play. Working-class immigrants seldom had the means to buy or build a grand villa; a crudely embellished timber cottage on an unmade street was often the best they could afford. But if the forms changed, the underlying expectations were often much the same. What the immigrants sought, and what their homeland often denied, was domestic independence. Freedom from the neighbours, freedom from the landlord, freedom from the boss: these, as much as the moral, aesthetic, sanitary and social ideals of the ideal English middle class, were the homeland dreams on which the Australian home was founded.

A century after Governor Arthur Phillip had cast anchor in Botany Bay a more recent English immigrant, Thomas Dobeson, was living in a humble wooden cottage on the swampy northern shore of the bay. Dobeson was an unlucky immigrant: he had arrived in the early 1880s just as the railway boom was about to collapse and by 1888 he was out of work more often than in it. He raged against those 'lying vipers', the immigration agents who had persuaded him to come to this supposed 'land of promise', and the politicians who denied the misery of the unemployed. There was little about Australia which he felt inclined to praise. 'Is there not a bright side of life? Something we enjoy?' he asked himself. Just two things, he decided, shone amidst the general misery of his life: the health of his children and his domestic independence.

> There is no landlord who has a habit of knocking at the Door every Monday morning in his three storied hat, a Black Bag and pocket book to receive the rent . . . We are our own landlord and glad of it too. Our house is 28 feet by 20 feet not quite finished yet but will do at present. Everything about our place is in excellent order. A good pump of clear pure water. Grass nicely cut and trimmed.[54]

'Our own home circle in our own house'—this was the ideal for which thousands of immigrants crossed the sea, and in which, even when all else failed, they continued to rejoice.

## Notes

1   James Backhouse, *Extracts from Letters* (1839); W. Pollock, *So This is Australia* (1937). These examples are drawn from the *Australian National Dictionary*.
2   James Broadbent, *The Australian Colonial House: Architecture and Society in New South Wales, 1788–1842* (Potts Point, NSW, 1997); Graeme Davison, 'Australia— The First Suburban Nation?', *Journal of Urban History*, vol. 22, no. 1, 1995, pp. 40–74.
3   Louis Hartz, *The Founding of New Societies* (New York, 1964), pp. 280–1; and for Australian applications of the 'fragment' idea, see A. W. Martin, 'Australia and the Hartz "Fragment" Thesis', *Australian Economic History Review*, vol. 13, no. 2, 1973, pp. 131–47, and J. B. Hirst, 'Keeping Colonial History Colonial: The Hartz Thesis Revisited', *Historical Studies*, vol. 21, no. 82, 1982, pp. 85–104.
4   Evidence of T. W. C. Murdoch to Select Committee on Emigrant Ships, Second Report, *British Parliamentary Papers (BPP)*, vol. 13 (349) 1854, q. 3740.
5   N. Pigeon to Select Committee on the Condition of the Working Classes of the Metropolis (SCCWCM), *NSW Votes and Proceedings*, vol. 4, 1859–60, q. 452.
6   This generalisation is based on an analysis of the 'Statistical Returns Relating to Emigration from and into the United Kingdom' in selected years between the 1870s and the 1890s, following a similar procedure to C. J. Erickson, 'Who Were the English and Scots Emigrants to the United States in the Late Nineteenth Century?', in D. V. Glass and Roger Revelle (eds), *Population and Social Change* (London, 1986), pp. 347–81, and Dudley Baines, *Migration in a Mature Economy: Emigration and Internal Migration in England and Wales, 1861–1900* (London, 1986), pp. 71–89. Also compare Maldwyn Jones, 'The Background to Emigration from Great Britain in the Nineteenth Century', *Perspectives in American History*, vol. vii, 1973, pp. 48–75; Eric Richards, 'British Poverty and Australian

Immigration in the Nineteenth Century', in Richards (ed.), *Poor Australian Immigrants in the Nineteenth Century* (Canberra, 1991), pp. 25–30. The Irish, who comprised about one-quarter of Australia's immigrants throughout the century, were also drawn from a somewhat higher stratum of the home population than Irish emigrants to the United States (see David Fitzpatrick, 'Irish Emigration in the Later Nineteenth Century', *Irish Historical Studies*, vol. 22, 1980, pp. 126–43), but while they may have been as eager to acquire land as their English counterparts, it may not have denoted the same desire for domestic privacy. See Fitzpatrick, 'Ambiguities of "Home" in Irish–Australian Correspondence' in Fitzpatrick (ed.), *Home or Away: Immigrants in Colonial Australia* (Canberra, 1992), pp. 23, 25.

7  M. Pescott, 'English Immigration, 1851–1891', in James Jupp (ed.), *The Australian People* (Sydney, 1988), pp. 385; Gareth Stedman Jones, *Outcast London* (Oxford, 1971), pp. 138–42; Ross Duncan, 'Late Nineteenth Century Immigration into New South Wales from the United Kingdom', *Australian Economic History Review*, vol. 14, 1974, pp. 60–5.

8  James Jupp, 'Migration from London and the South-East', in Jupp (ed.), *The Australian People*, pp. 392–6; B. L. Howarth, 'English Recruitment to Australian Elites', in *ibid.*, p. 452; M. Pescott, 'English Immigration 1851–1891', in *ibid.*, p. 385; Jones, *Outcast London*, pp. 138–42; also see geographical spread of 'Enquiries to Emigrants' Information Office' in Report of Emigrants' Information Office, *British Parliamentary Papers*, no. 73, 1888.

9  *Life and Labour of the People in London*, First Series: *Poverty* (London, 1902), vol. 1, pp. 48–50.

10  Ross Duncan, 'Late Nineteenth Century Immigration into New South Wales from the United Kingdom', *Australian Economic History Review*, vol. 14, no. 1, 1974, pp. 60–5.

11  *Paradise of Dissent*, 2nd edn (Melbourne, 1967), p. 183.

12  W. G. Rimmer, 'Workingmen's Cottages in Leeds', *Thoresby Society Publications Miscellany*, vol. 46, 1961.

13  Alice Mary Hadfield, *The Chartist Land Company* (Newton Abbot, 1970), p. 16.

14  'History and Effects of Peasant Proprietorship', *National Instructor*, 8 February 1851, p. 85, and 1 June 1850, p. 1; Eileen Yeo, 'Some Problems of Chartist Democracy', in James Epstein and Dorothy Thompson, *The Chartist Experience: Studies in Working Class Radicalism and Culture* (London, 1982), pp. 345–80.

15  *Builder*, 13 May 1843, p. 177; 14 October 1843, p. 438.

16  *Builder*, 27 August 1853, p. 552. For an account of the land societies, see Enid Gauldie, *Cruel Habitations: A History of Working-Class Housing, 1780–1914* (London, 1974), ch. 18.

17  James Begg, *Happy Homes for Working Men and How to Get Them* (London, 1866), pp. iv, 17, 113.

18  Edward Ryde (surveyor) to Select Committee on Town Holdings, *British Parliamentary Papers*, vol. xii, 1886, q. 7845.

19  Edward Hughes to Select Committee on Town Holdings, *ibid.*, vol. xiii, 1887, qq. 2428–9.

20  David Englander, *Landlord and Tenant in Urban Britain, 1838–1918* (London, 1983), p. 4; Martin Daunton, *House and Home in the Victorian City* (London, 1983), p. 198; Richard Dennis, *English Industrial Cities of the Nineteenth Century: A Social Geography* (Cambridge, 1984), pp. 142–4.

21  James Ballantyne, *Homes and Homesteads in the Land of Plenty* (Melbourne, 1871), p. 116.

22  R. T. Appleyard, 'International Migration and Social Mobility: An Australian Case-study', *International Migration*, vol. 6, no. 4, 1968, pp. 189–200.

23  'A Bundle of Emigrants' Letters', *Household Words*, vol. 1, 1850, pp. 21, 23.

24  Charles Booth, *Life and Labour of the People in London*, vol. 1 (London, 1889), as quoted in Albert Fried and Richard Elman (eds), *Charles Booth's London* (London, 1969), pp. 64–5.

25  Christopher Hodgson to Royal Commission on Friendly Societies, *British Parliamentary Papers*, vol. xxvi, 1871, q. 17 234.

26  J. Taylor, *ibid.*, q. 3794.

27  W. R. Selvey, *ibid.*, q. 3537.

28  'No Monopoly', *Argus*, 1 February 1850. The argument that home ownership would quell revolutionary aspirations became a leading theme in Australian political rhetoric: see Graeme Davison, *The Rise and Fall of Marvellous Melbourne* (Melbourne, 1978), pp. 176–80; Judith Brett, *Robert Menzies' Forgotten People* (Sydney, 1992), pp. 8, 45–7; Jim Kemeny, *The Great Australian Nightmare* (Melbourne, 1983), ch. 1.

29  19 November 1869, p. 58.

30  Friendly Societies Commission, *British Parliamentary Papers*, vol. xxiii, 1874, p. 247; Return of Building Societies incorporated under Building Societies Acts, 1880, 1890, *ibid.*, vol. lxxxiii (245), 1881, and vol. lxxix (154) 1890–91; Victorian Building Society Returns in *Statistical Registers*, 1874, 1880 1890.

31  William Senior, *Travel and Trout in the Antipodes* (Melbourne, 1880), pp. 28–9.

32  James Jupp, 'Migration from Northern England' and K. J. Melhuish, 'Migration from the South-West', in Jupp (ed.), *The Australian People*, pp. 398–406.

33  Damaris Rose, 'Home Ownership, Subsistence and Historical Change: The Mining District of West Cornwall in the Nineteenth Century', in Nigel Thrift and Peter Williams (eds), *Class and Space: The Making of Urban Society* (London, 1987), pp. 113–24.

34  *Lucky City: The First Generation at Ballarat* (Melbourne,1978), p. 190; John Lack, *A History of Footscray* (Melbourne, 1991), pp. 47, 120.

35  C. G. Pooley, 'Choice and Constraint in the Nineteenth Century City', in J. H. Johnston and C. G. Pooley (eds), *The Structure of Nineteenth Century Cities* (London 1982), pp. 199–235.

36  T. M. Devine, 'Urbanisation', in Devine and Rosalind Mitchison (eds), *People and Society in Scotland*, vol. 1, *1760–1830* (Edinburgh, c. 1988), pp. 41–7; R. J. Morris, 'Urbanisation and Scotland', in W. Hamish Fraser and R. J. Morris (eds), *ibid.*, vol. 2, *1830–1914* (Edinburgh, c. 1992), pp. 73–83.

37  As quoted in T. C. Smout, *A Century of the Scottish People, 1830–1950* (London, 1986), p. 40.

23

38   Morris, 'Urbanisation and Scotland', p. 83; Smout, *A Century of the Scottish People*, ch. 2; Frank Worsall, *The Glasgow Tenement: A Way of Life* (Glasgow, 1979). The relative weight to be attributed to supply and demand factors in accounting for the standard of Scottish housing has been the subject of a lively debate between Richard Rodger, 'The Invisible Hand, Market Forces, Housing and the Urban Form in Victorian Cities', in Derek Fraser and Anthony Sutcliffe (eds), *The Pursuit of Urban History* (London, 1983), pp. 190–211, and Martin Daunton, *House and Home in the Victorian City* (London, 1983), ch. 4.

39   Rev. James Begg to Royal Commission on Friendly Societies, *British Parliamentary Papers*, no. 26, 1872, q. 9059.

40   Dennis Chapman, *Wartime Social Survey: The Location of Dwellings in Scottish Towns*, new series no. 34, September 1943, quoted in Ian Adams, *The Making of Urban Scotland* (London, 1978), p. 176.

41   T. Brennan, *Reshaping a City* (Glasgow, 1959), quoted in Smout, *A Century of the Scottish People*, p. 39.

42   Maggie Brown Hoey, 'A Newtown Cottage', 1854, in Fitzroy History Society, *Fitzroy: Melbourne's First Suburb* (Melbourne, 1989), p. 32.

43   'Ambiguities of Home in Irish–Australian Correspondence', in Fitzpatrick (ed.), *Home or Away*, p. 25.

44   'Irish Emigration in the Later Nineteenth Century', p. 129.

45   Marian Pawsey to Select Committee on the Condition of the Working Classes of the Metropolis, *NSW Votes and Proceedings*, vol. 4, 1859–60, q. 1809. See also Oliver MacDonagh, 'The Irish in Nineteenth Century Victoria', in Jupp (ed.), *The Australian People*, pp. 578–82.

46   Lynn Lees, *Exiles of Erin: Irish Migrants in Victorian London* (Manchester, 1979), ch. 3; Graham Davis, *The Irish in Britain, 1815–1914* (Dublin, 1991), pp. 60–1; M. A. G. O'Tuathaigh, 'The Irish in Nineteenth Century Britain: Problems of Integration', in Roger Swift and Sheridan Gilley (eds), *The Irish in the Victorian City* (London, 1985), pp. 13–36; Francis Finnegan, 'The Irish in York', *ibid.*, pp. 59–84; Mervyn Busteed, Robert I. Hodgson and Thomas F. Kennedy, 'The Myth and Reality of Irish Immigrants in Mid-nineteenth-century Manchester: A Preliminary Study', in Patrick O'Sullivan (ed.), *The Irish in New Communities* (Leicester, 1992), pp. 26–51; Chris McConville, *Croppies, Celts and Catholics: The Irish in Australia* (Melbourne, 1987), pp. 32–9, 47–9, 86–8.

47   J. F. Hogan, *The Irish in Australia* (London, 1887), pp. 36–7.

48   David Ward, *Cities and Immigrants: A Geography of Change in Nineteenth-century America* (New York, 1971), pp. 109–15.

49   James Waldersee, *Catholic Society in New South Wales, 1788–1860* (Sydney, 1974), pp. 121, 124, 158; Shirley Fitzgerald, *Rising Damp: Sydney, 1870–90* (Melbourne, 1987), pp. 29, 214; McConville, *Croppies*, p. 49.

50   Michael Hogan to Mathew Hogan, 22 June 1856, quoted in David Fitzpatrick, *Oceans of Consolation: Personal Accounts of Irish Migration to Australia* (Ithaca, NY, 1994), pp. 171–2, and compare p. 165.

51   W. Ross Johnston, Brisbane: *The First Thirty Years* (Brisbane, 1988), p. 240.

24

52  Phillip Mahony to Lawrence Mahony, 18 August 1887, quoted in Fitzpatrick, *Oceans of Consolation*, p. 263.
53  William Stanley Jevons, 'Sydney in 1858: A Social Survey', reproduced from the manuscript in the Mitchell Library in *Sydney Morning Herald*, 7 December 1929. See Graeme Davison, 'The Unsociable Sociologist: W. S. Jevons and his Survey of Sydney, 1856–1858', in David Walker and Michael Bennett (eds), *Intellect and Emotion: Perspectives on Australian History, Essays in Honour of Michael Roe*, also published as *Australian Cultural History*, no. 16, 1998, pp. 127–50.
54  Graeme Davison and Shirley Constantine (eds), *Out of Work Again: The Autobiographical Narrative of Thomas Dobeson, 1885–1891*, Monash Publications in History no. 6 (Melbourne, 1990), p. 66.

# The Introduction of Order

## Chapter 2

*Susan Marsden*

26     This chapter surveys the progressive introduction of structural, fire and health regulations and their effect on housing design in Australia. The survey covers the period from the introduction of the first, limited regulations of the early nineteenth century through to the 1930s when a wide range of state and local government planning and building by-laws were in operation. The main theme is one of shaping space in a context of competing desires: the desire for order and the desire to escape order. As suggested in Chapter 1, colonists brought with them notions of property, family and independence which found form in the homes they made in Australia. The conflict between individuality and community persisted as a central tension in the designed garden suburbs of the early twentieth century (as argued in Chapter 8).

    The focus in this chapter is on the private house and its plot, designed and modified partly in response to regulation. These regulations include those now defined as building regulations and planning regulations: the former refer to building materials, room dimensions and other features of individual houses; the latter relate to block size, street layout and subdivision. Although planning regulations, so-called, date mostly from after the period considered in this chapter, some nineteenth-century regulations covered planning issues such as block size, including the very first, introduced in 1788. The chapter also considers why regulations were introduced, shaped by factors such as the influence of place of origin, government changes, fashion (in science, morality and consumption as well as in architecture), local physical influences and technology.

    This complicated history is simplified by dividing the chapter into three parts. The first two survey some of the influences outlined above and their outcomes in housing regulation. Part one provides a broad overview of overseas influences and the impact of Australian circumstances. Part two focuses on the roles of the colonial or state and local governments responsible for introducing and administering the regulations. Part three discusses types of regulation in more detail and their impact on housing design.

## Overseas influences and the impact of Australian circumstances

British influences and their adaptation were evident from the first in the plan for Sydney proposed by Governor Arthur Phillip and despatched to London in 1788 within months of his arrival. Streets were to be laid out to 'afford a free air', and 'land will be granted with a clause that will ever prevent more than one house being built on the allotment, which will be 60 feet in front and 150 feet in depth. This will preserve uniformity in the buildings, prevent narrow streets, and the many inconveniences which the increase of inhabitants would otherwise occasion hereafter.'[1]

As in any colonial society at the outset, existing British law was applied. New regulations were simply adopted by governors from those prevailing in Britain at the time they were preparing to leave for Australia. However, the attitudes of early administrators towards planning and the regulations they attempted to put in place depended mainly on their individual characters. Phillip's plan for Sydney as a grand city, while reflecting a British ideal, was his own conception; it was quite at odds with the British government's view of Sydney as a primitive convict depot. Phillip issued various orders relating to streets, building standards and pollution controls. He also hoped by regulation to *avoid* recreating the poor housing of industrialising England. This is obvious in his plan, which aimed to prevent construction of tenements by separating houses and permitting the circulation of fresh air. Similar concerns would inform regulations introduced later by colonial governments.

27

Phillip's regulations had some small impact, but freehold was substituted for the granting of land at the discretion of the governor—which had given governors some chance to control housing design. His successors did not care to hinder private builders nor to improve public building standards. Phillip's controls were restated in more detailed regulations by Lachlan Macquarie, who was like Phillip in his utopian views of Sydney's potential, unlike the intervening 'series of visionless governors and self-interested interim administrators'.[2] Like those of Phillip, Macquarie's regulations were concerned with civic standards, not simply, for example, with preventing fire, as he prohibited not only the flammable thatch but also fire-resistant mud walls.

British regulations were also the models for much ensuing regulation throughout the period under review. Their adaptation to Australian circumstances was mainly in terms of the time it took to reach local consensus on the need for such regulation. Most were set in place a long time after they were adopted in England. For example, the 1837 *Act for Regulating Buildings and Party-Walls, and for Preventing Mischiefs by Fire, in the Town of Sydney* was based on Cromwell's act of 1656, not even on the later *London Building Act* of 1774. The Sydney act and later building acts were concerned solely with fire and did not deal with other aspects such as safety and lighting. C. Paris argues that in most countries, including Australia, the 'rate at which governments have introduced such regulatory frameworks has been the result of the combination of economic growth (which has enabled provision) and recognition of need'.[3]

Not only were there long delays in introducing regulations in Australia, but most were generally ignored. Such minor regulation as was introduced by newly created local government of the 1840s and 1850s fared little better. Australian colonists were motivated to escape regulation, to buy their own plot and to use it as they wished, building homes without restriction. One factor in the early suburbanisation of Australian cities was an expression of this desire to escape restrictions introduced by city councils, such as the Melbourne *Building Act*, passed in New South Wales in 1849. Enforcement of the expensive specifications affected settlement because people who wished to use cheaper designs and materials were encouraged to move beyond central Melbourne, the area of jurisdiction and the city council's boundaries. In the 1850s this encouraged the suburban settlement of areas like East Collingwood and Brunswick.[4]

If there was little housing regulation in the city centres, there was almost none in the outer, semi-rural and rural areas. As discussed further in Chapter 4, while the authorities attempted to impose order in the central areas, people built as they liked where they could still find cheap land or could squat. This distinction held, even following a wave of municipality formation in the 1860s to 1880s when there was a great increase in the pace and extent of suburbanisation, especially in Sydney and Melbourne. The process is aptly described by Birch and Macmillan as 'this mass search for the individual's utopia in the suburbs—the bungalow cottage, unique yet so alike, set in its modest block of land'.[5]

Some variation in regulation and housing outcome reflected British response to the Australian environment, the regional differences in climate, building materials, and the problems of vermin attack, particularly by termites. Providing for ventilation and in hotter inland and northern climates for cross-ventilation, was more important in Australia than in Britain, as explained in Chapter 3, and this was reflected in building regulations.

Local regulations were also a response to public scares, sometimes in dramatic circumstances, such as the outbreak of bubonic plague in Sydney in 1900. Other regulations followed specific building failures or catastrophes, especially in matters such as structural safety and fire hazard. Local scares were not the sole, or even the main, basis for the introduction of structural, fire and health regulations: by the end of the nineteenth century every colony had introduced similar acts. Local factors influenced their timing, but most were copies of regulations introduced elsewhere. D. H. Coward usefully sums up the British precedents, colonial borrowings and local catalysts for the public health acts. The first was Victoria's *Public Health Act 1854*, modelled on the English act of 1848 with later amendments similar to those made in Britain. Queensland took precautionary action against an outbreak of smallpox in 1872 by setting up a temporary Central Board of Health, like that in Victoria, maintaining it under the *Health Act 1884*, which derived from the English *Public Health Act 1875*. South Australia borrowed from the English and Victorian Acts in its *Public Health Act* of 1873, amending it in 1884 after a smallpox scare by updating from the English act of 1875 and the amended Victorian act. Tasmania in 1885 and Western Australia in 1886 followed suit with provisions also derived from the English act of 1875. Underpinning most of these acts were theories such as the miasma theory, which were even more widespread. Its replacement by the germ theory informed the New South Wales *Public Health Act 1896*.[6]

The history of these public health acts illustrates influences which were cumulative rather than immediate in effect. Although poor housing was prevalent—indeed, axiomatic—from the time of first settlement, apart from sporadic promulgation by governors there was scarce public concern with the problem until after the mid-nineteenth century. From that time public health concerns formed the basis of new regulations, which included some attempt to improve housing standards.

For example, South Australia's *Public Health Act 1873* set up a central and local health boards, and authorised inspection of dwellings and the disposal of household rubbish. Subsequent amendments empowered health boards to deal with substandard and overcrowded dwellings and to administer building regulations. Inspectors soon returned scandalised reports of Adelaide's housing, duly publicised by the central board, such as this one of 1875.

29

> In old and dilapidated cottages which are really unfit for habitation, often consisting of only two or three rooms, as many as twelve or thirteen persons have been found huddled together, as regardless of decency as of health. This is a state of things which calls for grave consideration, and the remedy is not easy whilst the lower class of tenements are in such demand, and building operations are so costly. Many of these tenements are inhabited by workmen and labourers who receive high wages; and to the disregard of ordinary notions of cleanliness and comfort much of this unfortunate state of things is to be attributed. Around these dwellings are found dilapidated closets, built and exposed without regard even to decency—cesspits overflowing, stagnant drains, and filth abounding in every shape. There are several of these districts within the city [of Adelaide], which experience has shown to be hotbeds of disease.[7]

This statement bears close analysis because it expounds views prevailing in the Australian colonies that informed the regulations widely introduced in the remaining years of the nineteenth century. The concern with stagnant drains reflected the influential 'scientific' miasmatic theory of disease transmission and the related 'fresh air' movement, and recognition of the threats to personal and public health posed by overflowing sewage and uncollected rubbish. Adelaide's town clerk nicely expressed these notions: 'in many instances in the more densely populated parts of the City the very foundation of the houses suffer from fluid of the vilest description draining under them, that the occupiers are inhaling deadly gases resulting in certain death'.[8] The health board's reference to 'hotbeds of disease', confirmed by high rates of infant mortality, intimated that such housing posed a threat to Adelaide's entire urban society.

Mention of 'ordinary' notions of cleanliness, supposedly disregarded by workmen who could afford better, suggests how much housing regulation was class-based. Enforcing designs providing more numerous rooms and washing amenities, not to speak of segregating children and adults—and later, boys and girls—into separate sleeping quarters, expressed middle-class preoccupations and prejudices against working-class life. (The same may be said of the anti-slum movement as a whole, as Alan Mayne has argued.) Chapter 7 discusses such concerns in terms of 'cultural fetishes' and elaborates upon their impact on housing design and the furnishing of rooms.

The 'moral function' of housing—how its design and amenities shaped the behaviour of residents, especially women and children—became a pre-dominant concern of would-be regulators. This was a strong factor in argu-ments for broader town planning measures, which aimed not only to improve the standards of individual dwellings but to shift them altogether from insalubrious urban settings into idealised garden cities, that is, into suburbia. This is not to deny that housing conditions were often appalling and that most inhabitants wished for improvement and, if they realised their desires, thereby improved their class status.

The 1875 report also touched on the features of housing likely to draw attention by regulation: size, segregation of family members, provision for toilets and washing facilities, age and physical dilapidation. Use of the term 'old' in 1875 was hardly warranted: no dwelling was more than twenty-eight years old, and the term is really shorthand for the original small colonial buildings of pisé and timber. No-one worried about the bag humpies and bark huts typical of rural districts. Housing regulation was concerned principally with urban housing. The introduction of regulations—with some exceptions—displayed a chronology of earliest introduction in the original centres of settle-ment, then moving outwards as suburban settlement expanded, and in the larger regional towns.

Nineteenth-century regulators were reluctant to recognise the connection between housing standards and poverty, despite the 1875 report's oblique reference to the high costs of building. This report prefigures campaigns for 'slum' abolition, which became a recurring feature of town planning and public housing movements of the early twentieth century.

Similar concerns informed all public health regulations, although more than forty years separated the Victorian act from the last, enacted in New South Wales. Some regulations had contradictory effects. Legislation setting up 'workmen's blocks' aimed to assist unemployed families by providing them with small blocks where they might raise chickens and grow vegetables as well as improve their standard of housing. But the agrarian ideal at the heart of such schemes ran counter to threats to public health from farmyard practices in built-up districts. Tuberculosis from backyard dairies and disease spread by rats in fowlyards were serious problems, and so the keeping of cows, goats, pigs and large numbers of hens was progressively and eventually eliminated by local councils. Typically, the timing of these regulations was an expression of the outward movement of urban settlement.

Regulations were also influenced by design and technological changes, the introduction of new materials and household goods, and by the activities of architects, engineers, builders and lending institutions. These influences are too many to detail here. A single technological change, such as the introduction of electricity in domestic housing from the 1890s, meant that subsequent building regulations had to include specifications for safe wiring. New building technologies, such as the use of reinforced concrete, brought corresponding changes in nineteenth-century acts. South Australia's 'amended *Building Act* of 1923 was designed to address modern methods of construction, and was a further means of protection against fire. It . . . was an honest endeavour to base modern architectural construction upon sound engineering principles'.[9]

Three changes which contributed to changes in housing and housing provision were the creation of large housing markets, the growing role of the state, and the use of houses as a means of transferring wealth.[10] Paramount in the design of Australian housing from around the mid-nineteenth century was the role of builders and building firms as part of the process of the commodification of housing. 'Land subdivision was little more than a gamble, in which profit, not housing needs, was the first consideration.'[11]

The history of state housing policy, of which building regulation forms part, was largely a contest over the consequences of such speculative building. As speculative development reached a fever pitch in the eastern capitals in the 1870s and 1880s, resulting in deteriorating housing standards, these pressures were resisted by new colonial and municipal regulations. 'Thus,' in D. Kilner's words, 'one has a picture of conflict between a private sector which pushed housing towards lower standards and a regulatory state sector which pushed back against this trend.'[12]

The New South Wales *Local Government Act 1906* 'required dwellings to maintain a reasonable degree of health and sanitation'. It specified minimum sizes for allotments and rooms and established standards of light and ventilation. However, these were negative or prescriptive controls, intended as a minimum standard; they 'instead became a maximum as jerry-builders erected street after monotonous street of uniform houses. Although general health improved, aesthetics continued to deteriorate.'[13]

The conflict between builders and regulators was repeated in later building booms. As the president of the Master Builders Association protested in Sydney in 1925, 'building, health and other regulations make it impossible to erect a home at a figure that had any possible relation to the average worker's income . . . It was [once] possible to put up a dozen brick terrace homes on the minimum frontage required for half a dozen detached cottages.'[14]

31

From about 1910, government impact on houses was augmented by direct intervention in subdivision and the designing, building and financing of homes. Such intervention, together with an increasing pace of urban regulation, remained principally a state government role. As explained in Chapter 18, after Federation in 1901 the new Commonwealth government displayed little interest in this area of policy.

The style of domestic architecture changed after World War I and builders and architects favoured the Californian bungalow form. This was then adopted as the norm by councils, especially as this was a period when government housing schemes built thousands of new homes in the suburbs of the main cities. The style had a great influence on the 'Queensland house' for the whole of the inter-war period, mainly because of the role of the Workers Dwelling Board which produced standard designs of bungalows and built large numbers of timber houses. The bungalows changed very little in that time. 'Design No. 47, from the 1935 Workers Dwelling booklet featured outdoor sleeping verandahs, typical of bungalows a decade or more earlier.'[15]

Canberra provides a model case of total government control of housing design as the new federal capital was built from scratch by Commonwealth agencies after the site was opened in 1913. The first cottages of the 1920s were designed by private and public service architects for the Department of Works and Railways and the Federal Capital Commission. Dwellings offered to public servants who came to live in the suburbs of Ainslie, Eastlake (Kingston), Westlake and Blandfordia in the 1920s and early 1930s were all variations of the free-standing suburban villa.[16] As the Commonwealth continued to build most of Canberra's houses until the 1970s, they express most fully the intentions of government regulation and planners and the interactions with prevailing health, style and moral attitudes.[17]

## The roles of governments with relation to housing standards

There were three phases of government which strongly determined the timing and nature of regulations affecting housing. The first phase was the period of administration by appointed British governors, which lasted from the time of first settlement in each colony (between 1788 and 1836) to the 1850s. The second phase dated from the 1850s when, following the *Australian Colonies Act* of 1850, each colony (except Western Australia) became separate and self-governing. The third phase dates from about 1910, when the labour movement arrived as an organised political force at all levels of government.[18]

The early governors had sweeping powers, although in practice these were limited by the governors' own capacities and by the interests of the colonists. The jurisdiction of the New South Wales governor until 1851 included all of eastern Australia, and thus regions that were later the separate colonies of Queensland, Victoria and Tasmania. Even the most limited regulations, therefore, had far wider effects than any subsequently introduced by the separate colonial governments or by local councils.

In 1810, Governor Macquarie laid down Australia's first building regulations, requiring dwellings to be of brick or weatherboard, with brick chimneys and timber shingle roofs. But little heed was paid to these regulations and in fact, during his administration (1810–21) Macquarie's regulations had less effect in Sydney than in the smaller regional settlements in New South Wales and Van Diemen's Land (Tasmania). In 1810, Macquarie declared that six new towns were to be laid out in the Hawkesbury district and at Liverpool, and ordered that plans of all houses to be built in those towns were to be inspected to ensure that they met building regulations.[19]

Early governors also attempted to influence building standards by tying them to the issue of land grants or sales. In New South Wales Foveaux illegally but pragmatically issued freehold grants to lease-holders who had built 'excellent dwelling houses'. Macquarie, hoping to encourage improved building standards, recommended the same policy should apply to all persons 'as are willing and able to erect substantial and handsome buildings in the town'.[20]

In Hobart Macquarie allocated town allotments only on lease, but the entitlement varied in accordance with the type of building the lessee was prepared to construct. A two-storey house of at least 40 by 50 feet, built of brick, stone or weatherboard, properly glazed and roofed, would get a 21-year lease on a block measuring 98 by 131 feet. A smaller house earned a shorter lease on a smaller block.[21] A carryover from this older system to the freehold system in Melbourne was evident in the governor's stipulation in the first town sales of 1837 that a permanent building worth at least £50 be put up within a year. 'This requirement would surely have been very difficult to enforce over freehold property, but it had a marked effect on the development of the town.'[22]

The third governor to attempt through regulation to improve housing and the health and amenity of colonial towns was Ralph Darling. In 1829 he issued surveying regulations which specified certain widths for blocks of land 65 by 328 feet with buildings set back 14 feet from the footpaths. These regulations had some influence on the many towns within the jurisdiction of the New South Wales governor—including Brisbane and Melbourne—which were established in the 1820s and 1830s.

However, before the separation of Victoria, Tasmania and Queensland in the 1850s, the New South Wales governors generally had little interest in regulating development or providing amenities in the far towns of Melbourne, Hobart and Brisbane, let alone the smaller settlements. This meant that Brisbane, for example, lacked 'the kind of municipal utilities usually found in a nineteenth-century town' until after it became capital of a self-governing colony in 1859.

Apart from Sydney and Melbourne (1842), and briefly, Adelaide, local government was formed after the establishment of colonial (later, state) governments in the 1850s and has remained legally and financially the 'creature' of those governments. During the nineteenth century, the powers of local government in New South Wales, for example, were marginal. The 1906 *Local Government Act* permitted little more than helping administer the 1896 *Public Health Act*, cattle slaughtering, road-making, pipe-laying, control of

33

nuisances, and the regulation of balconies and lodging houses. Even those powers were not granted automatically to councils, but upon application to the government. Until the 1919 *Local Government Act*, councils had no power over land subdivision and buildings.

Quite apart from the legal and financial constraints on local government, the property-related restrictions on municipal voters in most of the colonies kept councils conservative. Effectively, most councils represented ratepayers, landowners and local businessmen, the very people who opposed regulations on housing and other building that might curtail their rents and profits.[23]

Since the mid-nineteenth century (and 1890s in Western Australia) the colonial or state governments have been the principal actors in urban policy and urban government, operating directly and through a multiplicity of boards and authorities, while devolving a 'minutiae of local affairs', such as building regulation, onto local government.[24] During this second phase of government in Australia, housing design was addressed by various regulations but not as part of a deliberate housing policy. Nineteenth-century colonial governments acted on concerns about low structural standards, unhealthy premises and overcrowding, in fear of disease, crime and political discontent. The pattern of regulatory response varied widely, although roughly similar regulations were introduced in each colony.

There seems to be general consensus that, except for basic public health measures, nineteenth-century regulations had little impact on housing, although this should be qualified by some success in curtailing the expansion of poor housing. Deliberate housing policy and direct intervention in finance and construction as well as wider regulation emerged after the Labor Party won parliamentary seats in the 1890s and won government around 1910.

In summary, the Australian colonial and state governments were slow to introduce building regulations covering all aspects of structural safety, health and general amenity, but by early in the twentieth century all six states had regulations in place. These powers were reserved to them rather than to the new Commonwealth government at Federation in 1901. In practice, though most of the relevant regulation was administered by local government and so was widely divergent in character, timing of introduction and impact.

## Regulations and their impact on housing design

Many laws concerning building requirements (mainly concerned with safety and health rather than housing amenity), as well as subdivision and zoning, date from the nineteenth century. These were mainly colonial or state laws but much was contained in local council by-laws made under the *Local Government Acts*. There was in effect a *de facto* hierarchy of regulations reflecting the degree of concern about problems relating to housing. As disease posed a universal threat, measures dealing with public health were introduced early, and followed up by more comprehensive acts which were enforced by the government throughout the colony. Fire risk and low building standards were of less concern because their impact was more localised or restricted to the lower classes, and so control over buildings was left to 'discretionary municipal control rather than mandatory central authority'.[25] Kilner argues that, until about 1910, state regulation and state services were aimed at drawing a line below which building and health standards were not permitted to fall. 'On the one hand this meant raising the standards of existing areas and on the other it meant fighting the replication of such problems in new areas.'[26]

Another expression of this 'hierarchy of concerns' was the formation by colonial governments of departments and authorities that operated alongside municipalities but in a wider sphere, concerned with health, public transport, water, sewerage and later, housing. Although it is impossible to list all the structural, fire and health regulations, let alone the regulations of these state authorities that had some effect on housing design, it is important to emphasise that the latter did affect housing design. Quite possibly, given their metropolitan-wide scale of operations, they had wider effects than many building by-laws passed by local councils.

For example, the operations of the New South Wales Water and Sewerage Board originally covered the County of Cumberland, and from 1916 were extended to include towns such as Wollongong. Under the *Metropolitan Water and Sewerage Act 1880*, owners or occupiers of a house or land within 150 feet of the board's main were liable for payment of water or sewerage rates. In 1924 this was extended to 250 yards for water and 250 feet for sewers.[27] From that time, then, quite apart from specific regulations concerning cesspits and washing facilities, it was sensible to assume that the purchasers of new suburban houses would soon pay for the privilege of sewered toilets and piped water and so to include those features in the designs. Real estate subdividers and builders could also ask higher prices if the board's sewers were already in place. On the other hand, in Melbourne, where 'transportable' weatherboard houses were more prevalent, some residents in sewered areas who did not wish to pay the steep connection fees to the Melbourne and Metropolitan Board of Works 'bodily removed their houses beyond the reach of the Board's sewers'.[28]

Even if we consider only the acts passed by the colonial and state parliaments regarding structural, fire, health and general building matters, there is a bewildering variety to choose from. D. H. Coward lists sixteen acts passed in New South Wales between 1833 and 1886, from the *Police Offences Act 1833* to the *Public Health Act 1896*, all of which dealt with some aspect of public health (most of them, by extension also touching on housing standards).[29] As in the other colonies, these acts included acts setting up or enlarging the responsibilities of local government, with further legislation enacted in the early twentieth century. Other relevant New South Wales acts included the *Real Property Act 1900*, *Housing Act 1912*, *Local Government Act 1919*, *Encroachment of Buildings Act 1922*, *Sydney Corporation Act 1932*, *Housing Improvement Act 1936* and the *Local Government (Regulation of Flats) Act 1940*.[30] The multiplicity of local councils makes detailed consideration of council regulations and their impact impossible.

One general point should be noted again, and that was the difference in urban, suburban and rural housing. This was determined in part by the prevalence of building regulations in the city councils, followed much later by suburban and town municipalities once they had sufficient housing and population, and then a gradual extension of usually less strict (or less strictly applied) regulations into the countryside. This was another expression of the 'hierarchy of concern'. Strict building controls were introduced earliest in the worst areas, that is the inner city, and then were progressively adopted by other councils. This progression is nicely illustrated by the dates of adoption of the 1881 *Building Act* in metropolitan Adelaide. The act was adopted by the Adelaide City Council in 1882 and then in 1884 by the adjacent and densely populated municipality of Kensington and Norwood. In 1909–10 the last councils to adopt the act, among them Brighton, Woodville and Enfield, were still rural as much as suburban in character and more distant from the city.[31]

How effective were regulations in changing housing design and what was the impact of specific controls? It is easier to make broad generalisations about the effect of regulations than to isolate specific features as consequences of particular regulations. J. M. Freeland goes so far as to claim that the introduction of comprehensive building regulations 'spelled doom' for an emerging colonial style. He dates this event from as early as 1838, when Sydney's building regulations came into effect. Freeland also touches on another phenomenon of building regulation: its focus on urban centres and its gradual spread outwards. 'Only in the ragged fringes of the outback, whose limits have been pushed steadily further inland and where the necessary but deadening hand of bureaucratic control has lain but lightly, have the outgoing natural forces been free to develop in an organic way.'[32]

These 1837 building regulations, like those enacted later in the other colonies, were aimed solely at fire control, an omnipresent danger during the Australian summer in the colonial towns with their tents and timber dwellings. Such regulations also reflected the influence of insurance companies. The concern with fire risk rather than with other features of housing design was evident in most building acts, which did not actually prohibit timber buildings but required them to be 'insulated' (that is, isolated) by a prescribed distance from lot boundaries. In effect, these regulations shifted the emphasis to masonry rather than timber materials, and to roof coverings of slate, tin or tile rather than thatch and wooden shingles. Other impermanent materials also disappeared rapidly wherever the new regulations took force.[33]

Another significant feature of the Sydney act was the provision for different rates of buildings. Each rate or class was determined by its use, size and proximity to the street and other buildings, and each required owners to comply with different standards of construction.[34] The regulations also set down thicknesses of external and party walls, and requirements for the construction of fireplaces and chimneys. To keep inflammable materials away from building exteriors, two further requirements were transposed from London. All timber was to be kept at least four inches from the face of the building and all projections except those essential to copings and door and window dressings were banned. The effect, writes Freeland, was instantaneous as verandahs, window shutters and roof overhangs disappeared. Protests, most vociferously by builders and architects, soon brought amendment; verandahs returned, but party walls and other requirements remained.[35] One complaint, that the legislation encouraged 'large stores and mansions while persecuting small buildings',[36] could with justification be applied to most subsequent regulation affecting housing design in Australia.

Sydney's 1837 *Building Act* was also significant because of the extent of its eventual influence. Like most of these regulations it applied initially only to the core of the city, but this area was later expanded. Similar regulations were introduced in Hobart in 1840, and the first building regulations introduced by the city commissioners in Adelaide in 1849 were an amalgamation of Sydney's 1833 and 1837 acts.[37] The Sydney act was 'transmogrified' in 1852 into a Brisbane *Building Act*.[38] By contrast, Melbourne's 1849 *Building Act* was an independent piece of legislation.

I have already referred to the role of the Melbourne act in promoting suburban development and, by default, the construction of small timber dwellings no longer permitted in the city. D. A. L. Saunders proposes that this outcome was a deliberate policy. 'The new regulations were deliberately not extended to the new areas [such as Carlton] because urgently needed houses could more quickly be built by carpentry.'[39] The same events occurred after wooden houses were forbidden in the Town of Sydney, although P. Ashton describes this a ploy by owner-builders and modest speculators simply to evade control by building wooden cottages just beyond the defined town limits.[40]

The effectiveness of these building regulations in preventing the construction of the kind of housing condemned in the city centres is indicated by the findings of later 'slum investigations'. For example, in South Australia the *Building Act Inquiry* report of 1940 found that substandard houses were almost entirely confined to the oldest working-class districts in the Adelaide, Port Adelaide, Hindmarsh, and Kensington and Norwood councils. Outside those areas there were only 'isolated' examples of substandard housing.[41] The impact of specific municipal by-laws can also be illustrated by differences even in adjacent subdivisions. R. Allom observes distinct differences in allotment size and housing type in two former local council areas at Clayfield (Brisbane). In Bonney Avenue on the high side (Hamilton) are large allotments and houses, and on the low side (Windsor) are small lots with working-class cottages. 'Using an old map of the pre-1925 municipal boundaries, similar observations of physical differences can be made right across the city.'[42]

Regulations governing the size of blocks were highly influential, especially from the late nineteenth century as the movement for minimum allotment size gained strength, partly influenced by the English Garden City concept (Chapter 8). In Brisbane the search for building blocks further and further afield from the city centre was encouraged by the *Undue Subdivision of Land Act 1885*. This introduced a minimum size for suburban blocks and precluded

37

narrow streets.[43] Fuelling a postwar suburban boom in Sydney were regulations under the *Local Government Act 1919*, which also specified a minimum lot size. Other examples include building setback, building materials, permitted uses of house and garden, standards governing interiors as well as exteriors, and the progressively increasing standards governing size of rooms, light and ventilation. Their impact was soon evident in the design of new houses and, more slowly, in the 'modernisation' of existing houses.

The *Town Planning and Development Act 1928* of Western Australia was the first to give local government the power to control the use of private land. Similar legislation was enacted in every other state except South Australia by 1945. Only the Greater Brisbane Council approached uniform control of housing development across the whole metropolitan area when it gained a measure of control over land use in 1935, extended by the *City of Brisbane (Town Plan) Act 1959*.[44] Greater Brisbane Council was formed in 1925. Greater Brisbane was defined as an area within 'natural' boundaries approximating a 10-mile radius from the GPO.

The main effect of these planning acts was on the design of new suburban housing, as few overall planning schemes were actually prepared and even fewer came into operation. In P. Harrison's words, 'There was a general reluctance to interfere with the rights and consequently the values attaching to property ownership.' Less onerous and less contentious forms of land control continued to be used by councils, the principal purpose of such controls being the 'preservation of residential amenity'.[45] Such regulations aimed not only to prevent commercial and industrial intrusions, but also to ensure that new suburban housing was of an acceptable type and standard.

In Sydney, these powers had been used since the *Local Government Act 1919*, which had enabled a council to proclaim part of its area a 'residential district', prohibiting both non-residential and unacceptable residential uses, such as blocks of flats. The richer suburbs used such zoning far more frequently than the poorer suburbs, with the effect of concentrating industry and poorer types of housing in those parts of Sydney least able to get government approval for residential zoning.[46] Yet there was some truth in the contemporary assertion that the effect of the act's building regulations

> [was] not confined to the wealthier houses but is even more marked in what might be termed artisan suburbs ... ten years ago the terrace house as a home for the working man was then almost the rule ... In those days the jerry builder employed his evil devices in secret. Now he has to expose all his tricks beforehand to ... council meetings ...[47]

P. Spearritt suggests that this commentator did not foresee the increasingly prominent role that real estate agents would play in such council deliberations, but their involvement confirms just how much of an impact local government decisions would have on private house-building. Above all, the regulations confirmed the prevalence of detached bungalows in gardens,

38

which remain the predominant form of housing in Australia. My survey of these building regulations confirms an observation I made twenty years ago after researching the history of a suburban council:

> So it is that the *Building Acts* have had a predominant influence not only on the character of most of Adelaide, but in most of urban Australia, as the situation was everywhere more or less the same. By insisting upon minimum block sizes and detached houses, they have enforced *by law* the Australian 'suburban ideal'. They have helped create the suburban sprawl that is as typical of Woodville as anywhere else in Australia.[48]

## Notes

1   Governor Phillip's despatch to Lord Sydney, 9 July 1788, in A. Birch and D. S. Macmillan, *The Sydney Scene, 1788–1960* (Melbourne, 1962), pp. 30–1.
2   G. Aplin, 'Collaborative Planning? Macquarie and Greenway', in R. Freestone (ed.), *The Australian Planner: Proceedings of the Planning History Conference, 1993* (Sydney, 1993), p. 34.
3   C. Paris, *Housing Australia* (Melbourne, 1993), p. 12.
4   D. Dunstan, *Governing the Metropolis: Melbourne, 1850–1891* (Melbourne, 1984), p. 66.
5   *The Sydney Scene*, p. 237.
6   D. H. Coward, *Out of Sight: Sydney's Environmental History, 1851–1981* (Canberra 1988), pp. 167–8.
7   Report of the Board of Health, 1875, in M. Barbalet, *The Adelaide Children's Hospital, 1876–1976* (Adelaide, 1975), p. 5.
8   Town Clerk's report, 1872, in *ibid.*, p. 8.
9   P. Stark, S. Marsden and P. Sumerling (eds), *Heritage of the City of Adelaide* (Adelaide, 1990, 1996), p. 40.
10  Paris, *Housing Australia*, p. 9.
11  County of Cumberland report, quoted in Birch and Macmillan, *The Sydney Scene*, p. 237.
12  'The Evolution of South Australian Housing Policy, 1836–1987', PhD thesis, University of Adelaide, 1988, p. 79.
13  W. Bunning, W. H. Ifould, C. R. McKerihan and S. J. Luker, *The Housing Problem in Australia: Papers Read at the Winter Forum of the Australian Institute of Political Science, Wollongong 1947* (Sydney, 1947), p. 4.
14  Quoted in P. Spearritt, *Sydney since the Twenties* (Sydney, 1978), p. 23.
15  M. Kennedy, 'Domestic Architecture in Brisbane in the Late 1930s', in I. Kelly (ed.), *Papers and Proceedings, Society of Architectural Historians Australia and New Zealand, 1993 Annual Conference* (Perth, 1993), p. 64.
16  D. Dunbar, 'The Manuka Grouped Houses', in P. Freeman (ed.), *The Early Canberra House* (Canberra, 1996), p. 121.
17  See essays in ibid.

18  See Kilner, 'The Evolution of South Australian Housing Policy', pp. 232–8.

19  Aplin, 'Collaborative Planning?', p. 34.

20  M. Lewis, 'Darling and Anti-Darling in the Plan of Melbourne', in Freestone (ed.), *The Australian Planner*, pp. 43, 44.

21  *Ibid.*, p. 44.

22  *Ibid.*, p. 45.

23  A. Parkin, *Governing the Cities* (Melbourne, 1982), pp. 106–7.

24  *Ibid.*, pp 59, 63.

25  Kilner, 'The Evolution of South Australian Housing Policy', p. 76.

26  *Ibid.*, p. 77.

27  Coward, *Out of Sight*, p. 225.

28  T. Dingle and C. Rasmussen, *Vital Connections: Melbourne and Its Board of Works, 1891–1991* (Melbourne, 1991), p. 102.

29  *Out of Sight*, p. 170.

30  Information provided by R. Coles, Urban Research Program, Australian National University, 1997.

31  Kilner, 'The Evolution of South Australian Housing Policy', table 2.1, p. 76.

32  J. M. Freeland, *Architecture in Australia* (Melbourne, 1972), p. 85.

33  M. Lewis, *Melbourne: The City's History and Development*, 2nd edn (Melbourne, 1995), p. 79.

34  P. Ashton, *The Accidental City: Planning Sydney since 1788* (Sydney, 1993), p. 19.

35  *Architecture in Australia*, pp. 84–6.

36  *Ibid.*, p. 86.

37  Most sources give 1857 as the date of the first Building Act in Adelaide, which banned the use of flammable materials.

38  Freeland, *Architecture in Australia*, p. 88.

39  'Three Factors behind the Form of Melbourne's Nineteenth-century Suburbs', in P. N. Troy (ed.), *Urban Redevelopment in Australia* (Canberra, 1967), p. 9.

40  *The Accidental City*, p. 19.

41  Building Act Inquiry Committee, *Third and Final Report* (*SA Parliamentary Papers* 1940, no. 34).

42  Allom, 'The Built Environment as an Historical Resource', in Brisbane History Group, *Brisbane: Public, Practical, Personal* (Brisbane, 1981), p. 14.

43  K. Conmee, 'Subdivision Boom, Building Bust: The Slow Settlement of Norman Park', in R. Fisher and B. Shaw (eds), *Brisbane: People, Places and Progress* (Brisbane, 1995), p. 93.

44  Harrison, 'City Planning', in P. Scott (ed.), *Australian Cities and Public Policy* (Melbourne, 1978), pp. 155–6.

45  *Ibid.*, p. 142.

46  Coward, *Out of Sight*, pp. 240–2, 244.

47  Spearritt, *Sydney since the Twenties*, p. 23.

48  S. Marsden, *A History of Woodville* (Adelaide, 1977), p. 177.

# Making Do

## Chapter 3

*Miles Lewis*

The early use of local materials in Australian building is distinguished from that in most other colonial societies in four main ways. The first is that indigenous building traditions had almost no impact on European settlers, to which generalisation the use of bark is the only, partial exception. The second is that the nature of the materials called for changes in building form and technology. On the one hand they presented problems: for instance because Australian timber was too hard to cut with British tools, tools had to be introduced from Germany and America. On the other hand they presented opportunities: for instance a number of timbers could be readily split for construction purposes. The third distinctive feature is the way in which, in the first half of the nineteenth century, travelling splitters and sawyers spread advances in building technology down the eastern seaboard so that they acquired the status of endemic vernacular traditions. The fourth is the fact that owner-building was encouraged by specific historical factors.

The materials offered by the Australian landscape were otherwise comparable with those of Britain, or at least of Europe. Sods or turfs were available in some locations, though not so ubiquitous as in Europe. A variety of thatching materials grew locally, though as soon as cultivation advanced sufficiently the straws of wheat and other crops were used, just as in Europe. Clay suitable for bricks was widespread. Building lime could be obtained in many locations from limestone, shell middens, or occasionally coral. Building stones were generally not as good as in Europe—or, if they were, they were inaccessible for ordinary commercial use—but for the purposes of dry walling and other vernacular forms, most European stone types were paralleled in Australia somewhere or other.

In housing generally the impact of Australian materials is almost entirely confined to non-urban areas. Imported timber was used for most building work

41

in the ports and major cities until late in the nineteenth century, and even when local timber did come into use for framing, it was largely concealed from view. It is true that shingles and palings split from local timbers were used in urban areas, but they were entirely prohibited in central areas under the various building acts (Chapter 2), and even in the suburbs were soon displaced by corrugated iron. Local clay was of course used to make bricks, but these looked much the same as British or American bricks. Industrialised materials were absorbed into the vernacular with great rapidity, though their acceptance in the hinterland had generally to await the arrival of the railway lines. Corrugated iron is so fundamental a part of the Australian building tradition, even in the outback, that it is difficult to remember that until 1926 every bit of it was imported, mainly from Britain. Similar things could be said of almost all the common iron components, and of some others as well.

It is probably more obvious in Australia than anywhere on the globe that building, even at its most rudimentary level, is strongly informed by culture. Regardless of the availability of materials, of the characteristics of the local climate, or of the prevailing social and economic conditions, ethnic traditions frequently supervene. Within the Anglo-Celtic majority of the settlers, the Cornish can be identified by their round chimneys in almost every nineteenth-century mining field, especially in South Australia but also in locations as remote as Port Essington in the Northern Territory. Elsewhere, as in western Victoria, there are Irish settlements with whitewashed cottages surrounded by potato farms. The single-storey urban cottage, so typical of Scotland, but so atypical of England, is prevalent.

The effect of the minority ethnicities is even more striking. German *lehmwickel* construction (discussed in detail below) has been identified in all the eastern colonies, among German settlers of widely different origins. Chinese characteristics are restricted to the vernacular, in the total absence of Chinese professional designers, and they occur in cane constructions in the Northern Territory, blue bricks on the Bendigo goldfields, and in the form and style of what would otherwise be—in construction terms—entirely European joss houses. Even the Afghan camel driver has left a distinguishable imprint on the vernacular of Central Australia.

These separate traditions were fostered by the process of land selection after the 1850s. While the precise mechanisms varied from one colony to another, and from one year to the next, the general effect in New South Wales and Victoria was to put onto the land people with little money, who were required not only to survive but to make improvements and/or payments on their holdings. With no money to buy materials or to engage labour, each selector tended to fall back upon the materials offered by the land and the experience of his ethnic background. Structures differed markedly from one farm to the next, not because of the practical constraints but because the proprietors were of different ethnic origins.

The tradition of self-building continued into the twentieth century, and is the subject of Chapter 4, but it is worth noting that the average male in

Australia, to a much greater extent than his overseas counterparts, could still handle many of the less specialised aspects of building. And he had an incentive to do just this, because he owned, more often than not, the house in which he lived. The materials he used were mainly the product of his native soil, albeit in manufactured form—the timber, bricks, tiles, lime and plaster, and in due course the cement, the steel and the window glass. What he produced, however, was no longer very distinctively Australian.

## Bark

Certain common Australian trees produce bark which can be stripped off in large sheets and used for building. There is no exact parallel in any other country, for although the birch is stripped for various purposes in Europe and North America, the sheets it produces are smaller and thinner.[1] But these Australian barks present special problems because they warp and twist. If they are nailed at the four corners they will tear apart as they shrink. If they are not nailed, they will curl up, and finally blow off.

The European settlers devised an ingenious roofing system to overcome these problems. The sheets were flattened by one or more processes: smoking them over a fire, soaking them in salt water, or leaving them flattened under weights.[2] They were not nailed to the roof but tied on by the corners, which allowed for some degree of movement. The best cord was greenhide, because it was elastic, but in the case of stringybark an adequate rope could be made— as the name implies—from the bark itself.

This was sufficient to hold the bark onto the roof, but not to prevent it curling and lifting. Therefore logs or poles, best described as *ledgers*, were laid along the surface lengthwise, or transverse to the slope, to weigh the sheets down. But the ledgers could not be nailed or otherwise fixed through the bark because of the same problem of tearing, and so they were supported from above. Sloping poles or *saddle poles* were placed over them at right angles and attached by lashing or by pegs. These poles ran up to the ridge and were similarly fixed together where they crossed. Thus a complete grid of poles was laid over the roof, but resting on it rather than fixed to it, and there were no nails or metal fixings in the whole system.[3]

The Aboriginals were skilled in selecting suitable trees and in peeling the bark for canoes and other purposes, and in some areas for the construction of shelters. These were either lean-tos or large bark sheets bent into an inverted V form, and one of the first illustrations of the latter type appears in *The Voyage of Governor Phillip to Botany Bay*.[4] But the European settlers waited more than quarter of a century, to about 1815, before they made any use of bark. It was well after this again, possibly towards 1840, that the canonical settler's bark roof emerged, but when it did it swept the eastern seaboard.

This raises a number of questions about European adaptation to the Australian environment. Why was it so long before any use was made of a

43

building material that was so readily available? Was the final roof form literally an invention by the settlers? Or was it a combination, deliberate or otherwise, of elements which occur separately in disparate thatching traditions in Europe? Or did it derive from somewhat similar form of construction of *atap* palm thatch roofing in Sumatra, and if so was this by way of direct experience, or from the illustration first published in 1811 in the third edition of Marsden's *History of Sumatra*?[5] Or, finally, did it derive from an analogous form of bark roofing used by a very small minority of North American Indians,[6] and if so, how was this transmitted to Australia?

## Logs and poles

One might expect that the difficulty of sawing most local timbers would have encouraged log building in accordance with the post-neolithic traditions of northern and central Europe, and later of North America, and there are indeed some buildings of this character. But, perversely enough, log building is most extensive in areas of native pine—*Callitris*—and in forms which require extensive cutting and working.

    The traditional log cabin, a stack of horizontal logs halved together at the corners, is rare in private use, though it is widespread in police lock-ups. The pine buildings of north-western Victoria, the Riverina of New South Wales, and occasionally of western Queensland, are on the entirely different principle of *log panel* construction. A complete frame is built of sawn or split timber, and into this frame are packed small logs running horizontally. This has also been a traditional European form since neolithic times. It is found in other colonial cultures, especially in the French settlement of Acadia (later Nova Scotia),[7] and in later Canadian building, in which both logs and slabs placed in this way are referred to as *pièce-sur-pièce* or *poteaux en coulisse*.[8]

    The means of connecting the infill logs to the frame is a critical aspect. Traditional European, and earlier Australian, practice was to form grooves in either side of the vertical posts, and to trim the log ends into the form of tongues which could be slotted into the grooves. Later Australian practice avoided the labour of cutting the groove by nailing on a pair of vertical strips, or cleats. This method was hardly feasible when nails had to be individually and expensively forged by a smith, so it came into its own only when mass-produced nails became available, especially wire nails from about 1870.

    Thus this common Australian vernacular construction was dependent upon a mass-produced and imported product. Similar comments can be made of most of the Australian vernacular. Apart from bark construction, which can be done with wooden pegs and cords made from the stringybark itself, most construction depends upon imported materials or tools—on saws and axes, nails and galvanised wire. Even earth construction (apart from cob, which is the form least used in Australia) depends upon sawn timber formwork assembled with European fixings.

44

## The splitters

A distinctive aspect of Australian vernacular construction is its reliance upon split timber, though this derives directly from British and Irish traditions. Australian timber was generally harder than European timber, and rapidly blunted or broke the usual British saws and axes. Governor Arthur Phillip complained about poor tools at the outset of settlement, and four years later was still seeking replacements for British tools which had worn out. There was no substantial improvement prior to the arrival of the American axe towards the mid-nineteenth century.

On the other hand many Australian species were, in varying degrees, amenable to splitting with a maul and wedges, so that split timber came into common use for post and rail fences, framing members, slabs for walling, palings for fencing and roofing, and shingles for roofing. James Atkinson lists among the items an emigrant should bring to the colony, 'Two sets of cleaving wedges, with iron rings for mauls' and 'Cleaving axes or knives for splitting palings, shingles, and laths'.[9] He clearly regarded these as items which would be understood by his reader, and would be readily obtainable at home. Peter Cunningham describes the wedges as being long and thin 'with an irregular indented groove up the middle, to make them draw, and be retained better, from the hold the irregularities of the groove give'.[10]

'The trees for splitting', according to Cunningham, were 'singled out by the straightness of their stem, its freedom from notches, and the smooth, straight-grained nature of the bark, the swirly bark always denoting a swirly fibre in the wood.' Alexander Harris describes splitting blackbutt in the 1820s, so true that it could scarcely be distinguished from sawn stuff, and with hardly a splinter.[11] Atkinson distinguished blue gum as a timber which would split well, except that grown in the County of Argyle which was smaller in size, while the 'black-butted gum' (blackbutt) and forest or water gum were, by implication, similar in properties. Ironbark was identified as a timber that would split easily, and made excellent shingles and fence rails, while stringybark, and by implication turpentine, were readily split for building timbers, fencing and palings. Forest oak (known in England as Botany Bay wood or beef wood), and the rather similar swamp oak, were both used for shingles, the former splitting from heart to bark.[12]

Splitting from heart to bark—that is radially—was the normal principle in Britain, and Cunningham describes how it was done in Australia. But most Australian timbers were split tangentially,[13] especially messmate stringybark, which yielded pieces up to $2^1/_2$ by 5 feet.[14] Atkinson gives an account of tangential splitting, using blue gum, ironbark, stringybark (not the messmate of Victoria and Tasmania) or box:[15]

> The tools used in splitting are a cross-cut saw, scoring axe, set of seven wedges, and two mauls or beetles . . .

> They . . . select the straightest and freest grown trees, fell them with a cross-cut saw, cut them off to proper lengths, and billet them out into as many divisions as the size of the tree will admit; they are then split or run out with wedges into rails or posts; not from heart to bark as is practised in splitting woods in England, but across the silver grain.

According to W. T. Pyke, some of the older trees required gunpowder for the first split.[16]

The best time for splitting or for felling was late autumn. Then, it was held, the new wood had reached maturity, but the sap was at the minimum. If the work was done in spring, the grain would contract unevenly; the timber would become more open, cracked and loose, it would last less well, and it would be more susceptible to rot, grubs and white ants.[17] Shingles, palings and slabs were always of split timber; fenceposts and rails usually were. In rural areas split timber was used even in place of sawn for work such as stud frames.

## Slab construction

46

Slab construction comes in two main forms, depending upon whether the slabs are placed horizontally or vertically, and both types rely upon a timber frame to support them. Robert Irving has concluded that slab construction was not used in Australia before Macquarie's time,[18] and William Thornley's description of a farmhouse in Van Diemen's Land dates from that period, though it may have been standing for some time before he saw it in 1817. It was about 30 feet long and 'built of the logs of the stringy-bark tree, split in half, and set on end'.[19] The earliest illustration of slab construction is of the miller's cottage at Marsden's mill near Parramatta in 1820,[20] and the earliest local descriptions after Thornley's date from later in that decade. By that time, to judge from Alexander Harris's reminiscences, slab buildings were becoming common.[21] Cunningham speaks of split timber and plaster as a standard type of construction.[22] Plastered-over slabs were used for the first military barracks and detached cottages at Moreton Bay (Brisbane) in 1825, and then for a number of further buildings in 1826.[23]

Within two decades, the construction had become standard throughout large areas of the eastern colonies. Edward Beckham, Crown lands commissioner for the Lachlan District, in 1841 visited fifty-two squatting stations, the buildings on which were of slabs in fifty-one cases, and brick in one. In 1844 he visited 144 stations, all with slab or bark buildings, and in 1855 he visited 155, of which 150 were of slabs, in combination with weatherboard in four cases and bark in one.[24]

Where vertical slabs were used, their upper ends were tied or nailed to a horizontal member which spanned between the main upright posts, or alternatively there could be two horizontal members with the slab-ends sandwiched between them; the lower ends would commonly rest directly on or in the ground. The earliest descriptions of vertical slab construction, in the 1820s, include both the cruder type, with the ends of the slabs resting in the ground, and the more sophisticated type set into a complete frame. Andrew Lang's house Dunmore in the Hunter Valley, of 1826, was 'formed of rough slabs of split timber, the lower ends of which were sunk into the ground, the upper extremities being bound together by a wall plate'.[25] This was the simplest and crudest method of building with slabs, and was commonly used for outhouses, while more important buildings were of horizontal slab construction.

Alexander Harris describes the main posts as being 10 feet high with about 2 feet set in the ground, and part above ground squared off with an axe. The wall plates, on the ground and at the top, were squared off only on the sides facing each other, and in these faces were cut grooves about $1^1/_2$ inches wide by 2 inches deep to take the ends of the slabs.[26] The specification for the national school at Drayton, in 1831,[27] describes essentially the same system, and H. W. Haygarth, writing some years later, gave a more complete account:[28]

> four posts are sunk in the ground to a depth varying with the height and size of the building, and form the four corners: these support long beams, or wall-plates, grooved on the under side, and immediately beneath these again wooden sleepers are laid in the ground, a little below the surface, which are grooved similarly to the wall-plates, and are, in fact, the main foundations of the building: the sides, or wooden walls, are formed of slabs, the ends of which are respectively fitted into these grooved plates, and the sides are smoothed off with the adze to make them fit close together.

The slab hut at Delegate, southern New South Wales, is one of the oldest surviving slab buildings in the country, and is built on this basic system of fitting slabs into grooved top and bottom plates. The marks of close-set auger holes used to start the groove are still visible. The hut is believed to have been an outstation or manager's hut for the Delegate station, which was a subsidiary of Robert Campbell's Duntroon, and was built in the 1840s (though later extended). Essentially the same system of vertical slabs set in grooved plates appears to have been used in another building thought to date from the 1840s, Gum View, off Brookman Road near Kuitpo, South Australia.[29]

External walls made of split slabs could be made smooth and windproof by several methods: covering them with battens, sealing up the joints with plaster or mud, or plastering the wall surface completely. Generally the use of battens seems to have been more common in Victoria, and plastering in New South Wales. 'Rusticus' (W. N. Chauncy) in 1855 advised the Victorian settler to nail strips of wood over the joints,[30] and there are a number of surviving examples. The construction is also used in Don Bank, formerly St Leonard's Cottage, North Sydney, a building almost certainly dating from 1854 in its present position (though a date of 1823 has been claimed, and it may have been moved in whole or in part from a nearby site). In Queensland battened slab buildings are common in the south-west, particularly Tambo.

47

In all these cases it is uncertain whether the cover strips are original or were added, but they would certainly be unlikely in 1823, for the method was suitable only after the mid-century when nails became comparatively cheap. Most commonly, according to Donald Watson, battens were a later addition to slab buildings which, even if fitted tightly when first built, soon gaped as a result of shrinkage.[31]

Complete plastering of slab buildings was common in New South Wales, but there is no specific reference to it being done in Victoria. The slabs were chipped all over with an axe to provide a key, and then plastered with a mixture of alluvial soil, cow dung, and chopped grass, which was put on with a light spade and then smoothed with a trowel.[32] Haygarth, writing of New South Wales in the 1840s, speaks of using lath and plaster over the slabs, the face of it lined in imitation of stonework.[33] Precisely this was being done in the 1860s at Hill End, New South Wales.[34] It is occasionally found in Tasmania,[35] and Louisa Meredith spoke derisively of the house she was forced to occupy near Port Sorell as Lath Hall because it was built of slabs internally lathed and plastered. and externally lathed but not plastered—though doubtless intended to be.[36] In Western Australia, Cook's Park homestead on the Leschenault Estuary, of about 1862, had wattles nailed over both the internal and external faces of the slabs, which were then plastered.[37]

The majority of squatters' houses were of horizontal slabs fitted into slots in the sides of the vertical posts, as at Wambiana hut, Queensland.[38] Often such a groove was formed by drilling wide auger holes at fairly close intervals, and then cutting out the wood between them; the circular traces of the auger at the bottom of the groove can often be seen today. Later it became more common to form the groove by nailing a pair of vertical cleats onto the posts, once again a practice that grew as nails became cheaper. This is the case at Bygoo north of the Murrumbidgee, dating from about 1870,[39] and in one of the north barns at Moray homestead, Research, near Melbourne.

In horizontal, just as in vertical, slab construction, the slabs might on occasion be sawn rather than split, and really would be better termed *planks*, or even *boards*. John Cotton built a house of sawn timber slabs at his property Doogalook on the Goulburn in 1843.[40] At Coonanga homestead, on the Murray, circular-sawn redgum slabs were used in 1866, some of them with beaded edges. This refinement seems to have been something of a Riverine speciality, for it is found also on the cypress pine planks at Bygoo homestead, referred to above, notwithstanding the fact that they are only pit-sawn.[41]

There is a traditional English precedent for horizontal plank construction in timber partitions,[42] and it was used at the Hudson's Bay Company's buildings at Fort Vancouver, Canada, in 1839, where it was said 'posts are raised at convenient intervals, with grooves in the facing sides. In these grooves planks are inserted horizontally, and the walls are complete.'[43] This construction was known as *bois en coulisse*.[44] As the name indicates, it is essentially the same as the framed log construction in Canada discussed above. It seems likely to remain a

48

moot point whether the Australian version of the method was independently developed, but even if this is not so it remains one of the nearest things we have to a distinctively local system of construction.

Sometimes split logs, or flitches with one curved face, were used in panels, so there is a complete spectrum between log panel and horizontal slab construction. Of the outbuildings at Albacutya homestead at Rainbow, in the Wimmera region of Victoria, there survive two out of the original seven built between 1849 and 1857, and these have been removed to a folk museum. They are of half-logs placed in the same way as horizontal slabs. The posts are squared, and have battens nailed up them to form a groove for the logs; the half round side of each log faces outward, and it is chamfered off at the end to fit into the groove, each panel being about 3 feet wide. Horizontal flitches are also found at the homestead of Old Drumbanaghar in the same region, dating from the 1860s. The homestead at Newcastle Waters near Darwin, similarly appears to have been of horizontal flitch construction. Split logs were used for two successive homesteads at Big Willandra station in western New South Wales, the first of the 1860s and the second of 1884,[45] in the stables at Buckburraga in the vicinity of Bathurst.[46]

The logs of the Albacutya buildings appear to fit fairly closely, but in the average hardwood slab building, assembled when the timber was green, the slabs shrank apart from each other to leave wide gaps.[47] Georgiana McCrae wrote in 1846 of her house as being:

> built of gum tree slabs supported, horizontally, by grooved corner posts and the same artifice (used again) for windows and doors. The biggest room has been furnished with a table and chairs, but no pictures—long lines of actual landscape appearing at interstices between the planks, instead! In addition to the house proper, we have recently erected a suite of wattle-and-dab rooms, which only need plastering before we begin to flatter ourselves on the possession of as comfortable an establishment as one could reasonably wish.[48]

The slabs were of stringybark, and the building still stands.

## Earth construction

The various forms of earth construction in Australia were derived from European and other overseas sources, and as no one variety was nearly so common as slabs, they can be treated more briefly here. There are basically four types of earth building—sod, cob, adobe and *pisé de terre*, as well as an infinite variety of combinations with timber and other materials.

Sods were simply cut or turned up with a plough from an area of grassy ground, which had been scythed or mown as close as possible beforehand. They were a traditional building material in many parts of the world, but especially the British Isles and Scandinavia. In Australia sod walling in buildings is associated especially with Irish settlers, and sod farm walling and stob thatching—thatch pegged into a substrate of sods—with the Scots. It is more difficult to establish the source of true sod roofing, but the Irish are the logical suspects. There were also some groups of Aboriginals who built in sods in Western Australia and Victoria,[49] but they are less likely to have influenced the European settlers.

Sods were used in the first years of Hobart,[50] and later in many other parts of Van Diemen's Land. One of the first identifiable examples in Sydney was the house of Paddy Welch at Potts Point, already abandoned by 1828,[51] and sods were common use around Bathurst by 1822 because of the shortage of timber.[52] And so it continued. When the Reverend Thomas Hassall obtained a land grant at O'Connell Plains, he built a house 'after the usual fashion in the Bathurst district then' of sod walls with a grass thatched roof: 'The sods were cut with a spade in squares, at right angles to the surface, and laid upon one another with the grass side downwards. The soil was a black clay. When the walls were up, the outside was smoothed down and stuccoed with lime, so that it looked as if built with brick or stone.'[53] His son, J. S. Hassall, reported that he found the building in good condition thirty years later. Another of the sort was built on the Bathurst road for the use of the troopers, and gave rise to the name of the place as The Sod Walls.

Today the only surviving sod-walled building in New South Wales is the house at Blayney, in the Bathurst district, built by the Irish family of Ewin. The remains of sod buildings survive at Burra and Freeling in South Australia. In Victoria nothing survives of the sod houses which largely constituted the Irish settlement of Belfast (Port Fairy), though there are sod-roofed and stob-thatched barns to be found elsewhere.

The adobe, or unbaked brick, generally derives from Spain and hence from Mexico and California, though there is an independent English 'clay lump' tradition in Norfolk,[54] which may have had some effect in Australia. Despite various unauthenticated reports of adobe structures from 1819 onwards in the Hunter Valley and around Bathurst, the use of adobe cannot be confirmed until the 1850s, except in the German settlements of South Australia,[55] and it seems likely that it was brought by gold diggers from California. Adobe is found in a number of German settlements in Victoria, Central Australia and Queensland, even though it is not generally regarded as a common German material, and occasionally elsewhere it is referred to as 'German brick'. Sometimes, too, it is called 'Egyptian brick',[56] though this less likely to be a genuine ethnic connection than a reference to the Biblical episode of the exiled Israelites making bricks without straw.

By 1911 the official *Farmers Handbook* of New South Wales included instructions for adobe construction,[57] and in the 1920s adobe was being deliberately revived in Queensland by the Department of Agriculture and the Town Planning Association.[58] By 1935 Justus Jorgensen and other artists and camp followers at Eltham, near Melbourne, had begun to use the material,[59] and it was partly on the basis of this experience that G. E. F. Middleton of the Commonwealth Experimental Building Station published his *Earth-Wall Construction* as an official report, followed in 1953 by the book *Build Your House of Earth*.[60] The outcome was that adobe construction became, and has remained, a technique in regular use by self-builders, and especially those of an artistic or environmental bent.

Cob construction is more primitive than adobe, and is the traditional earth construction of England. The earth is mixed with water and usually with straw, and piled on the wall in a plastic state. The wall can proceed only slowly, as each course of about 150 millimetres must be allowed some weeks to set before the next is placed. The surface is irregular, and must be trimmed true with a spade or other tool, and the straw creates tubes which can house vermin in the finished house. Cob was increasingly condemned by housing reformers in mid-nineteenth-century Britain, and this may account for its relative scarcity in Australia.

There are a few explicit references to Devonshire cob technique being used in South Australia.[61] In Victoria there is a remarkable surviving house of the 1840s, Bear's Castle at Yan Yean near Melbourne, made of cob in the Hampshire manner, and a settler's guide published in Melbourne in 1855 contains what may be the only local description of how to do it.[62] Many less specific descriptions of earth buildings probably imply cob; and there are many more references to earth in combination with timber frames of various sorts, where the earth is much the same as cob, though the term *pug* is better used in these circumstances.

*Pisé de terre*, or rammed earth, is the most substantial of all these materials. The earth is ideally a gravelly loam, rather than a clay such as is preferred for adobe, and it is used nearly dry, by contrast with cob. It is rammed hard into a timber-lined formwork of the desired shape, and is crisply shaped, dense, durable, and strong enough to build several storeys high if required. It is traditional in the Lyonnais of France, and in Spain, and hence in Mexico and California. It was used in Britain only in a few experimental examples of the late eighteenth and early nineteenth century, and most British settlers in Australia would have had no direct experience of it. However, it had been well publicised in Britain by the early nineteenth century, and appeared in many farming texts and settlers' handbooks used in the colonies. Other settlers, notably William Kelly, had become familiar with it in California, and put their experience into effect locally.[63]

Pisé is quite widespread in Australia, though never a part of the common vernacular. It was well-known in western New South Wales[64] and in the Riverina, where the architects Macknight, *père et fils*, specialised in it until the 1950s. But the story is otherwise much the same as for adobe. The material was publicised by state agricultural departments, before being enthusiastically promoted by G. E. F. Middleton, and since that time has been taken up in the modern revival of earth building.

51

## Hybrids

There are many combinations of timber and earth to be found in Australia, and a misleading tendency to refer to them all as wattle and daub. This term correctly applies only to basketwork (wattle), plastered with mud (daub). Versions are found in many parts of the world, but in British practice it is usually found as panels in a framed or half-timbered building. Vertical rods are put in first, and then lighter twigs or split rods are interwoven between to create a basketwork. In England hazel is the commonest material for this weaving, but in Australia, as in South Africa, the acacia has been found the most suitable and flexible timber, and it has been given the common name 'wattle' for this reason. The daub can be any suitable mud mixture, but it may contain lime and animal hair. Only a few identifiable examples survive, and it seems never to have been very common.

A more specifically Australian technique is pole and pug, in which vertical structural posts have horizontal saplings nailed to either side at intervals of about 100 millimetres, and then the whole frame is packed with mud and daubed smooth on the face. Although there are some overseas analogies, in France[65] and among Ukrainian settlers' buildings in North America,[66] the technique seems to have evolved separately in Australia. These buildings appear most commonly in mining areas in New South Wales, Victoria and South Australia. In such areas occasional examples have been reported, or survive, of a version in which stones rather than mud are packed into the frame. Given that similar pole framing packed with stones is found in tin and lead mines in Britain, it seems likely that pole and pug construction evolved locally out of mining practice.

A German technique is used rather like wattle and daub, to fill in the panels of a *fachwerkbau* (framework construction) building; it is called *lehmwickel*, or earth winding. A mixture of mud and straw is rolled around a timber stake with pointed ends, and this is placed vertically in the panel with the points in holes or grooves at top and bottom. The material is used more often for ceilings, with rows of these mud-covered stakes spanning between the joists. It is now thought that it was widespread in medieval times, and certainly examples from the seventeenth century have been found in Brittany as well as in Germany. Later examples are found in Hungary and other Eastern European countries, apparently associated with the immigration of Germans, and it is also found in German buildings in North America. Examples or reports have been found in German buildings in Queensland, New South Wales, Victoria, South Australia and possibly Tasmania.[67]

Probably related to *lehmwickel*, and found most commonly in German settled areas at least in South Australia and Victoria, is palisade and pug. Vertical stakes are used rather as in *lehmwickel*, but instead of earth and straw being wound separately around each, the whole panel is plastered with mud directly over the stakes. Elsewhere the same is done in full-height sections of walling, not merely within the panels of a frame. This is not necessarily a local corruption of *lehmwickel,* for it also found in Europe, at least in Germanised areas of the Czech Republic,[68] though not so far reported specifically in Germany itself. In South Australia this is traditionally known as pine and pug, but this term is not generally applicable because the technique is by no means confined to pine.

## Conclusion

Vernacular building traditions are usually developed over long periods of time. By a process akin to natural selection, they represent the optimum response to the environment and resources of a particular locality. Thus the alpine architecture of Macedonia, parts of Spain, Nepal, and parts of South America is almost interchangeable, regardless of the ethnicity and culture of the population.

In some parts of the world, such as northern Syria, the vernacular has remained unchanged for four or five thousand years, because the conditions have been largely unchanged. But when a population is dislocated and must apply its traditions to a strange environment, an experiment in cultural survival takes place. There has never been a grander experiment of this sort than in Australia, especially in a period of land selection. Settlers from Cornwall, Germany and China may have been on adjoining blocks, subject to the same conditions, and each drawing on their own memory or folk memory. Which building tradition will prevail, and to what extent will they merge? We cannot answer the question with any precision, but we can say that the culture of building is as complex as any other aspect of culture in Australia, and more fundamental than most of them.

**Notes**

1 John Fitchen, *Building Construction before Mechanisation* (Cambridge, Mass., 1986), p. 216; R. G. Knapp, *China's Vernacular Architecture* (Honolulu, 1987); Eric Sloane, *An Age of Barns* (extracted edition, no place, 1976 [1967]), n.p.

2 Mabel Brookes, *Riders of Time* (Melbourne, 1967), p. 70; Harriet Daly, *Digging, Squatting, and Pioneering Life* (London, 1887), p. 50; W. T. Pyke (ed.), *Bush Tales by Old Travellers and Pioneers* (2nd edn, Melbourne, 1893 [1888]), p. 71; C. J. Ellis, *I Seek Adventure* (Sydney, 1981), p. 54.

3 'Giacomo di Rosenberg' [James Tucker], *Ralph Rashleigh*, ed. Colin Roderick (Sydney, 1952 [1929]), p. 44; Peter Cunningham, *Two Years in New South Wales* (2 vols, London 1827), vol. II, p. 161; Robert Dawson, *The Present State of Australia* (London, 1830), pp. 431–2.

4 Arthur Phillip, *The Voyage of Governor Phillip to Botany Bay* (London, 1789), facing p. 119.

5 William Marsden, *The History of Sumatra* (Kuala Lumpur, 1975, reprint of 3rd edn, 2 vols, London 1811 [1783]), vols I and II, p. 57 and plate XIX, 'A Village House

in Sumatra'. The book was first published in 1783, but the plate is labelled 'Published by W. Marsden. 1810' and so must have appeared for the first time in this 1811 edition.

6 Peter Nabokov and Robert Easton, *Native American Architecture* (New York, 1989), pp. 22–3.

7 Harold Kalman cites a report of dovetailed log construction in Texas in 1685 as being 'in the manner of Canada': *A History of Canadian Architecture* (2 vols, Toronto, 1994), vol. I, p. 83.

8 Thomas Ritchie, *Canada Builds, 1867–1967* (Toronto, 1967), p. 156; E. Arthur and P. Whitney, *The Barn* (New York 1988 [1972]), pp. 122–3.

9 *An Account of the State of Agriculture and Grazing in New South Wales* (London, 1826), p. 127.

10 *Two Years in New South Wales*, vol. II, p. 165.

11 *Settlers and Convicts* (Melbourne, 1953 [London, 1847]), p. 29.

12 Atkinson, *Agriculture and Grazing in New South Wales*, pp. 14–16.

13 Cunningham, *Two Years in New South Wales*, vol. II, p. 165.

14 C. B. Mayes, *The Australian Builders' Price-Book* (Melbourne, 1862), p. 49.

15 *Agriculture and Grazing in New South Wales*, p. 92.

16 *Bush Tales*, p. 71.

17 R. W. E. MacIvor, in Jonathan Periam [adapted R .W. E. MacIvor], *The Pictorial Home and Farm Manual* (Sydney, 1885), p. 662.

18 'The First Australian Architecture', MArch thesis, University of New South Wales, 1975, p. 191.

19 *Adventures of an Emigrant in Van Diemen's Land*, ed. John Mills (Adelaide, 1973 [London, n.d. (1840s)]), p. 22.

20 Joseph Lycett, 'Mill, near Parramatta, New South Wales, the property of the Revd. Sl. Marsden', watercolour, 1820: in Tim McCormick et al., *First Views of Australia, 1788–1825* (Chippendale, NSW, 1987), p. 263. The original construction of the cottage cannot be made out, but the later skillions appear to be unequivocally of vertical slabs.

21 *Settlers and Convicts*, pp. 23, 29, 41, 79, 144, 182.

22 *Two Years in New South Wales*, vol. II, p. 162.

23 J. G. Steel, *Brisbane Town in Convict Days, 1824–1842* (St Lucia, Qld, 1975), p. 56.

24 Peter Freeman, *The Homestead: A Riverina Anthology* (Melbourne, 1982), p. 23.

25 J. D. Lang, *A Historical and Statistical Account of New South Wales* (2 vols, London, 1834), quoted in R. M. Deamer, 'Houses Erected on Original Land Grants in the Lower Hunter, Paterson and William River Valleys between 1800–1850', MArch thesis, University of Newcastle, 1971, p. 196.

26 Harris, *Settlers and Convicts*, p. 41.

27 Donald Watson, 'Outside Studding', *Historic Environment*, vol. vi, 2–3, 1988, p. 22, quoting an unidentified specification from the Mitchell Library, Sydney, in the Drayton School file, History Unit, Queensland Department of Education.

28 *Recollections of Bush Life in Australia* (London, 1848), pp. 15–16.

29 Paul Stark, *Meadows Heritage* (Meadows, SA, 1983), p. 116.

54

30  *How to Settle in Victoria* (Melbourne, 1855).

31  *The Queensland House* (Brisbane, 1981), pp. 12.1–12.2.

32  Cunningham, *Two Years in New South Wales*, vol. II, p. 162.

33  *Bush Life in Australia*, p. 14.

34  At Beyer's Cottage, c. 1865, and English Cottage (before 1869): in the latter (from inspection) the laths are diagonal across the face of the slabs and are covered first with mud and then with a finish coat of lime plaster. These dates are those given in Geoff Ashley, 'Two Centuries of the Western NSW Dwelling', *The Australian Dwelling: A Conference* (Hay, NSW, 1990), p. 4. Another example, not necessarily as finely finished, is 'Mutton's Falls', Tarana.

35  As in the original settler's house at Grantham, Bothwell, illustrated in Frank Bolt, *Vanishing Tasmania* (Kingston, Tas., 1992), p. 15.

36  Vivienne Rae-Ellis, *A Tigress in Exile* (Hobart, 1990 [1979]), p. 137.

37  Molyneux, *Looking Around Perth* (East Fremantle, WA, 1981), p. 97.

38  Ray Sumner, *Settlers and Habitat in Northern Queensland* (Townsville, Qld, 1974), fig. 10.

39  Freeman, *The Homestead*, pp. 120–1.

40  John Cotton to William Cotton, October 1843, in George Mackaness (ed.), *The Correspondence of John Cotton* (2nd edn, 3 vols, Dubbo, NSW, 1978), vol. I, p. 29.

41  Freeman, *The Homestead*, pp. 282–5, 120–1.

42  C. F. Innocent, *The Development of English Building Construction* (Cambridge, 1916), p. 116.

43  *Builder*, vol. 2, no. 60, 30 March 1844, p. 169.

44  A. J. H. Richardson, 'A Further Note on French-Canadian Roof-cover and Timber Walls', *APT Bulletin*, vol. 8, no. 1, 1976, p. 66.

45  Geoff Ashley, 'Two Centuries of the Western NSW Dwelling', in Peter Freeman and Judy Vulker (eds), *The Australian Dwelling* (Red Hill, ACT, 1992), p. 79.

46  R. I. Jack, 'History', illustration 18, in Hughes Trueman Ludlow, *Evans Shire Council Heritage Study* (2 vols, no place, 1987), vol. I, no page,

47  James Armour, *The Diggings, the Bush, and Melbourne* (Glasgow, 1864), p. 13.

48  Hugh McCrae (ed.), *Georgiana's Journal* (Sydney, 1934), p. 196; N. W. Thomas, *The Natives of Australia* (Melbourne, 1906), p. 51.

49  Thomas, *The Natives of Australia*, p. 51.

50  John Shillinglaw (ed.), *Historical Records of Port Phillip: The First Annals of the Colony of Victoria* (Melbourne, 1879), p. 13.

51  Barrie Dyster, *Servant and Master* (Kensington, NSW, 1989), p. 35.

52  Barron Field, 'Journal of an Excursion Across the Blue Mountains of New South Wales, October 1822 . . .', in George Mackaness (ed.), *Fourteen Journeys over the Blue Mountains of New South Wales, 1813–1841* (Sydney, 1965), p. 132.

53  *In Old Australia* (Brisbane, 1902), p. 187.

54  Emil Mercer, *English Vernacular Houses* (London, 1975), p. 135.

55  John Archer, *Building a Nation* (Sydney, 1887), p. 53; Gordon Young, 'Early German Settlements in South Australia', *Australian Journal of Historical Archaeology*, vol. 3, October 1985, p. 50.

56  Ellis, *I Seek Adventure*, pp. 8, 9, 11, 29.

57  Clough Williams-Ellis, *Cottage Building in Cob, Pisé, Chalk and Clay* (London, 1919), p. 59.

58  *Architectural and Building Journal of Queensland*, vol. 8, no. 87, 10 September 1929, pp. 27–32.

59  Peter Cuffley, *Australian Houses of the Forties and Fifties* (Knoxfield, Vic., 1993), pp. 129–30.

60  *Earth Wall Construction* (North Ryde, NSW, 1946); *Build Your House of Earth* (Sydney, 1953).

61  G. S. Kingston to G. F. Angas, 25 December 1837, Mortlock Library PRG 147, transcript kindly supplied by Don Langmead; Jim Faull and Gordon Young, *People Places and Buildings* (Adelaide, 1986), pp. 45, 66–7.

62  'Rusticus', *How to Settle in Victoria*, p. 20.

63  William Kelly, *Life in Victoria in 1853, and Victoria in 1858* (2 vols, London, 1860), vol. I, pp. 296–9, 318–19.

64  A. L. Green, 'Unfired Earth Walls: The Promotion and Use of Sod, Sun-Dried Brick, Cob and Pisé Walling in New South Wales from 1788 to 1960', MBltEnv thesis, University of New South Wales, 1989, passim.

65  Georges-Henri Rivière, 'La Maison Rurale des Pays Normands', in *Chantier 1425* (reports of a survey of vernacular architecture, early 1940s, held in the library of the Musée des Arts et Traditions Populaires), p. 20.

66  Christopher Martin, 'Skeleton of Settlement: Ukrainian Folk Building in Western North Dakota', in Thomas Carter and B. L. Herman (eds), *Perspectives in Vernacular Architecture, III* (Columbia, Miss., 1989), p. 86 ff; David Murphy, 'Building in Clay on the Central Plains', in *ibid.*, p. 81; Blanton Owen, 'The Great Basin "Mud" House: Preliminary Findings' (abstract), in *ibid.*, pp. 245–6.

67  Miles Lewis, 'Lehmwickel', in Paul Oliver (ed.), *International Encyclopedia of Vernacular Architecture* (London, 1997), s.v.

68  Vaclac Mencl, *Lidova Architektura v Ceskoslovensku* (Prague, 1988), p. 182.

56

## Chapter 4

# Necessity the Mother of Invention, or Do-It-Yourself

*Tony Dingle*

> There is some of the same fitness in a man's building his own house as
> there is in a bird's building its own nest.
>
> HENRY DAVID THOREAU

'I reckon we can build our own little place', declared Bill Brown as he despaired of finding a house any other way at the height of the housing shortage after World War II.[1] He was about to follow in the footsteps of many Australians. There is a great Australian tradition of building one's own home, although it has gone largely unnoticed. In Aboriginal Australia all home building was do-it-yourself. Since European settlement there has also been much owner-building, although it is difficult to estimate how much before the 1950s. Of course, numbers are dependent upon which definition of owner-building is used. The Australian Bureau of Statistics (ABS) defines an owner-built house as one 'erected . . . by the owner or under the owner's direction without the services of a contractor who is responsible for the whole job'.[2] This embraces a wide variation in the extent of involvement in physically constructing the structure, from doing all of it oneself to doing nothing more than co-ordinating the work of tradespersons. In this chapter my primary concern is with the people who both plan and build some part of their house, that is, those who think about the kind of home they can build and then dirty their hands on site constructing a large part of it.

Shelter is a fundamental human need, but we need to ask why anyone in a market economy would want to build their own house? Specialisation is a central feature of such societies. Builders build houses, just as bakers make bread. They have acquired the necessary skills and equipment to enable them to do so. They are better builders than people who do not have their knowledge and tools. Under normal circumstances people can purchase their housing needs in the market from a stock of professionally built houses. My central hypothesis is that only when this becomes difficult or impossible will owner-building reach significant levels. Some will build for themselves if they can afford the materials but not the skilled labour needed to construct a house.

More will do so if there is a shortage of both houses and builders so that the only way in which to get a roof over their heads is to build it themselves.[3] Under these circumstances we might expect a decline in the quality of housing being constructed because amateurs are involved.

The conditions of economic development in Australia since 1788 have tended to create periodic housing shortages. During the nineteenth century the land and the mineral resources it contained were exploited through a massive importation of capital and labour. Once a resource had been identified and a method of utilising it had been worked out, expansion was usually rapid, largely because there were markets in Europe eager to buy what was produced. This was most obviously true in the case of gold, but the wool industry, and later wheat-growing, also expanded their output with breathtaking speed. As new resources were brought quickly into production by a rapidly expanding labour force, typically in locations where there was little or no accommodation, housing shortages were inevitable. This was the situation during the formative years of most of the capital cities, during the gold rushes and other mineral finds, and also with the opening up of the pastoral and later the farming frontiers. In such places housing shortages continued until the building industry adjusted sufficiently to supply both the materials and the skilled labour required. Meanwhile those desperate for accommodation built something for themselves. The extent of owner-building can be seen therefore as a measure of the magnitude of the housing shortfall.

## 'The structures of pioneer days are not for permanency'[4]

Amateurs built some of the first private residences in the capital cities. During the earliest days of settlement in Sydney convicts used the timber of the cabbage-tree palm, plastered it with mud and fashioned roofs thatched with rushes, to build modest huts for themselves on land set aside for the purpose. Better-housed observers described them as hovels. They were not well adapted to the city's heavy downpours, which played havoc with the mud-plastered walls, but they were the first modest efforts of owner-builders in Australia.[5] The convicts were also directed to build accommodation for others, thus making them, at the same time, the first European builders in Australia.

The comments of early visitors to other capital cities suggest that similar developments took place there also for, although the circumstances of their settlement differed, they all suffered from a chronic lack of shelter. In Melbourne free labourers built huts made from the local tea-tree, their frames interwoven with wattle and plastered with mud. One young journalist described the results as 'a nucleus of huts, embowered in a forest foliage', which he thought looked more Indian than European.[6] Here too a nascent building industry developed quickly, although in Melbourne it was market forces which stimulated its emergence as some people began to specialise in building these mud huts for those recent arrivals from Van Diemen's Land who could afford to buy them rather than build themselves.[7]

In both places the activities of the early home builders were somewhat anarchic, with their huts located without reference to the wider uses of the nascent urban space. The desire of the authorities to impose order on the growing settlements and the activities of their agents, the surveyors, seems to have quickly checked owner-building in what were becoming central areas, but it continued where people could still find cheap land or could squat undisturbed (Chapter 2). This was true of the Rocks in Sydney where some simply built on land to which they had no claim.[8] In Newtown (later Fitzroy) and Brunswick in Melbourne, Garryowen remembered 'bunches of cabin residences . . . formed of sods, brick, wood, canvas, or any other sort of material available'.[9]

In the bush the first owner-builders also operated outside the law as they squatted on Crown land. These squatters took their name from their English forebears, who were so labelled because they quickly threw up their cottages on the wastes or common land to which they had no title. The buildings which the antipodean squatters erected have been widely described and illustrated, so it suffices now to point out that they shared with urban owner-builders a preference for using whatever materials were available locally and for simple construction methods. It has sometimes been suggested that the dwellings were makeshift largely because of a lack of secure tenure of the land that they occupied, so that even wealthy squatters made do with modest shelters.[10]

Those seeking to settle on the land legally and to cultivate it were more likely to be constrained in their housing choices by a scarcity of capital and the need to use it on productive activities. 'The time and expense bestowed upon setting up the requisite buildings, are among the greatest drawbacks upon the success of a new Settler', declared James Atkinson in 1826, as he urged farmers to use the materials to hand and spend as little as possible on housing.[11] *Mann's Emigrant's Guide* of 1849 offered intending settlers both a justification for building their own home and a sketch of how to do so. The settler of modest means

> will necessarily proceed in the most economical style possible. And one of the first things he will proceed with, will be the erection of a house for himself and family, if he have one. Very often, however, the settler does not build his house until the land has been ploughed, cropped, and got into decent condition; being satisfied in the meantime, with a canvass tent . . . When at length he finds sufficient time to put up a house, it is after a very homely description. The first house is generally of turf pise, or slab; afterwards as wealth increases, a brick or stone house is erected.[12]

Once the *Selection Acts* attempted to open up the land to the small farmer on favourable terms from the 1860s, far more people went on to the land with little capital. The impetus to build oneself and save scarce capital was intensified by the conditions imposed on the selector by the legislation. A minimum number of improvements, including the construction of a house, fences, and the clearing of specified amounts of land, had to be completed within a three-

59

year period. Numerous selectors' diaries describe how they and their spouses and children substituted their relatively plentiful labour for scarce capital and made themselves as comfortable as they could with a shelter constructed of whatever materials were easily available to them. But this was seen to be only an initial stage in their settlement. Financial success on the land, once achieved, could be displayed conspicuously by having a grander and more ornate house constructed by a builder. This replaced their own modest effort, which could then be relegated to the status of an outhouse. Such a progression of buildings can sometimes be seen still on rural properties.

The built evidence for such a progression is not found so easily in the cities because the higher value of urban land has discouraged the survival of relics, but some families progressed in the same way. Stefan Pikusa has charted the housing progress of William Finlayson and his wife in and around Adelaide in the 1830s. Finlayson began by building an 8-foot square reed hut with a roof that leaked. After six weeks he helped a married friend to build a larger hut about 20 by 10 feet. This was partitioned into a room each for the two couples, while both men combined to build a like hut for Finlayson in Rundle Street. This was a respectable small cottage with windows and a stone chimney in which he lived for some time. A subsequent trip to the bush where he built another cottage was not financially successful, but after eight years he returned to Adelaide and could afford to have a substantial house built for him.[13]

In the nineteenth century miners also had to build themselves a house because usually no one else would do it for them. Minerals were found in remote areas, far from existing housing, and few mining companies were willing to provide company housing. The Cornish copper miners in South Australia began the tradition, building low whitewashed stone cottages at Moonta and elsewhere, just as they had long done in Cornwall.[14] Gold-mining was the most frenetic and unstable sector of the industry, but it also attracted most labour. Finds might be exhausted in weeks or months, but shelter was vital while the work went on. Photographs and drawings of the early fields show a motley collection of shelters, part tent and part hut, thrown together cheaply and quickly with whatever materials were to hand. The miner's cottage emerged as an ideal form of shelter. The simple one- or two-roomed oblong hut, 10 by 20 feet or thereabouts, consisted of a peaked roof of shingles, and later corrugated iron, on a light wooden frame clad in weatherboards and lined on the inside with hessian. A brick chimney would be added at a gable end. On the wall facing the street a window on either side would flank the front door. Such a structure was cheap and quick to build, and small and light enough to load onto a bullock dray to be moved to a new location when necessary. If there was insufficient room for a growing family, another hut could easily be built or placed alongside the first. In this way the distinctive zigzag roofline of the miner's cottage was created.[15] It was built in great numbers from Ballarat to Broken Hill.

In order to succeed in their task, all owner-builders in the nineteenth century had to meet several requirements. They needed to buy or collect materials from which to build a shelter. They also required the skills, knowledge and equipment necessary to fashion a house from these materials. Building took time, time that could not also be used for earning an income, so that builders needed to sustain themselves during construction. Finally they needed to acquire a site on which to build.

Amateur builders used whatever materials were plentifully available and therefore cheap or free. Houses were of wood where that was easily utilised, stone where it could be got without too much effort, but in the earliest years especially the humble earth in its various forms—sod, pisé and wattle and daub—was widely employed (see Chapter 3). The cost to the builder was the labour time necessary to prepare the materials. Relatively plentiful labour could be substituted for scarce cash, a vital requirement for many who needed shelter. Later, with the availability of machine-made or prepared materials, notably corrugated iron roofing and machined weatherboards, miners particularly seem to have been willing to meet the cost of these materials in return for the greater speed and ease of construction that they offered.

It is unclear how many migrants brought with them building skills or knowledge. Although people came from societies in England, Scotland and Ireland where there was a tradition of rural self-building, probably few of them had personally tried their hand at, say, wattle and daub construction.[16] Migrants from the towns would have had little opportunity to do any construction work in the high-density, brick-built, and landlord-owned environments they had inhabited. This was unlikely to have been a significant handicap, however. Probably all that was necessary was for a handful of people to have the requisite skills so that others could watch and copy their methods. This was the way in which the first wave of alluvial goldminers had learnt to mine, and they could as easily have watched how their neighbours built their shelter.[17]

From the perspective of the late twentieth century it is worth reminding ourselves that the male migrants who came in the nineteenth century were overwhelmingly manual workers. They laboured or worked at a trade or a craft, and manipulated tools and fashioned things with their hands. They were literally handy in a way that is no longer true; consequently, using their hands to build a house was an extension of a familiar activity. Some instruction manuals were written to help the amateur builder, but few of the dwellings that we know were constructed by owner-builders in the nineteenth century look much like the ambitious structures in these manuals. Intending migrants could have got some idea of how people were housing themselves in the new country from the more general guides to emigrants, such as *Mann's* which was quoted earlier.

Albert Facey's biography is revealing about how people learnt to build. As a child he watched his Uncle Archie and his brothers build a simple but effective house out of poles set vertically in the ground. Some years later he watched a neighbour build a mud and stone house, while as a teenager he made mud bricks for one new house that an uncle would build and also helped in the construction of another. Later again we find him confidently taking

61

charge of the design, costing and construction of a house made from 'bush timber' and corrugated iron. It cost about £100 for iron, hessian, nails and an oven, took three weeks to build. He was 'very proud of it, especially the chimney. I had never built a chimney before, but after a lot of working out and changing around, it worked fine—without smoking'.[18]

The time constraint—the need to build accommodation and also earn a living—was tackled in various ways. Factory work hours made owner-building difficult but by no means impossible, as we will see later. The miners at Moonta had to squeeze their building activity in among their regular shifts, and wives helped. Young men intending to marry set about building the family home just as they were to do in the suburbs a century later.[19] Many amateur builders in the nineteenth century did not work for wages on an hourly basis. The early alluvial miners worked on their own account; so too did the squatters, although in effect they were paying their station hands to build for them. The selectors, too, could allocate their time, and that of their wives and children, as they saw fit. This made it far easier to fit building activity around other, often seasonal, work requirements. The other strategy to economise on time was to build as quickly as possible, using the speediest methods. Simple huts could be erected in two or three weeks, and small places could be expanded piecemeal as the demand arose and time was available.

It was necessary to find land on which to build. The cheapest solution was to squat on a piece of land without possessing any legal claim to it. So long as little capital was embodied in the structure, this was a risk worth taking. It was the approach taken by squatters in the bush and in the early towns. After 1855 the miner's right in Victoria allowed the holder to build a house on unoccupied Crown land in return for a small annual payment. Although only those who were mining were supposed to do this, in practice many took out a miner's right simply to obtain cheap land to build on.[20] At Moonta miners were allowed to build on the mining leases free of charge. This left them without title to the land and vulnerable to eviction if they displeased the company, but at one time six thousand of them preferred to build here rather than on the surveyed town lots that they would have to purchase. They reasoned that the mine might soon close, which would push down property values.[21] Selectors, too, had access to cheap land on which to build, for they simply chose a site on the agricultural land they were already buying on term payment without incurring any extra charge.

This brief survey suggests that owner-builders in the nineteenth century who lived outside the major cities paid little or nothing for the land on which they built. Urban land values rose appreciably as towns and cities expanded rapidly in size, and this may have made it increasingly difficult for amateurs to build in the cities. Some did still operate there, although they are not easily identified. Thomas Dobeson, the disillusioned English migrant, built a small cottage measuring 20 by 28 feet for his family in the Sydney suburb of Botany in 1889, but unfortunately does not explain how he acquired the block on which he built.[22] Dobeson was not an amateur, for although not trained in the building trades he had been earning a part of his precarious living from building small shops and cottages. During the boom years in the 1880s, some builders, carpenters and others in the building trade had invested in suburban expansion by building houses to sell or rent. Typically they constructed the first house of a planned terrace and lived in it themselves while they completed the remainder of the row as funds allowed.[23] Although technically this made them owner-builders, they were not amateurs either.

## Holiday homes and humpies

During the twentieth century the economy has been rather less susceptible to sudden large geographical movements of the workforce, mainly because resource exploitation has increasingly relied on capital rather than labour. Large mining projects have required more machinery but relatively few workers, and highly capitalised companies have usually been willing to provide accommodation for their employees in remote locations. Nevertheless, circumstances have sometimes combined to create a mismatch between the demand for housing and the supply of it.

63

In some respects the environment in which owner-builders operate has also become less congenial from the early years of the twentieth century. Governments became increasingly concerned to establish minimum housing standards for public health reasons and also in the interests of town planning. Local authorities also acquired by-law powers and used them in some places to prevent the building of small houses. Such developments, which are detailed in Chapters 2 and 18, made it harder for typical owner-builders to construct the cheap, low-quality accommodation they had built during the nineteenth century. Richard Harris has argued that self-help building flourished only beyond the reach of the planning and health regulations in North American cities, in other words that owner-builders and regulators were antipathetic.[24] Their houses could be distinguished from the products of the building industry in part because they did not conform to regulations. The growth of what have been called 'network technologies' posed additional problems.[25] In the form of reticulated water, sewerage, gas and electricity supplies, they all introduced technical complexities into house construction which were beyond the competence of, or forbidden to, most amateur builders. It became necessary to employ expensive specialists to install the equipment.

There was a serious housing shortage after World War I, but there is no sign of any increase in self-help activity in the capital cities. This is surprising because there appears to have been an obvious stimulus to self-build. In Europe shortages forced many people to build their own homes and encouraged some governments to assist them in their efforts.[26] It may simply be that there was intensified activity in Australia but historians have not yet unearthed evidence of it; this seems unlikely given the clear indications of activity after World War II that are easily found in the press and elsewhere. An alternative explanation is that the efforts by both federal and state governments to provide housing finance on favourable terms to low-income groups successfully housed those who might otherwise have been forced to build for themselves.[27] Upwards of one-third of the large number of houses built in Melbourne during the 1920s were financed by such schemes, with the War Service Homes Scheme the most important single source of finance.[28]

Outside the major cities, owner-builders were more in evidence. Large amounts of labour were required in the La Trobe Valley in Victoria in the 1920s and 1930s, as the massive brown coal deposits located there were developed to produce electricity on a large scale. The State Electricity Commission (SEC) of Victoria, which was in charge of the development, set about building the township of Yallourn on garden city principles as a model town for its employees. The well-designed, substantial houses were to be rented out at 10 per cent of their capital cost. It quickly became evident that these rents at 22s 6d a week were too high for the majority of SEC workers on the basic wage. In an area where there was little alternative housing, such workers gravitated to an older unplanned mining settlement, known as Brown Coal Mine. Here they could rent a plot of land from the SEC for one shilling a year and build their own house with whatever materials they could lay their hands on. They threw up their houses anywhere except on the road, using traditional bark and slab construction but also packing cases from the mine, flattened kerosene tins, and sacking treated with a cement and lime wash. Similar shanty towns sprang up in other locations nearby, with some SEC workers applying for a miner's right and then building a home on the land they claimed. The SEC was embarrassed by this but was unable to come up with accommodation at an affordable price. Its initial attempts to demolish the shanty towns gave way eventually to the provision of basic services such as water and sanitation in order to combat health problems.[29]

Self-help building activity became increasingly evident in new locations from early in the twentieth century. During the previous century only the very wealthy had been in the position to afford holiday homes, but somewhat higher wages and longer holidays, combined with the growing popularity of open-air recreation at the beach and elsewhere, led to modest attempts to ape the wealthy. Camping in a tent at the beach during the summer holidays could lead to the construction of a small 'bungalow' on the foreshore if it was possible to get access to land. Clusters of holiday shacks grew up in places around the coast during the inter-war years where private land could be purchased cheaply or where there was a reasonable prospect of building on public land without being disturbed. Bonnie Vale on the shores of Port Hacking in New South Wales began as a collection of fishermen's huts after 1918. During the 1920s they became holiday homes for some, but by the 1930s many people out of work and desperate for accommodation were living there.[30] This pattern was repeated along the West Gippsland coast of Victoria, where driftwood combined with materials scavenged from the state coal mine at nearby Wonthaggi was converted into rudimentary holiday homes, which subsequently housed an increasing number of families as unemployment drove them there.[31] The makeshift structures that resulted did not please the eye of the health officer or the municipal inspector.

In 1915 the Royal Commission on the Housing Conditions of the People in the Metropolis in Victoria examined the shoreline of Port Phillip Bay from Black Rock to the town of Frankston.[32] It found that private land behind the beach had been subdivided and sold off to people who wanted holiday homes, and increasingly to families looking to build their own family home and so escape from the rents in Melbourne's established suburbs. 'Bungalows' were crammed together onto these blocks with what officialdom identified as inadequate water supply and drainage. There are close parallels between these kinds of developments and what was happening along parts of the British coast and waterways, where weekenders were springing up to provide what Dennis Hardy and Colin Ward have called 'Arcadia for All'.[33]

Many of those who built their own shelters in the inter-war years were in a different situation to their nineteenth-century counterparts. It was their destitution rather than a shortage of accommodation that drove them to build. Because they could not afford to rent or buy existing properties they were simply not in the housing market. Their poverty was reflected in the rough structures that they erected wherever they could find free land and free or cheap materials. These were clearly and identifiably far inferior to the existing housing stock and to the houses built by the building industry during this period.

Some of the families trying to make their way as farmers in the Closer Settlement and Soldier Settlement Schemes after World War I were forced to live in bag humpies that they erected on their blocks because they could not afford anything better. One returned soldier pointed out: 'It is a mistake to think that because we were willing to crawl into a dug-out or shell-hole and call it home, a few years ago, that we have acquired a taste for that mode of living.'[34] As the economy slumped into the Great Depression at the beginning of the 1930s, more people found themselves in a similar situation. The unemployed had time but no money, and some of those who had lost both income and home exercised their ingenuity in constructing temporary accommodation out of whatever materials came freely to hand. Waste land in the cities sprouted ramshackle accommodation. Dwellings on the West Melbourne tip at Dudley Flat became known widely by the ironic name of 'Dudley Mansions'.

The river flats outside country towns offered free land, water and waste disposal facilities. Outside Mildura in the mid-1930s, 225 huts had been built by their occupants:

> Constructed in the main of timber frame covered with bags, these 'shacks' and 'humpies' house approximately 1,000 people, of whom approximately 50 per cent. are children . . . these dwellings have been erected on the river frontages, are mostly without floors and are subject to periodic flooding. No regular system of sanitation has been provided by either municipality, and the shack dweller is

65

therefore obliged to make his own arrangements for disposal of nightsoil. This is particularly dangerous and objectionable as most of the shacks are erected adjacent to the river.[35]

For the first time in the 1930s there was some modest government assistance to those wishing to build themselves. This may have been stimulated by recognition of the precarious position of self-help builders, as well as by knowledge of ambitious schemes for assistance overseas, especially in Sweden.[36] The Housing of the Unemployed Trust set up in New South Wales in 1934, built and sold 833 houses by 1943; it also financed the purchase of building materials which were used by 1946 borrowers to build or extend houses with their own labour.[37] There were also community building projects at Matraville and Stockton, where local companies raised funds and labour to build housing for war widows and the war disabled.[38]

## The postwar boom

66     After World War II a period of rapid family formation and heavy immigration, following on the heels of wartime disruptions to residential construction, created the biggest housing shortage the nation ever experienced. Residential building had collapsed during the Great Depression of the 1930s and had not recovered fully before World War II broke out in 1939. There was virtually no private construction after the attack on Pearl Harbor and the Commonwealth Housing Commission established to investigate the housing situation estimated that Australia faced a shortfall of 300,000 dwellings in 1945.[39] There was considerable overcrowding, especially in the cities. The 1947 census indicated that there were only 877 dwellings for every 1000 households, while a 1949 opinion poll found that in metropolitan areas one house in four contained an extra family or individual who would have moved into their own accommodation had any been available.[40] Towards the end of the war people ranked better housing second behind full employment on their list of priorities for change.[41] There was a rising public expectation that everyone would have better housing in the new postwar world, and specifically that every family deserved to occupy and own its own detached home.[42]

People looking for a place of their own could explore various possibilities. Most of them were eligible to apply for public housing and many did, but they faced enormous waiting lists. In Victoria, for example, the Housing Commission was building nearly 3000 dwellings a year but its waiting lists had blown out to almost 43,000 applicants, all of whom went into regular ballots to choose tenants.[43] The odds were obviously not good, and many quickly concluded that their prospects of being housed by the state were negligible. Although there had been expectations that public housing would provide up to a half of all housing needs in the immediate postwar years, it is clear from Figure 4.1 that this level of provision was not remotely achieved. Nor was the private rental

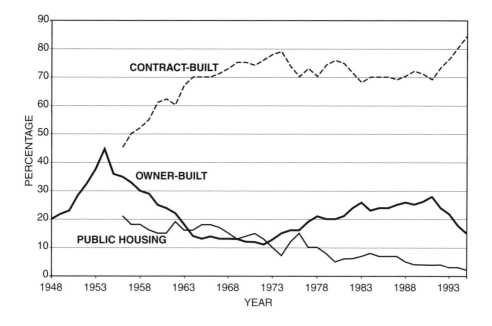

**Figure 4.1** Proportion of houses built annually in Australia by private contract builders, owner-builders and the public sector
*Source:* ABS, Building and Construction series.

market a viable alternative for home seekers because it was shrinking in size. The continuation of rent controls, which pegged rents at prewar prices during an inflationary period, meant that landlords earned poor returns. In such circumstances there was no incentive to build new private rental accommodation, and existing landlords sold their properties to their tenants.[44]

The alternative was to try to buy a house or build for onself. Many turned to the private building industry. Here they faced the prospect of long delays caused by materials and labour shortages, rapid increases in price, and poor workmanship. Some were so desperate to get out of crowded accommodation that they would not wait months or a year until a builder could begin building them a house. Ray and Kay Jones decided to build their own house as a last resort once they had failed to persuade any builder to do it for them within what they considered to be a reasonable time.[45] This way they could at least control the building process and try to search out scarce building materials personally; they could console themselves with the thought of the cost savings they were enjoying. There was a hint that this might happen when a Gallup poll of people sharing accommodation in 1945 revealed that one-third of them planned to build their own house rather than buy one once conditions allowed.[46]

It was for these reasons that owner-builders emerged in large numbers and set to work in the capital cities as well as in small towns and rural areas. As in the nineteenth century it was the shortage of housing, this time both public as well as private, which persuaded people to build for themselves. The architect Robin Boyd identified them as 'a new social phenomenon'.[47] The playwright David Williamson, growing up in the 1950s, remembered:

> I had an extreme anxiety attack when I went out to my cousin's place at Niddrie in Melbourne's outer suburbs. I saw all these guys building their houses. It used to be the Australian pastime; they'd work all week and then spend the weekends building these homes-to-be so they could get married. I thought this was a rite of passage and it was obligatory that every male had to build his own house. I was hopeless at carpentry and I had nightmares that when I reached 21 I'd have to go out to Niddrie and build my own house.[48]

68   Figure 4.1 shows the proportion of all houses completed each year by owner-builders, private contract builders and the public sector throughout Australia between the beginning of the 1950s and the early 1990s. The graph is dominated by the peak level of more than 40 per cent of all houses built by their owners in 1954, but the average throughout the 1950s is around one-third. This was roughly in line with the experience of the United States, and probably Canada at the same time.[49] The number of owner-builders then shrank dramatically as the housing shortage was eliminated, partly at least as a result of their efforts.[50] A decade later they were completing less than one-third of all houses, and for a time they built fewer houses than the public sector.

This seemingly straightforward relationship between the magnitude of housing shortages and the level of self-help activity at the national level is modified somewhat by an examination of regional variations, because there were large differences in the level of owner-building among the various states. In New South Wales, Tasmania, Victoria and Western Australia, owner-builders were responsible for 40 per cent or more of house completions in the early 1950s, but in South Australia and Queensland only between 20 and 25 per cent. In other words there was proportionately twice as much self-help building in New South Wales as in Queensland and South Australia. It seems that there was an inverse relationship between the level of public housing provision and the volume of owner-building. It was in those states where people perceived they had little chance of getting public housing that they were willing to build themselves.[51] The South Australian Housing Trust built proportionately more than twice as many houses as its counterparts in Tasmania or in the other states with high levels of self-help activity.

Neither the Commonwealth nor the State governments offered aid to self-help builders during these years. This was not even considered as an option during the planning of postwar housing policy, despite the modest moves in that direction which had been in the 1930s and knowledge of successful Swedish experiments. But they did allow owner builders access to building materials. This was permitted despite serious materials shortages and opposition from the building industry. Without access to materials no self-help building of substantial housing, as opposed to shacks, would have been possible. Each State appears to have made a percentage allocation of the available materials between public housing, private housing and non- residential construction. In NSW and Victoria an upper size limit was imposed on new houses to make materials go as far as possible, but anyone who did not already own a home could apply to build one. South Australia and WA kept a tighter rein on building and would only give permission to build if the necessary materials were available, and then on a priority basis.[52]

Finding the building materials that they needed remained the most challenging task facing owner-builders. Once their house plans had been formally approved by the municipality, they could go along to building suppliers to buy what they needed but they faced long and frustrating delays. *Australian House and Garden* explained to home builders that 'you must be prepared to crawl and crawl *and* crawl to get your materials. No builders' suppliers will come running to accept your order. You're the one who'll be doing the grovelling. You're one of the "no second order" types, you poor owner builder you.'[53] The folklore of self-help during the 1950s revolves around stories of cement or bricks acquired in roundabout ways, of green framing timber carted straight from mills in the forest. It was a time when a load of bricks made a welcome wedding present.[54] The search was complicated by the existence of minimum specifications for building materials; unwary amateurs could end up buying roofing tiles made in India that were rejected by the building inspector. No longer could they use local or secondhand materials as their predecessors had done.

The houses which owner-builders constructed after the war were more complex and sophisticated than those erected by their predecessors, but a lack of building skills does not appear to have slowed their progress. Newspapers and magazines were quick to offer self-help builders information, advice and encouragement. *Australian Home Beautiful* designed what it called a 'Pay your Way House' and over several months provided detailed and illustrated instructions on how it could be built, making no assumptions about prior knowledge of building techniques.[55] *The Australian Carpenter*, written as a textbook for apprentice carpenters, quickly went through eight editions and sold 80,000 copies to self-helpers in search of instruction in the skills that they needed.[56] The Small Homes Service was started by the Royal Victorian Institute of Architects in Melbourne in 1947, in conjunction with a daily newspaper, the

*Age*, and was directed by the architect Robin Boyd. He set out to encourage and advise owner-builders in his weekly column in the newspaper, and the service offered architect-designed house plans that were simplified specifically for amateur builders.[57]

Owner-builders who have been interviewed recall approaching their task confidently, even when they had no background in building or handicraft skills. Their main source of help and information was usually other builders in the vicinity, both amateur and professional, whom they could talk to and whose work they could examine and copy. In this way they were following a tradition well over a century old. Alva Jones's husband decided to build his own house after visiting another amateur and concluding 'if he could do it, so could I'.[58] Typically they used weatherboard or fibro-cement sheeting as wall cladding, rather than bricks, partly because these were cheaper but mainly because they were easier to use with limited skills.

Most postwar owner-builders were wage earners with regular working hours. It took determination and commitment to work at a job all week before spending each weekend or summer evening labouring on the house for two years or more until it was finished. They were no longer constructing small, simple miners' cottages that could be thrown up quickly. Those who persevered faced the difficulty of travelling considerable distances from their lodgings in the inner suburbs to their outer-suburban block. Many wanted to live on their block in temporary accommodation to save travelling time while they built. Some erected simple huts, brought in caravans or old railway carriages, or pitched tents, while others tried to build structures that they could later turn into garages. This provoked conflict on the suburban frontier between owner-builders and municipal building inspectors because any temporary structures had to be approved by the municipality. Municipalities varied in how strictly they tried to enforce their by-laws. Typically they seem to have been willing to allow someone to erect a temporary hut once they had made significant progress in building their home. Whenever people had lived in temporary accommodation for a year or so without signs of progress on their house, municipalities threatened to demolish their hut. Shanty towns sprang up in some areas while outer suburbs filled 'with building frames which appear to have settled into a state of permanent incompletion'.[59]

Owner-builders required finance to buy both the land and the materials they needed to begin building. Some institutional lenders in the housing market refused them mortgages. In Victoria, the State Savings Bank, the traditional provider of low-interest housing loans, insisted that a registered builder must construct the houses against which it would lend. The federal government subsidised the War Service Homes Division, which provided low-interest loans of up to 90 per cent of valuation to ex-servicemen, but it also refused to lend to owner-builders. It did, however, lend on completed houses that met its construction standards, thus allowing some ex-service owner-builders to raise short-term finance to build and then transfer to a War Service loan. Commercial banks varied in their willingness to lend to owner-builders and would not lend more than 85 per cent of valuation at commercial rates of interest.

Terminating co-operative building societies were established in New South Wales from 1937 and Victoria from 1944. They raised funds from banks and other financial institutions, aided by a government guarantee of repayment. They lent up to 90 per cent of valuation to their members, and the government indemnified the society if a member defaulted. These rapidly became popular; by 1946 there were well over three hundred such societies in New South Wales with more than 31,000 members. A decade later society numbers had more than tripled and membership had doubled. In Victoria they became 'the popular choice of the man [sic] who wants to build his own house but has limited finance'. He had to begin building with his own money, 'but when he gets the frame up he is entitled to a progress payment based not only on 75 per cent valuation of the work done but of his land, too'. One Victorian society estimated that 60 per cent of its members were building their own homes.[60] These co-operative terminating building societies (called housing societies in Victoria) rapidly became the most important lenders for residential construction in both states.

Other states did not follow the example of New South Wales or Victoria. This may have made it somewhat more difficult for owner-builders to raise finance in those states, but too much should not be made of this because it seems that a significant amount of self-help activity was not financed through formal lending institutions. It has been estimated that lending institutions financed only a little over a half of all houses built in the decade after the war, while public housing authorities financed less than one-fifth and private mortgages less than one-tenth. This left one house in five to be financed out of the owners' own resources.[61] Owner-builders were probably disproportionately represented in this group. Forced wartime savings as well as war gratuities were used to buy cheap, unserviced building blocks on the suburban fringes and to start building. Subsequently the rate of construction was tailored to the rate of saving, as well as to the rapidity with which materials could be acquired. Frequently it took several years to complete the house, but there were exceptions. Newly married Alva Jones and her husband believed they should not borrow to buy anything, even a house. This did not prevent them from financing and building their house to lock-up stage in only nine months.[62] The number of people able to proceed in this way despite rapidly rising prices was a reflection of the high level of savings accumulated by the end of the war and the fact that wages were keeping pace with price rises.

Much self-help activity in Europe was co-operatively organised, and there were examples of formal, voluntary co-operation in the building of houses, as well as in financing them, in Australia also. The South Australian Home Builders Club, formed in 1946, bartered the labour of its (male) members. Each member contracted to repay with his own labour the number of hours of work that others had expended on his house. Its members built three hundred homes over fourteen years.[63] The Victorian Home Builders Club worked on a

71

similar principle and was probably patterned on the South Australian organisation. It appealed particularly to immigrants, who were beginning to arrive in increasing numbers and needed accommodation.[64] There were co-operative ventures in Sydney also. The Metropolitan Homes Community Advancement Society built about three hundred homes between 1953 and 1960, although it is not clear how much of the building was done by owners.[65] The best-documented and most ambitious scheme of this kind was the Peter Lalor Home Building Cooperative Society, which set out in 1947 to create a new suburban community in Melbourne run on co-operative lines. While it employed tradesmen, it also used the labour of future owners extensively.[66] There may well have been other co-operative ventures of this kind, as well as companies such as Broken Hill Proprietary, which helped its workers to build their own homes at Port Pirie.[67] Nevertheless, such formal arrangements constituted only a tiny fraction of all self-help activity.

Men did most of the construction work. Women often laboured for them, fetching and carrying materials and tools and holding things in place. They also fed them on site and sometimes controlled the finances, but the act of building was seen to require skill, strength and stamina. Wives as well as husbands believed these to be essentially masculine virtues; consequently the building of the family nest was seen to be primarily a male achievement.[68] Slowly, often painfully slowly, houses were completed and became homes. Their owners frequently moved in long before everything was finished so that interior work stretched on for years, being carried on spasmodically amid the routines of family life. Some felt that their lives had been enriched and ennobled by the act of building a home, but for others the worry, the financial pressures and the incessant work left them profoundly damaged.[69] Some did well out of it financially, selling their homes at a handsome profit. A few built a second home, and a handful enjoyed the experience so much that they became professional builders. Owner-builders saw themselves as suburban pioneers, rightful heirs to those who had opened up new farming land in the nineteenth century.[70] They had transformed muddy paddocks into a tranquil domestic environment far superior to the overcrowded inner city they had left.

Their achievements are impressive. They contributed largely to solving the nation's housing crisis. They did so by building substantial parts of the new ring of suburbs forming around the great capital cities, a location where their predecessors of the nineteenth and early twentieth centuries had found it difficult to operate. Owner-built houses from this era are not distinguishable from the professionally built houses in the same neighbourhood. Graham Holland has pointed out that this indicates that owner-builders wished to conform to majority tastes in housing style and design.[71] It also indicates that amateurs were able to match the standards of professional builders and meet all the requirements of the building regulations. This is a tribute to the skills that they managed to acquire, but it also results from the emergence of an environment that allowed them to act as they did.

In Australia the essential ingredients for self-help building were cheap building blocks, buoyant incomes and full employment, combined with a cultural preference for simple, single-storey detached homes of wood or brick veneer, as well as governments that were half-hearted about town planning and did not prohibit amateurs from obtaining building materials. The contrast is with Britain, where there was little owner-building in these years. There, rationed building materials directed largely to the public sector, effective zoning of costly building land, combined with a preference for complex two-storey row or semi-detached houses of solid brick, offered few openings to the enthusiastic amateur with limited equipment and skills, despite growing incomes and full employment.

## Epilogue

Owner-builders did not stop their work once the postwar housing shortage had been overcome. As can be seen from Figure 4.1 they have continued to build one-tenth, and sometimes as many as one-quarter, of all houses each year for more than three decades. The story of this activity remains to be told. These builders were not reacting to major housing shortages as their predecessors had done in the decades before. Holland has surveyed owner-builders who were active in Sydney in the late 1970s and asked why they were doing it themselves rather than having a house built for them. Generally they were not short of accommodation. They earned higher-than-average incomes and they built themselves in order to get the kind of house they wanted at a price they were willing to pay. They built conventional designs using conventional materials.[72]

A different kind of owner-building gathered pace in some rural areas in the 1970s as groups and individuals interested in self-sufficiency and a simpler life went into the bush to build cheaply and often in sympathy with their surroundings. For some this was a financial necessity, but for others it was a deliberate choice to adopt a new lifestyle. They built cheaply and sometimes innovatively, using local and secondhand materials. Often their homes did not conform to local building regulations, which led to conflicts between builders, councils and older residents in places such as Nimbin.[73] In some respects this was a return to nineteenth-century approaches to owner-building.

One further development needs to be included in any discussion of recent self-help building. A widening range of hand tools powered by small electric motors have invaded backyard sheds and empowered home handymen to believe that there is nothing they cannot tackle with their trusty Black and Decker in their hand. Do-it-yourself activity in the form of extensions and renovations to the home has absorbed increasing amounts of family time and expenditure since the 1960s and transformed many houses.

73

1  *Argus*, 24 April 1946.
2  *Commonwealth Yearbook 1960.*
3  This is not to deny that there have always been some people for whom building their own home is a creative challenge they wish to undertake even though they could afford to house themselves in other ways.
4  Mary E. Fullerton, *Bark House Days* (Melbourne, 1964), p. 1.
5  James Atkinson, *An Account of the State of Agriculture and Grazing in New South Wales* (Sydney, 1975, facsimile edn [London, 1826]), pp. 76–7.
6  A. G. L. Shaw, *The Port Phillip District: Victoria Before Separation* (Melbourne, 1996), pp. 68, 72.
7  *Historical Records of Victoria*, vol. 2A (Melbourne, 1982), p. 188.
8  Grace Karskens, *The Rocks: Life in Early Sydney* (Melbourne, 1997), p. 28.
9  M. Weidenhofer, *Garryowen's Melbourne* (Melbourne, 1967), p. 45.
10  Margaret Kiddle, *Men of Yesterday: A Social History of the Western District, 1834–1890* (Melbourne, 1961), p. 54.
11  Alan Atkinson, 'Taking Possession: Sydney's First Householders', in Graeme Aplin (ed.), *A Difficult Infant: Sydney Before Macquarie* (Sydney, 1975), p. 94.
12  Robert James Mann, *Mann's Emigrant Guide to Australia, including the colonies of New South Wales, Port Phillip, South Australia, Western Australia, and Moreton Bay* (London, 1849), pp. 22–3.
13  Stephan Pikusa, *The Adelaide House, 1836 to 1901: The Evolution of Principal Dwelling Types* (Adelaide, 1986), pp. 6–8.
14  Oswald Pryor, *Australia's Little Cornwall* (Adelaide, 1962), pp. 64–5.
15  Miles Lewis, *The Essential Maldon* (Melbourne, 1983), pp. 32–3.
16  Miles Lewis, *Victorian Primitive* (Melbourne, 1978), pp. 1–2.
17  Tony Dingle, *The Victorians: Settling* (Sydney, 1984), p. 42.
18  A. B. Facey, *A Fortunate Life* (Melbourne, 1990), pp. 19–20, 49, 105, 194–5.
19  Pryor, *Australia's Little Cornwall*, p. 65.
20  John Hirst, *The World of Albert Facey* (St Leonards, NSW, 1992), pp. 20–1.
21  Pryor, *Australia's Little Cornwall*, pp. 64–5, 69.
22  Graeme Davison and Shirley Constantine (eds), *Out of Work Again: The Autobiographical Narrative of Thomas Dobeson*, Monash Publications in History no. 6 (Melbourne, 1990), pp. 65–6.
23  Max Kelly, 'Eight Acres: Estate Sub-Division and the Building Process, Paddington, 1875 to 1890', *Australian Economic History Review*, vol. 10, no. 2, 1970, pp. 155–68; A. E. Dingle and D. Merrett, 'Landlords in Suburban Melbourne, 1891–1911', *ibid.*, vol. 17, no. 1, 1977, pp. 1–24.
24  'Self-building in the Urban Housing Market', *Economic Geography*, vol. 67, 1991, pp. 1–21, and also his 'The Unplanned Blue-Collar Suburb in its Heyday, 1900–1940', in Donald G. Janelle (ed.) *Geographical Snapshots of North America* (New York, 1992), pp. 94–7.

25  Joel Tarr and Gabriel Dupuy, *Technology and the Rise of the Networked City in Europe and America* (Philadelphia, 1988).
26  Richard Harris, 'Slipping through the Cracks: The Origins of Aided Self-help Housing, 1918–1953', *Housing Studies*, forthcoming.
27  P. Williams, 'The Politics of Property: Home Ownership in Australia', in J. Halligan and C. Paris (eds) *Australian Urban Politics: Critical Perspectives* (Melbourne, 1984).
28  A. J. Ward, 'The Development of Melbourne in the Interwar Years', PhD thesis, Monash University, 1983, p. 378; Robert Murray and Kate White, *A Bank for the People: A History of the State Bank of Victoria* (Melbourne, 1992), p. 210.
29  Meredith Fletcher, 'Yallourn the Planned, and the Township of Brown Coal Mine', in Tony Dingle (ed.), *The Australian City: Future/Past*, Office of Continuing Education, Monash University (Melbourne, 1997), pp. 65–72.
30  *Age Good Weekend Magazine*, 17 January 1998.
31  Bill Hayes, 'Miners' Huts on the Bunurong Coast' *Gippsland Heritage Journal*, no. 17, 1994, pp. 2–11.
32  Royal Commission on the Housing Conditions of the People in the Metropolis, *First Report* (Government Printer, Melbourne, 1915).
33  *Arcadia for All: The Legacy of a Makeshift Landscape* (London, 1984).                    75
34  Marilyn Lake, *The Limits of Hope: Soldier Settlement in Victoria, 1915–1938* (Melbourne, 1987), p. 154.
35  Housing Investigation and Slum Reclamation Board, *First (Progress) Report*, 1937, p. 81.
36  Harris, 'Slipping through the Cracks'.
37  N. G. Butlin, A. Barnard and J. J. Pincus, *Government and Capitalism: Public and Private Choice in Twentieth-century Australia* (Sydney, 1982), p. 229.
38  Patrick Troy, 'The Evolution of Government Housing Policy: The Case of New South Wales, 1901–41', *Housing Studies*, vol. 7, 1992, p. 224.
39  Commonwealth Housing Commission *Final Report* (Canberra, 1944), p. 11.
40  Australian Gallup Polls, *Australian Public Opinion Polls* (1949), pp. 590–9.
41  *Ibid.*, pp. 170–9.
42  Kate Darien Smith, *On The Home Front: Melbourne in Wartime, 1939–1945* (Melbourne, 1990), p. 12.
43  Warwick Eather, 'We Only Build Houses: The Commission, 1945–60', in Renate Howe (ed.), *New Houses for Old: Fifty Years of Public Housing in Victoria, 1938–1988* (Melbourne, 1988), pp. 71–2.
44  G. Bethune, 'Urban Home Ownership in Australia: Some Aspects of Housing Demand and Policy', PhD thesis, Australian National University, 1978, pp. 165–6.
45  As part of a larger study of housing and suburban development in postwar Melbourne, extended interviews of 2–3 hours duration have been conducted with owner-builders and others who lived in the suburbs during the 1950s and 1960s. Pseudonyms have been used in the text in accordance with the conditions under which the interviews were conducted.
46  Australian Gallup Polls, *Australian Public Opinion Polls* (1944–45), pp. 241–8.
47  *Age*, 28 March 1951.

48 *Australian Weekend Magazine*, 18–19 September 1994.
49 Harris, 'Slipping through the Cracks'.
50 Tony Dingle, 'Self-help Housing and Co-operation in Post-war Australia', *Housing Studies*, vol. 14, no. 3 (1999), p. 346.
51 *Ibid.*
52 Walter Bunning, W. H. Ifould, C. R. McKerihan, Sidney Luker, *The Housing Problem in Australia* (Sydney, 1947), pp. 11–12, 62–5.
53 June 1949.
54 P. M. Rehak, 'Stoking up Dreams: Some Aspects of Post-war Housing in the Suburbs of Melbourne', MA thesis, Monash University, 1988, p. 118.
55 August 1953.
56 *Age*, 22 April 1952.
57 Tony Dingle and Seamus O'Hanlon, 'Modernism versus Domesticity: The Contest to Shape Melbourne's Homes', *Australian Historical Studies*, vol. 28, no. 109, 1997, pp. 38, 42–3.
58 Interview (see note 45, above).
59 Pru McGoldrick, *When the Whistle Blew: A Social History of the City of Sunshine* (Morwell, 1989), pp. 205–6; *Age*, 22 April 1952.
60 *Age*, 21 November 1950.
61 M. R. Hill, *Housing Finance in Australia, 1945–1956* (Melbourne, 1959), p. 133.
62 Interview.
63 Archer, *The Great Australian Dream*, pp. 190–1.
64 *Age*, 10 October 1950.
65 Graham Holland, 'Cooperative Housing for Australia', Department of Architecture, University of Sydney, Paper 6, 1973, pp. 5–6.
66 Mary Johns, 'Building a Suburb: The Peter Lalor Home Building Co-operative Society', Melbourne State College, Occasional Papers, vol. 1, no. 2, 1978.
67 Archer, *The Great Australian Dream*, p. 191.
68 Interviews. There appear to have been a handful of women who built houses on their own.
69 Rehak, 'Stoking up Dreams', pp. 127–38.
70 Barbara Davison and Graeme Davison, 'Suburban Pioneers', in Graeme Davison, Tony Dingle and Seamus O'Hanlon, *The Cream Brick Frontier: Histories of Australian Suburbia*, Monash, Monash Publications in History (1995).
71 'Owner Building as an Expression of Popular Culture', *People and Physical Environment Research*, no. 52, 1997, pp. 20–7.
72 Graham Holland, *Emoh Ruo: Owner-Building in Sydney* (Sydney, 1988).
73 John Rockey, 'Architecture Arcadia', *Architecture Australia*, vol. 71, no. 4, 1982, pp. 46–51; Alison Louise Taylor, *Retreat or Advance: New Settlers and Alternative Lifestyles in the Rainbow Region* (Armidale, 1981); Graham Holland, 'Planning and Building Regulations and Alternative Lifestyles: Conflict and its Resolution in New South Wales, Australia', *Journal of Architecture and Planning Research*, vol. 3 no. 1, 1986, pp. 65–77.

76

# The Industry Time Forgot

## Chapter 5

*Glenn Mitchell*

The construction of Australian homes has been a significant economic and social activity since European settlement began in January 1788. From the early days of the colony, building work was a fundamental craft and trade. It employed large numbers of workers and made substantial contributions to the wealth of the colony.

Figures for the latter are not available but there are data on the workforce. A little over one hundred years after settlement, building workers were a significant part of the workforce. In 1891, the Census of New South Wales recorded 24,379 workers engaged in the construction of houses and buildings. With one exception, these were male workers. The Census listed all building workers under a category known as Order 19, and under sub-order 1, group 4 it listed the largest group of workers—carpenters, joiners, turners and labourers.[1]

A century later, little had changed. The building industry generated considerable wealth—in 1989–90 private expenditure on dwelling construction exceeded $18 billion, or approximately 5 per cent of non-farm gross domestic product[2]—and employed a major part of the nation's workforce. In 1989 a survey by the Australian Bureau of Statistics (ABS) found that the Australian residential sector employed more than 124,000 workers,[3] more than 40 per cent of all employees in the Australian building and construction industry.

For politicians, 'home' and home building had different meanings. Robert Gordon Menzies, as an ambitious backbencher sharpening his political skills, gave a radio broadcast in which he identified themes and issues that he would return to time and again in his long political career. He saw the family home as one of the nation's fundamental institutions. He asserted that the nation's homes were 'the foundation of sanity and sobriety' and that its 'real life' was to be found in 'the homes of people who are nameless and unadvertised'. He went on to say:

The material home represents the concrete expression of the habits of frugality and saving 'for a home of our own'. Your advanced socialist may rage against private property even whilst he acquires it; but one of the best instincts in us is that which induces us to have one little piece of earth with a house and a garden which is ours, to which we can withdraw, in which we can be among friends, into which no stranger may come against our will . . . My home is where my wife and children are; the instinct to be with them is the greatest instinct of civilised man; the instinct to give them a chance in life is a noble instinct, not to make them leaners but lifters.[4]

Ten years after this broadcast and through the electoral support of many nameless and unadvertised home dwellers and home owners, Menzies became prime minister. Another observer, Robin Boyd, said: 'Yet the small house, probably more than anything else that man has done, had made the face of Australia and to an extent the faces of Australians. Australia is the small house. Ownership of one in a fenced allotment is as inevitable and unquestionable a goal of the average Australian as marriage.'[5]

However, to describe, define and quantify the Australian building and construction industry is a complex task. There are several competing sets of data and competing interpretations of their quality. The late Noel Butlin has drawn attention to the richness of this material—those sources of historical evidence which the English historian R. H. Tawney called 'the shrivelled tissue'[6]—when he described 'the vast wealth of statistical information' available to the urban researcher. Butlin described this material as 'a veritable laboratory' and urged researchers to use it.[7]

In 1948, J. Hamilton and J. Wark argued that 'building has been neglected more than any other major Australian primary or secondary industry; its statistics are largely unassembled, its history is unwritten, its organization is virtually unknown'.[8] The eminent urban researcher Max Neutze wrote in 1981, 'Apart from the level of employment, very little was known about the building industry in Australia prior to a special ABS survey of construction establishments in 1978/79.'[9]

However, the competing claims and academic debates over the size of the Australian building industry and the historical materials which might be used for its description and analysis cannot hide the considerable changes which have occurred since January 1788.

## Innovative, timeless or just plain conservative?

Raymond Postgate has eloquently testified to the timeless qualities of the building trades. In his history of these trades in England for the National Federation of Building Trade Operatives, he drew attention to the ancient record: plasterers plied their craft on the pyramids in ancient Egypt more than four thousand years ago, and masons used their skills in the construction of

King Solomon's temple; and building workers covering a range of crafts and skills attempted over many centuries to form combinations, guilds, associations or unions. He wrote:

> For thousands of years the crafts of plasterwork, carpentry, masonry, bricklaying and tiling have been handed down from father to son, and the history of the trade is written all over the world, not in pen and ink, but in brick and stone and wood. In every age that has not been utterly barbarous and degraded, in which there has been some pleasure and colour in life for the workers, the builders have left their enduring monuments. Carpenters, masons and bricklayers have expressed the ideals and civilisation of their age as much as and as well as writers, soldiers and statesmen.[10]

W. S. Hilton was more forthcoming when he said that an Egyptian building worker 'might not understand the language but could work (with a contemporary worker) all day till sundown without suspecting that four thousand years lay between them'.[11] Others are less sympathetic to this continuity of noble tradition, craft and skill when they say that 'a peg-board chart or a type-written schedule count in the literature as newsworthy management innovations'.[12]

A study by the Australian Centre for Innovation and International Competitiveness challenged this view of an insular and innovation-resistant industry when it concluded that there had been 'a wide range of innovation'[13] in the housing industry. The report also noted that much of this innovation was in organisation rather than building technology.

Home owners and builders have consistently challenged and redefined the use of 'traditional' building materials as the only materials. Weatherboard cottages or triple-fronted, red-brick dwellings with tiled roofs are no longer the norm. In the 1940s, steel framing, plastic cladding, fire-resistant insulation, prepainted roofing iron using 'intelligent' polymers, and specialist labour to build or install particular components were yet to be devised; yet contemporary home building uses them regularly.

Some commentators see innovation in terms of building technologies, building materials and the way building work is organised. Using these categories, they proceed to make judgements about 'progressive' or 'primitive' home building practices. But are these the only categories? Organisational and technological innovations may not be the only criteria by which to judge a progressive industry.

For example, could we consider efforts by building workers to identify and define the moral and ethical worth of their work as 'innovative'? In an interesting but sadly forgotten address to building workers, John Short made the case for all building workers to pursue moral, ethical and social imperatives:

> Through negotiation and discussion you have a role to play in setting priorities. In any building programme the number of office blocks has to be balanced

against the number of houses needed. Building workers need to think about such priorities if they are to be involved in pressing governments for more funding.

　As building workers you have a legitimate concern with the types of building that you construct. Your working experience allows you to identify safe and unsafe dwellings, desirable and undesirable buildings, good and bad environments. Construction workers need to consider the social implications of buildings. Rather than seeing a building project as just so many jobs, you have to ask who gains and who loses; construction jobs at any price is too high a price to pay. I am asking you to consider the social consequences of your labour. Construction workers have a duty and a right to be concerned with the types of city they are building. You and your families have to live in the cities you build.[14]

In the light of Short's assessment, the quest for an eight-hour day by stonemasons in nineteenth-century Victoria could be seen not only as morally and ethically based but also as 'innovative'. Masons wanted a balance in their working and social lives, and fought for a fairer distribution of time for work and recreation throughout the day.[15] So could the campaign by militant building workers after World War II who opposed the diversion of scarce building materials to luxury housing rather than homes for ordinary folk. The founding federal president of the Building Workers Industrial Union (BWIU), Ted Bulmer, has spoken of the union's commitment to an innovative housing program following the war:

> It was a pity you know, that the government and building firms didn't let us look after housing after the war. We would have done a bloody better job than anyone else!! We saw the problems very clearly and I think we had the answers too. Building workers, especially those in the home building game, were more than workers. They had brains as well as skills. That's because they had a real feel for building things.[16]

The Green Bans,[17] imposed by the New South Wales branch of the Builders Labourers Federation (BLF) to prevent the demolition of working-class accommodation in Sydney and its replacement with office towers and luxury apartments, could also be seen as innovative. Building workers loudly and critically evaluated, and in some cases rejected, proposals by government planning authorities and housing developers. One such case was Kellys Bush. In 1967, residents of Hunters Hill, a northern middle-class Sydney suburb, became concerned about the future of an area of bushland known as Kellys Bush. A smelting works had closed and relocated, and rumours about other developments began. Jack Mundey, the state secretary of the BLF, argued:

> In a modern society, trade unions must broaden their vision and horizons and become involved in wide-range social, political and environmental activities.

> The struggle for improvement in wages and conditions must continue, but the broader issues should be addressed. Not only has the trade union movement the right to intervene, it has the responsibility to do so.[18]

Green Bans made a significant contribution to Australian urban planning and the determination of what constituted fair and equitable development. This legacy continues, not only in spirit but also in law. Section 94 of the *New South Wales Environmental Planning and Assessment Act 1979* requires developers to address increases in demands for 'public amenities and public services' associated with building projects.

## House building and house builders

Although many works have looked at histories of building workers and their attempts to fight for wages and conditions, there are few studies of workers in the Australian home building industry. Indeed, most histories of that industry ignore the roles of building unions or industry associations.[19]

Whatever the ebbs and flows of struggles by building and construction workers on large building sites, similar industrial and political struggles have not taken place in the home building industry. Battles between large, in some cases multinational, construction firms, employer groups, industry associations and large federal industrial organisations have not found their way to the quarter-acre block. The broad sweep of collective action and industrial activity by building unions has largely bypassed the construction of the humble suburban cottage. Some Australian building unions and their English counterparts, however, have long recognised the inherently conservative nature of a craft union.[20]

These progressive unionists argued that, if the industrial organisation of building work remained segmented and spread over several unions, each representing a different craft or trade, employers would never meet an industry challenge or a united front for industrial demands.

Thus, in February 1918, when a conference of the Federated Building Trades Unions met at the Sydney Trades Hall and agreed to form 'one big union' of the building trades and to seek a federal award, what appeared to be the promise of an organisation that would cover all manner of national building activity was, in fact, something less grandiose and more utilitarian. Leaving aside the important matter that this union never came into being, the principal players attempting to create it had little or no intention of unionising workers on home building sites. This would have been a union for big building sites. The same can be said of similar attempts in 1921 and 1922 to form one building union, the Building Workers Industrial Union.

Big building sites, rather than suburban homes, also cast shadows over the moves made by two craft unions in the 1940s to establish an industrial building union, also called the Builders Workers Industrial Union (BWIU). The

81

Amalgamated Society of Carpenters and Joiners of New South Wales and the United Operative Bricklayers Trade Society of New South Wales began moves to create a large amalgamated building union—in effect, another 'one big union' like the earlier attempt in 1918. They wanted the BLF to be a third partner, not because its membership would give the new union more opportunities for industrial action on suburban home building jobs, but because the combined membership of the three craft unions would give the new union greater coverage and more efficient industrial muscle on large building sites.[21]

Both the BWIU, from the time of its formation in 1942, and the BLF, from the time of its transformation from an allegedly corrupt organisation to a progressive industrial organisation with the election of Mick McNamara as NSW state secretary, concentrated their separate and sometimes collective attention on large building sites. The reason was simple: it was easy to get to large numbers of building workers who worked on sites in Sydney's central business district. These sites also had tactical and strategic significance—a strike on one or several large sites could drive home a union's point very quickly. By comparison, domestic construction lacked the easy access to members and the strategic significance afforded by large sites.

82      Building unions fought for a variety of places. At Kellys Bush the NSW BLF and a coalition of resident groups opposed the construction of townhouses on the site of bushland in Hunters Hill. Residents finally learned that Australia's largest land developers, the A. V. Jennings Company, planned to build three eight-storey high-rises and forty-two townhouses there. Protests, deputations and the usual manner of community objections failed to stop the Jennings proposal. When unions such as the Federated Engine Drivers and Firemen's Association, whose members operated bulldozers and heavy digging equipment, and the BLF, whose members would be involved in many aspects of building work, placed bans on the site, the Jennings homes failed to proceed. To this day, Kellys Bush remains undeveloped bushland.

The BLF did not confine its industrial action about the worth and location of home building to Kellys Bush. It began to apply moral, ethical, legal, political and environmental tests to other sites—Victoria Street in Kings Cross, Woolloomooloo, and the urban heritage area of The Rocks at Sydney Cove. In all, the BLF agreed to more than forty Green Bans, stopping more than $3000 million of building work—work which Mundey derisively labelled 'so-called development'.

Put simply, the BLF and resident action groups had begun to apply definitions to 'useful' housing or, more accurately, to highlight the differences in the utility and worth of certain houses. These definitions had at their core different understandings of the word 'development'. Terrace housing in The Rocks had a substantial monetary worth for developers, but it had a different worth for its working-class occupants—the simple utility provided by a family home.

Some members of the BLF destroyed building work on houses carried out by non-union labour while a Green Ban was in place: recently-completed brick walls were destroyed. Although this was an example of the union making a political and social comment on building work, the union's executive regretted the actions.[22]

The building unions, both the BLF and the BWIU, recognised that ordinary houses were more than pieces of assembled shelter. Each house was a political statement about the worth of its inhabitants, and each house was a site for the expression of skill, craft, tradition and the combination of these qualities to form a fierce pride. Ted Bulmer, a hard and experienced union official as well as a loyal member of the Communist Party of Australia, could point to joinery work in the family home he built, to shelves and cupboards he crafted in union offices, and to the beauty—his word—of the expression of building skills in all housing. He saw this work as appropriate and in keeping with the times. He saw the pre-fabricated home—which some might call innovative—as a backward step and the antithesis of building work. As far back as 1935, the official journal of the bricklayers and carpenters had drawn the attention of its members to this development. 'We have mass-production motor-car bodies, and now, apparently, we are to have ready-made houses en-masse. One firm is turning out "prefabricated" houses at the rate of *fifty complete houses a day*. This is something for the building worker to ponder over seriously.'[23]

83

## The conservative nature of the industry?

Some talk of the 'conservative' nature of Australia's residential building industry. But what do they mean: are they concerned only with the crafts or skills used in homebuilding? Or are they interested in the ends (products) and purposes of the buildings in whose construction various crafts and skills are deployed? Are these products 'conservative'? Have conservative crafts and skills in the way buildings are used impeded the development of the industry? Many building crafts and skills have long traditions and histories. The suggestion that the residential building industry is conservative might be simply a confusion of 'tradition' and 'historical use' with 'conservative'.

The progressive building unionists who attempted to form amalgamated or industrial unions in 1918, 1921 and 1922 recognised that organisation of industrial groups around skill or craft meant division, which led to industrial weakness. Such a fundamental industrial weakness brought with it the prospect of defeat. Employers had long recognised the industrial strengths which attended a united front. In 1873, Sydney's master builders had formed the Builders and Contractors Association, a forerunner of the Master Builders Association.

Building crafts and skills, no matter their vintage, were not the problem; rather, it was the way these skills were organised into traditional industrial groupings. With the exception of pride in the application of building skills, the existence of a multiplicity of building unions was seen as conservative, old-fashioned, even downright dangerous.

There has also been a very conservative approach in another area—writing about building workers and building work. Bob Reckman has noted:

> The academic/historical sources reveal an interesting pattern. There are many books on related topics: the technologies of building, the architectural aesthetics of various historical periods, the history and documents of carpenters' organizations and contractors' associations, etc. But no one has focused on the central figure on whose labor all of these separate questions turn—the working carpenter. The roles and problems of the actual mechanic—the person who does the work and is most responsible for or affected by changes in each of the other areas—has somehow been overlooked in the grand sweep of engineering, art, or labor history as written 'from above'.[24]

When we consider the nature and historical development of building crafts and skills, clearly there has been a long and honourable tradition of handing down skills and crafts, such as those referred to earlier by Postgate. Typical of this tradition was the course in carpentry by C. Lloyd. Lloyd was an instructor at Swinburne Technical College in Melbourne, and his book *The Australian Carpenter* ran through five reprints between January 1948 and May 1950. His books revelled in restating the master–servant relationship between builder and apprentice and emphasised that carpentry skills could not be learned quickly.[25]

84

## Conclusion

European housing in Australia has continued to draw on the innovation, capacity for change and ingenuity displayed by colonial settlers. When the settlement began at Sydney Cove on 26 January 1788, one of the first tasks of the English settlers was the unpacking of the colonial governor's accommodation. This was a prefabricated house, which came packed in a large wooden crate in kit form, ready to assemble. Australia is probably the only nation which commenced its housing construction with one packed in a wooden box and ready for assembly. And in more than two hundred years, building workers, firms and government agencies have built millions of homes which have given, and continue to give, shelter and meaning to a population.

**Notes**

1   *Census of New South Wales, 1891*, Occupations, pp. 618–19.
2   A recent report by ACIL Australia Pty Ltd noted that 1989–90 was a boom year and that an annual figure of 4–5 per cent would be more appropriate. See ACIL Australia, *Structure of the Housing Industry. Report for the Australian Housing Industry Development Council*, Occasional Series No. 5, Housing and Urban Developmnent Program (Canberra, 1993), p. 3.

3  ABS, 1988–89, Unpublished Construction Industry Survey, quoted in *ibid.*

4  Quoted in J. Brett, *Robert Menzies' Forgotten People* (Melbourne, 1992), pp. 7–8.

5  R. Boyd, *Australia's Home: Its Origins, Builders and Occupiers* (Melbourne, 1991), Preface.

6  Quoted in R. Samuel, 'Local History and Oral History', *History Workshop*, no. 1 (Spring 1976), p. 204.

7  *Australian Domestic Product, Investment and Foreign Borrowing 1861–1938/39* (1962), p. 3.

8  'Building Industry Statistics', *Economic Record*, December 1948, p. 204.

9  *Urban Development in Australia: A Descriptive Analysis* (Sydney, 1981), p. 164.

10  *The Builders' History* (London, 1923), p. 1.

11  *Industrial Relations in Construction* (London, 1968), p. 1.

12  Kaiser Engineers, *Innovations in Housing Design and Construction Techniques as Applied to Low-Cost Housing.* Report prepared for the Department of Housing and Urban Development, 1969. Quoted in G Runeson, *Economics of Building* (Petone, New Zealand, 1983), p. 123.

13  Australian Centre for Innovation and International Competitiveness, *Innovation in the Housing Industry.* Occasional Series No. 4, Housing and Urban Development Program (Canberra, 1993), p. ix.

14  *The Humane City: Cities as if People Matter* (London, 1989), Appendix 3: A Note to Building Workers, p. 140.

15  H. Hughes, 'The Eight Hour Day and the Development of the Labour Movement in Victoria in the Eighteen Fifties', *Historical Studies*, 9, 1961, pp. 396–412.

16  Ted Bulmer, personal interview.

17  W. S. Ramson (ed.), *The Australian National Dictionary: A Dictionary of Australianisms on Historical Principles* (Melbourne, 1988), pp. 289–290.

18  'From Red to Green: Citizen-Worker Alliance', in D. Hutton (ed.), *Green Politics in Australia* (Sydney, 1987), p. 107.

19  For one example, see G. Mitchell, *On Strong Foundations: The BWIU and Industrial Relations in the Australian Construction Industry, 1942–1992* (Sydney, 1996).

20  Ted Bulmer, personal interview.

21  A detailed discussion of these developments occurred in G. Mitchell, Ted Bulmer, personal interview.

22  Jack Mundey, personal interview.

23  *Trade Union Review*, 15 September 1935.

24  'Carpentry: The Craft and Trade', in A. Zimbalist (ed.), *Case Studies on the Labor Process* (New York, 1979), pp. 73–102.

25  C. Lloyd, *The Australian Carpenter* (Melbourne, 1950).

85

# Embracing the New

*Kimberley Webber*

In Australian households at the beginning of the nineteenth century, two essential tasks were, if not marginalised, at least encouraged to take place on the outskirts of domestic life. By century's end, one was being enthusiastically embraced as constituting 'the heart of the home' while the other remained on its margins. One was comparatively well equipped with cooking stove, specialised utensils, sets of matching crockery and cutlery, and the paraphernalia of that most Victorian of ceremonies, the tea party. The equipment of the other remained rudimentary: wash tubs and bucket, with the possible addition of a wringer. The first room was, of course, the kitchen and the second the laundry.

This chapter is not a history of the kitchen and laundry, but rather an analysis of the technologies that became available in Australia in the period 1850 to 1900, their potential to transform the processes involved in food preparation and laundry work, and the response of Australian households to them. It seeks to explain why the most hated task—washing—remained unmechanised and marginalised while other technologies—such as food preparation—had, as the Sydney store Anthony Hordern's proclaimed in 1895, 'all the science of the century' applied to them[1] and their workplace was increasingly regarded as central to the home.

## 'Stipulate for a stove': The technological challenge to the cheerful fireside

The Australian kitchen of the early 1800s was rarely, except in the homes of the wealthy, a special-purpose room. The kitchen also served as general living space, bathroom, classroom and, at times, bedroom. Indeed, with little by way of equipment, no running water and simple one-pot cooking, there was no need for a 'kitchen' as such. Furthermore, within the household economy, cooking was low on the hierarchy of work compared to the more obviously productive tasks such as spinning, weaving and dairying. Simple one-pot meals were prepared over an open fire, and if baking was done, it was in a brick oven.

The equipment of Australian kitchens in the first decades of settlement was thus a modest, portable, basic collection of tools largely unchanged since those found in Europe in the twelfth century, when chimneys (and fireplaces set into the wall) had begun to replace a round hearth in the centre of a room.[2] It was, as James Atkinson wrote in *An Account of Grazing and Agriculture in New South Wales* (1826), a bucket, an iron pot, a frypan, a kettle, tin dish, plates, pannikins, a knife, a steel mill for grinding, and a sieve for dressing coarse flour.[3] With these, colonists could readily prepare their typical diet for much of the nineteenth century—boiled meat, damper and tea—a diet that (with the exception of tea) had been common in England since the seventeenth century.[4]

The change implicit in the introduction of the stove—with its closed oven and loss of sight of the fire—was far more significant than the need to incorporate a new piece of equipment. By replacing a general-purpose open fireplace that the entire household could use—not only for cooking but also for warmth, for light to read by, and a hearth to sit around—with a cast iron box intended for cooking and heating water, the process of room specialisation began. More importantly, it challenged the ideal image of the Victorian family. For the hearth was the heart of the home—a meaning evident in the use of 'hearth' as a metonym for home—and the replacement of the open fire with such an obviously industrial product directly challenged the domestic ideal of the home as removed from industry, and the family as gathered harmoniously around its hearth.

The strength of this ideal is evidenced by its ready transfer from Europe to Australia, despite the considerably milder climate. Ada Cambridge wrote of 'The glorious log fire of the country—the most beautiful piece of house furniture in the world'.[5] Paintings and drawings of colonial interiors invariably depict a fire blazing in the hearth.[6] Indeed, the alternative of an empty fireplace would be taken to represent dire poverty, desolation or even death.[7] A witness to the 1860 inquiry into working-class housing in Sydney described a particularly poor house as having 'not a spark of fire in the place'.[8] As a result, the desire for the open fire persisted long after the technological necessity for it had gone.

This is apparent in the ambivalent response of Australian consumers to cast iron cooking stoves which had been available in colonial New South Wales from the early 1800s. The kitchen at Government House, Parramatta, had a cooking range probably installed by Macquarie in 1812. In 1813, the *Sydney Gazette* advertised a closed kitchen range with 'oven, boiler, Hot Plate and Hot Closet; calculated to Bake, Boil, Roast, Steam, Stew and heat Flat Irons by a small Fire with a continued Supply of Ten Gallons of boiling Water'.[9]

87

Yet, as a collection of Sydney auction notices from the 1840s reveals, this acceptance of stoves was far from universal. Out of a total of forty listing household contents, only five have stoves, including the Reverend Dr Bodenham with Gravely's 'patent cooking apparatus (new)' and Hannibal Macarthur's 'large range and fender'.[10] Rather than a cooking stove, the most common apparatus mentioned was a fender—a surround that prevents wood and coals falling onto the hearth—indicating that for the majority of households, cooking generally took place over an open fire or at best with a simple grate.

However, over the next half-century, economic and practical considerations forced a re-evaluation of the cooking stove and a reworking of the space in which it would reside. Cooking with a naked flame was undeniably dangerous. Further, the heat, dust and smoke generated made it often a doubtful pleasure, as is evident in Annie Baxter's vivid description of roasting meat:

> In the bush, we have immense fireplaces . . . I remember one day we had a large piece of beef roasting—the chimney smoked furiously—and we were putting up with this, for the sake of a fresh morsel of beef! The old man who was turning it, kept on running out every now & then to breathe the fresh air—altogether it was enviable—when in came three visitors, one of them a lady—I do suppose she thought I cried with delight to see her—for my eyes were full of tears from the smoke![11]

More importantly, open fireplaces were extraordinarily inefficient. Generally built to measure 6 feet wide by 3 feet deep, they consumed huge quantities of wood, yet only 12 to 14 per cent of the heat generated entered the room and most went up the chimney.[12] This was not a particular problem while wood was plentiful and cheap, but by the 1880s and 1890s urban development and population increases were beginning to push up the price of wood.[13] Significantly, it was at this time that stove manufacturers began to promote the 'economy' of their products. Thus, a 1906 advertisement for the Sam Weller claimed that it used 75 per cent less fuel than any other stove,[14] and an advertisement for the Younger pointed to the fact that it would soon 'pay for itself' since it used only $2^1/_2$ tons of coal a year.[15]

But if fuel costs were the catalyst, the successful introduction of stoves depended on manufacturers and retailers overcoming social and cultural resistance to them. The strength of this resistance is evident in Sydney, where high prices should have made a more fuel-efficient method of cooking desirable but where, even by the late nineteenth century, cast iron stoves were far from universal. Only one reference could be found to a cooking stove in selected New South Wales insolvency records surveyed for the 1870s, 1880s and 1890s: the saddler, John Owen, had one in his Wollongong kitchen.[16] Most people cooked on an open fire or simple grate, using the same basic equipment that Atkinson had recommended a half-century before. John Shiel, a Murrumbateman contractor, was typical. Although his parlour featured a clock and sewing machine, the kitchen could boast only a table, bucket, small quantity of crockery, tea kettle and frying pan.[17]

Even when a household had a stove, traditional cooking methods were preserved and there was considerable resistance to roasting meat in the oven. Furthermore, a collection of 1920s and 1930s auction records reveals that this uneven distribution continued well into the next century. Of the thirty houses auctioned, although the majority had a gas stove, two households still cooked with a wood stove and one used a kerosene stove. A 1955 survey of household equipment in Australian capital cities found as many fuel stoves as electric in use, with 18 per cent of Brisbane housewives surveyed still preparing meals on a fuel stove despite the hot climate.[18]

Contrary to what Siegfried Giedion in Europe, and Beverley Kingston and Kerreen Reiger in Australia have suggested,[19] the introduction of the cast iron cooking stove was not simply the story of the replacement of one technology by another cheaper and more efficient one. The ultimate abandonment of the open fire required far more than a desire for economy. In the end, it was a process of acceptance and rejection, with manufacturer and retailer jockeying for position in a market where cost saving and fuel efficiency were just two considerations.

It was only when social and cultural changes occurred that the stove became not just practical but desirable. As Chapter 7 argues, the allocation of rooms became more specialised in the course of the nineteenth century and the dining room was no exception. Dining had taken on a new importance and the image of the family gathered before a cheerful fire was increasingly replaced by a more formal portrait of them seated at the table. Whereas in the eighteenth century, dining had been a casual activity which often took place outside the home, during the 1800s it became far more ritualised and, as such, a symbol of family life. Kenneth Ames has suggested that dinner in middle-class Victorian America became a ritual of bonding where people were united by eating the same food off matching dishes with matching silverware and glasses.[20]

Underlying this change was a new attitude to the importance of food and cooking which, with the end of many forms of household work capable of generating a cash income, became an increasingly significant household task and one regarded as central to women's role in the home and the essential ingredient of a happy marriage. This was reflected in the rising importance of domestic advice literature, and particularly of cookbooks. Auction notices from the 1840s reveal that works such as Mrs Rundell's *Domestic Cookery*, *Lady's Own Cookery*, Johnson's *Cookery* and *The Practical Cook* were all popular in the colony.[21] The first cookbook to be published for a specifically Australian audience, albeit a middle-class one, was Edward Abbott's *The English and Australian Cookery Book* (1864). Within a decade an enormous outpouring of cookbooks written by Australian women brought them within the reach of all.[22]

Research by Martyn Lyons and Lucy Taksa on Australian reading has shown that the cookbook was the commonest source of household advice

89

across all social classes.[23] Although no sales figures survive, some indication of their popularity can be drawn from the number of editions. By the early 1900s, Mrs Harriet Wicken's *Kingswood Cookery Book* (first published in 1885) had run to six editions, with 30,000 copies sold. *The Presbyterian Cookery Book* went into six editions between 1895 and 1902, selling 30,000 copies and claiming, 'it is significant that many discerning women have made it a habit to give a copy . . . to every new bride of their acquaintance'.[24]

The success of the cookbook provides a clear indication of the new importance of cooking—and the kitchen—in family life. Indeed, reading nineteenth-century domestic guides, it is surprising how often reference was made to the close links between a well-fed man and a happy home. The underlying implication was that food was more reliable than sex as a satisfier of men's appetites and, what was more important, cooking could be learnt. As the anonymous author of *Men and How to Manage Them* puts it:

> No man grumbles after a good dinner, and, provided that he does not suspect that his pet dishes have been furnished to further some design upon him . . .
> he can be moulded like wet putty when dinner is over, and he wants to expand himself. This is the time to let him go, and if you are wise he will go your way. I know a woman who used to get all she wanted out of her husband by merely sitting near him after dinner and peeling walnuts for him, a feat she performed very neatly, and with much patience, finding herself, as she used to say, very well paid for it.[25]

If women wished to preserve their financial and emotional security, they must ensure that their households were well run and their meals worth coming home to.

By the last quarter of the nineteenth century, the new importance attached to homemaking and meals in Australian family life encouraged households to move away from the open fire to the cast iron stove because the latter enabled food to be cooked on top of the stove while pastries and other dishes were baking within. But it was not sufficient for the cooking stove to simply do the job: it must also look the part, and thus this pre-eminently industrial object needed to be domesticated. 'Romancing' the stove was achieved, first, by the application of romantic names to different models, and second, by replacement of the aesthetic of the factory with that of the parlour.

Of all the industrial products targeting at the domestic market in the nineteenth century, the cooking stove outstripped all others in the sheer range of models available and the ingenuity of their names. Rathbone, Sard and Co. (a major American manufacturer who exported their stoves to Australia) listed seventy-one different models in their 1890 catalogue, each available in at least four different sizes. Their foundry was therefore producing parts for 284 stoves.[26] The names given to stoves were quite extraordinary and as far removed from any suggestion of industry as possible. For example, an 1887 catalogue from McLean Bros of Melbourne listed the Ascot, Derby, Gipsy Queen,

90

**ANTHONY HORDERN & SONS, HAYMARKET ONLY, SYDNEY.**

# ELECTRIC LIGHT RANGE.
## FOR EITHER COAL OR WOOD.

This Stove has been specially constructed for Australian requirements. One of its strongest recommendations is the number of moveable rings on the top plate, there being four over the oven and two over the fire, so that the boiling capacity is far in excess of what is usually the case. The Range has a deep Fire Box, Central Flue, Automatic Damper, and **Fall Down Grate to admit logs of wood.** It is strong and well finished, with bright mouldings round the hob and in front. The Oven is large and well ventilated, and hinged on left hand of Range. Altogether this Stove makes a handsome addition to the furniture of the kitchen.

| | Width. | Height. | SIZE OF OVEN. Width. | Depth. | Height. | |
|---|---|---|---|---|---|---|
| No. 7 ... | 29in. ... | 23in. ... | 15in. ... | 15in. ... | 8½in. ... | £2 10s. 0d. |
| „ 8 ... | 32in. ... | 24in. ... | 17in. ... | 17in. ... | 9½in. ... | £3 0s. 0d. |
| „ 9 ... | 34in. ... | 25in. ... | 18½in. ... | 18½in. ... | 10½in. ... | £3 12s. 6d. |

Prices include Ring Lifter, Scraper, Poker, Brush, and 4 feet of Pipe to fit Flue.

**PACKING FOR COUNTRY, 2/6 EACH, EXTRA.  See remarks on page 53.**

### DUPLICATE PARTS OF STOVES.

It must not be supposed that, because some of the parts of your Stove gets cracked or lost, the Stove is done for. Even as **there is many a good tune played on an old fiddle,** so, by sending to us for duplicates of missing or broken parts, many an excellently cooked family feast will follow the repairs. We stock duplicates of top and bottom plates, oven linings, rings, cups, and fire-bricks in connection with any of the Stoves in this Catalogue. Prices on application.

The Stoves listed on this and other pages can be recommended as the best in the market; but, should other Stoves be required, we shall be pleased to send quotations and full particulars by return of post.

**ALL PRICES IN THIS CATALOGUE ARE SUBJECT TO MARKET FLUCTUATIONS.**

**Plate 6.1** The Electric Light Range, Anthony Hordern & Sons Catalogue 1895. With its rounded corners, 'bright mouldings' and claw feet, the Electric Light was proclaimed to be 'a handsome addition to the furniture of the kitchen'. (Powerhouse Museum, Sydney)

St Leger, Stenben, Uncle Sam, Empress and Enchantress;[27] and an 1895 catalogue from Anthony Hordern's incuded the New Matron, Dover, Criterion, Orient, and Electric Light.[28] Names never refer to any quality of the stove or distinguish between different capacities. Rather, this most banal of products required associations with the exotic, the patriotic or the classical in order to be desirable.

By the second half of the nineteenth century, stove manufacturers both in Australia and overseas were beginning to pay almost as much attention to the appearance of the stove as to its workings. As one wrote in 1900:

> A merchant who has an eye to the appearance of his store will be delighted with the effect of a nice assortment of Buck's Steel Ranges when lined up as if for dress parade. When a customer enters he [sic] cannot but be struck with the imposing display, and a sale is half made without a word being spoken . . . It is true that 'Beauty is but skin deep', nevertheless it is of paramount importance in making a sale that the purchaser falls in love with the range 'at first sight'.[29]

Curved legs and rounded corners, embossed decorations on the front and sides, pierced shelves, decorative handles and nickel plating all gave the stove the aesthetic of the parlour, of rounded edges, shiny, polished surfaces and 'appropriate' decoration.[30] The importance of such features is evident in Mrs Lance Rawson's endorsement in 1886:

> The American Stoves are strong and useful, as well as being ornamental, and take very little extra trouble in cleaning: they are more expensive in the beginning, but last longer than an oven, and burn far less wood or coal . . . the Colonial oven is anything but an ornament to the kitchen, while an American stove is the same to the kitchen that the piano is to the drawing room—a handsome piece of furniture.[31]

As the American historian Ruth Schwartz Cowan has argued, a network of social relations determines the choices made by consumers.[32] By 1900, the most important factor that limited the acceptance of the cast iron stove—the image of the family gathered around the hearth—was disappearing from popular memory and being replaced with other rituals, notably that of dining.

The cast iron cooking stove presented an obvious challenge to the 'cheerful fireside', and consumers resisted its attractions until both the domestication of the stove and changes in its social significance made it desirable. Central to the stove's success was the identification of cooking as a key factor in maintaining a stable home, while the ideology of separate spheres underlined the financial dependence of women upon their husbands and fathers. In 1895, with the benefit of hindsight provided by her own experiences of the uncertainties of married life, Wilhelmina Rawson advised her readers: 'Let me suggest to prospective brides that they should stipulate for a stove if marrying a Bushman. A man will promise anything before marriage, very little after. I was wise in my generation, and stipulated for a stove and a mangle, in preference to a piano, and got all three'.[33] Wilhelmina Rawson was fortunate: her stove not only served to keep her family happy, but through her recipe books and guides it also gave her a living.

## 'Machinery for the household': Scientific management and the introduction of gadgets

The kitchen could absorb a major new piece of technology in the form of the cooking stove, but it does not follow that Australian households wholeheartedly embraced the new or that the charms of the nineteenth-century kitchen rapidly gave way before the relentless advance of the laboratory. Certainly retailers such as Anthony Hordern's applauded the value of 'science in the cottage' and proclaimed:

> Now-a-days everything is done by machinery, from crushing tons of iron to stoning cherries or raisins. Natural forces are drilled into the service of domestic life, and whether the housewife has potatoes to peel or rats to catch, she may start on her job with the assurance that all the science of the century supports her, and that inventive genius has been puzzling its brains and scratching its head on her behalf.[34]

93

There is little evidence to suggest that this commitment to science was anything more than a marketing ploy. An examination of the means used to promote 'scientific management'—principally cookbooks, domestic guides and women's magazines—reveals that these mechanical wonders faced the same resistance and for much the same reason as had the cooking stove. Furthermore, since there was little that could be done to disguise the cogs and wheels of the egg-beater or to soften the mechanical appearance of the meat mincer, this was a resistance that was even more difficult to overcome.

Originating in the United States in the 1880s, scientific management—which, in the home, became domestic economy—sought to apply the principles of industrial life and, through a rational, methodical and objective approach, raise housework above mere drudgery and make the housewife as much a professional as her husband.[35] It was, in the words of Mrs Wicken (founding instructor in Domestic Economy at Sydney's Technical College), 'the science which teaches us the right way to manage our households'.[36]

However, it is clear from an examination of textbooks, curriculums and training programs that the commitment of nineteenth-century home economists to science was, in general, superficial, and the Victorian ideals of thrift and economy in household management acted against major investment in domestic appliances. As a result, the very movement that is most often seen as a catalyst for the use of labour-saving technologies in the home—and for the transformation of the kitchen from 'heart of the home' to laboratory—in fact

**Plate 6.2** Cookery class at Warrnambool School, photographed about 1890. Studiously concentrating on the task at hand and with their boards, bowls and rolling pins laid out with a laboratory-like precision, these girls appear the embodiment of their motto, 'Cookery is here elevated into a science'. Yet aside from the gas stoves, there is no evidence of machinery or gadgets. Furthermore, the tea things and cakes arranged on the table suggest that, once the photographer is finished, the students and their teacher will engage in the far more appealing ritual of afternoon tea. (National Library of Australia)

worked against such change. Thus, in the 1892 syllabus for a one-year course in 'Domestic Economy and Cookery' at Sydney Technical College, the majority of student time was spent on food preparation, with less than one-sixth being given over to 'science'. In all, some thirty lessons were spent preparing puddings, cakes and sweets, while the 'chemistry of food' was covered in a single lesson, as was 'arranging household work'.[37] As for the food itself, it generally drew upon old favourites with little evidence of concern for diet, nutrition or calories. Similarly, although the 1890s saw attempts to move Australians away from their traditional 'British' meat diet—notably by Philip Muskett[38]—the Cookery Instruction Cards from the Victorian Department of Public Instruction concentrated on roast meat, grilled chops, rissoles, and the correct way to make toast and tea.[39]

The experienced Australian domestic science teacher Mrs Fawcett Story blamed her students for this conservatism. She claimed they were more interested in preparing 'dainty meals' than in science:

> As it is, when girls do attend cookery classes for a term or two, it is generally only with the idea of learning to make scones and cakes, nice little supper dishes for company &c., and very rarely, indeed, with the object of making themselves so thoroughly acquainted with the art and science of cookery as to fit them to take charge of households.[40]

Conservative in what was being taught and traditional in the way it was carried out, domestic economy did not encourage either potential home-makers or established ones to embrace new technologies. If Australian women bought gadgets, they did so despite their home economics training and not because of it. 95

Furthermore, although the use of labour-saving appliances was a major tenet of nineteenth-century home economics, few writers on the subject actually came out in favour of them. Although Mrs Wicken argued that the proper equipment of the kitchen ought to be the first priority of the new householder, 'for a cook cannot be expected to send up a good dinner without proper utensils', there was little evidence of any commitment to labour-saving appliances in her books. Indeed, the only appliances mentioned in 'Australian Cookery Recipes and Accessory Kitchen Information' were agate iron ware, 'a little more expensive in the first place . . . [but] unbreakable, and therefore cheaper in the end'; a small sausage machine, 'very necessary'; and a good stove.[41] In *The Australian Home* she recommended against having too many things in the kitchen: 'it is better to use the simplest utensils, and not have too many about, or one is apt to get confused'. Indeed, the list of kitchen equipment she provided was notable for the absence of mention of anything mechanical.[42]

Although Mrs Rawson provided a more extensive list in *The Antipodean Cookery Book*, only three gadgets were listed, despite the author's enthusiasm for labour saving appliances:

> In the Bush, where servants come and go like angels' visits, the housewife finds the benefit of the many labour-saving machines now in existence. I can speak from a personal experience of many of them, and can assure my readers that a lady—no matter how unaccustomed to work, provided she be willing to do it—

can do the whole of her housework with very little exertion or fatigue to herself if she has the following machines:

1. A washing machine
2. A wringer
3. A mincing machine
4. A knife cleaning machine
5. Small kerosene stove
6. Patent egg-beater
7. Scrubbing brush with long handle
8. A brass box iron
9. Mangle
10. A good American stove
11. A chain pot-cleaner![43]

Although they were decidedly the products of the industrial revolution, a meat mincer, knife cleaner and egg-beater could not be expected to transform the comfortable kitchen of the 1800s into a scientific workplace, particularly when even the cheapest and simplest—the egg-beater—was not unequivocally recommended. As Mrs Rawson added, it was 'merely optional; for my own part I much prefer a fork'.[44]

It can be concluded therefore that the promotion of science by Australian domestic writers in the late nineteenth century reflected contemporary enthusiasm for 'scientism' rather than any real commitment to 'science' and to change.[45] In reality, the advice of authors like Mrs Wicken or Mrs Rawson differed little from that given by Mrs Darling in the first Australian domestic guide, *Simple Rules for the Guidance of Persons in Humble Life*. Published in 1837, it laid much the same emphasis on order and cleanliness as the more 'scientific' works written fifty years later. Just as Mrs Wicken ended the introduction to *The Australian Home* with the advice 'Have a place for everything and everything in its place', so, a half-century earlier, 'Mrs Shepherd' had advised her young friend Sarah Brown that there were three rules in housekeeping:

1. Do everything in its proper time.
2. Keep everything for its proper use.
3. Put everything in its proper place.[46]

In the last quarter of the nineteenth century, the promotion of the home as a sphere for science by manufacturers, retailers and domestic scientists had the potential to raise the profile of machinery in the home and to transform the kitchen into a laboratory. Yet if we look at the particular impact of these changes, it is clear that the 'scientific cottage', so beloved by manufacturers and retailers alike, was still far from fruition. Women clung to their traditional ways of doing things and to their traditional tools, and they embraced the new only when it helped to reinforce those traditions rather than sought to revolutionise them. For despite all their cogs, wheels, gears and levers, domestic gadgets neither simplified work practices nor improved the quality of domestic life. Perhaps they appealed to men, but men were not meant to use them and had far less opportunity to buy them. It was quite apparent to women that they threatened to bring all the clutter and noise of the factory into the home, with none of the consequent benefits. And whereas a sewing machine looked like a fine piece of furniture and held the promise of fashionable dress, a meat mincer offered only shepherd's pie.

## 'I was the machine myself': The failure to mechanise drudgery

In contrast to the respect afforded to food preparation, the washing of clothes and household linen was regarded as the most onerous domestic task of all, and almost universally loathed. Whereas there was some room for creativity and imagination in the preparation and serving of food, washing was unequivocally hard work. Furthermore in the course of the nineteenth century, it only became worse. In sixteenth- and seventeenth-century Europe, clothes were washed infrequently, undergarments were minimal and household linen was sparse. By the early 1800s the fortnightly wash had become common practice; as the century progressed, increasing amounts of starched white underclothes, cotton shirts and dresses, and vast quantities of starched white table and bed linen added to the chore.[47]

Although it is impossible to calculate exactly how much wash was being done in nineteenth-century Australia, what indications there are suggest that it was large. Evelyn Barwick, a domestic servant in rural New South Wales, reported in her diary for 7 January 1890, 'We did the washing and we had such an awfully big wash. We had forty-six bedroom towels, and such a lot of sheets and two white counterpanes.' And on 21 December 1893 she wrote, 'One washing day this month, I think it was the 12th, we had seventeen dozen of clothes in the wash.'[48] Furthermore, in an age of uncertainty about social standing and class, cleanliness had become the measure of a man (and his family).

George Horne, an unemployed clerk of Glebe, went bankrupt in 1890 owing £95 1s 2d, including a debt of £29 3s 6d accumulated over the previous three years for washing, ironing and mangling.[49] The 1860 New South Wales Committee of Enquiry into the Housing of the Working Classes was particularly concerned about the lack of washing facilities in the homes of Sydney's poor. Cleanliness had become so central to civic behaviour that its absence was regarded as tantamount to spiritual decay and social ruin. Witnesses spoke of the 'loathsomeness' of slum housing, where 'inside and out, everything is an object of disgust'. They argued that the inevitable consequence of such dirt was destruction of the family:

> The father, finding all in disorder and confusion at home . . . seeks consolation
> . . . at the public house, which is always close at hand. The wife, neglected by her
> husband, unable with all her efforts to maintain cleanliness and order, becomes

dirty in her habits, slatternly in her appearance, generally indifferent to domestic comfort, and probably at last has recourse to that which seals the ruin of her family—the rum bottle.[50]

The indefatigable Mrs Rawson provided a detailed description of how such despair could be avoided by thoroughly explaining the correct way to wash in her *Australian Cook and Laundry Book*. After soaking the clothes overnight:

> Start your washing as early as you can next morning. If you are quick you will get a boilerful on before breakfast . . . A washing board is a great help to a woman who has her own work to do, but like everything else she must learn how to use it properly or she will scrub the skin off her hands . . . As you wash each piece shake it out and put it in the boiler . . . When your clothes have boiled the half hour and been properly poked under with the 'pot stick' so that everything has been boiled, they are ready to come out. Place a tub close to the boiler . . . drain the clothes . . . let them down into the tub, cover with clear cold water and rinse well up and down to get all the soapy water out, then wring out each piece, shake it, turn it and plunge into the blue water, rinse about in it and wring out again, shake and throw into your basket to be hung out on the line to dry.[51]

98

Although this passage was written at the end of the nineteenth century, only two pieces of technology were mentioned—the washboard and the wringer—and Mrs Rawson assumed that the wash would be done out of doors. Indeed, given the amount of water being used and the mess inevitably created, it is impossible to see how it could have been otherwise.

Not surprisingly, laundrywork was the most hated of all domestic chores, and paid laundryworkers the lowest on the hierarchy of domestic servants.[52] Whenever it is mentioned in diaries and letters, it is invariably in terms of resignation. In his 1860 description of the family's chores, Joseph Elliott referred to washing day as 'the worst day in the week . . . [Becky] is generally very tired after it but yet sometimes, she gets her ironing done in the evening!'[53] Whereas the preparation and presentation of food was often portrayed as essential to domestic harmony, there was nothing romantic about doing the wash. Paintings of women doing such work are rare, and when they do exist, they leave no doubt as to the arduous nature of the task. Thus in Vida Lahey's painting 'Monday Morning 1912', her two sisters have their sleeves rolled up to reveal muscular arms, and both are hard at work in the laundry of their family home in Indooroopilly, Brisbane. One lifts washing out of the steaming copper, while the other rubs soap into dirty clothes. They are both bent over their work and, although the youth and beauty of her subjects softens the atmosphere of industry, it is not an environment of seduction or romance.[54]

Indeed, the heavy labour involved in doing the wash was a direct challenge to the domestic ideal. The space in which it occurred, although a

**Plate 6.3** Unidentified family, Gulgong, photographed by Beaufoy Merlin about 1872. This photograph is a testament to the importance of cleanliness as evidence of respectability. Despite the mud and the crude accommodation with its very basic laundry equipment—a water cask with a saucepan for a pitcher stands next to two washtubs raised to a comfortable height by rough-hewn logs—these women dress themselves and their children in impressively clean clothes. (Mitchell Library, State Library of New South Wales)

woman's space, was not a feminine one. The Lahey sisters were fortunate to have a room for their laundry—and the luxury of running water—but the cement tubs, rough walls and uncurtained window remind the viewer that this is a workplace. For the majority of Australian women the wash took place in the space that Chapter 10 identifies within the garden as workplace, the area by the back door that houses toilet, wood pile, and bench or lean-to with wash tubs and buckets.

The very fact that laundrywork was so universally loathed was a major factor in preventing either its mechanisation or its acceptance into the charms of the domestic circle. This does not mean, however, that an attempt to mechanise was not tried. Indeed, experimentation with mechanising the laundry process—through washing machines, wringers and mangles—came

**Plate 6.4** The Wolter & Echberg Washing Machine. The handle on the right swung the washing machine back and forth. The manufacturer made the surprising claim that it also had the 'remarkable advantage that it can be used either as a washing machine or as a churn' but gave no suggestions as to how to get the butter out before putting the clothes in. (Powerhouse Museum, Sydney)

100

about as a by-product of the textile industry. As Siegfried Giedion has shown in *Mechanization Takes Command*, this was an area always prolific in invention. By the 1870s more than two thousand patents had been issued for washing machines in the United States.[55] Even in Australia, where there was far less inventive 'activity', washing machines attracted one of the highest levels of patents among domestic appliances.[56]

Numerous solutions were proposed for the problem of the wash. The starting point was an attempt to imitate the to-and-fro motion of the hand and scrub clothes clean. One of the most successful Australian washing machines was patented by Hans Echberg of Victoria in 1877. Shaped like a double-ended torpedo, its interior was lined with corrugations. When loaded with laundry and water, it was 'swung to and fro' by the operator and the clothes agitated clean. As a washing machine it claimed to do a wash in five minutes, although it is not clear how much laundry it could hold.[57] Far more common, however, were the imported English and American machines, generally in the form of a wooden box or tub with internal corrugations and a mechanism that beat the clothes against the sides (in the form of paddles turned by a handle or by being rocked back and forth).

There was an equally wide range of boilers available, both imported and locally manufactured. A surviving flyer for the Victoria Patent Domestic Boiler, manufactured in Melbourne, claimed that all the proud owner had to do was 'Boil twenty to thirty minutes; then lift the clothes from the boiler into the rinsing water, which should be changed twice, thence through the wringer into the blue water, thence through the wringer, when they will be ready to hang out on the line.' Of course, this was still a substantial amount of work—particularly when one considers that in most households the machine would have had to be filled by hand—and therein lies the problem of all hand-powered washing machines. For even with a machine, the heavy work remained—filling tubs with water, emptying, lifting wet washing and wringing out—and all of this created a considerable mess. In her autobiographical *Childhood at Brindabella*, Miles Franklin described the washing machine in her grandmother's laundry as 'a species of cradle swung on a stand, [it] took two to rock it. The chore was generally the refuge and wonderment of the untrained men visitors from overseas.'[58] More than half a century later, the owner of a 1920s manual vacuum pump machine (which was still being used in the 1960s) described its operations: 'The only problem was that if you put too many clothes in you didn't get circulation. Your arm would get tired—it was hard work. I used to get the missus to have a go, but mostly I had to do it all. It ended up I was the machine myself'.[59]

The failure of the concept of the washing machine to reach any sort of 'closure' in the course of the nineteenth century is indicative of its fundamental inability to significantly reduce either the time or the labour involved in the wash.[60] Whereas manufacturers fairly quickly solved the problem of sewing two pieces of cloth together and a standard sewing machine emerged by the 1870s, the concept of what constituted a washing machine remained fluid and continued to offer an almost open field to the inventor. It was not coincidental that, while other domestic technologies were quickly dominated by a small number of British and American manufacturers, washing machines had a comparatively high proportion of local manufacturers.[61] But the extravagant claims of local and international manufacturers alike—'Washing Day no longer Dreaded'—could not be matched by the capabilities of the machines.

The poor performance of washing machines combined with the low status of laundry work gave households little incentive to mechanise the wash in the same way that sewing had been or that cooking was in the process of being. Money spent on the laundry meant taking resources away from the domestic circle, rather than reinforcing it. Thus, American women surveyed about their 'home equipment' in 1926 consistently stated that they would prefer to spend what money the family had on services or products of benefit to all, rather than on labour-saving machines. Mrs J. L. G. of Missouri wrote that she 'would rather have a telephone than a power washer'. Furthermore, since there was no getting away from the hard labour involved, it was impossible to romanticise either the work or the machine. Clean clothes were of critical importance to social standing and respectability but were achievable without mechanisation.

Mrs Rawson neither expected her readers to have a laundry—'I myself had none until quite lately'—nor much by way of laundry equipment: 'I believe a copper boiler is the best, but never having used one, I cannot speak confidently . . . I have seen a common kerosene tin used for the purpose, and answer very well . . . As for washing machines, "I have very little to say, for my own part I do not care for them." '[62]

Not surprisingly, therefore, little evidence could be found for ownership of washing machines in Australia. William Tanner, a founder of the colony at Swan River in Western Australia, brought a washing machine worth £3 3s with him from England in 1831, together with two ironing machines (worth 19 shillings), nine irons for laundresses (13 shillings) and three mangles (6 shillings).[63] Sarah Midgley's father brought one home from town in the 1850s and she later wrote, 'today we have washed a fortnight's washing with the new machine'.[64]

Such instances were the exception rather than the rule. Auction notices and insolvency records indicate that neither the houses of the Establishment nor those of the middle classes commonly had such equipment. A surviving inventory of the laundry at Parramatta's Government House reveals that it contained 'one complete mangle', an ironing table, two water casks, three round washing tubs, one clothes horse, a table and washing stool and a copper.[65] Nor do washing machines appear in Sydney auction notices of the 1840s. After the iron, the most common piece of laundry equipment listed (aside from washing tubs) was the patent mangle. Indeed, the laundries of professional and working people were surprisingly similar in the simplicity of their equipment. John Usher, a publican from Muswellbrook, had three tubs and a boiler in the laundry; Timothy Henery, a Woollahra coachman, had wash tubs, bucket and a mangle, as did John Owen, a saddler from Wollongong.[66]

Throughout the nineteenth century, therefore, the traditional practices, tools and location for laundrywork prevailed. Even the Monday wash persisted. In most households, as in Evelyn Barwick's, Monday was identifiable as the day when typically, 'We rose early and did our washing and mangling'.[67] The laundry was more often a bench and tubs than a room specially set aside for the purpose, although copper and sink could be bricked in to form a wash house outside the back door. Washing inside was to be avoided at all costs. Regarded as a sign of poverty, it would produce 'great discomfort and inconvenience to the whole family'.[68]

Whereas the introduction of the cooking stove was a major factor in the development of a specialised kitchen, and the sewing machine was reworked to make it acceptable in the parlour, the washing machine and wringer remained peripheral to the development of housing design until well into the twentieth century. Once piped water became available, a room was given over to the laundry, but this was often either a lean-to by the back door or the closed-in end of a verandah. Not until after World War II was it incorporated into the house proper and never does it exhibit the same attention to fittings and finishings as the kitchen. At Calthorpe's House in Canberra (an intact 1928 house), the kitchen and bathroom have the most up-to-date tiled walls and floors. The result is a sparkling white industrial surface and an overall atmosphere of hygiene and efficiency. The laundry, on the other hand, is not incorporated into the main house at all but accessed through the verandah. It has bare brick walls, a cement floor and only cold running water. Stepping into that room it is immediately clear that, although other household tasks could readily be embraced within the 'domestic circle', laundrywork remained unequivocally 'work' and, as such, removed from family spaces into a utilitarian workspace.

However, if the wash was not welcome in the home, it was not rejected altogether. The cooperative laundry movement was just as unsuccessful as that for the cooperative kitchen and, even today, Ann Oakley has found British housewives resistant to using laundromats; as one woman said, 'They don't seem to get the clothes clean—you have to boil them when you get back.'[69]

## Conclusion

In 1996, the *Australian Magazine* published an article on the kitchen as the arbiter of social change, claiming it was 'the domestic indicator of our sense and sensibilities'. Entitled 'The Heart of the Home', it presented an ideal kitchen that was a curious mix of nostalgia and modernity, with a dishwasher under the 'American oak' bench tops contrasting with a bright blue enamel Aga stove in the corner. Its owner, architect Irena Lobaza, explained her choice: 'I wanted a country-style kitchen that was inviting.'[70] While there is much that could be said about this choice of fittings and equipment—and the degree to which this can be regarded as representative can certainly be questioned—what is significant for this paper is that even today no-one would aspire to make the laundry inviting.

The Australian home, its organisation and equipment, is the result of a complex interweaving of romantic ideals about the family, the practical demands of feeding and caring for its occupants, respect for traditions and desire for the new. Within this web of competing demands, new technologies have had the potential to revolutionise the home. However, as the histories of the washing machine, the cast iron cooking stove and gadgets like the meat mincer and egg-beater indicate, it is only when the home has been able to romance the machine, to incorporate it within the charmed circle of domestic life, that these technologies have succeeded.

103

## Notes

1  *Anthony Hordern and Sons Catalogue* (Sydney, 1895), p. 79.
2  See F. Braudel, *The Structures of Everyday Life* (New York, 1985), p. 10; S. Mennell, *All Manners of Food* (Oxford, 1986), pp. 47–9; C. Davidson, *A Woman's Work is Never Done* (London, 1983), pp. 44–72.

3   See R. Walker and D. Roberts, From *Scarcity to Surfeit* (Sydney, 1988), p. 141.

4   The essential components of seventeenth-century diet as described in English agricultural literature were bread, boiled meat (enlivened by a sauce of available vegetables) and cider or beer, with the possible addition of a boiled pudding: L. T. Ulrich, *Good Wives* (Oxford, 1983), p. 19.

5   *Thirty Years in Australia* (Sydney, 1989 [1903]), p. 28.

6   T. Lane and J. Serle, *Australians at Home* (Melbourne, 1992), p. 18.

7   The Hazens point out that in nineteenth-century literature the fireless grate was used to represent terrible suffering, and cites the example of the Hummels in Louisa May Alcott's *Little Women*: M. H. Hazen and R. M. Hazen, *Keepers of the Flame* (Princeton, 1992), p. 107.

8   *New South Wales Parliamentary Papers, Legislative Assembly: Report from the Select Committee on the Condition of the Working Classes of the Metropolis*, 1860, p. 1434.

9   Lane and Serle, *Australians at Home*, pp. 7, 211.

10  *Catalogue of Elegant Household Furniture: At the Residence of the Rev. Mr Bodenham* (Sydney 1848), p. 8; *Catalogue of Excellent Household Furniture, Cabinet Pianoforte: In the Insolvent Estate of H. H. Macarthur* (Sydney, 1848), p. 11.

11  L. Frost (ed.), *No Place for a Nervous Lady* (Melbourne, 1984), p. 92.

12  Hazen and Hazen, *Keepers of the Flame*, p. 170; P. Brewer, ' "We have got a very good cooking stove": Advertising, Design and Consumer Response to the Cookstove, 1815–1880', *Winterthur Portfolio*, vol. 25, no. 1, pp. 35–54.

13  Davidson, *A Woman's Work*, p. 22.

14  *Lassetter's Complete General Catalogue* (Sydney, 1906), p. 181.

15  *Agricultural Society of New South Wales Intercolonial Exhibition 1869* (Sydney, 1869), n.p.

16  J. Owen, Insolvency Records, 1887, State Archives Office of New South Wales, n.p.

17  J. Shiel, *ibid.*, n.p.

18  *Council for Advertising Research in Australia* (1955), table 2.

19  Giedion, *Mechanization Takes Command* (New York, 1975 [1948]); Kingston, *My Wife, My Daughter and Poor Mary Ann* (Melbourne, 1975); Reiger, *The Disenchantment of the Home* (Melbourne, 1985).

20  *Death in the Dining Room and Other Tales of Victorian Culture* (Philadelphia, 1992), pp. 76–7; see also S. Williams (ed.), *Savory Suppers and Fashionable Feasts* (New York, 1984); K. Grover, *Dining in America* (Amherst, 1987).

21  Mrs Maria Rundell, *A New System of Domestic Cookery: Formed upon Principles of Economy and Adapted for the Use of Private Families* was one of the first cookbooks to enjoy commercial success. It was published in 1806 and reprinted throughout the nineteenth century. *Lady's Own Cookery* was first published in 1840; the title page stated that it was 'adapted to the use of Persons living in the Highest Style, as well as those of Moderate Fortune'. For a history of cookbooks, see E. Quayle, *Old Cook Books* (New York, 1978). For examples of auction notices mentioning cookbooks, see *Catalogue of Elegant Modern Household Furniture: Property of Mr Samuel Lyons* (1836), p. 15; *Henry G. Bohn Covent Garden: New Valuable and Most Important Books* (1848), p. 18.

22  The publication of Mrs Lance Rawson's *Cookery Book and Household Hints* in 1878 was followed by an 'Old Housekeeper's *Australian Housewives' Manual* (1883),

104

'A Practical Cook's' *Australian Plain Cookery* (1883), Mrs Harriet Wicken's *Kingswood Cookery Book* (1885), and Margaret Pearson's *Cookery Recipes for the People* (1888). For a bibliography of Australian cookbooks, see B. Austin, *A Bibliography of Australian Cookery Books Published Prior to 1841* (Melbourne, 1987).

23 *Australian Readers Remember* (Melbourne, 1992), pp. 104–8.

24 *The Presbyterian Cookery Book of Good and Tried Receipts* (Sydney, 1922), n.p.

25 'An Old Housekeeper', *Men and How to Manage Them* (Melbourne, 1885), p. 22.

26 *Acorn Stoves and Ranges* (Albany, 1890), n.p.

27 *Catalogue of Ironmongery, Hardware, Metals etc.* (Melbourne, 1887), p. 114ff.

28 *Anthony Hordern and Sons*, p. 423ff.

29 *Buck's Stove and Range Co.* (St Louis, 1900), p. 16.

30 R. L. Bushman, *The Refinement of America* (New York, 1993), p. 109.

31 Mrs L. (Wilhelmina) Rawson, *Mrs Lance Rawson's Cookery Book and Household Hints* (Rockhampton, 1886), pp. 5–6.

32 'The Consumption Junction: A Proposal for Research Strategies in the Sociology of Technology', in T. J. Pinch, T. Hughes and W. E. Bijker (eds), *The Social Construction of Technological Systems* (Cambridge, Mass., 1987), pp. 261–80.

33 Mrs L. (Wilhelmina) Rawson, *Australian Cook and Laundry Book* (Melbourne, 1897), p. 6.

34 *Anthony Hordern and Sons*, p. 79.

35 B. Berch, 'Scientific Management in the Home: The Empress's New Clothes', *Journal of American Culture*, vol. 4, 1980, pp. 410–15; see also Reiger, *The Disenchantment of Home*.

36 H. F. Wicken, *The Australian Home* (Sydney, 1891), p. 1; see also J. I. Peacock, *A History of Home Economics in New South Wales* (Sydney, 1982), p. 16.

37 *Calendar of Sydney Technical College for 1892* (Sydney, 1892), pp. 104–8.

38 *The Art of Living in Australia* (London, 1894), pp. 114–25.

39 *Cookery Instruction Cards* (Melbourne, n.d.); see also L. Shapiro, *Perfection Salad* (New York, 1986), p. 63.

40 In 1886, Mrs Fawcett Story had been appointed lecturer and demonstrator in Cookery and Domestic Economy at Hurlstone Training College in Sydney. This college trained young women as instructors of cookery for schools: F. Fawcett Story, *Australian Economic Cookery Book and Housewife's Companion* (Sydney, 1900), p. iv.

41 Muskett, *The Art of Living*, p. 251.

42 Wicken, *The Australian Home*, p. 21.

43 Mrs L. (Wilhelmina) Rawson, *The Antipodean Cookery Book and Kitchen Companion* (Melbourne, 1895), p. 6.

44 *Ibid.*, p. 8.

45 Jackson Lears has defined 'scientism' as a 'superstitious faith in the powers of science: 'Some Versions of Fantasy', *Prospects*, vol. 9, 1984, pp. 389–90.

46 E. Darling, *Simple Rules of the Guidance of Persons in Humble Life* (Sydney, 1837), p. 13.

47 R. L. Bushman and C. L. Bushman, 'The Early History of Cleanliness in America', *Journal of American History*, vol. 74, no. 4, 1988, p. 1220.

48  H. Ashford (ed.), *The Diary of Evelyn Barwick* (Scone, 1988), pp. 31, 77, 142.

49  G. Horne, Insolvency Records (1890), n.p.

50  *New South Wales Parliamentary Papers*, 1860, p. 1271.

51  Rawson, *Australian Cook*, pp. 102–3.

52  B. Dyster quotes the wages given to female domestic servants on John Blaxland's estate as cook, £25 a year, sempstress £20, housemaid £13 7s and lady's maid £12, with the laundress coming last at £10 3s: *Servant and Master* (Sydney, 1989), p. 146; see also A. Oakley, *The Sociology of Housework* (Oxford, 1988), pp. 85–97.

53  *Our Home in Australia* (Sydney, 1984), p. 81.

54  Lane and Serle, *Australians at Home*, p. 389.

55  Giedion, *Mechanization*, pp. 560–2.

56  *Index to New South Wales Letters of Registration of Inventions* (Sydney, 1891), p. 108; *Index to New South Wales Letters Patent Registered 1 August 1887–31 December 1891* (Sydney, 1894), pp. 651–97.

57  *Australasian Ironmonger*, 1 September 1889, p. 399.

58  Sydney, 1981 [1963], pp. 148–9.

59  L. Donovan, Interview with Inara Walden, Powerhouse Museum, Sydney, 1992, n.p.

60  Trevor Pinch and Wiebe Bijker argue that when new technologies are under development there is a great deal of flexibility in the definition of that technology. 'Invention' is not a single event but a process that can extend over many years. 'Closure' occurs only when there is a single accepted solution to the multitude of problems presented by the object: 'The Social Construction of Facts and Artifacts', in Pinch, Hughes and Bijker, *The Social Construction*, pp. 17–50.

61  For example, at Melbourne's Centennial Exhibition local manufacturers included L. Harrison of Marrickville, G. Hardley of North Melbourne, S. Lower, W. F. Manson, and Wolter and Echberg: *Official Record of the Centennial International Exhibition* (1890), pp. 456, 616.

62  Rawson, *Mrs Lance Rawson's Cookery Book*, p. 8.

63  P. Statham (ed.), *The Tanner Letters* (Perth, 1981), Appendix 1.

64  H. A. McCorkell, *The Diaries of Sarah Midgley and Richard Skilbek* (Melbourne, 1967), pp. 59, 62, 64.

65  Lane and Serle, *Australians at Home*, p. 389.

66  J. Usher, Insolvency Records, 1887, n.p.; T. Henery, Insolvency Records, 1874, n.p.; J. Owen, Insolvency Records, 1887, n.p.

67  Ashford, *Diary of Evelyn Barwick*, p. 72.

68  *New South Wales Parliamentary Papers*, 1860, p. 1320.

69  *The Sociology of Housework*, p. 55; see also D. Hayden, *The Grand Domestic Revolution* (Cambridge, Mass., 1982), pp. 115, 116, 120, 130, 155.

70  S. Symons, 'The Kitchen: The Heart of the Home', *The Australian Magazine*, 9 March 1996, p. 6.

## Chapter 7

# Making Oneself Comfortable, or More Rooms than Persons

*Nicholas Brown*

'Our community believes in the family', Walter Burley Griffin declared in 1920. He was the Director of Design and Construction of the new Australian national capital. 'Even though we might not be agreed upon the status of the other functions or any other forms of our social organism, we are satisfied that nothing must be allowed to absorb or supplant the existing segregation of families.' This segregation entailed larger blocks of land and more privacy to mark the boundaries between the home and a wider world. It also required— through what restraints Griffin did not specify—'no further dispersal of the activities that belong to home life into general eating houses, nor external services to replace . . . household activities'. Within the home, there were other forms of segregation to be secured, especially in the privacy of bedrooms for parents and for children of each sex. 'Though man is a gregarious being', Griffin advised, 'to the extent of the family group, he is an individual soul' and must have personal space in which to express that identity. The 'basic house' that Griffin proposed to secure these precepts, five rooms shown in plan, was uncompromisingly 'modern'—even down to directing the location of furniture in modular units placed hard against the walls and in the corners of each room. With such regularities guaranteed, however, Griffin could let others relax: whoever it was who cooked and cleaned was termed a 'worker' in their own right, and was entitled to 'household equipment' that approximated to the standard of 'a laboratory' if not 'a factory'; and 'dining in the living room' was one way in which to celebrate this ethic of efficiency as it could now transform older anxieties about segregation into 'the adaptability of a single space alternatively to each purpose'.[1]

If this statement had the tone of a manifesto, it hardly appeared in a radical medium. The *Real Property Annual* kept pace with trends in building, design and decoration rather than forcing them, and Griffin—to a considerable extent—was only drawing together a range of themes then emerging in discussions of the Australian home. His synthesis might have been confronting—the plan dispensed almost completely with a hallway or formal entrance, and his precise mapping of furniture was far from the clustering around the bric-a-brac of the nineteenth-century home, all according to conventions of 'taste' architects had rarely troubled to prescribe. Even so, the elements of this ideal, from the prompts to efficiency to the psychology of privacy, were increasingly current in a diverse range of magazine and newspaper journalism dealing with the making of a home. Here was a neat encapsulation of early-twentieth-century ideas of comfort, organisation and behaviour in domestic spaces, defined at the intersection of a range of influences: of class identities, technological change, gendered and generational aspirations, and prevailing moral economies.

What is striking about Griffin's ideal, however, is the ways in which it marked a transition from what had been possible to expect of Australian housing in the last decades of the nineteenth century. Between the 1880s and the 1920s there occurred a marked shift in the relationship between housing form and cultural values as they were acted out in the Australian home—so marked that it seems to hold in microcosm much of what came before and after that period. The focus of this chapter is on aspects of this shift as they provided the preconditions for Griffin's manifesto, and for the emergence of the twentieth-century suburban home. For the purpose of this survey, and in the context of this book, I want to deal in particular with the intersections noted above at two points: the ways in which rooms, as the spaces in which people organised the minutiae of their lives (their 'individual souls', as Griffin had it) were reconfigured in this transition; and the comforts of the home, as reward or solace, as they were often defined in opposition to something existing beyond the home, and which the home kept at bay. At these points of intersection we can see the complexity of much that we might still take for granted in the spaces in which we live.

First, to set the scene: European settlement in Australia took place just after the bourgeois ideal of the home, centring on domestic life and comfort, and disaggregated into discrete rooms, had taken hold across northern Europe, all ready to be transported.[2] There are many striking images in Australian history of such rooms dislocated, disarrayed, latent but unrealised in the search for familiarity in a strange landscape. There was the foundational symbol of Governor Phillip's prefabricated home, its modular rooms now marked out in hatchings spilling from the pavement to the roadway of Bridge Street. There are images of the first settlers at Swan River, who set out for Western Australia with 'carriages of all sorts, pianos and harps and sumptuous wardrobes' only to be hastily landed in June 1829 and left with 'all their belongings, both luxuries and necessities . . . strewn about them on the sandy shore'.[3] In 1839 there is Henry Parkes's image of his wife, sitting 'on a box I had brought with us from the ship . . . with her newborn infant in her arms' in the only room, 'dirty and unfurnished', he had been able to find after their disembarkation—a room that offered a status no better than the convicts from which such free immigrants fought to distinguish themselves.[4] And there is the cultivated exoticism of Harden Melville's 1850 painting of 'The Squatter's Hut', subtitled 'news from Home'—an image widely popularised, becoming almost a genre of its own, and in 1851 paired by George Baxter with his 'News from Australia'. At 'Home' there is an ordered, feminised room, a violin, a spinning wheel at rest, in contrast to Melville's rustic masculine chaos in a room 'up country', a trumpet cast among a saddle and rifle, carcasses on the dirt floor, the bush beyond the door.[5]

Diaries and letters indicate the intense investment made in the concept of 'home' and 'hearth' by settlers lacking any larger community in this new landscape. By the latter half of the nineteenth century, so Graeme Davison notes, this ideal was further seasoned with a Victorian sentimentality regarding the home as 'haven' of the nuclear family. 'Home is the congenial soil of the purest affections of the noblest virtues of the heart', wrote Emma Thompson in 1857, as society around her in Western Australia acquired a more reassuring appearance.[6] Henry Handel Richardson in *The Fortunes of Richard Mahony* paid close attention to rooms as symbols in the relentless odyssey of her central character: rooms that were makeshift, exclusive ('a room that was all his own'), self-conscious spaces; rooms of emigration and arrival, to be packed and unpacked, renovated or let; 'unnatural-looking rooms' she describes them in one passage. The attempt to divide, replicate and cultivate spheres of personal, domestic and intimate life in rooms reveals much about the aspirations and anxieties of those who sought to make or find their homes in Australia.[7]

109

For the first hundred years of European settlement the search for comfort was often conducted in whatever rooms were available. Official inquiries and regulations as early as 1810, keen to establish minimum dimensions and standards in this almost prematurely suburban society, prescribed the number and size of rooms, and by the second half of the century, their overcrowding had become a perennial anxiety among social reformers. The concern was not so much with itemising the function of discrete spaces—in general, houses would continue to be described by the number of undifferentiated rooms they had until World War II ('five rooms at Woolloomooloo, a healthy and eligibly situated locality')—but rather with estimating the extent to which rudimentary colonial life was approximating to standards of health, morality and civilisation. 'In the smallest dwelling I entered, I never saw less than two apartments'—this last term being used in a very literal sense: the breaking-up of otherwise undefined space, the securing of at least some privacy and relief from excessive propinquity.[8] William Jevons recalled one 'Robinson-Crusoe-like construction' that he slept in while travelling in the Illawarra in 1857:

> The cottage had in reality but one apartment, a low partition without any door shutting off the part represented by the bedroom. About ten o'clock I retired to bed, if getting into bed with two other men can so be called, Moran and one of

the younger men, his brother I think being my bedfellows. His wife and the young woman slept in the other half of the hut on the ground before the fire.[9]

Against these experiences, however, and in many ways defining the concerns they registered, was the ideal of the home as envisaged for the new colonist. In the 1830s, for example, local advocates of emigration to New South Wales—those, perhaps, who lured Parkes—promised emigrants 'that domestic comfort which every labouring man should be enabled to enjoy'. Once in the colony, 'each would have a home', they guaranteed—drawing out a wide significance for that term: 'a direct interest in the maintenance of social order'. Such a home, affording a couple of rooms and invested with 'courtesy and self-respect', would remedy the condition of families 'crowded into a single and often narrow apartment' in Britain: a bedevilled space in which 'woman, a drudge in dirt, loses her attractions' and where the children grow up without 'reserve'.[10]

Courting the respectable labourer, such manifestos framed comfort with reference to distinct gender and familial identities which would continue to be refined into the twentieth century: the comfort to which a man comes home, which redeems a woman, which secures the children from the streets. There were plenty of prompts to such comfort. The Reverend G. H. Stanley outlined for the Sydney Mechanics Institute in 1851 his ideal of domestic comfort: a clean home—a place, Stanley insisted, where 'a man shows himself as he is'. It was decorated with some simple pictures of 'taste and refinement' readily available as engravings, a shelf of 'immortal works of genius' also available in cheap editions, and a few busts of great men ('but a few shillings'). A version of what this ideal might have looked like in practice is exactly recorded in Joseph Elliot's account of his Adelaide cottage in the 1860s, where evangelical literature had its place on the dining table, and reproductions of the Duke of Wellington and the death of Nelson on the parlour walls. The kitchen was papered with posters inviting audiences to 'Go See the Nigger Postman Tonight', and in a drawer in the bedroom there was a baby's caul, kept to protect the child from drowning, and a book of lockets of hair from deceased members of the family. Each room, in these ways, mapped out a distinct sphere of solace, pleasure and contentment.[11]

These ideals, prescriptions and experiences jostled each other through the first century of European occupation. By the end of the 1880s, as Noel Butlin noted with a statistician's exactitude, housing in Australia 'had grown to such an extent that the number of rooms in "permanent" houses, 3,058,000, almost exactly matched the number of people, 3,003,692'. For the first time, taking census aggregates at face value, each white Australian had a room to her or himself. 'By the turn of the century', Butlin continued, 'there were actually 100,000 more rooms than persons', and these rooms were bigger and better built than those inhabited by earlier settlers. Through this index Butlin identified a first phase of maturity in Australian housing, catching up with population growth and mobility since the 1850s. Although these new rooms were far from evenly distributed, their quantum was read as an indication of 'the social tendencies of the people' (as early statisticians put it), and it heralded a more powerful image of the home as a normative device and aspiration. Graeme Snooks observes of the same period that household multiplication then replaced economic growth as the dominant economic stimulus in the Australian colonies. This transition involved not just technological change and more efficient resource utilisation, but substantial realignments in 'the internal dynamics of the household sector'. Australians, it seems, quite markedly began to prefer living in smaller family groups in more houses, even if the preference was pursued 'at the expense of household living standards'.[12]

Accompanying this preference, architectural histories recount another transition. The cottage or row-house of boxy, largely undifferentiated rooms along a 'skittle alley' hallway had been the predominant house form in the colonies, endlessly replicated and adapted on narrow blocks by speculators. It was replaced by the bungalow form, at its purest on a wider suburban frontage, single-family focused, individualised, more often owner-occupied and better serviced.[13] With its diverse, more rectangulated spaces, this new form began to approach that advocated by Griffin ('the adaptability of a single space'). It was observed by Robin Boyd as providing, by the inter-war years, the 'informality' of a 'triumvirate of entertaining rooms—hall, dining and sitting room', and a diversity of address to the street and garden.[14] By the 1920s, so the statisticians recorded, an average private house had five rooms and 4.15 occupants. The *Real Property Annual* was already celebrating this transformation in 1911 as a 'complete revolution' not just in housing form, but in the lives that might be lived in such spaces. What was it about rooms and ideas of comfort that lay behind, and were caught up in, these transformations of the ideal home around the turn of the century?

It is impossible to recreate an accurate sense of these rooms as lived-in spaces, especially as we move away from more regularised patterns of life in cities and suburbs and into areas where the reach of such ideals was moderated by distance and local conditions. Innovation and adaptation have always been a characteristic of making a home in Australia: these traits were recognised by *The Australian Enquiry Book*, for example, in advising that homemakers could do much with packing-cases, shirtboxes, horseshoes and horns (covered in velvet), and that even the wings of a parrot might make an attractive ornament to a fire-screen.[15] But it is possible to convey the kinds of meanings attaching to the making of a home, and the aspirations encouraged and deviations scrutinised in the process.

From one perspective, the Victorian age dripped with comfort. Comfort was promoted by industrial innovation and increasing levels of mass consumption, by the consolidation of a middle-class sensibility longing for the 'cosy' and the 'quaint', and a social conscience of 'pious self-congratulation'.[16] From another perspective, 'comfort' could amount to a strict discipline of thrift and a more subjective retreat into the privacy of the family for those who strove for the virtues of domesticity from further down the class hierarchy.[17] Across

111

this compass, these meanings could also become integral to concepts of entitlement. The clearest, and most resonant, example of this synthesis came in 1907 when H. B. Higgins sought to determine in the Commonwealth Arbitration Court what might constitute 'a wage sufficient' to secure 'frugal comfort' for the working man, his wife and two children—a regimen including books, newspapers, furniture, sewing machines, amusements, and acceptable consumption of intoxicating liquor and tobacco.[18] The full range of such domestic comfort—from solace and self-improvement to status and display—was present in commentary on housing in this transitional period, setting up new tensions as the home steadily reflected not just social stratifications but the segregated stages on which to enact modern personalities.

The comfort of ostentation is easily recalled now from roped-off restorations in heritage houses. It seemed to some—such as Richard Twopeny, writing in the early 1880s—that this form was only exaggerated in the prosperous colonies among those indulging a prevailing taste for the 'grandiose', the 'heavy' and the 'frowsy', without any corrective metropolitan influences.[19] And it was a fashion, Twopeny argued—in a refrain that runs across generations of disgruntled commentators on the 'featurism' of untutored Australian sub-urbanites—that easily spilled over into the lower ranks, where 'quality and quantity' only suffered further in imitation. Something of what Twopeny meant can be glimpsed in the catalogue that the society magazine *Table Talk* offered in 1885 of a new mansion in Kew, 'the residence of Mr W. Greenlaw, general manager of the Colonial Bank of Australia, and one of Victoria's essentially representative men'. The dining room was 'in the Medieval style', with friezes depicting scenes from Scott's Waverley novels; the drawing room was 'modern Italian', with floral motifs and a touch of Japan; the breakfast room was 'Italian renaissance', 'very elaborate', with paintings in the 'Watteau style'; the hall was populated by cupids, holding family crests and gasburners.[20]

This was comfort-as-pleasure and display, an eclectic catalogue of the voguish Aestheticism then gripping the colonies, and advocated in its 'early English' mode at the 1880 Melbourne Exhibition—that celebrated stimulus to the spread of 'elegance', 'artistry', 'enterprise' and 'judgement' through colonial society. This Exhibition had the standing of a kind of mission delivering, Ada Cambridge recalled, a desperately needed awakening of 'taste' in the arrangement of 'artistic things' in the home, from Persian rugs to Venetian glass. And to these styles could be added the 'soul-stirring Gothic' advocated by the *Argus* that same year as a remedy for those in the colonies homesick for all they had left behind.[21]

This opulence, then, had its own sensitivities in relation to status and culture. From its launch in 1885, *Table Talk* celebrated the popularity of the 'at home' and all it represented, offering advice on the intricacies of hosting such occasions and on suitable comportment when attending them. The style of this advice was less exacting than the prescriptions of the etiquette manuals also current at the time—which decreed, for example, that no call should last for less than fifteen minutes or more than thirty. Even so, the formalities of the 'at home' synthesised the privacy and intimacy of the home and the public display of status, right down to minute details: 'books, papers, music, work-baskets (pretty ones), all should be in our receiving rooms. These furnish conversation when we are receiving, as oftentimes there is a break in conversation.'[22] Beyond such injunctions, these practices revealed the ways in which the comfort of the home was becoming increasingly crucial to the rituals that consolidated and perpetuated class identities. 'The glory of hospitality has revived among the colonists', J. A. Froude observed in 1885, perhaps partly because they had become sufficiently confident in their hierarchies to allow these divisions to be enacted in drawing rooms, at parties, and during 'recherché suppers'.[23]

Comfort, as these examples suggest, was not perceived to be innate within the home, but something to be cultivated and carefully balanced in dealing with a range of concerns, resources and threats. Mrs Wicken, an 'instructress in Domestic Economy' at Sydney Technical College, indicated how pervasive the gradations of comfort and 'station' could be in her 1891 'handbook' when she advised that 'if there are not two chairs alike in the room so much the more are we in fashion'—so long, she promptly added, as homemakers observed 'what is suitable to our position in society'.[24] That profusion of objects of Victorian sentimentality—those 'artistic things' the arrangement of which tested sensibilities—were strict arbiters of individual and class identities. As well, very often, they allocated distinct forms of comfort: the chairs in which a man might 'lounge'; the straighter, lower-backed equivalent for women. They determined the repose and conduct—as David Malouf suggests—of bodies 'differently conceived or differently seen' as they moved through the various rooms of the home.[25]

Although the home was often marked out as women's space, it was the comfort of men which emerged as central to the meaning of home by the end of the nineteenth century. As Mrs Beeton's trusted household manual lectured from 1861 onwards, 'men are so well served out of doors—at clubs, hotels and restaurants—that to compete with the attractions of these places, the mistress must be thoroughly acquainted with the theory and practice of cookery, as well as the arts of making and keeping a comfortable home'. By 1900 Mrs Aronson was advising in *Twentieth Century Cooking and Home Decoration* that the 'mistress' must take special care to provide congeniality for the 'sterner sex'. This could be achieved, perhaps, by dropping reference to the forbidding 'drawing room', calling it a 'smoking room' instead, and furnishing it in ways enabling 'menfolk to rest'. This message could be stripped back to its essentials for the less well-off. In 1885 the *Australian Housewives Manual*—advising housewives on 'small incomes' on achieving 'decent comfort'—recommended that a wife should build her domain out from the stove and around a regime of 'self-denial'. Her kitchen should be run so that, if the house lacked a dining room, she might still be capable of serving a meal neatly in the sitting room, then clear it away, wash up, and return to her husband's side before he had finished his first pipe: she might then talk gently to him, or quietly sew, 'according to his mood'.[26]

In these formulations, then, the division of the home into discrete rooms—kitchen, dining room, sitting room, drawing room or smoking room—was being invested with complex, intersecting meanings. As the case of the dining room, or at least its equivalent zone, indicates, there were many elements to this concern: those of appropriate behaviour; the consolidation of the home away from the 'external' and the 'general' corruptions that Griffin feared; and—equally importantly—a model of the hygienic, fit and well-adjusted citizen. The catalogue of the Sydney store Anthony Hordern's in 1909 advised that the 'dining room was surely the most important apartment in the house': its decoration should be 'strictly conventionalised' to keep the room conducive to the ease, peace and good digestion. Appropriate furnishing for such a room might include a couch or an armchair—presumably to mark further the distinction between those who waited to be served, then withdrew from the table, and those who served. 'It must be a pleasant room', *Building* magazine insisted in 1910: if it encouraged the family to take time over their meal, it was a 'health helper'; if it instilled discipline, order, a regularised policing of manners, it was even more an asset. As Kimberley Webber observes in Chapter 6, in the nineteenth century great emphasis was placed on the

rituals of formal dining. Mrs Wicken had been quick to indicate the ways in which even the setting of the table could stimulate 'a wholesome rivalry' among daughters needing to understand the importance of order, 'however well-born'.[27]

These dictums were not without challenge in the name of the 'informality' championed for the new century, but even then it was clear that rooms defined carefully scrutinised boundaries. Anticipating Griffin's relaxation about eating in living spaces, in 1902 John Sulman, a prominent progressive architect, advocated breaking down the division between kitchen and dining room as a challenge to 'the intense conservatism of the average middle-class man, and especially woman' in an increasingly servant-scarce society.[28] Although these walls might be made more permeable in middle-class homes, where comfort might reside in more open exchanges, it is revealing that they should be made more exclusive in the homes of a working class whose social identities were, presumably, less secure or reliable. So, in 1920, in the course of extensive inquiries by the Royal Commission on the Basic Wage, the status of the dining room in working-class homes was still of considerable interest. Further refining Higgins's determination of the 'frugal comfort [of] the worker's household', by then scrutiny was shifting from concerns with the moral economy of familial discipline and the regularity and hygiene of the body, to the 'new science of the household' as championed by the commission's chairman, A. B. Piddington.[29] In the minutes of evidence it was noted that, if a house for a family of five had four rooms, the tendency was to allocate a common function of 'kitchen and living-room . . . combined'; if there were five rooms, however, a 'dining room' would be specifically allocated to that fifth room as a discrete space. These observations reflected a concern that food was being prepared in the space where it was to be eaten—the implied problem being a lack of clear boundaries in domestic conduct as much as hygienic and organisational disorder. Although the final report of the commission recorded the necessity for workers of a fifth room as a 'sitting or social room', with its function in 'preserving decency in the home' and 'maintaining a good standard of manners and civilisation', the emphasis in the minutes from a range of witnesses was also on encouraging that practice available to 'people occupying five-roomed houses' who 'generally have their meals in the dining room'—and all that such a practice might represent.[30]

If dining rooms prepared the healthy, well-mannered citizen for a world of order and efficiency, more subjective identities were being mapped out in bedrooms at the intersection of pressures towards hygiene and discipline, and also that increasing interest in the expressive dimensions of the 'individual soul'. Throughout the nineteenth century bedrooms were often under the cloud of being 'unwholesome' spaces, where enclosed air and prone bodies were most liable to lassitude and sickness. In 1891 Mrs Wicken had, in the interests of economy, suggested bedrooms be furnished as alike as possible, and kept free of unnecessary ornament because dust and disease quickly accumu-lated in carpets, curtains and discarded clothes. Well into the 1920s the glossy magazine *Home* could still enthuse that 'the bedroom is slowly but surely coming round to the hygienic, well-lit, easily cleansed, bacteriologically sterile hospital ward'—stripped of suffocating bed canopies (single beds were always preferred), heavy carpets and dust-accumulating furniture.[31] The decoration of bedrooms 'must not in any way stimulate the brain', so the injunction ran: they were places of rest, for physical rejuvenation not emotional indulgence—and, only when appropriate, for 'duty to the race' rather than sensual pleasure. The bedrooms of the poor came in for particular scrutiny in the 1917 Royal Commission on Housing Conditions in Melbourne. There it was asserted that there was 'a definite association between the number of rooms and the morality of the individual'. This precept led to the insistence that 'no male above ten years of age shall use a room used as a sleeping room by females; nor shall any unmarried female use a room in which any male above ten years of age sleeps; and two males above ten years of age shall not occupy the same bed'. The commissioners detected, in a revealing formulation, a 'patent' link between a decline in the 'physiological grounds' of 'ordinary comfort' in crowded bedrooms especially, and the rise of 'evil moral influence'.[32]

Yet, alongside these anxieties, another role for the family in the 'social organism' was acquiring greater importance. This was its role in the education and adjustment of children, especially those nearing adulthood. Young people increasingly had to find their place in an urban and suburban society which valued their living in the parental home until marriage while also engaging more freely with the emerging concept of adolescence.[33] The failure of the home to adequately serve the needs of the adolescent was often indicted as discontent mounted from the 1880s onwards regarding the behaviour of young men. They were perceived to be restlessly urbanised, able to find well-paid if unskilled work, and to assert an aggressive identity on the streets. By the early

1900s, adolescence was being defined in terms of a fragile balance between nostalgia for an ideal of home (mostly among girls) and a restless independence (predominant for boys). It was argued that, especially in those years of self-formation, an increase in 'comfort' was required to lift adolescents above their 'instincts'.[34] And this burden fell heaviest in the bedroom—that room where, as Griffin put it, 'each individual must have the greatest obtainable privacy'. In their bedrooms children might create their own 'realm', as *Home* put it in 1920, yet must also avoid being 'oppressed'.[35] By 1925 the *Australian Home* was counselling that 'a girl should be encouraged to take personal pride in her room': 'to feel that there she may have peace and privacy for girlish dreams, hopes and aspirations, and then the department will blossom out into a fitting and beautiful environment for the tenderness, sincerity and artistic ideas which should be the attributes of a woman'.[36] There was no equivalent commentary on the requirements of a bedroom for boys. They, sometimes along with their fathers, were consigned to the bracing climate of the 'sleep-out', their potency checked in a space neither in the home nor in the world beyond.

This emphasis on the regulated development of personality indicates a variation of the idea of comfort as pleasure or solace. Comfort was instead becoming the modern domain in which to achieve psychological adjustment between self and society. And this association was especially marked in those rooms which mapped out new domains of efficient parenting. 'Children are always anxious to copy grown-ups', another article on bedrooms argued in 1925, 'and like to be treated as little men and women with their own special rooms in which they can be taught to take a pride.' A formidable decorative progression was projected to assist the emergence of maturity. As the child advanced, 'artistic panels will take the place of the nursery rhyme wall-paper, brilliant prints will be replaced by softer and less meaningless pictures, and maturer judgement will banish the joyful primary colours and contrasts so pleasing to the eyes of youth'.[37]

All of this was based on clear assumptions, and on the recasting of space and ornament in the home to accord with these new identities. For parents, the scrutiny of the physiological and the psychological development of their children began increasingly early. The admonishment for mothers, for example, from the 1910s onwards was that children should sleep in their own space, with their own clean air, and at best their own room, specifically furnished for them. The tendency of child-care experts then was to see the lack of such space as a sign of maternal ignorance and carelessness. There may well have been a connection between falling rates of child mortality and the tendency of smaller families to live in houses of four or five rooms, but for those without access to such housing, just as for the many who offended against the sleeping dictates of the 1917 Royal Commission already noted, there was scope for little sympathy: it was morality rather than political economy which shaped the analysis of the home and its medicalised role.[38]

Certainly, the recognition of such norms and expectations provided an opportunity for protest on the part of those excluded from such privileges, and there were powerful indictments of a society which left so many outside this 'revolution' in housing. There were the rooms of sweated labour, for example, provoking outrage in William Lane's *Workingman's Paradise* in 1892:

> At the open window of a small room, barely furnished with a broken iron bedstead, some case boards knocked together for a table and fixed against the wall, a couple of shaky chairs and a box, a sharp-featured woman sat working at a machine, as if for dear life . . . For the first time in his life, [Ned] felt ashamed of being an Australian.

Revealingly, Lane contrasts this image with the rooms of the artists whom Ned, his central character, meets. These rooms equally challenged prevailing conventions, being 'long, low and not very broad, running the whole width of the house', and divided only by 'folding doors' and 'curtains'.[39] There were the utopian rooms of collective housing as envisaged by Bertha McNamara in 1894, rejecting completely the subjectivised privacies of the cottage and the bunga- low. These were rooms, instead, to which the working man returned at the end of his day's labour, bathing in a separate block before 'he slips into a dressing garment and proceeds to his room; he is soon arrayed in decent and becoming attire'—and then 'just a peep into the dining room. Oh, . . . fine pictures adorn the wall'.[40] Most protest, however, was directed more simply to securing greater access to a housing form which would secure health, privacy and familial integrity. In 1908 W. G. Spence, president of the Australian Workers Union, was reporting British inquiries that showed 'a difference in height of three inches and in weight of 7 lbs in children of the same age when forced to live in one room'. From these perspectives, the absence of space was a denial of justice: to live in a single room, another prominent reformer, Professor R. F. Irvine, insisted in 1913, was 'soul-destroying'.[41]

117

It was not only that new housing forms were becoming more capable of allocating discrete spaces within the family. There was also a larger social context reaffirming and refining this process. Histories of leisure in Australia, for example, have identified 'a gradual move to more carefully limited social intercourse' from the 1880s into the twentieth century, a shift associated with an increasing rigidity of customs linked to suburbanisation and the steady formalisation of holidays, trading hours and patterns of public transport. In this process the familial home came to the fore as the site of recreation, expression and moral instruction in such matters as frugality, industry and sobriety.[42] 'Comfort', loosing the explicitly classed overtones of consolation and display, settled emphatically within the nuclear family circle. It was affirmed in any number of ways—including, for example, the popularity of the 'parlour song', a form geared to gathering the family around the piano, and one in which the Australian composer, May Brahe, excelled. Among Brahe's most successful compositions, appropriately, was 'Bless this House': a perfect example of domestic retreat and piety, written in a style that Brahe calculated precisely to capture a feminised amateurism, 'a source of solace and personal enjoyment', as she put it, of women giving 'pleasure to their own circle'.[43] Into the 1920s radio brought other dimensions to this process of shaping the intimacy of the family unit around a cultural medium which, as Lesley Johnson argues, ever more intricately constructed both familial relations and the contacts between 'listeners-in' and the world outside. In its programming and categories of taste, radio even began structuring the day around a progression from room to room, from the kitchen in the morning to the fireside at night. Into the 1950s television only refined this process further, bringing—as Raymond Williams observed—abstracted images of 'out there' into the senti-mentality and the privacy of familiar rooms, and further influencing the modalities of social engagement.[44]

This focus on the nuclear family brought with it its own scrutiny of what defined the comforts of the home, and who was excluded from them. Beyond the familiar markers of respectability—the scarcely used front 'parlour', the careful allocation of sleeping space—there was a more exacting sense in which rooms marked out the fulfilment of identities as well as the expression of taste. For the unmarried or the childless woman there was no comfort:

> What can a helpless woman do?
> Rock the cradle, and bake, and brew;
> Or if no cradle your fate afford
> Rock your brother's wife's for your board
> Or live in one room with an invalid cousin
> Or sew shop shirts at a dollar a dozen.[45]

For unattached women, the house itself emphasised the basic incongruity of living outside the family. The house form was predicated on such a unit: in the arrangement of rooms along hallways which marked domains of privacy, and in the increasing centrality of kitchens and in internal bathrooms. In 1903 a feature in the *New Idea* on 'The Women Who Toil' reproduced photo-graphs of the drawing room and parlour from the homes of 'a better class of factory girl' (those 'who do not spend all their earnings on their backs'), teasing away at the trade-off between skill, wages and worldliness on the one hand with the security and innocence of domesticity on the other.[46] These rooms, well-furnished, but empty of the familial presence, begged the question: how could women live in both worlds, and what unhappiness must there be for those whose lives fell so far short of the purposes and ideals of such allocated rooms?

Increasingly, then, rooms tested identities not just of class but also of a more individualised adjustment to modern roles. As Sulman had anticipated, the symbol of the 'the servant problem', whatever the reality, influenced much discussion of houses for the more affluent after World War I. As *Home* candidly put it, 'that section of the community from which the old trusty domestic servant was drawn has advanced in its . . . intellectual development' and was no longer prepared to work long hours in other people's homes.[47] For the advocates of modern comfort, however, the decline of 'Mary Jane' was also the making of efficient, technologically advanced homes—homes in which there was now even more opportunity to stamp rooms with a personalised taste. Servants were associated with dark passages, draughty rooms and dirty kitchens. With their passing, houses might become informal and integrated: living rooms leading into dining rooms leading into kitchens (tiled and 'painted in white or lemon to raise your spirits') and out on to verandahs and gardens beyond—all this without ever needing to cross into another's domain.[48] Yet in uniting these spaces there came new challenges. Articles in the *Real Property Annual* carried titles such as 'Art and Comfort in the Home: Personality in Furnishing', or advised that 'it is the higher duty of every man and woman'—note the combined parental obligation—'to provide for themselves, and for their children, surroundings that uplift and soothe'.[49] In this context, the assembly of 'artistic things' that Ada Cambridge had admired in the 1880s, or the conservative and highly feminised forms of Victorian handiwork—the doilies, mats, cloths and samplers carrying the moral injunctions to order, neatness, duty and cleanliness—began to be replaced by other objects. Now the message was directed more to refining a sense of identity in a modern world, as testaments to creativity and fashion under the influence of the arts and crafts movement, for example, and enthusiasm for greater simplicity. There was even a stylised nationalism and mechanisation in design and motif.[50]

119

These changing concepts of comfort were also being mapped out in rooms that coupled informality with gendered and social identities to be registered within the home, and within the family, rather than in transactions between the home and the world outside. From this perspective, that vestige of Victorian comfort, the drawing room, was coming into a scrutiny of its own. Perhaps, it was argued in 1919, the drawing room might be replaced by a small study for the husband and a sewing room for the wife? If retained, 'it might be recessed with deep window seats, alcoves etc. in order to allow two or three friends to chat in an informal way'.[51] Eventually it might be gradually reconfigured entirely as a living room, positioning its occupants not for conversation so much as consumers of the new mass culture of phonograph and radio. In the 1880s, *Table Talk* had offered literary strictures on deportment and entertaining 'at home'; by the 1920s its pages had been transformed into photographic essays on how Hollywood celebrities lived in their highly individualised houses, and how readers might replicate the same 'fads' in their own homes. The registers of comfort were changing as the handful of rooms in which you reflected your social standing and role became the suite of rooms in which you—however problematically—expressed yourselves.

It is difficult to single out any factor which explains this transformation more powerfully than any other—from the economic 'maturity' of the 1880s to the increasing province of 'science' and 'efficiency' in the 1920s. It is the intersection of them all which is most remarkable, and most productive in explaining the importance of this period in the history of housing European Australians. Certainly, these changes provided a whole new market. The department stores which, since the 1880s, had been enticing customers into more intimate spaces of sexuality and gender—the men's and the women's sections, fitted out accordingly—were also beginning to court a larger market among those whose houses and rooms fell within a wider domain of consumption. In 1917 *Real Property Annual* noted that the leading furnishing firms, producing suites to furnish the whole house in a common style, were replicating rooms in their displays, thus 'educating the public taste'. It was insisting that domestic comfort was more a feature of the homes of people of modest means who truly lived as a family.[52] There was also a considerable impetus coming from technological change. On the eve of World War I, electricity was still in combat with gas for the provision of domestic heat and light—the campaign being waged in familiar terms (and endorsed by medical opinion) such as 'electricity stagnates, while gas . . . causes circulation of the air and efficient ventilation'. Even so, the imagery of electricity was dauntingly modern—clean, reliable, efficient, and servant-free. Advertisements itemised its applications for each room of the house: for the kitchen, a thermostatically controlled oven, a griller, vegetable steamer, cereal cooker, kettle and iron; in the bedroom, movable lighting, curling tong heater and a smaller kettle for the morning cup of tea; an egg boiler, toaster and coffee percolator for the dining room; decorative, dimmable lighting in the drawing room; a radiator easily transported from room to room in the course of the day's itinerary.[53] A crucial aspect of the 'electric home' was that each room became more than ever self-defining, and experienced in terms of an ease of movement: a switch activated its special functions; an appliance brought it to life, and gradually influenced its form (the radio in the living room by the 1920s, for example, or the 'rational cooking stove' in the kitchen).

Yet, important as all of these factors are, perhaps the most significant feature of this transition from a cultural point of view is the way in which it shaped new ways in which the home was seen to relate to the lives of those who lived in it. If rooms are, as Gwendolyn Wright argues, 'our culture's fetishes', then these homes between the 1880s and the 1920s were being carefully disaggregated into new zones of reverence and accountability.[54] In the process, the rooms of entitlement, of solace and display, became the rooms of personality. In 1924 Leslie Wilkinson, Professor of Architecture at the University of Sydney, contended that 'house building has become, for the majority, a much more personal matter than in the past' in its financial and design accessibility. 'This increased personal interest must, in the long run, make for good', Wilkinson continued, while adding a revealing qualification: 'but in the early stages of the advent of individuality there are the pitfalls of ignorance, of self-confidence and lack of public spirit, which have played sad havoc with the creation of sound building tradition'.[55] Here were the seeds of new and enduring preoccupations in the commentary on housing. The colonial scrutiny of health, over-crowding and self-improvement was becoming the modern scrutiny of the intelligence and social adjustment of those who lived in the nation's housing. Wilkinson's registers of transgression in taste are revealing of his time—his concern, in 1919 for example, at the proliferation of 'Bolshevistics generally' in the chaos of design and decoration in the average home.[56] Each generation of critics since has defined and policed its prevailing fetishes in its scrutiny of the family home.

In the 1880s the journalism of the slum problem rarely ventured into the houses concerned: in those rooms, it was assumed, 'lurked all the horrors of civilised degradation, and . . . modern barbarism'. Yet when a few righteous eyes did brave this darkness, they found in many homes that 'every room, even under the most disadvantageous circumstances, was scrupulously clean; and in many the attempts at refinement and ornamentation were very marked'.[57] By 1925, in a very different mode, the *Australian Home* published an essay which proclaimed that 'the homes of comfort and of affluence should be the pride of the nation, not only for the refined and gently nurtured citizens they breed, or for the beauty they bring to cities and towns, but for what they represent in human endeavour'. 'No state', the article insisted, 'can ever substitute individual effort in the getting together of a home.'[58] In a similar vein, and a little under twenty years later, R. G. Menzies made the homes of 'the forgotten people'—modest, insular, independent—the bastion of the best social 'instincts', to be held out against those who wanted to intervene in private life (see Chapter 5). Clearly, a new series of threats and oppositions began to condition concepts of comfort as the 1920s led into the 1930s and beyond, and as anxieties about compulsion and the resilience of the individual came to matter more than those of degeneracy and the collapse of necessary hierarchies. But to a large extent these new debates were building on and refining the transitions in housing form and the values ascribed to domestic space which had been already marked out. The post-1945 house might have seen an acceleration in the tendency to disaggregate, extend and elongate rooms and 'segregate' family identities, but the 'revolution' had already occurred. In 1998 Neil Clerehan, one of the vanguard of the post-1945 generation, described the 'Battle for Modernism in the 1940s':

121

> The attack was aimed at just one wall—between the dining room and the kitchen. By 1945 walls between front halls and sitting rooms and sitting rooms and dining rooms had already gone. The new and exciting openness was defeated by two new forces: the 1940–60 birth rate and TV. Six people couldn't find true happiness in the New Space so a wall was sent up between the dining room and the living room, and the family room was born in 1961.[59]

The specific objectives and the countervailing forces here are clearly more familiar to us than the debates of the 1880s to the 1920s, but they exist in a continuity with those concerns. It is instructive, and perhaps sobering, to reflect on such enduring preoccupations, and on the kinds of contexts which so formatively shape both the structures and the values in which we live.

1 W. B. Griffin, 'The Problem of the Basic House', *Real Property Annual*, vol. 9, 1920, pp. 30–1.

2 W. Rybcynski, *The Home: A Short History of an Idea* (Harmondsworth, 1987), p. 77.

3 Baron C. von Hugel, *New Holland Journal: November 1833–October 1834*, trans. and ed. D. Clark (Melbourne, 1994), p. 32.

4 A.W. Martin, *Henry Parkes: A Biography* (Melbourne, 1984), p. 28.

5 T. Bonyhady, *Australian Colonial Painting in the Australian National Gallery* (Melbourne, 1986), p. 146.

6 G. Davison, *The Rise and Fall of Marvellous Melbourne* (Melbourne, 1978), pp. 138–40; Thompson's diary reproduced in M. Aveling (ed.), *Westralian Voices: Documents in Western Australian Social History* (Perth, 1979), p. 277.

7 See especially H. H. Richardson, *Ultima Thule* (Ringwood, Vic., 1978), p. 96.

8 J. Archer, *The Great Australian Dream: The History of the Australian House* (Sydney, 1996), p. 24.

9 W. S. Jevons, *Papers and Correspondence*, vol. 1, ed. R. D. Collison Black and R. Konekamp (Clifton, NJ, 1972), p. 173.

10 J. Macarthur et al., *New South Wales: Its Present State and Future Prospects: Being a Statement with Documentary Evidence, Submitted in Support of Petitions to His Majesty and Parliament* (London, 1837), pp. 160–2.

11 G. H. Stanley, 'The Homes of Our People', *Sydney Morning Herald*, 30 September 1851; J. Elliott, *Our Home in Australia: A Description of Cottage Life in 1860*, ed. Stephan Pikusa (Sydney, 1984), pp. 33, 54, 59.

12 N. G. Butlin, *Investment in Australian Economic Development, 1861–1900* (Cambridge, 1964), pp. 215–23; G. H. Knibbs (1917), 'Modern Methods of Census Taking', *Statistician's Report: Census of the Commonwealth of Australia, 1911*: Melbourne, p. 8; G. Snooks, *Portrait of the Family within the Total Economy* (Melbourne, 1994), pp. 137–42; see also Lynette Finch, *The Classing Gaze: Sexuality, Class and Surveillance* (Sydney, 1993), pp. 10–13.

13 A. King, *The Bungalow: The Production of a Global Culture* (New York, 1995).

14 R. Boyd, *Australia's Home: Its Origins, Builders and Occupiers* (Ringwood, Vic., 1968), p. 81.

15 L. Rawson, *Australian Enquiry Book of Household and General Information* (Sydney, 1894), pp. 205–12.

16 J. Gloag, *Victorian Comfort: A Social History of Design, 1830–1900* (Trowbridge, 1973), p. 211.

17 E. Zaretsky, *Capitalism, the Family and Personal Life* (New York, 1976), p. 51.

18 H. B. Higgins, Ex Parte H.V. McKay, *Commonwealth Arbitration Reports*, vol. 2, 1907–08, p. 4.

19 R. E. N. Twopeny, *Town Life in Australia* (Sydney, 1973), pp. 33, 38–48.

20 'A Spendid Mansion', *Table Talk*, 26 June 1885, p. 4.

21  A. Garran, *Australia: The First Hundred Years* (Sydney, 1974), pp. 178–9;
    A. Cambridge, *Thirty Years in Australia* (Kensington, 1989), p. 113; *Argus*
    reproduced in J. Grant and G. Serle (eds), *The Melbourne Scene, 1803–1956*
    (Sydney, 1983), p. 176.
22  Anon., *Australian Etiquette* (Sydney, 1985), p. 242; 'At Homes', *Table Talk*, 3 July
    1885, p. 2; 'Tea Table Talk', *Table Talk*, 7 August 1885, p. 7.
23  Froude quoted in M. Gilding, *The Making and Breaking of the Australian Family*
    (Sydney, 1991), p. 33.
24  Mrs Wickens, *The Australian Home: A Manual of Domestic Economy* (Sydney, 1891), p.
    111.
25  D. Malouf, *12 Edmondstone Street* (London, 1985), pp. 61–6.
26  I. Beeton, *Mrs Beeton's Household Management* (London, n.d.), p. x; F. B. Aronson,
    *Twentieth Century Cooking and Home Decoration* (Sydney, 1900), p. 305.
27  *Anthony Hordern and Sons, General Catalogue* (Sydney, 1909), p. 2051; 'A Livable
    Home—The Dining Room', *Building*, 12 April 1910, p. 12; Wickens, *The
    Australian Home*, p. 127.
28  J. Sulman, 'The Twentieth Century House', *Report of the Ninth Meeting of the
    Australasian Association for the Advancement of Science* (Hobart, 1902), p. 671.
29  See K. Reiger, *The Disenchantment of the Home: Modernising Australian Domestic Life*      123
    (Melbourne, 1985), pp. 67–9.
30  *Minutes of the Royal Commission on the Basic Wage* (Melbourne, 1920), pp. 28, 34,
    40, 49; *Report of the Royal Commission on the Basic Wage* (Melbourne, 1920),
    pp. 20–1.
31  Wickens, *The Australian Home*, p. 123; W. A. Osborne, 'Architecture in Relation to
    Hygiene', *Home*, vol. 5, no. 3, 1924, p. 54.
32  *Second Progress Report from the Royal Commission on the Housing Conditions of the People
    in the Metropolis* (Melbourne, 1917), pp. 14–15.
33  A. Larson, 'Growing Up in Melbourne: Transitions to Adulthood in the Late
    Nineteenth Century', PhD thesis, Australian National University, 1986,
    pp. 110–17, 223.
34  G. S. Hall, *Adolescence: Its Psychology in its Relation to Physiology, Anthropology,
    Sociology, Sex, Crime, Religion and Education* (New York, 1904), vol. 1, pp. 31, 47;
    vol. 2, pp. 375–83; see also J. Kociumbas, *Australian Childhood: A History* (Sydney,
    1997), ch. 8.
35  'Cool, Neutral Tones Best for Australian Bedrooms', *Home*, vol. 1, no. 2, 1920,
    p. 34.
36  'Furnishing a Girl's Room', *Australian Home* , vol. 32, no. 896, 1925, pp. 4–5.
37  'Bedrooms for Children', *Australian Home*, vol. 32, no. 891, 1925, p. 5.
38  See P. Mein Smith, *Mothers and King Baby* (London, 1997), p. 98.
39  W. Lane, *The Workingman's Paradise* (London, 1948), pp. 19–20, 55–7.
40  Mrs W. H. McNamara, 'Working Men's Homes', in *Three Essays on Social Items*
    (Co-operative Printing Company, Sydney, 1894), p. 13.
41  W. Spence, *The Child, the Home and the State* (Sydney, 1908), p. 2; R. F. Irvine,
    *Report of the Commission of Inquiry into the Question of the Housing of Working Men in
    Europe and America* (Sydney, 1913), p. 11.

42 M. Indian, 'Leisure in City and Suburb: Melbourne, 1880–1900', PhD thesis, Australian National University, 1980.

43 K. Dreyfus, 'Capturing the Ear of the Populace: May Brahe and the Domestic Song Market, 1912–1953', in N. Brown *et al.* (eds), *One Hand on the Manuscript* (Canberra, 1995), p. 49.

44 L. Johnson, *The Unseen Voice: A Cultural Study of Early Australian Radio* (London, 1988); Raymond Williams, 'Drama in a Dramatized Society', in *Writing in Society* (London, n.d.), pp. 14–21.

45 Unattributed verse quoted by Louisa McDonald, 'The Economic Position of Women', *Australian Economist*, vol. 3, no. 11, 1893, p. 370.

46 H. Down, 'The Women Who Toil', *New Idea*, 6 July 1903, pp. 14–16.

47 'Household Services, Limited', *Home*, vol. 2, no. 6, 1921, p. 16.

48 M. Barlow, 'A Servantless House', *Real Property Annual*, vol. 6, 1917, p. 63.

49 'Art and Comfort in the Home', *Real Property Annual*, no. 1, 1911, p. 55; Elizabeth Sergeant White, 'The Home and What Makes One', *Real Property Annual*, no. 9, 1920, p. 24.

50 See J. McPhee, *Australian Decorative Arts, 1900–1985* (Canberra, 1988); J. Broadbent, 'The Chore and Art of House Furnishing', in A. Toy *et al.*, *Hearth and Home: Women's Decorative Arts and Crafts, 1800–1930* (Sydney, 1988), p. 32; E. Wright, *Soft Furnishings, 1788–1930* (Sydney, 1995).

51 C. Keeley, 'Home and Environment: Refinement the Keynote', *Real Property Annual*, vol. 8, 1919, p. 22.

52 'Setting the House in Order', *Real Property Annual*, vol. 6, 1917, p. 40; see also Gail Reekie, *Temptations: Sex, Selling and the Department Store* (Sydney, 1993).

53 See *Electricity: A Journal to Record the Progress of Electricity for Light, Heat and Power*, vol. 1 no. 2, 1911.

54 G. Wright, 'Prescribing the Home' in Arien Mack (ed.), *Home: A Place in the World* (New York, 1993), p. 216.

55 L. Wilkinson, 'The Recent Development of Domestic Architecture in Australia', *The Home*, 1 March 1924, p. 11.

56 L. Wilkinson, 'Domestic Architecture', in S. Ure Smith and B. Stevens (eds), *Domestic Architecture in Australia* (Sydney, 1919), pp. 5–6.

57 'The Rookeries of the City', *Daily Telegraph*, 7 January 1881.

58 'The Home of Comfort', *Australian Home*, vol. 32, no. 909, 1925, p. 5.

59 N. Clerehan, Letters to the Editor, *Weekend Australian*, 31 January–1 February 1998.

## Chapter 8

# Planning, Housing, Gardening

*Robert Freestone*

Where did house and home fit into early town planning reforms? This chapter examines the idea of the planned garden suburb, primarily within the context of the foundational planning movement in the early twentieth century (1900–39). It looks at the 'garden suburbness' of the house and garden, and revisits meanings embedded in the detached house in a garden and grouped setting, meanings revolving around the garden suburb as an improver of human life, well-being and morality. The chapter disaggregates the garden suburb into its constituent components, relating these to the Australian suburban ideal and the particularistic ideology of the early planning movement. It also seeks to go further to uncover the human experiences of early planned residential environments.

125

## Everyday life and the garden suburb

The bottom-up view is usually silenced in planning studies, particularly in planning history. The 'insurgent historiographies' recently gathered together by L. Sandercock collectively challenge official history and received wisdom in liberating other stories where the telling factors become class, gender, race and cultural difference.[1] Such critical perspectives reflect broader movements in social theory, postmodernism and cultural studies. The focus shifts from inclusion to exclusion, from global to local, from theory to practice, from behavioural codes to individual lives, and from triumph to darkness.

The underside of mainstream planning history in Australia has never been far from the surface.[2] A recent classic, Mark Peel's sobering study of planning's legacy in the former showpiece new town of Elizabeth in South Australia, connects social dislocation, community organisation and policy critique.[3] But just as meanings of home are ignored by macro planning and housing policies,[4] planning history tends to cling to its supply-side perspective. The direct privileging of human experience is rare in the literature. R. Finnegan's retrieval of 'manifold personal narratives from residents of a neighbourhood of the British New Town of Milton Keynes stands out as an application of story-telling processes in the context of planned development.[5] But more explicitly historical studies are harder to find. Notable exceptions in an Australian context are F. Adams and L. Johnson, who both expose the chasm between planners and the planned-for in the Cumberland County Council era in Sydney from the 1940s.[6] Johnson talks of planners' visions grounded in synoptic representations of cities as spatial entities; adopting a totalising 'as if from above' standpoint, which diminishes or ignores 'the lived experience of the urban.' Her concern is the human impact of early green belt policies in western Sydney. D. Chambers continues the story through to the 1970s, telling often gruelling stories of 'battles between the council and planning authorities and members of the local community'.[7]

Concentrating on the residential sphere, the reality of individual lives is documented less in traditional scholarly discourse than in anecdotes, images, ephemera, and oral history. The Internet, with its subversive power to democratise the dissemination of information, has unsurprisingly emerged as a formidable resource. Various documentary projects are preserving the collective memory. The Levittown project in New York goes beyond both the mythic creation of its developer and the barbs of critics of postwar suburbia to reveal a heterogeneity which is 'testimony to the resilience of the community'.[8] A local example is the Australia Street project, which explores, through a range of family portraits, how generations of Australians have organised their lives and expressed their experiences in house and garden settings.[9] Glimpses into the more public realities of contemporary social life in a garden suburb, from organising for local heritage battles to the humdrum rhythms of community events, can now also be browsed on the World Wide Web.[10]

The site planning and townscape impacts of the garden suburb movement in Australia have already been broadly delineated.[11] Retelling this design history from a more humanist perspective, let alone actually revisiting the lived experience of early planned communities, is severely hampered by the passage of time and the lack of primary source material. The *modus operandi* here has been to trawl the historical record for evidence of garden suburbs as lived, rather than planned, spaces. The outcome is a broad but fragmented view of diversity, struggle, satisfaction, ordinariness, and tension between individuality and community. In the realities of living, ideal planning projects were inevitably compromised, undermined, and certainly shaped by the complexity and contradictions of individual actions, memories, behaviours.[12] But the various components of the house-and-garden suburb must first be assembled, starting with the dwelling.

126

## 'For every man his own home'

This section takes its name from the book—which did have families in mind—edited by Melbourne architect Harold Desbrowe-Annear in the early 1920s.[13] As unassailable as it seemed, the planning movement was vigorous in its advocacy of the ideal of the detached house for traditional families. Put simply by John Sulman, 'the single storey cottage is the ideal aimed at'.[14] In 1919 Charles Reade, writing as Ebenezer Howard, emphatically affirmed 'the economic and social utility of the Australian one-family detached house'. Anything less was a risk to public health, a threat to industrial efficiency and productivity, a recipe for immorality, drunkenness, and epidemic diseases, and a catalyst for 'social unrest generally'.[15]

'Space-saving' housing was anathema to early planning advocates. There was little support for, and few experiments with, medium-density housing. Radical options, such as the co-operative housekeeping ideal which might have released women from 'domestic drudgery', were not seriously explored. Flat and tenement life was a poor substitute for the comforts of the home. Even the semi-detached house was frowned upon, contradicting the vernacular Australian tradition.[16]

Home ownership went hand-in-hand with the detached housing ideal, with many quotable statements as to the ideals of patriotism and citizenship that were at stake. Victorian bank executive George Emery returned from an overseas visit in 1925 convinced that good housing was an imperial mission:

> The supply of homes for the people is, I consider, a most important enterprise from a National point of view, because every man who can call the dwelling he occupies with his family his own private property is a citizen that can be relied upon to support the National honour and do whatever duty patriotism may require of him. Love of home is the basis of patriotism, but a man who has no home, and no interest in the rooms he occupies from time to time, is not so sure to develop a love for his country as one who permanently occupies his own dwelling; and the children who are brought up in such a permanent home are likely to be better citizens also.[17]

Cultural preferences for detached cottages were reinforced and shaped by improvement ideology and government policy. For all the progressivism of the built form, the social ideology of the planned garden suburb was deeply conservative.

## The big backyard

The garden setting was integral to the house and to home ownership. Gardens were not just an investment in land, although owning 'the rose in the garden' was as important as escaping the domestic prison of 'rented rooms'. The actual practice of gardening intersected with other strivings for space, autonomy, freedom, and definitions of self. The front yard was both a zone of display and a social contract, a semi-public space of neatness encoding a statement about individual personality in the context of community. Backyards were always more private; they were 'one of the few areas in our lives where we have real power, make decisions, and put them into practice'.[18] The functions of the backyard have changed through time in response to the growth of public infrastructure, changing household structure and needs, cultural change, and local government policing. In the metropolitan setting at least, the outhouse has made way for the paved outdoor entertainment area, the woodheap for the barbecue, and the fowl run for the swimming pool.

The quintessential traditional element in the Australian backyard was the vegetable patch. A badge of economy and resourcefulness, if not self-sufficiency, it was an invaluable supplier of fresh fruit and vegetables during times of depression and war, and even today it connects with notions of environmental sustainability.[19] The big backyard was the domain of F. W. Eggleston's 'self-contained man'.[20] That it was self-contained 'man' also highlights the gendering of suburban space. While the house was female, the yard was the male domain.[21]

128

## The garden suburb

The garden suburb was the improvers' response to, in contemporary parlance, the 'jerry-builder', the 'land-jobber' and the 'pocket-handkerchief' allotment. It was not your average house-and-garden suburb, but an environment of harmoniously grouped houses which self-consciously committed individuals to be parts of a whole. The planning ideas appeared elsewhere in fragmented or partial form—detached houses, setbacks from streets, nature strips, open spaces, attention to street picture—but in the garden suburb these were integrated in an ideal holistic scheme. The garden suburb was seen to embody the best suburban ideals: healthy, family life, social stability, respectability; and the moral and physical sanitation of working-class culture. 'The well-to-do', John Sulman assured his social peers, could still 'easily look after themselves.'[22]

Albert Goldie, a journalist and publicist for Sydney developer Richard Stanton, defined the garden suburb in 1913 as 'a community of interests by which every individual enters into an implied contract to contribute in the planning of his home life to a scheme of beautification'.[23] This balancing of privacy and community was a central tension in the garden suburb. It could be seen as an ideal intermediate between rural isolation, freedom and individuality, on the one hand, and inner-city conformity, sameness and uniformity, on the other. The garden suburb became a transactional space between liberty and cohesion.

The dialogue between these two states was one of the many forces under-cutting the integrity of Australian garden suburbness, compared to British prototypes developed under stricter co-partnership principles or leasehold conditions. Contrasting Australian individualism with more selfless collectivism evident overseas, Sydney architect James Peddle complained that 'one great difficulty with us is, that we are too individualistic . . . we think of my piece of land, of my lot, of my garden . . . we . . . will do anything to make our place beautiful, and we fence it in, and keep it exclusively for our own pleasure'.[24] It is perhaps not surprising that the impact of garden suburb ideology was less evident in Queensland—where the collective consciousness of planning has wrestled most vigorously with the individualism of private property rights during the twentieth century—than in any other Australian state. A female delegate to the second Australian Town Planning Conference in 1918 empha-sised that Queenslanders simply 'do not have that fondness for stereotyped garden suburbs in prescribed areas' like their southern counterparts.[25]

Although responsible for a mere fraction of housing production in the first half of the twentieth century, the garden suburb movement did produce an array of exceptional environments, the best of which now receive the blessing, if not the protection, of heritage authorities. The garden suburb could be a device to sell land, just as the idea of an artistic bungalow was a device to sell property.[26] The archetypal speculative garden suburb was the first: Haberfield in Sydney, 'the place of beautiful homes'. The great variety of types is documented elsewhere: estates sponsored by federal and state governments, voluntary and private projects. The best and most enduring results came where planning was integrated with housing production and service provision.[27]

## The garden suburb house

The sorry reality of the garden suburb movement in Australia was its mani-festation as primarily a better subdivision movement, stressing the orderly geometric laying out of public and private spaces quite distinct from the actual erection of houses. Where the third dimension came into view, the ruling dictum was for the grouping of housing and the overall street picture to be always valued over individual structures.

But what was the ideal garden suburb house? Several ideas were advanced by developers and architects (for example, Plate 8.1). One of the most interesting was by non-architect planning advocate Charles Reade. His plan (Plate 8.2) eliminated passageways, provided sleep-out accommodation, and responded to the Australian climate.[28] Despite a pervasive ideology that under-lay such theoretical schemes, there was a variety of design ideas and no standard style. The ideal house responded differently to regional, local and temporal variations. Over time the common drive was toward modernisation and simplicity, with bungalow forms predominating. The bungalow was artistic, rustic, individual, modern, comfortable; it was adaptable, and had a verandah

129

130

**Plate 8.1** The garden suburb housing ideal. The detached single family cottage was universally regarded as the town planning ideal. The Exhibition in conjunction with the national planning conference held in Brisbane in 1918 featured two 'model homes' erected in garden settings on Machinery Hill at the Brisbane Showground. The cover of the conference proceedings featured an 'ideal' three-bedroom timber bungalow designed by local architect A. E. Brooks. (Volume of Proceedings of the Second Australian Town Planning Conference and Exhibition, Brisbane, 1918)

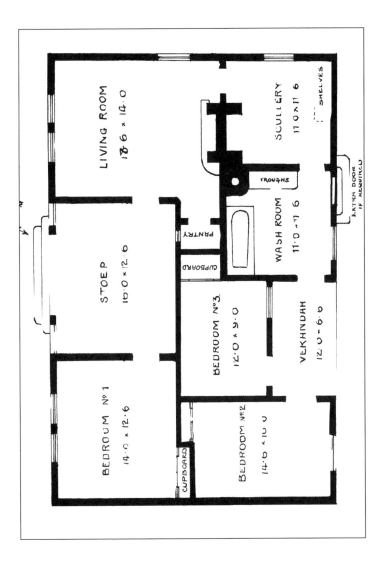

**Plate 8.2** Floor plan of an ideal garden suburb house. Leading town planning advocate Charles Reade prepared his own rather impractical scheme for a 'cheap cottage' designed to adapt the best qualities of cool-climate garden suburb architecture to the Australian setting. Reade uses the Dutch term 'stoep' to designate the front verandah. (*The Salon*, June 1915)

for enjoying outdoors. Diversity of facades in group housing could also mask considerable uniformity in internal floor plans.[29]

Model cottages were constructed at several speculative garden suburbs—an early version of the project house. At the A.A. Company suburb in Newcastle, New South Wales, houses designed by local architect F. G. Castleden were erected 'both by way of opening and developing the land and as a lead to buyers as to the type or grade of building that is expected'.[30] Early focal points for the Endowment Lands project in Perth were two model cottages, one in brick and another in timber, designed to stimulate development.[31]

Some of the more distinctive homes were testimony to the import of British design ideas. At Lutana in Tasmania, where architect Walter Butler took his inspiration from the arts and crafts movement, the Australian Heritage Commission duly describes 'a uniquely English, picturesque village style'.[32] The 180-odd houses erected at Garden City in Melbourne were a minuscule number of the nearly eight thousand houses built throughout Victoria in the 1920s by the State Savings Bank under the provisions of the *Housing and Reclamation Act 1920*.[33] Breaking Sulman's rejection of the style as 'unsuited to the Australian climate', the double-fronted, two-storey 'cindcrete' houses designed by G. Burridge Leith were directly inspired by British housing schemes at Letchworth and Welwyn Garden City and London County Council's Becontree Estate.[34] Providing few clues to the economy-minded mass public housing program that came after World War II, in 1936 adjacent to the original Garden City a small group of quality model homes were designed in 'Tudor-bethan' style by Percy Everett for the Public Works Department. They provided an even more literal connection with British vernacular architecture.[35]

## The garden suburb garden

The garden suburb was seen as democratising access to a private garden. The garden provided 'direct contact with nature', opportunities for healthy outdoor activity, and even a return to agrarian ideals. In one sense it was the yeoman idyll in a suburban setting, and the desire for a well-kept garden setting was said to be 'in the soul of every individual'.[36] As noted, the front garden generally was a buffer between the private home and the public street.[37] In the planned spaciousness of the garden suburb setting, this juggling of neighbourliness and privacy took on added importance.

There was early enthusiasm for the American idea of gardens without front fences, creating the park-like street. Landscape gardener Harry Davey returned from California impressed by the greensward quality of fenceless residential streets: 'to walk along one of these suburban streets is like going through a Botanical Gardens with the addition of homes set amongst the green'.[38] There was also a security logic attached to this approach: the exposure also inhibited the anti-social behaviour of burglars and peeping toms. Daceyville in Sydney was the first garden suburb to dispose of front fences, an

133

**Plate 8.3** A classic garden suburb garden. Alfred Knight's Antirrhina featured in the front garden of his cottage in Lutana, a model factory village developed by the Electrolytic Zinc Company of Australasia outside Hobart. By 1922, Lutana was 'a blaze of flowers'. (*The Electrode*, December 1922, State Library of Tasmania, Hobart)

experiment criticised in state parliament as promoting a 'sort of socialistic equality among the tenants'.[39] Little enthusiasm was shown thereafter; space in the garden suburb had to be demarcated as elsewhere.

The maintenance of front gardens was vital in order to attain the coherence of the garden suburb street picture, which secured a demonstrable sense of community. This was pursued by moral imperative, if not by government policy. At Daceyville, leases specified not only that premises should be kept in 'good and substantial repair' but also that 'the garden ground attached to the premises' should be kept 'in good order'. Garden competitions with cash prizes were judged by a staff member of the Botanic Gardens. Lawn mowers were loaned out, a cheap purchase scheme was instituted, working bees were formed to keep up appearances, and a branch of the Horticultural Society of New

South Wales was established.[40] In 1917 the State Housing Board assumed liability for excess water rates to maintain 'the garden character' of the suburb.

Interventionist public landlords similarly regulated private gardens in other states. In the 1920s, the Federal Capital Commission in Canberra set in train a long-standing policy of government subsidy of garden needs and regular maintenance of front hedges. In Yallourn, every March, the head gardener of the Victorian State Electricity Commission would score garden quality out of 100.[41] In Garden City in Melbourne, determined to make the estate 'worthy of its name', the State Savings Bank also sanctioned garden competitions through the local progress association. But the onus was largely on residents to visibly demonstrate their own individual commitment to community through the public streetscape. It did not take much to undermine the desired effect. Gardening was central to early Lutana life (Plate 8.3), and taken seriously enough for complaints to surface in *The Electrode*, the company journal, about uncooperative tenants 'spoiling the general effect'. But generally the mainten- ance of the character of the garden suburb was made possible as self-interest aligned with public-spiritedness and tapped into deeper social pressures. 'All the best instincts in human nature compel obedience', argued Albert Goldie in reference to the well-kept and well-laid-out gardens at Haberfield: the resident 'who would allow his ground to run to weeds and waste would be regarded as a pariah, a social outcast, so strong is local feeling on this matter'.[42]

Occasionally the reformers' gaze would descend upon the state of backyards. The early annual reports of the New South Wales Housing Board contrasted photographs of model versus 'ill-kept' backyards at Daceyville. Ever the busybody, Sydney planning advocate Florence Taylor invoked environ- mentalist logic in endorsing the remodelling of untidy backyards:

> With a little labour and care, a back yard can be transformed, in one short year, into a veritable fairyland of brightness, where children may play and learn to love the flowers, the foliage and the bright sunshine. There is nothing more indicative of bad living than a back yard littered with bottles, pots, tins and other rubbish. It reflects also upon the neighbours as being careless and uninterested in the health and welfare of the community. The effects of untidy back yards must have a very bad effect upon the minds of the young. In times of reverse and through days of bitter trouble, the garden always offers solace and pleasure. It also brings cheer and adds brightness to the declining days of the aged.[43]

But as in wider civil society, the back garden was seen primarily as a zone for exclusive use and access. The side of the house was a utilitarian space. The growth in demand for garage space for a motor vehicle during the inter-war years was often accommodated there. Daceyville, the original state housing suburb, was planned before World War I without the motor vehicle in mind. By the 1920s, the garden suburbs of Canberra were distinguished by garages, usually set back on the side of the allotment so as not to disturb the rhythm of the front house elevations.[44] Many a garage doubled as, or was extended for, a workshop for Dad, underlining the maleness of the yard domain.

134

## Living in a garden suburb

Having sketched the particular elements and distinctiveness of the garden suburb package, we now finally turn to the garden suburb as a place to live. The classic dilemma of suburban history is how communities lose identity and merge into the overall metropolitan fabric.[45] So too the fate of the garden suburb, whose historical evolution soon steers away from the special planning conditions which may have created it in the first place. The trajectories, interrelationships and real meanings of individual lives inevitably also lose meaningful contact with the planned setting.

The planners' concept of the orderly environment is usually not central to the behaviour, emotions, and memories of residents. The realities of lived space diverge from the geometries of planned space. Typically, as with more prosaic suburbs, there was a strong sense of community spirit in the early years, often when communities were relatively isolated. This gradually dissipated, with housing and infrastructural development making the suburb whole, albeit often over many years. But things can be cyclical. Since the 1980s heritage consciousness has been a strong factor in redefining community identity for some places.

One of the few detailed sociological studies of garden suburb life is by Fitzjames Henry in Colonel Light Gardens in Adelaide.[46] It documents in considerable detail aspects of early community organisation and perceptions. Early disharmony is recorded when the state government redesigned and increased the housing density of the southern half to accommodate the 1000 Homes Scheme. Familiar-sounding fears were entertained that mass house-building would depreciate land values in the locality. Some of the early occupants of the state scheme were seen as 'no-hopers', identified by a lack of interest in their homes and gardens. Within a few short years, however, it was difficult to distinguish the divide between private and state housing. The residents of Colonel Light Gardens evaluated their suburb not in terms of the famous 1918 bird's-eye view by D. W. Crawford, but in terms of their immediate neighbourhood.[47] One major finding by Henry was residents' positive valuation of the amenity and flexibility of the 'detached house suburb' in offering privacy, security and adaptability to change. Residents generally liked the open layout, but difficulties of maintenance early emerged for older residents. 'It's hard for me to get the garden in good order', said one resident; 'nowadays it takes me two days to cut the lawn.'[48] Ironically, the spacious street reservations with generous grass verges may have also actually inhibited neighbourly interaction; while chats over the side-fence were common, 'little contact was made with people living on the opposite side of the street'.[49]

Elsewhere we are left with anecdotal experiences of garden suburb life, snippets not so different from conventional house-and-garden settings. In his pioneering study of Daceyville life, historian Ian Hoskins engaged in detailed discussions with long-term residents to record intimate details of everyday life. The garden suburbness of the place dissolves in stories of home, play and work. We get glimpses of a darker side of life, tales of drunkenness, neglected

135

children and battered wives. Seldom was life conducted with explicit reference to planners' ideals. Such personal narratives are 'inherently subversive in that they explode the monolithic constructions of spatial meaning presented by . . . the planners'.[50] Further south on Sydney's Anzac Parade at the Matraville Soldiers Garden Village, Paul Ashton has trawled the surviving historical record to recall 'the harsh realities of daily existence' belied by the two-dimensional organisation of John Sulman's 1917 site plan.[51]

In recent years a vigorous local history industry has produced a rich store of original material recording life growing up in the archetypal planned twentieth-century city of Canberra. Numerous 'insurgent historiographies', including those of construction camps and transitory suburbs,[52] now comple-ment the official history of the planners. The planning and production of Canberra's early garden suburbs to exceptional physical standards exemplifies bureaucratic embrace of garden city principles adapted to Australian condi-tions.[53] Their human side of early occupation from the 1920s is captured in memories recorded by the Canberra Stories Group.[54] The stories tell mainly of kitchen smells, wood stoves, household chores, cubby houses, fruit trees, and chooks behind the garage. Houses become homes and places of 'joys and disappointments'. At the same time, there are relatively few stories which specifically recall the planners' suburbs, beyond the regular hedge trimming by government gardeners and the pushing of prams across paddocks and dodging open drains to distant planned shopping centres. These comments flesh out Hugh Stretton's observation of the 'inconvenience' of the pioneers' life amidst the 'mannered geometry' of Canberra's garden suburbs.[55]

Life in some model developments was clearly not all that it was cracked up to be. Many houses in the 'group' state housing schemes developed in Sydney and New South Wales regional centres in the early 1920s appeared to have more than their fair share of structural defects. 'Almost without exception [they] provided sources of considerable trouble and of incipient unrest.'[56] The Littleton munitions village developed near the Lithgow Small Arms Factory by the Commonwealth government during World War I ran into similar problems. Planned by John Sulman, this estate was distant from shops; there were delays in getting electric lighting and gas supplies; and, according to a Sydney journalist, the roads in wet weather looked like 'the front line in Flanders'.[57] Similarly, Yallourn may have been what poet Ted Hopkins called 'an intelligent arrangement of form in space', but there are also enduring memories of inces-sant noise from the power turbines, the grinding of the open-cut dredgers, and a 'constant rain of coal dust' from the briquette factory.[58]

Residents could sometimes resist the planners' ideal of the garden suburb. Their ambitions and dreams were often about being like everyone else; per-haps this reflected a peculiarly Australian way of thinking. Serious divergences between the professional consciousness and everyday life could emerge. In the mid-1950s when the first generation of Victorian public housing estates were criticised by architects for their 'lack of any aesthetic cohesion' because of the variety of house types, a Royal Commission revealed that 'this is exactly what

137

**Plate 8.4** Inside a garden suburb home. A rare contemporary photograph of the interior of a semi-detached cottage in Daceyville, Sydney. Florence Taylor extracted the 'very spirit of the room' as suggesting 'a clean wife, nicely cooked and dainty meals, children clambering over the knees of the parents, perhaps hospitality when a few friends are entertained with a little music, kind thoughts for the children's future'. Her imagination was instilled with mainstream improver ideology: 'everything uplifting to the race could emanate from such a home as this.' (*Building*, January 1913)

the tenants want' because this diversity was 'the usual pattern of private housing development'.[59] The natural evolution of the state-sponsored garden suburb conceived in the 1910s was toward the large public housing estate which introduced more standardised and uniform approaches in the era following World War II. As the scale of estates increased, so did aesthetic uniformity and social stigma. Public housing policy has now retreated toward a different policy: a mix of housing scattered across suburbs and preferably indistinguishable from private housing. Transforming car-taming cul-de-sac layouts based on the 'Radburn' principle into more mainstream house-and-garden streetscapes is the latest manifestation of the desire to return to 'basic Australian values of an appropriate level of privacy, security, a front door facing the street, a vibrant street environment, and safety in public spaces'.[60]

## Conclusion

Australian cities are predominantly 'freehold' cities. The co-partnership and leasehold estates which helped set the stage for the emergence of the modern garden suburb in Britain were absent. An ingrained Australian ideology of individual property rights worked against the logic of planned grouped housing.[61] The planned garden suburb did become a reality in the Federation era. Despite all its specialness in professional and planning theory terms, however, when realised it was no more or less than a physical framework for everyday life.

Although we learn more and more about garden suburb architecture and site planning, we know less of garden suburbs as lived environments. Despite their distinctive status in planning history terms, ultimately they were engulfed by broader cultural aspirations and Australian ways-of-doing-things, with early community aspirations ultimately giving way to natural individualism. What was distinctive on paper, even in built form, was always less exceptional in human terms. This is hardly a profound observation, but it is a valuable and humbling perspective. Built forms 'can only provide possibilities and not imperatives for people to act'.[62]

There were diverse house types in garden suburbs, but even more diverse lives were lived therein. Garden suburbs as lived spaces were 'somewhere acted upon by people who invest the space of home and locality with meaning through communal and self-identification'.[63] The house interiors were always private, and photographs on the public record are few (Plate 8.4). Although we might consider the garden suburb as home, there are still deeper meanings and experiences which the observer can never access: things more personal and subjective 'which can be only glimpsed and guessed'.[64]

138

**Notes**

1  L. Sandercock, *Making the Invisible Visible: A Multicultural Planning History* (Los Angeles, 1998).
2  R. Freestone and A. Hutchings, 'Planning History in Australia: The State of the Art', *Planning Perspectives*, vol. 8, 1993, pp. 72–91; L. Sandercock, *Property, Politics and Urban Planning: A History of Australian City Planning, 1890–1990* (New Brunswick, 1980).

3 *Good Times, Hard Times: The Past and the Future in Elizabeth* (Melbourne, 1995). A related examination of ordinary lives in a planned postwar housing estate, drawing on qualitative methods, is L. Bryson and I. Winter, *Social Change, Suburban Lives: An Australian New Town, 1960s to 1990s* (Sydney, 1999).

4 S. Thompson, 'Home: A Window on the Human Face of Planning', in R. Freestone (ed.), *Spirited Cities: Urban Planning, Traffic and Environmental Management in the Nineties* (Sydney, 1993), pp. 150–62.

5 *Tales of the City: A Study of Narrative and Urban Life* (Cambridge, 1998).

6 F. Adams, 'Re-reading the Space(s) of the City, Sydney 1948: Ruth Park's *The Harp in the South* and the Cumberland County Council Plan', unpublished paper, Faculty of Architecture, Building and Planning, University of Melbourne, 1997; L. Johnson, 'Feral Suburbia: Western Sydney and the "Problem of Urban Sprawl"', in H. Grace et al. (eds), *Home/world: Space, Community and Marginality in Sydney's West* (Sydney, 1997), pp. 31–65.

7 'A Stake in the Country: Women's Experiences of Suburban Development', in R. Silversone (ed.), *Visions of Suburbia* (London, 1997), p. 89.

8 Levittown: Documents of an Ideal American Suburb (Peter Bacon Hales) <http://www.uic.edu/~pbhales/Levittown.html>. The website URL addresses cited here and in subsequent notes were all current in May 1999.

9 Australia Street: Great Australian Dreams (The Australia Street Archive) <http://www.australiast.uts.edu.au/>.

10 Welcome to Hampstead Garden Suburb (London) <http://www.hgs.org.uk/index.html>; Colonel Light Gardens (Adelaide; Colonel Light Gardens Historical Society Inc) <http://www.cobweb.com.au/~pknight/ clghs/index.htm>; and Haberfield (Sydney; The Haberfield Association) <http://linus.socs.uts.edu.au/~colville/habas/>.

11 R. Freestone, *Model Communities: The Garden City Movement in Australia* (Melbourne, 1989).

12 M. de Certeau, *The Practice of Everyday Life* (Los Angeles, 1984).

13 *For Every Man His House* (Melbourne, 1922).

14 *An Introduction to the Study of Town Planning in Australia* (Sydney, 1921), p. 190.

15 E. Howard the Younger (C. Reade), 'Towns and Industry', *Science and Industry*, vol. 1, 1919, p. 111.

16 R. J. Lawrence, 'The Organization of Domestic Space', PhD thesis, University of Cambridge, 1977, p. 238.

17 G. Emery, 'General Manager's Report to the Commissioners on his Visit to Great Britain to Enquire into Housing', December 1925, p. 5, State Savings Bank of Victoria Archives.

18 G. Seddon, 'The Australian Backyard', in his *Landprints: Reflections on Place and Landscape* (Cambridge, 1997), p. 161.

19 P. N. Troy, *The Perils of Urban Consolidation* (Sydney, 1996).

20 F. W. Eggleston, *State Socialism in Victoria* (Melbourne, 1932), p. 331; see also Chapter 9 in this book.

21 Seddon, 'The Australian Backyard', p. 155.

139

22  *An Introduction to the Study of Town Planning*, p. 189.
23  'The Garden Suburb Idea', *The Lone Hand*, vol. 13, 1913, p. 163.
24  'Some Lessons We Can Learn from our American Neighbours', *Building*, January 1917, p. 98.
25  E. Young, 'Written Criticisms', *Volume of Proceedings of the Second Australian Town Planning and Housing Conference and Exhibition* (Brisbane, 1918), p. 138.
26  A. D. King, *The Bungalow: The Production of a Global Culture* (London, 1984).
27  Freestone, *Model Communities*, ch. 8.
28  C. Reade, 'Cheap Cottage for Australia', Part 2, *The Salon*, vol. 4, 1915, p. 163.
29  C. Garnaut, 'Model and Maker: Colonel Light Gardens and Charles Reade', PhD thesis, University of South Australia, 1997, p. 188.
30  Quoted in the 1913 *Annual Report* of the Australian Agricultural Company, AA Company Papers, 78/1/87, Noel Butlin Archives Centre, Australian National University.
31  H. J. Selwood, *Residential Development Processes in Perth: Two Case Studies*, Geowest 14 (Department of Geography, University of Western Australia, 1979).
32  Lutana Village, Lutana, Tasmania, in Australian Heritage Commission, Register of the National Estate Database <http://www.environment.gov.au/heritage/>.
33  D. Routt, 'Classic Homes for the People: The State Savings Bank Housing Scheme of the 1920s', *Transition*, Summer 1987, pp. 45–51.
34  S. Tuxen, 'Town Planning and the Working Man', *Australian Home Beautiful*, September 1927, pp. 61–2; cf. Sulman, *An Introduction to the Study of Town Planning*, p. 190.
35  M. Nankervis, 'A Museum of State Housing: Port and South Melbourne', *Heritage Australia*, Autumn 1991, pp. 17–20.
36  'The Housing Problem', *Building*, January 1920, p. 81.
37  A. Ravetz with R. Turkington, *The Place of Home: English Domestic Environments, 1914–2000* (London, 1995).
38  'America: Impressions in General', *Home and Garden Beautiful*, November 1915, p. 198.
39  I. Hoskins, I., 'Constructing Time and Space in the Garden Suburb', in S. Ferber, C. Healy and C. McAuliffe (eds), *Beasts of Suburbia: Reinterpreting Cultures in Australian Suburbs* (Melbourne, 1994), pp. 1–17.
40  A. W. Price, 'Dacey Garden Suburb', BArch thesis, University of New South Wales, 1969.
41  P. Read, *Return to Nothing: The Meaning of Lost Places* (Cambridge, 1996), p. 79.
42  'The Garden Suburb Idea', p. 164.
43  F. M. Taylor, 'Home Surroundings and Influences', *Building*, November 1915, p. 98.
44  R. Freestone, 'Planning Canberra in the 1920s', in P. Freeman (ed.), *The Early Canberra House: Living in Canberra, 1911–1935* (Canberra, 1996), pp. 11–26.
45  A. M. S. Roberts, 'The Study of Suburban History', *Teaching History*, vol. 17, no. 3 (1983), p. 31.
46  F. S. Henry, 'Colonel Light Gardens: A Study of the Garden Suburb in Adelaide, South Australia', MA thesis, University of Sydney, 1955.

47  C. Garnaut, *Colonel Light Gardens: A Model Garden Suburb* (Sydney, 1999), p. 33.
48  Henry, 'Colonel Light Gardens', pp. 185, 217.
49  B. Y. Harper, 'Colonel Light Gardens: Seventy Years of a Garden Suburb',
    *Australian Planner*, vol. 28, 1991, p. 67.
50  Hoskins, 'Constructing Time and Space in the Garden Suburb', p. 16.
51  P. Ashton, 'Reactions to and Paradoxes of Modernism: The Origins and Spread of
    Suburbia in 1920s Sydney', PhD thesis, Macquarie University, 1999, p. 240.
52  A. Gugler, *Westlake: One of the Vanished Suburbs of Canberra*, Canberra from the
    Ground Up, Series Two (Canberra, 1997).
53  Freestone, 'Planning Canberra in the 1920s'.
54  Canberra Stories Group, *My First Home in Canberra: Canberra Residents' Memories of
    Their First Homes, 1920–1990* (Murrumbateman, 1994).
55  *Ideas for Australian Cities* (Melbourne, 1970), p. 30.
56  Housing Board of New South Wales Annual Report, *New South Wales Parliamentary
    Papers*, 1922, p. 2.
57  *The Sun* (Sydney), 20 July 1921.
58  Read, *Return to Nothing*, p. 77.
59  'Report of the Royal Commission to inquire into the Operation of the Housing
    Acts of Victoria and the Administration of the Housing Commission', *Victorian
    Parliamentary Papers*, No. 45, 1956, p. 64.
60  R. Woodward, 'Paradise Lost', *Australian Planner*, vol. 34, 1997, p. 27.
61  L. Wilkinson, 'Domestic Architecture', in 'Domestic Architecture in Australia',
    *Art and Australia*, Sydney, 1919.
62  Lawrence, 'Organization of Domestic Space', p. 2.
63  Hoskins, 'Constructing Time and Space in the Garden Suburb', p. 10.
64  Ravetz with Turkington, *The Place of Home*, p. 224.

# The Household Production of Subsistence Goods

THE URBAN PEASANT THESIS REASSESSED

*Patrick Mullins and Chris Kynaston*

142     This chapter aims to reassess, and then extend, an argument formulated in the late 1970s:[1] that Australian urban households had, until the middle of this century, operated a highly developed and unique domestic economy. This economy produced a great number of goods (as well as services) for household consumption and for exchange, and the goods ranged from foodstuffs grown, hunted, gathered, and processed, to those manufactured in the household in the form of clothes, furniture, and even owner-built housing. In all of this, the dwelling and the yard were the capital for producing this income.

The term 'urban peasantry' was introduced as a concept to identify and define this elaborate subsistence-based domestic economy. This economy had evolved in the nineteenth century, but began to disappear in the late 1940s as the postwar economic boom (1945–72) took effect. The rise of mass consumer capitalism during the boom enabled households to earn a relatively high cash income from wages, thus allowing them to buy many goods formerly produced within the household. Conversely, since consumer capitalism mass-produced goods relatively cheaply, it became more expensive to produce them within the household, thus pushing urban households into buying goods they had once produced. A marked change in the urban household economy had thus occurred. In this regard, it now seems pertinent to ask whether a similar dramatic change has occurred during the period since 1972: whether the ongoing economic, political, and social crises of the last twenty-five years—with their rolling recessions and high unemployment—have ushered in a new (post-industrial) urban household economy.

As originally formulated, the urban peasant thesis was based upon few empirical data and, although it seemed to have a conceptual and theoretical logic, the absence of detailed data has left doubts about whether it is true in practice. Furthermore, no interest has been shown in testing the argument empirically since it was first published. Now, in reassessing the argument, this chapter draws together a wide range of data from a number of sources.

The chapter is divided into five parts. The first defines the meaning of the household, and specifically the household economy. Then we summarise the urban peasant thesis, and we test it empirically. The fourth part considers the empirical relevance of the thesis for contemporary urban Australia. Finally, we explore an argument about the urban household economy in the late twentieth and early twenty-first centuries. This argument claims that now, more than at any other time in history, the work undertaken by household members is directed towards accessing a cash income from whatever sources are available. Contemporary life is now defined by the consumption of goods produced in the market—from designer-label clothes to cars, and from Big Macs to Pepsi—and only cash can provide legal access to these desired goods.

More broadly, this chapter seeks to show how changes in a society's formal (capitalist) economy texture the changes in the household (domestic) economy. In particular, changes in the long waves of economic development not only transform the formal economy, but influence household work strategies as well, and thus the household economy.

143

## Defining households

The chapter's general goal is to emphasise the importance of understanding households in any attempt at comprehending housing and urban development, both now and in the past. The household has been ignored as a social actor in urban development, especially in the housing question. Certainly, it has long been recognised as an important demographic entity, but its role as a social actor has largely been neglected. There is need, then, to consider households in the same way as, for example, social classes: that is, as a social actor contributing to change.

During the 1980s and 1990s attempts have been made to identify the household's place within cities and societies, and specifically to show its role in shaping the contemporary world. This has taken two major, but separate, conceptual and theoretical paths. One comes from North America, having been constructed by I. Wallerstein and his colleagues who have examined the role played by households in the capitalist world economy.[2] The other approach was formulated in Britain by R. Pahl and his colleagues from analyses of work strategies used by British households in securing income during the period of radical socio-economic changes of the 1970s and 1980s.[3]

The defining feature of households, according to Wallerstein and Smith, is the way members work to obtain income from a range of different sources, and then pool this income for purposes of household consumption—for basic individual and social survival.[4] Income is both cash and in kind. Thus, to understand households and the role they play in urban development we must understand how they obtain income, how they allocate labour to obtain income (from whatever source), and how the income produced is then distributed among household members in the form of consumption.[5] Indeed, whether households can obtain sufficient income to survive determines the nature of household formation. Nuclear families, for example, are widespread only when conditions enable enough income to be accessed to maintain a husband, a wife, and children. In this regard, Australian households were 'born modern'[6] because stable nuclear families were established early as a result of people's relatively easy access both to a good cash income from the formal economy, and to a good subsistence income from the household economy. In difficult times, like the 1980s and 1990s, nuclear family households have declined as a proportion of total households, at least partly because many men and women have had difficulties earning sufficient income to maintain this type of household.[7]

When we think of income, we usually consider only cash obtained from the formal economy. Yet there are other cash incomes, including government transfers, gifts, inheritances, rent, and cash from the informal economy. Equally importantly, there is in-kind income; the most easily recognised is the goods and services, such as meals and cleaning, produced daily within the home. Less widely noticed is the home production of a wide range of goods, which occurred in the past. These goods were created by household labour for household consumption and for informal exchange. They included foodstuffs, such as vegetables, fruit, and poultry; and food processing—bottling and canning, for example—of food produced and bought. Food was also obtained from hunting, fishing, and gathering and firewood was collected. Other goods were manufactured, such as clothes, and the household may even have built the dwelling.

What we do not know empirically are the proportions of income that households derived from these different sources, and how these proportions changed over time. With the rise of capitalism, a wage income predominated. In-kind income remained important, but it is arguably of far less importance today, at the turn of the new century, than in living memory. Still, it remains important. If we generalise from G. Snooks's analysis about the total Australian economy,[8] household production—even today—comprises one-third of the value of total production. Changing proportions of household income from different sources can be observed; these are undoubtedly tied to long waves of economic development (Kondratieff cycles), because the nature and pro- ductivity of the capitalist economy determine the types of income that households access and the labour used. As capitalist economies rise and fall over, say, fifty-year cycles, so also do households' strategies for obtaining income. While a cash income was critical for household survival before 1945, in-kind income was also significant over this period. The 1945–72 economic boom became, arguably, the first time in history when full employment and a good cash income relieved households of the need to access, as widely as in the past, income from other sources, particularly from within the household itself. In the 1970s to 1990s, however, cash is more important than ever although, for many, it is far more difficult to obtain through employment compared with the postwar economic boom. Government transfers have now become crucial as a 'substitute' for a wage income for many households.[9]

## The urban peasant thesis

Ideas about urban peasants evolved from research undertaken in Brisbane in the early 1970s in an old, inner-city, working-class area threatened by freeway construction.[10] This area housed a large middle-aged and elderly population who had lived there for many years, and it was their accounts of life in the area before the 1940s that provoked the ideas. Households seemed to have been involved in a highly developed domestic economy, producing a wide range of goods and services.

The urban peasant thesis had four strands. The first was the 'capital' involved.

> The ownership of single-family housing epitomises the economic base of the urban peasantry [while] the major productive component of this residential life was the domestic labour that went with it: a domestic economy . . . appeared in the form of extensive 'do-it-yourself' skills that were used productively as non-capitalist labour. [It] . . . was clearly seen in the 'tilling of the smallholding' for vegetable and fruit production, and in the keeping of fowls for eggs and meat. A workshop/toolshed existed for repairing the house and for building and repairing household items [e.g. furniture] and in making leisure goods. Within the house there was a 'sewing room' for making clothes and in fact the house itself might even have been built by the householder and rooms added as the household grew. Moreover, many households supplied their own water from storage tanks, which had accumulated rainwater from the roof, and household waste was disposed either in a compost, for the garden, or in the outhouse located at the end of the yard [or more recently in septic tanks].[11]

145

Second, the labour was intensive, in that considerable amounts of time were spent on different activities; extensive, in that the activities covered the production of a great range of goods and services; and highly skilled, in that considerable ability was demanded. Importantly, it was largely female labour.

> What was striking about the domestic labour of the urban peasantry . . . was the high level of skill and the intensity and extensiveness demanded of this labour . . . Although men provided some of the domestic labour [e.g. repairing and modifying the house and yard, and preparing and tending the vegetable garden] . . . women were largely responsible for the day-to-day operation of the economy: 'harvesting the crops'; looking after the poultry [e.g. feeding, collecting eggs, killing and dressing poultry for the table]; processing some of the food produced, specifically bottling fruit and vegetables produced [and

bought] for the winter months; making and repairing clothes for husbands, children and themselves . . .; exchanging goods and services with neighbours, etc. Women were also noted for their cooking skills, although this was not so much in the provision of meals (which were 'simple and wholesome'), but in the production of confectionery, ranging from scones, biscuits, sponges, cakes, etc., to such noted Australian and New Zealand delicacies as lamingtons and pavlova.

Women, then, played a distinctive economic role under the urban peasantry . . . Australian women . . . came to be totally encapsulated in domestic labour [before the 1940s], with very few being employed as wage labour.[12]

Third, this domestic economy became a key component of the form of 'urban community' of that time.

Life in the urban peasant community came to be centred on the house and yard. The nuclear family spent its time working this unique (non-capitalist) domestic economy. In this way the urban peasant community came to be characterised by privatisation and individualism and . . . was characterised by a loose-knit social structure, comprising a system of sparse social ties of kinship, friendship and neighbour relations.[13]

Finally, this household economy began to disappear with the rise of consumer capitalism after 1945. Goods were now more easily and cheaply bought from the market.

Suburbanisation . . . spelled the demise of Australia's urban peasantry, for the vegetable garden, the fowl run, the fruit trees and the highly developed domestic economy were replaced by mass consumption, where food could now be bought more easily and cheaply at supermarkets and the availability of other consumption items also meant that goods once made, cultivated and consumed in the small holding are now bought. Moreover, an increase in personal income ensured this continued rise in consumption, enabling the hiring of artisans for repairing and maintaining the house. 'Do-it-yourself' skills wane and tend to live more in folklore than in reality.[14]

This chapter addresses only the first and fourth issues. This is not to negate the importance of the other two, but the aim here is to assess the nature and level of the production identified and defined by the concept 'urban peasantry'. In this regard, it is important to emphasise that the chapter focuses on goods only and not services, and so it does not consider housework in general. Moreover, and in regard to the goods produced, the chapter will not consider meals, arguably the most important of the goods produced within households.

## Testing the urban peasant thesis

In order to test the argument summarised above, it is necessary to have longitudinal data of a quantitative kind. These would allow trends to be traced over time and thus enable us to see whether there was a significant level of household production before 1950 and a decline after that time. Unfortunately, few quantitative data are available, so it has been necessary to draw evidence from a range of different sources. Unlike the formal (capitalist) economy, where there is an enormous amount of quantitative data from as far back as the nineteenth century, there is little historical evidence of a detailed quantitative kind on the nature, volume, and value of goods produced by households for household consumption and exchange. Snooks certainly provides information on the total value of goods and services produced, but he does not identify the nature and types of goods.[15]

We do not know the proportion of households over the years that have produced food, processed food, manufactured domestic goods, and hunted, fished, and gathered food and fuel. Nor do we know the proportion of total household income that has come from these sources. There is, nevertheless, a great deal of indirect data—both qualitative and quantitative—that point to something resembling an 'urban peasantry' in Australia.

QUALITATIVE EVIDENCE

It is often only diaries, autobiographies, biographical sketches and, more recently, oral histories that show the rich detail of 'urban peasant' production. However, important detail is lost because its 'everydayness' makes it unremarkable and it thus goes unrecorded. It is also lost because it falls outside prevailing academic paradigms and, in consequence, suffers from neglect. Academics have tended to interpret the world of work only through the set categories of 'waged work' and house work. Within the latter, work has been almost exclusively associated with the production of services and with consumption, rather than with the production of goods.

Even Janet McCalman, who provides an evocative account of everyday life and politics in the working-class suburb of Richmond in the early twentieth century, fails to acknowledge the importance of domestic production.[16] Her working-class informants made ample reference to domestic production in the taped interviews upon which her book is partly based (and which are, in part, included in the audiotape version of the book), but these references were edited out of the final text. And McCalman is not alone in overlooking the significance of domestic production.

Despite its general neglect, sufficient material exists to suggest that domestic production was an extremely important part of the working lives of many Australian households until the middle of this century. J. French recounts how she learnt 'the old Australian ideal of self-sufficiency' from her elderly next-door neighbour Jean, who represented a 'remnant' of the urban peasantry, for she had been brought up earlier this century.[17] Jean's meals provide valuable insight into just how extensive domestic production was in some homes:

> I remember my first dinner at Jean's. A roast chook—an Indian game, small and sweet—with the chicken taste I'd forgotten from my childhood . . . Potatoes, carrots, sweet potatoes, two sorts of beans and a small golden beetroot, all from the garden. Raspberries and cream for dessert—and through the window you could see the cow that gave the cream, chomping up the hill.
>
> It was sponge cake for supper, made with duck eggs, with home-grown passionfruit on top, and home-made raspberry jam and more of Sally's cream. Of the whole meal, only a little flour and sugar were not home-grown.
>
> Lunch was salad from the garden, and home-made cottage cheese. Breakfast was a soft-boiled egg and toast. Jean shopped only once a month. Apart from the cow (and in small areas you can substitute a goat) everything was grown on a plot as small as a normal suburban garden, and tended by a woman in her seventies.

Recollections such as this provide glimpses into a bygone era of extensive self-sufficiency. Of course, not all, or even most, homes would have been as self-sufficient, but there are enough passing references to urban domestic production for us to know that a degree of self-sufficiency was exceedingly common up until the middle of this century. References to the productive use of gardens are particularly widespread.

P. Cuffley, for instance, writing of urban Australian homes in the 1920s and 1930s, notes that, while front gardens were generally showpieces, 'the often extensive backyards were more likely to be utilitarian, with vegetable plots, poultry runs, workshops, wood sheds, fruit trees and the essential clothes lines'.[18] G. Karskens reaffirms this when she writes, in relation to homes in Sydney in the 1920s, that 'the backyard was . . . a vital source of food. Most people had large vegetable gardens and ran chooks.'[19] Betty Moffit writes in a similar vein about Sydney life in the 1930s, referring to the 'chooks and chokoes culture' of the suburb in which she lived.[20]

Queensland backyards and gardens were also regarded as being of a predominantly 'utilitarian' nature.[21] This is clearly and eloquently conveyed by David Malouf in his autobiographical novel *Johnno*, when he recalls his childhood home in inner Brisbane in the 1930s and 1940s:

> My memories were all of our old house in South Brisbane, with its wide latticed verandahs, its damp mysterious storerooms where sacks of potatoes and salt had been kept in the ever-dark, its washtubs and copper boiler under the porch, its vast garden that ran right through to the street behind, a wilderness that my grandfather, before he died, had transformed into a suburban farmlet, with rows

of spinach, tomatoes, lettuce, egg-plants, a shed where onions and garlic hung from the rafters, and a wired coop full of chooks.[22]

Moira Lambert's recollections of growing up in Melbourne in the 1920s are also punctuated with fond remembrances of the 'chooks' and ducks kept by the family, and of the vegetables and fruits grown in their gardens. She also recalls 'a pantry filled with homemade jams and preserved fruit'.[23] Not surprisingly, domestic manufacture of this nature was very common as it allowed surplus produce from the garden to be kept for later use. Indeed, just as in rural areas, there were definite seasons in the cities 'for making jam, sauce and pickles, for bottling fruit and vegetables, and for "putting down" eggs and fruit cakes'.[24]

Clearly, gardens were an important resource. They not only yielded produce for immediate consumption, but they also provided the base materials for the production of a number of processed foods. In addition, they provided householders with space for keeping animals; animals being another important source of food. Poultry keeping was particularly popular, for it offered householders a regular supply of protein-rich eggs and, on occasions, white meat as well. Some households also kept larger animals. The family of Violet Douglas, for instance, kept a cow, pigs, and goats, as well as poultry, in their Wollongong yard in the early 1900s.[25] Similarly, the daughter of an 'odd-jobber' in Albany recalls how her family 'used to keep lots of animals', including pigs and poultry. Indeed, as a young woman, she had once saved up her money to get her father 'a rather nice cow for Christmas'.[26] Of course, individual instances such as these do not allow us to ascertain how common it was for households to keep larger animals. However, some indication of the prevalence of this practice can be gleaned from the minutes of the old town council of Windsor (now part of inner Brisbane) in the early part of this century. These minutes contain frequent references to complaints about the problems created by stray animals, most particularly goats and cattle (and dogs).[27] Indeed, the goat (and dog) 'nuisance' became so pronounced that the owners of these animals were eventually required to register them. This obviously failed to fix the problem, for in the period 1914–16 owners of these animals were also required to pay a tax. In the Brisbane experience at least, the keeping of large animals was clearly not uncommon.[28]

In addition to harvesting the produce of domestically reared animals, a great many families were also able to avail themselves of freely provided 'bush' foods and sea foods, along with firewood. Rabbits and fish, for instance, were fairly common supplements to the diets of working people and, in some households, so too were kangaroos, wallabies, and bandicoots (the latter being said to taste like fish).[29]

As well as satisfying household needs, domestic production, plus hunting and gathering activities, sometimes spilled over into the petty entrepreneurial sphere, with surplus produce being routinely sold off. Edna Ryan makes this point: 'Suburban allotments enabled many housewives to have fowls, ducks and

149

geese, and to grow vegetables like pumpkins, marrows and chokoes, as well as a few fruit trees enabling the housewife to make pickles, chutney and jams for sale as well as eggs and poultry.'[30]

Given the potential for generating cash income through marketing home produce, it is not surprising that land and animals were sometimes given as gifts to widows in desperate straits, so that they might make a future for themselves and their children. At a particularly generous meeting in Castlemaine in the 1890s, for instance, concerned citizens raised £68 11s 'for the widow and five children of Norman McLeod to pay for funeral expenses and other debts, and found them a cottage, a paddock and some cows, pigs and poultry'.[31]

QUANTITATIVE EVIDENCE

Although these anecdotes generally point to the existence of 'the urban peasantry', they do not show the precise dimensions of this economy. This can only be gained from quantitative data of a longitudinal kind, enabling trends to be drawn over a long period of time and specifically over the years from the last century. Although there is not enough information to trace these trends precisely, a scattering of figures provides some insights.

Table 9.1 shows the best quantitative evidence available, even though it has major shortcomings. It gives an estimate of households' share of the total production and manufacture of certain foodstuffs, and of fish caught. Unfortunately, it is only for the period after 1950: there are no figures for the critical earlier years, when the urban peasantry is said to have been present. Nor do we know what percentage of households engaged in these activities, or what percentage of total household consumption came from them.

The table suggests a decline in domestic provisioning after 1950 and, with the exception of eggs, the total household contribution to Australian production was tiny. Households' share of vegetable production remained fairly constant over the forty years, but their contribution of potatoes, total fruit, poultry (meat and eggs), and butter has declined. Households' estimated share of the fish catch has remained surprisingly stable, and jam making—though a tiny contribution—appears to have increased somewhat. The household contribution to egg production has been surprisingly high, although later data cast doubt on this (see Tables 9.5 and 9.6). Thus, overall, the table tends to confirm the notions that the household production of goods declined after 1950 and what vestiges remain are small.[32]

Table 9.2 contains further information on household manufacturing—in this case the household construction of dwellings, or owner-building (see Chapters 4 and 12). It suggests a decline over the postwar years, although it also shows an increase from the mid-1970s. The significant owner-building activity after World War II reflects a major housing shortage in Australia, when for those with the necessary skills, owner-building became a way of securing good housing in difficult times.[33]

**Table 9.1** Household production of foodstuffs as a percentage of total production, Australia, 1951/52–1991/92

| Food production | % total production | | | | |
|---|---|---|---|---|---|
| | 1951/52 | 1961/62 | 1971/72 | 1981/82 | 1991/92 |
| Raising | | | | | |
|   Total vegetables | 5.5 | 6.5 | 5.3 | 5.1 | 4.8 |
|     Potatoes | 4.9 | 4.9 | 3.1 | 2.7 | 2.0 |
|   Total fruit | 2.8 | 1.7 | 1.4 | 1.7 | 1.2 |
|     Citrus | 4.8 | 4.9 | 4.5 | 5.0 | 5.0 |
|   Poultry: meat | n.a. | n.a. | 1.8 | 1.2 | 0.9 |
|   Poultry: eggs | 44.9 | 44.0 | 29.4 | 34.2 | n.a. |
| Gathering | | | | | |
|   Fish | 9.1 | 9.1 | 9.1 | 9.1 | 9.1 |
| Manufacturing | | | | | |
|   Jam | 1.6 | 2.3 | 2.6 | 2.9 | n.a. |
|   Processed fruit* | 0.5 | 0.2 | 0.3 | 0.5 | 0.4 |
|   Butter | 3.2 | 1.2 | 0.0 | 0.0 | 0.0 |

n.a. = not available.
*Notes:* *Canned apricots, peaches, pears, and pineapples only.
*Sources:* Commonwealth Bureau of Census and Statistics 1951/52 *Report on Food Production and the Consumption of Foodstuffs*; 1961/62 *Report on Food Production and the Apparent Consumption of Foodstuffs and Nutrients*, No. 17; 1971/72 *Apparent Consumption of Foodstuffs and Nutrients*, No. 10.10; ABS, 1981/82 and 1991/92, *Apparent Consumption of Foodstuffs and Nutrients*, Cat. No. 4306.0.

One of the problems with data about owner-building—particularly in recent years—is knowing how much of this activity is genuine household production and how much of it is done by self-employed tradespeople as their principal source of income: they sell the dwelling after completion. Graham Holland suggests that about 40 per cent of his sample of home builders had such building skills (e.g. they were carpenters), and this suggests that at least some of the houses that these people built were eventually sold.[34]

The problem with this information, then, is that it does not show trends before 1950, nor does it show good data for the post-1950 period. For this reason, and because Australia and New Zealand have parallel patterns of development, we have used New Zealand data to impute Australian trends. New Zealand has one set of historic statistics, the poultry censuses of 1921–66, that help pinpoint the probable trend in urban peasant activity in Australia. Because it requires relatively intensive labour, poultry keeping is arguably a good indicator of the urban peasant economy.

Australia and New Zealand share a common history; indeed, New Zealand was one of the Australasian colonies until 1901, when it declined an invitation to join the Commonwealth of Australia. In terms of urban development, the major difference between the two is the far more significant historic role played

**Table 9.2** Owner-built dwellings as a percentage of all dwellings, Australia, 1951/52–1984/85

| Year | % of all private houses completed | % of all dwellings completed |
|---|---|---|
| 1951–52 | n.a. | 32.4 |
| 1956–57 | 40.7 | 31.8 |
| 1961–62 | 27.1 | 18.9 |
| 1966–67 | 15.9 | 10.0 |
| 1971–72 | 13.2 | 8.3 |
| 1976–77 | 20.6 | 14.2 |
| 1981–82 | 24.9 | 16.4 |
| 1984–85 | 25.6 | 18.8 |

*Source:* G. Holland, *Emoh Ruo* (Sydney, 1988), p. 230.

by small towns in New Zealand—due to the country's intensive pastoralism—while Australia's largest cities have played the key defining role in the nation's development.[35]

As in Australia, urban peasant activity was highly significant in New Zealand from the nineteenth century. M. Fairbairn, for example, shows that a very large percentage of households were involved in this production during the second half of the nineteenth century. He points to the existence of a 'hybrid peasant/worker' in both urban and rural New Zealand who was involved in extensive hunting, fishing, and food gathering, with households making use of housing land for food production.[36] In the 1880s, half of all men owned land, with the wage earner drawing upon household production to add to the income from the formal economy.[37] Fairbairn also mentions that 'a frequent argument for shorter working hours for working men, a Saturday half day especially, was that they needed time to work in their gardens to raise produce to supplement wages'.[38]

This urban peasant activity in New Zealand continued into the twentieth century but declined after World War II, as suggested by Figure 9.1. Over half of New Zealand households kept poultry in the first quarter of this century, with the rural rate being much higher than the urban rate. The rate in both cases declined over the forty-five years to 1966, although the decline was not even. Three trends are worth noting here: the surprising decline during the hard times of the 1930s; the plateau over the good times of the 1950s; and the marked increase in the percentage of rural households having poultry in the 1950s. The 1950s trends may be related to three factors. First, the postwar boom enabled many more nuclear family households to be formed, because an adequate cash income could be obtained from the formal economy. Second, the fear of another depression—still strong after World War II—may have encouraged many households to maintain the urban peasant economy. Once this fear abated, and households were able to rely almost exclusively on the

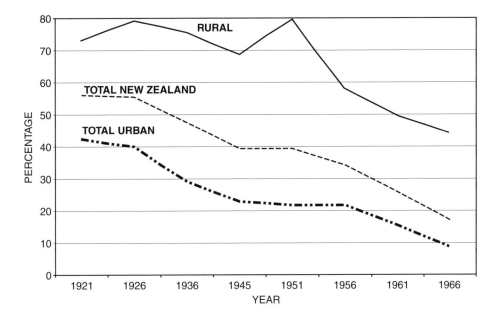

**Figure 9.1** Households with poultry: urban and rural New Zealand, 1921–66 (percentage of households)
Sources: New Zealand Census and Statistics Office, Results of a Census of the Dominion of New Zealand, 1921; New Zealand Census and Statistics Department, Population Census, 1936, 1945, 1951; New Zealand Department of Statistics, Population Census, 1956, 1961; New Zealand Department of Statistics, Census of Population and Dwellings, 1966.

formal economy for their income, household production declined. Of course, during the postwar economic boom it became cheaper for households to buy goods and services from the formal economy than to produce them. Third, the increase in rural household poultry production is probably related to the creation of new farm households. These were established after World War II as new farmland became available.

Figure 9.2 shows the percentage of poultry-producing households in urban centres. Clearly, the larger the centre, the less likely were households to have poultry, and vice versa. But in all cases there was a decline over the forty-five years after 1921, except for the 1950s plateau, and there was a very sharp decline in the 1960s. The lower levels of poultry production—and thus of the urban peasant economy—in the largest centres is probably associated with three forms of access provided by these centres. First, households could obtain a good cash income. Second, market goods were more readily available in the large centres. Third, these goods were likely to be cheaper in large towns. In

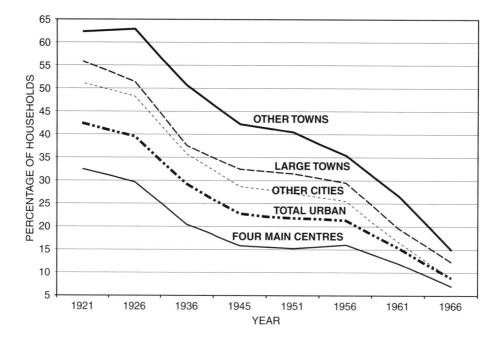

154

**Figure 9.2** Households with poultry: New Zealand urban areas, 1921–66 (percentage of households)
*Sources:* New Zealand Census and Statistics Office, Results of a Census of the Dominion of New Zealand, 1921; New Zealand Census and Statistics Department, Population Census, 1936, 1945, 1951; New Zealand Department of Statistics, Population Census, 1956, 1961; New Zealand Department of Statistics, Census of Population and Dwellings, 1966.

contrast, small centres were more likely to have highly seasonal labour and thus offer more insecure forms of cash income. Other sources of income—including those from the urban peasant economy—would therefore have been sought in these places.

Table 9.3 gives some additional New Zealand data, on vegetable production for the fifteen years to 1971: the end of the postwar boom in New Zealand and the last years of the fourth Kondratieff cycle.[39] What was shown above for poultry is generally reflected here, although vegetable production was more common than poultry production during these two periods.

If we can apply this New Zealand evidence to Australia, it seems that urban peasant activity was widespread in Australia over the early part of this century. It declined steadily to a plateau in the 1950s, and then contracted rapidly during the 1960s. What is of interest now is seeing the extent to which households produce, manufacture, and gather needed goods today.

**Table 9.3** Household production of home-grown vegetables as a percentage of total consumption, New Zealand, 1956 and 1971

| Share of total household consumption | Potatoes | | Other vegetables | |
|---|---|---|---|---|
| | 1956 | 1971 | 1956 | 1971 |
| All | 8.7 | 6.2 | 8.3 | 5.9 |
| Some | 41.5 | 28.0 | 52.3 | 45.3 |
| None | 49.8 | 65.8 | 39.4 | 48.8 |

*Sources:* New Zealand Census and Statistics Office, *Results of a Census of the Dominion of New Zealand*, 1921; New Zealand Census and Statistics Department, Population Census, 1936, 1945, 1951; New Zealand Department of Statistics, Population Census, 1956, 1961; New Zealand Department of Statistics, Census of Population and Dwellings, 1966.

## Urban peasant production in contemporary cities

Again we use a range of data to test whether the urban peasant thesis applies to contemporary cities and towns. Table 9.4 is drawn from a 1990 Brisbane survey of 372 households. This shows household production and manufacturing to be relatively insignificant, consisting mostly of vegetables, clothes and curtains. The proportion of total yearly household income from these sources was probably tiny.

Table 9.5 shows the household share of total Australian foodstuffs grown, gathered, or processed in 1992. The two most common goods produced or accessed by households are eggs and seafood, but, once again, it is hard to know the significance of these figures, particularly because we do not have separate figures for rural and urban areas.

Table 9.6 provides a better indication of today's domestic production. About one-third of Australian households grow fruit and vegetables, and a significant share (about one-fifth) catch fish. Moreover, a disproportionate share of household food production, food gathering, and food processing was done, overwhelmingly, outside the capital cities; that is, in rural areas, small cities, and towns. The exception was wine production. In New South Wales, home-produced wine was made almost exclusively in Sydney; in Victoria, it was mainly made in Melbourne. Also, Hobart households caught as much fish, relatively, as other Tasmanian households.[40]

So, food production, gathering and processing are relatively minor household activities today. It is unlikely that this household provisioning has much to do with necessity. It seems it is not cheaper for households to produce these goods than to buy them through the market. Those who do produce them may do this out of interest, specifically for reasons of taste, for recreation, and for environmental reasons.

**Table 9.4** Household production of goods, Brisbane, 1990

| Production | % of households |
|---|---|
| Food | |
| Poultry: meat | 0.3 |
| Poultry: eggs | 1.1 |
| Vegetables | 23.1 |
| Herbs | 21.5 |
| Fruit: tended | 10.5 |
| Fruit: untended | 11.8 |
| Other | 0.5 |
| Household manufactures | |
| Built house | 5.1 |
| Curtains | 29.6 |
| Chair covers | 11.6 |
| Children's clothes | 31.7 |
| Adults' clothes | 32.8 |
| Built-in furniture | 8.3 |
| Other furniture | 9.7 |
| Other goods | 9.1 |

*Note:* N = 372
*Source:* Brisbane Household and Residential Area Study: see
P. Mullins, *Exploring the Line of Descent in the Intergenerational
Transmission of Domestic Production*, Urban Research Program
Working Paper No. 55, Australian National University
(Canberra, 1996).

**Table 9.5** The household production of foodstuffs as a percentage of total production, Australia, 1992

| Food production | % total production | |
|---|---|---|
| | Home production | Commercial production |
| Raising | | |
| Vegetables | 5.3 | 94.7 |
| Fruit | 4.1 | 95.9 |
| Poultry: meat* | 0.4 | 99.6 |
| Poultry: eggs† | 11.1 | 88.9 |
| Gathering | | |
| Seafood | 12.3 | 87.7 |
| Manufacturing | | |
| Beer | 2.1 | 97.9 |
| Wine | 1.0 | 99.0 |

*Notes:* *Excludes Tasmania, Northern Territory and ACT. †Excludes Queensland and Western Australia
*Source:* ABS, *Home Production of Selected Foodstuffs, Australia*, Year ended April 1992, Cat. No. 7110.0.

**Table 9.6** Percentage of households producing foodstuffs, Australian states and territories, 1992

| Food production | % households involved | | | | | | | | |
|---|---|---|---|---|---|---|---|---|---|
| | NSW | Vic. | Qld | SA | WA | Tas. | NT | ACT | Total |
| Raising | | | | | | | | | |
| Poultry | 0.9 | 0.9 | 1.7 | 2.3 | 1.5 | 2.8 | 1.2 | 0.4 | 1.3 |
| Eggs | 4.7 | 6.1 | 8.1 | 9.9 | 8.3 | 10.8 | 7.2 | 2.3 | 6.6 |
| Fruit | 26.6 | 41.9 | 36.3 | 48.2 | 38.5 | 47.6 | 29.2 | 41.2 | 36.1 |
| Vegetables | 29.7 | 41.4 | 29.9 | 40.1 | 34.2 | 50.2 | 21.5 | 49.0 | 34.8 |
| Nuts | 1.8 | 2.8 | 4.6 | 7.4 | 3.5 | 3.2 | 2.4 | 2.6 | 3.2 |
| Gathering | | | | | | | | | |
| Seafood | 14.2 | 15.0 | 22.8 | 21.6 | 28.0 | 23.8 | 29.5 | 15.6 | 18.3 |
| Manufacture | | | | | | | | | |
| Beer | 3.2 | 2.6 | 5.8 | 4.6 | 4.1 | 6.2 | 8.0 | 4.1 | 3.9 |
| Wine | 0.5 | 1.1 | 0.3 | 1.0 | 1.0 | 1.4 | 0.2 | 1.1 | 0.7 |

*Source:* ABS, *Home Production of Selected Foodstuffs, Australia* Year Ended April 1992, Cat. No. 7110.0.

## Contemporary households and the cash imperative

The pursuit of cash is the focus of household labour at the end of the twentieth century/the beginning of the twenty-first century and because only cash enables households to satisfy the cultural imperative of consumerism, the demand that we consume more and more goods and services.[41] The consumption of culturally desirable goods and services—from Pepsi to the opera, and from new cars to overseas holidays—can only be satisfied with cash. Household labour, then, focuses on activities that obtain cash, rather than on those that produce subsistence goods, such as those of the urban peasant.

Employment, of course, is critical to obtaining cash, with the marked rise over recent years in two-income households reflecting the drive to ensure 'sufficient' cash to buy culturally prescribed commodities. Considerable cash is also obtained from the state in the form of government transfers, this being important for those unable to obtain cash from employment. Gifts and inheritances also provide cash.

Households are also obtaining cash in novel ways. Markets, fairs, and garage sales are among the most important, and magazines are now devoted to publicising the locations of markets and fairs around Australia, with information for both buyers and sellers. There is also the selling of illegal drugs: marijuana, for example, is Queensland's second-largest cash crop.[42]

Pseudo-cash transfers need also to be considered. Local exchange and trading systems (LETS), for example, reflect this development.[43] Here, goods and services are given monetary-equivalent values and so no money is exchanged.[44] Yet, if a cash income is central to satisfying the cultural demands of consumerism—with the desired goods and services only available for cash— LETS is unlikely ever to play a significant role in the *total* Australian economy. Indeed, it is likely to lose out to fairs and markets because, although all three have similar structures, fairs and markets involve the sale of goods (and services) for money. It is this cash nexus, then, which is likely to restrict the role that LETS play, relative to the role played by fairs, markets, and other informal economic activities based upon monetary exchanges. Labour that generates cash from the informal economy will therefore be far more important to households than any labour directed at non-monetary exchange of goods and services. Only cash enables people to consume culturally desirable goods and services, such as Pepsi. These cannot be directly exchanged through a system like LETS.[45]

GARAGE SALES AS A SOURCE OF CASH

158

One of the more important alternative cash sources—the garage sale—is worth examining in some detail. This is both because the dwelling is the retail site for this activity, and also because the garage sale shows how households are trying to obtain cash from sources other than from employment or from the state.

Garage sales have their beginnings in the socio-economic crisis of the 1970s, the decade coinciding with the rise of post-industrialism: the end of the fourth long wave of economic development (the fourth Kondratieff cycle) and the emergence of the fifth. Where the crest of the fourth long wave was a time of full employment and good wages, the current period is one in which many households are having difficulties obtaining sufficient cash from the formal economy to satisfy the cultural demand to consume more and more goods and services. Alternative sources of cash are therefore sought, and the garage sale is one of these alternatives.

What little research has been published on garage sales has focused on social and psychological contexts in which buyers and sellers find themselves.[46] No one seems to have analysed the critical relationship that exists between consumerism, the centrality of cash, and new ways in which households obtain cash during these difficult times.

We can test this proposition—that households use garage sales as a means of supplementing cash income—by asking two related questions. Are garage sales a phenomenon of the post-1970s period for reasons identified above; and are they more likely to be used by people who have difficulty obtaining a cash income from the formal economy? Answers to these two questions require different sorts of information. The first necessitates longitudinal data, which will show whether garage sales did, indeed, emerge during the 1970s and become significant in the 1980s and 1990s. The second question can only be answered from survey research: asking people whether they have held garage sales and, in doing this, noting the characteristics of the people involved.

An answer to the first question comes from a content analysis of classified advertisements in the Brisbane newspaper, the *Courier Mail*, over the years from the late 1970s. A separate advertising column for garage sales began in an intermittent way in late 1980, but it was not until early 1981 that it became a permanent feature of the 'Weekend Shopper' in the Saturday edition. The timing of this column suggests that garage sales were indeed a response to difficulties many households had, from the 1970s, in obtaining a cash income.

To see whether garage sales grew in importance over the 1980s and 1990s, a sample of Saturday editions from 1981 to 1995 was selected and their content analysed. Columns devoted to garage sales were measured in centimetres and these were summed for each year in order to show the volume of advertising. Figure 9.3 presents the findings. It seems to confirm the hypothesis, at least for the 1980s. Garage sales rose steadily from 1981 to 1987, then jumped to a peak in 1989. Thereafter the rate declined slightly, but it remained fairly constant during the 1990s. The peak coincided with a recession, but it is difficult to explain the 1990s plateau. It may be associated with the sharp increase in markets and fairs, whereby households now see better opportunities for steadier cash income from these sources than from the one-off effort proffered by a garage sale. Alternatively, more people, proportionately, may be using advertising avenues other than newspapers, such as posters on local lamp posts.

The analysis also showed that the largest number of garage sales was around Christmas, in November and December. This seems to suggest that households were jettisoning superfluous goods at this time to obtain extra cash to buy new goods for Christmas, both as gifts and for festivities, and this clearly suggests the power of consumerism.

Newspaper data indicate that garage sales as one means by which households are trying to obtain extra cash, but they do not provide information on who holds garage sales. This can only be gleaned from survey research and, for present purposes, data collected in 1997 from south-east Queensland residents are used.[47] This survey was part of a quality of life study, with respondents being asked, among other things, about their income sources.

Five per cent of respondents said that they had received income from garage sales over the previous financial year, and these were people who had difficulties accessing a good cash income. Compared with those who did not hold garage sales, they were far more likely (at a statistically significant level, 0.05) to be receiving social security benefits, to be in casual employment, to be poorly educated, and to be on the lowest personal (but not household) incomes.[48] They were not, however, more likely to be unemployed. This may be because, as Pahl has observed for Britain,[49] the unemployed are less likely to have the resources (e.g. the contacts) to obtain income from the informal economy, such as from garage sales and markets. Gender, age, and marital status were also not significant.

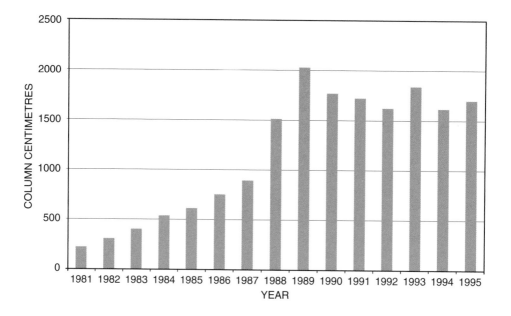

**Figure 9.3** Garage Sales advertised in Brisbane's *Courier-Mail*, 1981–95 (column centimetres)

Therefore, garage sales appear to be a response to difficulties experienced in the post-industrial age. This type of economic activity grew during the 1980s, and (apart from the long-term unemployed) it is those who have the greatest difficulty obtaining well-paid jobs and thus a good cash income in the formal economy who are most involved.

## Conclusion

This chapter has tested a theory about the way Australian urban households obtained income from the nineteenth century until the middle of the twentieth century. The evidence essentially confirms the presence of what has been called an urban peasant economy. However, the postwar economic boom (1945–72) led to a historically aberrant domestic economy. Households were able to rely significantly on cash obtained from labour in the formal economy, and they were (relative to the earlier period) little reliant on income produced in the domestic economy. The chapter has also argued that, over the twenty-five or so years since the end of the boom—a time when a new economy began to emerge—households have had to rely more (relative to the postwar period) on informal economic activities that generate income. However, unlike the urban peasant era, it is a cash income that is sought today, for only cash enables us to fulfil the cultural imperative to consume as many goods and services as possible.

Finally, this chapter has explicitly and implicitly emphasised the need to understand the way households obtain income in order to comprehend how people get by now and in the past. With few exceptions, this issue has been neglected. Certainly, a great deal of work has been done on housework, but this has not tackled the broad question about the way households use members' labour to obtain income from a range of different sources, both inside and outside the household. Understanding the domestic economy, as defined here, places the labour of household members into the context of the total economy, and this understanding will also clarify the way housing is used as capital by households to generate income.

## Notes

We are grateful to Frank Stilwell, and those attending the Summer Session of the Federated PhD Scheme in Housing and Urban Studies, 24 November to 6 December, 1996, for their comments on an earlier version of this chapter.

1   P. Mullins, 'Theoretical Perspectives on Australian Urbanisation, I: Material Components in the Reproduction of Australian Labour Power', and 'Theoretical Perspectives on Australian Urbanisation, II: Social Components in the Reproduction of Australian Labour Power', *Australian and New Zealand Journal of Sociology*, vol. 17, no. 1, pp. 65–76, and no. 3, pp. 35–43; see also P. Mullins, 'Is Australian Urbanisation Different?', in J. Najman and J. Western (eds), *A Sociology of Australian Society* (Melbourne, 1988).
2   J. Smith and I. Wallerstein (eds), *Creating and Transforming Households* (Cambridge, 1992).
3   R. Pahl, *Divisions of Labour* (Oxford, 1984).
4   I. Wallerstein and J. Smith, 'Households as an Institution in the World-economy', in Smith and Wallerstein, *Creating and Transforming Households.*
5   C. Kynaston, 'Patriarchy, Capitalism and Women's Subordination in Britain and Australia', PhD thesis, University of Queensland, 1997.
6   P. Grimshaw, 'Women and the Family in Australian History', *Historical Studies*, vol. 18, 1979.
7   See R. Easterlin, *Birth and Fortune* (London, 1980); W. J. Wilson, *The Truly Disadvantaged* (Chicago, 1987); W. J. Wilson, *When Work Disappears* (New York, 1996).
8   *Portrait of the Family in the Total Economy* (Cambridge, 1994).
9   Smith and Wallerstein, *Creating and Transforming.*
10  For example see P. Mullins, 'Social Implications of the Brisbane Northern Freeway', in J. S. Western and P. R. Wilson (eds), *Planning in Turbulent Environments* (St. Lucia, Qld, 1977).

161

11  Mullins, 'Theoretical Perspectives, I: Material Components', p. 69.

12  Mullins, 'Theoretical Perspectives, II: Social Components', p. 38.

13  *Ibid.*, p. 38.

14  Mullins, 'Theoretical Perspectives I: Material Components', p. 70.

15  Snooks, *Portrait of the Family*.

16  *Struggletown* (Ringwood, Vic., 1988).

17  *Backyard Self-Sufficiency* (Melbourne, 1992), p. 1.

18  *Australian Houses of the '20s and '30s* (Fitzroy, Vic., 1989), p. 150.

19  'A Half World between City and Country', in M. Kelly (ed.), *Sydney: City of Suburbs* (Kensington, 1987), p. 136.

20  'The Family Scene', in J. Rigg (ed.), *In Her Own Right* (Melbourne, 1969), p. 75.

21  C. Brouwer, 'Garden', in R. Fisher and B. Crozier (eds), *The Queensland House* (Brisbane,1994), pp. 92–3.

22  (Ringwood, Vic., 1987), p. 4.

23  M. Lambert, *A Suburban Girl* (South Melbourne, 1990), p. 18.

24  P. Grimshaw and J. Lack, 'Households', in B. Gammage and P. Spearritt (eds), *Australians, 1938* (Sydney, 1987), p. 201.

25  New South Wales Bicentenary Oral History Project, 1988.

26  J. Carter, *Nothing to Spare* (Ringwood, Vic., 1981), pp. 106, 109.

27  Windsor Town Council Minutes, 1907–19.

28  A. Gaynor has recently reviewed—for Perth—municipal by-laws that have restricted the household keeping of domestic animals: 'Regulation, Resistance and the Residential Area', *Urban Policy and Research*, vol. 17, no. 1, 1999, pp. 7–16.

29  See, for instance, Carter, *Nothing to Spare*, pp. 57, 106; A. Gollan, *The Tradition of Australian Cooking* (Canberra, 1978), pp. 51–2.

30  'Women in Production in Australia', in N. Grieve and A. Burns (eds), *Australian Women* (Melbourne, 1994), p. 261.

31  P. Grimshaw and C. Fahey, 'Family and Community in Nineteenth-century Castlemaine', in P. Grimshaw, C. McConville and E. McEwen (eds), *Families in Colonial Australia* (Sydney, 1985), p. 91.

32  How these estimates are made remains unclear, thus they seem only to provide a very rough indication of the level of production.

33  See G. Kelly, 'Portrait of a New Community', *Meanjin*, vol. 16, no. 4, 1957.

34  *Emoh Ruo: Owner-Building in Sydney* (Sydney, 1988), p. 151.

35  A. J. Rose, 'Dissent from Down Under', *Pacific Viewpoint*, vol. 7, no. 1, 1966.

36  M. Fairbairn, *The Ideal Society and its Enemies* (Auckland, 1989), pp. 103, 37–56.

37  *Ibid.*, p. 91.

38  *Ibid.*, p. 101.

39  Kondratieff cycles are roughly 50-year cycles of economic development, each rising to a boom and then collapsing. They are named after an early-twentieth-century Russian economist. S. Solomou, *Phases of Economic Growth, 1850–1973: Kondratieff Waves and Kuznets Swings* (Cambridge, 1987).

40  See Australian Bureau of Statistics, *Home Production of Selected Foodstuffs, Australia, 1992*.

41  P. Mullins, 'Households, Consumerism and Metropolitan Development', in
    P. N. Troy (ed.), *Australian Cities* (Cambridge, 1995); L. Sklair, *Sociology of the
    Global System* (New York, 1991).

42  Advisory Commission on Illicit Drugs, *Cannabis and the Law in Queensland:
    A Discussion Paper* (Brisbane, 1993), p. 59.

43  LETS appear to have had their beginnings in Canada in 1983: M. Jackson,
    'LETS—Creating a New Economic Space for Women', paper given at the Gender
    and Environments Conference, Adelaide, 1996.

44  M. Pacione, 'Local Exchange Trading Systems as a Response to the Globalisation
    of Capitalism', *Urban Studies*, vol. 34, no. 8, 1997; the special issue of *Environment
    and Planning A*, vol. 28, no. 8, 1996.

45  For a general overview of LETS, see C. Williams, 'The New Barter Economy',
    *Journal of Public Policy*, vol. 5, no. 16, 1996, and the special issue of *Environment and
    Planning A*, vol. 28, no. 8, 1996.

46  G. M. Herrman, 'Women's Exchange in the US Garage Sale', *Gender and Society*,
    vol. 10, no. 6, 1996; S. M. Soiffer and G. M. Herrman, 'Visions of Power',
    *Sociological Review*, vol. 35, no. 1, 1987; G. M. Herrman and S. M. Soiffer, 'For Fun
    and Profit', *Urban Life*, vol. 12, no. 4, 1984.

47  This survey was conducted as part of a larger Australian Research Council
    Collaborative project (1995–97) on the development of the South-East
    Queensland urban region. The principal investigators are Bob Stimson
    (Australian Housing and Urban Research Insitute at University of Queensland),
    Rod Simpson (Health Sciences, Griffith University) and John Western and Patrick
    Mullins (Sociology, University of Queensland), with the Queensland
    Government's Statistician's Office being the collaborative partner. A sample of
    1347 respondents were interviewed by telephone, the sample being drawn using
    random digit dialling.

48  These figures come from a multiple regression analysis. We are grateful to Andrea
    Lanyon for running these data for us.

49  Pahl, *Divisions of Labour*.

163

# In Her Master's House and Garden

## Chapter 1

*Katie Holmes*

164 In 1960 Robin Boyd described the process by which developers went about the construction of housing estates. First they had to select an area about 5 miles beyond the rim of a sprawling city, lay a grid of streets across it, remove all trees—native and fruit—and replace them by 'rows of electric and telephone poles and the wildflowers by tiny beds of English annuals'.[1] From what was left of the denuded landscape, gardens were built. Boyd was clearly dismissive of this particular 'Australian ugliness', condemning the small-mindedness that he perceived as leading not only to the destruction of the landscape, but also to the creation of inappropriate gardens. In his view, little of significance could some from such a suburban wasteland.

In Boyd's dismissal of the typical Anglo-Australian suburban garden, he failed, or perhaps refused, to recognise the layers of meaning which might be invested there. Whether they be formal gardens with beds of annuals, carefully pruned roses and neat, trimmed paths, or more wild and informal plantings, gardens carry important cultural and individual meanings. Since the early days of settlement they have been significant not only for their production of food, but for establishing the European presence in the landscape. Indeed gardens were one of those ideas the British brought with them when they colonised Australia, a means by which an alien people could create from this stolen land an image of their own making. By the beginning of the twentieth century, and especially during the inter-war years, as cities expanded and as the appropriation of indigenous land continued through the creation of suburbs, gardens and thus the space necessary for them were acquired by greater numbers of predominantly Anglo middle-class and lower-middle-class workers. Gardens did not lose their significance as markers of status and respectability, but greater numbers of people could share in their making and their meanings.

The meanings gardens carry are both individual and cultural. Gardens exist as both a physical and a metaphorical place, a place where nature and culture meet—indeed, as in the Garden of Eden, where humankind began and order was created out of chaos. They can evoke paradise; they can be a place of sensuality and sexuality, especially feminine sexuality; and they can harbour the phases of life and death, of regeneration.[2] For their owners and creators, gardens form an expression of creativity: a space invested with dreams and fantasies, where plants can evoke memories of other places and people, where desire and pleasure and skill can bring about the transformation of a desolate landscape into a secluded oasis, and where an immigrant people can create expressions of permanence and belonging.

Immigration, and the selective and adaptive attempts by successive waves of immigrants to recreate through their gardens the familiar and the affirming, is one of the recurring themes of this chapter. The period under consideration, 1900–60, was marked by significant population growth, provided mainly through immigration. In the earlier years of the century immigrants were pre-dominantly Anglo-Saxon; Britain remained the source of the largest number of immigrants throughout the period, but after World War II large numbers of Southern European immigrants markedly changed the ethnic mix of the population.

Accompanying this population growth was large-scale and largely unquestioned suburbanisation. As we have seen in other chapters, this brought new forms of housing, better serviced blocks and, by the end of the period, greater prosperity and thus greater leisure time for the home owner and gardener (see Chapters 2, 6, 11 and 14). It was also a period marked by what we have come to call the values of modernity: the house and garden were to reflect the concerns of social hygiene, efficiency, progressivism and environmental determinism. As the immediate environment within which a child was raised, the home was to provide the foundations for good citizenship, and the basis for a healthy, modern life. It was also the centre of the nuclear family, based on the heterosexual couple, with the consequent division of labour, unequal income and the power relations this usually implied. These developments were all reflected in the garden.

Australian gardens represent one of the key features of Australian suburban living. They have been characterised by a clear sense of boundaries and a demarcation between the front garden and the larger, functional back-yard. Yet when Captain Arthur Phillip decreed that it was his aim that 'every family should have a separate house in a separate allotment' (see Chapter 2), he can hardly have envisaged the extent to which this would become the hallmark of Australian suburban living. And just as Captain Phillip's vision was an expression of a set of values including order, decency and privacy,[3] so the garden has remained a space planted with the values of a community and culture.

In this chapter I consider the idea of the garden, the importance given to it in creating desirable citizens and suburbs, and the different uses and

**Plate 10.1** *A View of the Artist's House and Garden* in Mill Plains, Van Diemen's Land, by John Glover illustrates early ideas of what constituted an ideal house and garden—one filled with European plants. (Art Gallery of South Australia)

meanings that women, men and children have made of this space between the house and the world outside. The material I use is a mixture of domestic and garden manuals, journals and books, and personal manuscripts such as letters and diaries. Although these sources are drawn from a variety of Australian states, it is not my intention to canvass all the local variations in climate and topography surrounding the garden. The use of such litera-ture inevitably speaks to a fairly middle-class and European experience of gardens; it does not tell of the ways in which, for example, Aboriginal servants could be instrumental in both clearing the land on which gardens could be planted, and then assisting in the planting and care of the transformed landscape.[4] In gardens particular understandings of civilisation were planted; order and control over the environment was sought; the appearance of the landscape changed; and the history of its acquisition was both erased and celebrated.[5]

## House plus garden equals home

One of the most repeated pieces of advice offered by garden writers in the early decades of this century was that, when designing and building a house, thought should be given to the garden. Rather than building a house and then creating a garden from what was left, the two should be conceived and designed together. In 1911 the magazine *Home and Garden Beautiful*, positioning itself as the judge and purveyor of good taste and beauty, reflected on the shortcomings of colonial homes and gardens:

> In the early days of this settlement in this young country, life was made up of a mad rush for gold. Little thought was given to home building, and very much less to garden making, two matters which must always mean so much in the moulding of the future of a young country. Interest in these things has, however, improved; but at no time more than the present has it been necessary that a broad spirit of progressiveness should be shown in the erection of houses with an effective garden space as part of the architectural design.[6]

Good taste, however, did not come naturally. Many individuals would need to be taught to desire a 'fitness between a house and its garden',[7] but as the garden was the first impression people gained of a house, it was of 'primary importance'. Indeed, as the well-known Melbourne architect Mr Barlow noted in a piece on 'Architectural Gardening' for *Home and Garden Beautiful*, 'The garden is an integral part of a beautiful home, and forms a fit setting to an architectural success. In other words, the garden should combine and be composed of architectural features that bring it in perfect harmony with the house.'[8]

The celebrated garden designer Edna Walling wrote at length about the need to create harmony between the house and the garden, and recommended considering particular views from different parts of the house when planning a garden: 'To have a good garden view from a breakfast room window is a great possession; the morning light is so splendid in the garden. It is suggested that a sundial or bird's bath or a stone pedestal be set in the centre of the formal lawn onto which this window looks.'[9]

Walling's emphasis on a particular style of garden necessitated a particular class of client. Her advice was well and good for those able to afford to build their own home, and to employ assistance with designing the garden, but for the majority of Australians, the garden has been an area predetermined by existing fence and boundary lines, the layout of housing estates, and the limited means available for expenditure on things horticultural. Few suburban gardens would have boasted formal lawns and garden pedestals, let alone homes with a separate room for breakfasting. For much of the first sixty years of this century, front gardens have been marked by a neatly kept lawn, perimeter plantings of colourful annuals, standard roses and some low, carefully shaped shrubs, and perhaps an odd tree, often a lemon, planted in the centre of a rectangular lawn.[10] But although it did not need to be grand, a house needed a garden. Its absence suggested a want of home life.

Garden writers placed enormous emphasis on the need for a garden to make a house a home; its value was practical and moral. Lady Hackett in *The Australian Household Guide* (1916) stressed both: 'The House is a place to live in. To make it a home in the true sense of the word certain adjuncts are necessary, and among these none are more important than the home garden.' The influence of the garden on a home could be found in several factors: money was saved by growing one's own fruit and vegetables. Other benefits included lawns for children to play on, flowers for decorating the house, and the 'healthful exercise' of gardening. Lady Hackett espoused the values of hygiene, environmental determinism and child development. Gardening journals did likewise. According to the journal of the New South Wales Horticultural Association, *Garden Gossip*, gardens were crucial to creating a settled, domesticated citizenship. They were evidence of a 'civilised' society. Gardening inculcated 'uplifting thoughts and refining influences'.[11] Australians needed to be encouraged to garden more, and children needed to be educated into a love of gardening. The Melbourne-based journal *Garden Lover* was quite explicit about this: 'The love of horticulture implanted in the plastic years of youth will yield a harvest of public-spirited citizens with high ideals.'[12]

There is a distinct class dimension in the calls to plant gardens and beautify homes. This was clearly articulated by a member of parliament quoted by E. W. Cole in his curiously titled book, *The Happifying Gardening Hobby* (1918). The MP was speaking at 'A Pleasant Sunday Afternoon' where he deplored the fact that 'while you could see miles of cottages without a garden, yet you could often see twenty thousand people gathered to see forty men knock one another about at the violent game of football'.[13] Gardens were civilised, while football was decidedly uncouth. The workers would be better off gardening.

Class distinctions were evident in gardening competitions as well. In fact for all the talk about gardens breeding good citizens and promoting a settled life, it was only a particular type of garden which reflected the desirable qualities. Order and neatness were to reign supreme. In 1910 the Fremantle Horticultural Society sought to encourage the citizen 'to beautify his home by increased attention to his garden, his hedges, his lawns, his drains, and also his backyards, all of which, of course, is calculated to add attractiveness and charm to the street and municipality in which he lives'.[14] A series of awards was introduced, with preference 'given to neatness, cultivation, economy and amateur efforts, as against lavish expenditure, or expensive and rare plants, professionalism, or any costly appurtenances whatever'. Prize-winning gardens could be small and humble, as befitted an ordinary suburban block. The values of modernity also found expression: efficiency, order and cleanliness held sway, although the preference for the amateur over the expert marks an interesting divergence from other prescriptive literature such as that directed to mothers and home makers.[15] Perhaps the Fremantle Horticultural Society was particularly interested in the ways amateurs incorporated the advice of professionals into their gardens.

In the pages of gardening journals, magazines and books, the 'citizen
gardener' began to take on a particular identity. Nearly always represented as a
man, he was an earnest sort of chap who took seriously the task of beautifying
his patch, growing vegetables to feed his family, and upholding the values of
decency and moral order. Importantly, he was an amateur who, unlike those
who employed professionals to mow their lawns and sow their vegetables, dug
his own garden, pruned his own roses, and entered his own prize blooms in the
local gardening competitions.

The concern with citizenship, order and compliance, inflected as it was
with assumptions about class and gender, also found expression in the 'garden
city' movement of the early decades of the century. As Ian Hoskins's work has
demonstrated, town planners believed that the cramped living of workers in
England bred industrial militancy; the solution was to improve the living conditions of the urban working class. The early-twentieth-century urban reformer
R. F. Irvine had very definite ideas about how to do this: ' "Decent family life"
could not exist in a domestic environment where there were "no front gardens
and [only] small backyards".'[16]

169

Gardens reflected stability, a submission to duty, pride of home and
country. They were also an indication of what was going on in the lives of their
owners, the most visible expression of the state of play behind the front door.
Walter Bunning, writing at the end of World War II about inner urban housing,
was clear on the relationship between the state of the garden and the inhabitants of the house; he was also particularly damning of the effect that living in
confined spaces without adequate garden space induced: 'Few of these
houses . . . have any gardens in front; the doorsteps are on the street. At the
back they try to grow flowers—they grow sooty stunted flowers like their own
withered lives.'[17] It is little wonder that creating gardens was seen at times as a
national project of some urgency.

The encouragement of workers to create gardens of a particular style and
design could come in many forms. Tenancy inspectors could enforce clear
guidelines about the plants grown and the standards of neatness to be maintained. Those who rented houses had less scope to create their own designs
than home owners. As suggested, garden competitions were another way of
promoting a particular style of garden. Competitions might be organised by the
local horticultural society, perhaps in conjunction with the town council, and
promoted a particular style of garden—not that likely to be found amongst
Edna Walling's clients. Horticultural societies also held regular shows in which
prize blooms were exhibited and home produce displayed. The early editions
of *Yates Seed Annual* included comments from satisfied customers about their
seed-growing and success in local gardening competitions. Mr Walter Hart,
from Ipswich in Queensland, was positively chuffed with his achievements:
'I may tell you that I gained 27 Prizes at our last October Show for Flowers and
vegetables grown from your Seeds. The Cinerarias were splendid and took firsts

in all classes.'[18] Women also entered competitions. Mrs Thomson from Forbes in New South Wales believed she had found great value for money: 'Last year I got a 3d packet of your Pansy Seed and they were such a success that I exhibited at the local Flower Show and took a Prize, and the people could not credit they grew from a 3d packet.'[19]

One participant in a garden competition in the Perth suburb of Mount Hawthorn approved of strategies to promote particular styles of gardens. Mrs V. Clifford wrote to the local Town Planning Commissioner about a 1936 competition. She was delighted that the gardens of 'workers' were being recognised and encouraged:

> I do not think any of us had false ideas of just how good our small domains were, but I certainly do think we needed all the encouragement we could get for entering into the spirit of the thing, after all, we are the pioneers of the movement, on an occasion like this people are apt to expect too much from a prize winning garden comparing it with larger and more prosperous places, forgetting that the suburbs are composed mainly of working class homes and to make a suburb beautiful the workers must be encouraged.[20]

170

Garden competitions encouraged the display of horticultural skill, while their emphasis on order and neatness carried strong overtones of respectability. The emphasis in such gardens was on public display, with the orientation of the front garden toward the public face of the street and the community. Many upper-class gardens on the other hand, such as those of Edna Walling's clients, were secluded from view: hedges and fences kept out unwelcome eyes. Class and aesthetics combined to ensure that privacy in the garden was valued as much as privacy in the home.

The orientation of the garden was influenced by other factors. In lower-middle- and working-class areas the height of fences was often determined by developers and landlords, and while a low fence may have enabled the garden to be displayed, it also permitted children to play in the street within view from the house. Communication across fences was easy and conversations with passers-by possible. Garden city suburbs insisted on low fences to create a sense of community.

Although the style and design of a garden was heavily influenced by class, other factors were important. Changing architectural designs of the house, changing technology, and changing fashions in garden design and understandings of how gardens should be used, all generated significant shifts in the use and style of the garden. In the first edition of *Yates' Garden Guide* (1895), strict guidelines were provided on designing gardens:

> 'Walks'. These as a rule should not be less than four feet wide, and, except in special cases, should be laid out on a curve . . . All walks should be laid out on some system and with a purpose, and not taken aimlessly here and there as is so often done . . .

'Lawns'. Except in very small cottage gardens there should always be a certain amount of grassplot, nothing is so effective and sets off a garden so much as a good lawn . . .

'Flower beds'. These should be laid out in graceful curves.

The imperative 'should' reigned in *Yates' Garden Guide.* Even in 1916, when *Yates* admitted that the formal style of garden design had 'given place to a much freer and more individualistic treatment', 'shoulds' remained in abundance. Indeed, gardening books have long had a tendency to issue strict instructions with definite moral overtones. Brunning's *Australian Home Gardener* excelled in this with a chapter on the 'Ethics of Gardening' where the use of such things as soil, manure, drains and garden tools all had an ethical dimension.[21]

Changes in the architectural design of houses, especially the creation of areas such as the sunroom, the bay window and the breakfast room, all reflect ideas about the relationship between the house and the garden. As windows lengthened, especially from the late 1930s onward, shrubs outside were planted so as to be seen and enjoyed from inside the house. Not until after World War II, however, was there discussion of the garden as another room of the house, reflecting the increasing emphasis on the relationship between the internal and external environments. The picture windows of the 1950s and 1960s deliberately sought to bring the garden into the home and vice versa. Similarly, the fashion for patios and 'outdoor living' areas affected the design of the house as well as its use. In 1949 Nerine Chisholm advised that the garden 'should be thought of, and planned for, as another room of the house'.[22] Indeed Chisholm suggested segregating the garden into different zones: an open space (the front garden), a utility area (garage, drying yard, vegetables, etc.) and a private area. The design of the garden reflected the same organisation of space as did the design of the house.

This clear delineation between the front, the side and the back garden was not a new feature of Australian gardens. The back garden, or backyard as it was more commonly known, was the functional space. Indeed backyards rather than back gardens characterised the suburbs of the lower-middle and working class. Initially access to lanes was necessary for the nightcart to carry away the 'nightsoil'. As cars became more common, so driveways and garages made their appearance, most commonly down the side of the house with the garage situated between the end of the house and the back fence. A house and garden design competition run by *Home and Garden Beautiful* in 1914 short-listed ten plans for readers to vote on. Each had an area of the garden set aside for chooks, vegetables, a drying yard, and the fruit trees. The toilet, or WC as contestants called it, had by this time moved up from the back of the yard to become attached to the end of the house, usually near the wash house and woodheap. By the 1950s, some of the features still remained, but the function of the backyard was changing: it was to be lived in rather than merely used, and so it gradually became a garden rather than a yard, a place of leisure rather than predominantly of work. When R. G. Edwards published his work *The*

171

*Australian Garden Book* in 1950, he confidently asserted: 'The average home lover has a beautiful front garden because it meets the eyes of passers-by, he beautifies the service area in order to mask or disguise ugly objects, but his back garden he converts into an outdoor living-room for his family alone.'[23]

## Men and women in the garden

Within Mr Edwards's framework, the average home-lover was the man of the house and he held responsibility for determining the design of all sections of the garden. Perhaps this is in keeping with the 1950s model of the nuclear household, with the husband and father most definitely in charge. But a 1913 discussion of men and women in the garden presented a different picture:

> Where ever you find a garden beautiful—that is very beautiful—it is always safe to connect a woman with it . . . A garden of Roses and a sun-bonnet . . . a rapturous bed of Poppies . . . Violets and Snowdrops and two soft arms wet with dew and so on and so on—but the woman is always there in the garden very beautiful.
>
> A man always betrays his presence in a garden that is left solely to his management. His utilitarian instincts are found in the surreptitious smuggling of a Tomato vine or a bed of Lettuce in what he considered an out of the way corner, which a woman would regard as a treasure spot for some of the more delicate and beautiful blooms of her garden.[24]

There is much in gardening literature to suggest that men and women have different concerns in the garden: invariably she is portrayed among the flowers, her femininity aligned with the delicate style and perfume of the species she cultivates. Occasionally she can be found mowing the lawn, or digging a trench, but more often she bends gently to catch the scent of a flower, or stands elegantly, hose in hand, watering her blooming patch. He, on the other hand, is more often found pushing the wheelbarrow or tending the vegetable patch, than cultivating beauty among the flowers—unless of course, he is growing prize blooms for competition. In 1931 the New South Wales Horticultural Society's journal, *Garden and Home Maker of Australia*, ran an amusing article on gender differences in the garden titled, 'The Husband in the Garden: a warning as to the perils involved in having both'. Husbands and gardens were a dangerous mix: 'turn a man loose in a garden and the harm that ensues may take at least two planting seasons to correct'. Men, according to the article, were most inclined to the regimental style of planting—straight rows, squares—and an obsession with red flowers. They should never be let loose with the pruning shears: 'His form of gardening bliss lies in cutting off all possible branches and shoots. He wants to reduce all growth to six inches above the ground.'[25]

172

There is a sense here in which gender is something which is performed in the garden. Edna Walling reiterated such an idea in her discussion of the difference between men and women gardeners: men were more interested in gravel footpaths, prize blooms and impressing passers-by. So engrossed in show blooms was this type of gardener that he was often oblivious to his surroundings: 'in fact the idea of seclusion does not appeal to him very much, for he loves to hear the eulogistic remarks of the passer-by'. Masculinity was associated with display. For Walling, a garden should convey 'a hint of mystery, of gradual revealment, [give] play to the imagination and [keep] the spectator pitched to pleasurable expectancy'.[26] A garden, in other words, should seduce those who enter, keeping their senses permanently aroused, perhaps, we might surmise, to a level of withheld climax. The one-off, spectacular, prize-winning bloom, was not for Edna.

Walling's highly sexualised imagery betrays other meanings. As noted, the display garden, with its prize blooms, was more often found in working-class suburbs than among those who would have comprised Walling's clients. Class intersected with gender in the garden. Indeed for Mrs Clifford, the entrant in the Mount Hawthorn garden competition, the two could produce interesting tensions:

173

> my husband is the gardener, still I love all flowers, particularly the so called common flowers, in my opinion at least, they are the backbone of the garden, like faithful dogs they are there when everything else fails. I refer to one in particular—'the geranium' . . . my husband pulled most of ours out, telling me that we had no chance of winning a competition with those common flowers in, he has replaced them with more expensive creepers that will take years to make any show at all and have to be looked after like a lot of sick babies all the time, not only that, they only bloom once a year whereas the old geranium is ever blooming making a riot of colour all the year round, folks say they harbour pests I find less pests on them, than any other plant in the garden, they need little water and the poorer the soil the better they like it, what more could we wish for.

Mrs Clifford was clearly more interested in a garden of colour and pleasure: plants were to be familiar and domestic, as comfortable as friends might be, and as undemanding. Not for her the special needs of exotic species which gave so little in return for so much.

Upper-class couples also experienced tension over whose vision of the garden would be realised. Una Falkiner had quite a different understanding of the garden to her husband, the wealthy Riverina pastoralist Otway Falkiner. Her vision was of a retreat, a place of beauty and joy. It was a buffer zone between the house and the world of sheep, horses, manure and making money. For Otway, the garden differed little from the paddocks beyond its fence: it should be a useful place, neat and functional. Una used her diary to record disagreements with Otway about the garden, and at the same time highlighted the performance of roles within it:

Had a talk with Otway about the rose arches going up. I had such *lovely* high
ones, 10 ft high, but my lord wants them waist high, so I agreed in a nice wifely
way, & then we walked around the garden with the new gardener & he thinks
Otway a lamb, as Otway kept appealing to him, telling him things & saying 'isn't
that your experience gardener'. Of course it was his experience! . . . Old Chips,
the Carpenter came up blowing his nose, & I called out that it was quite right of
him to cry about his arches. I felt like it too. [8 July 1920]

Una Falkiner sought allies for her position. The choice of gardener was
crucial: 'I was also worried about losing my gardener, who understands his job
& has the garden looking beautiful, but Otway doesn't like him & says he is no
good on the electric light & engine for pumping. The new man I can see only
understands engines' (12 October 1920).

Una valued beauty over utility and sought workmen who shared her
values. She resisted Otway's attempts to exert his control and influence over a
place she wished to reign. A gardener appointed by Otway would be answerable
to him, and Una would lose the grounds of her authority. When it came to the
garden and conflict with Otway, Una practised a little insubordination and
slowly succeeded in establishing the garden as her own.[27]

174

But gardening could also provide a common interest for couples. Wendy
O'Dowd's letters to her aunt in the 1950s recount some of the difficulties in her
relationship with her husband, who, it seems, was prone to drinking and
violence. Attention to the garden became one way for him to demonstrate his
attempts to reform: it was a mark of respectability. The letters also reveal the
sorts of plants and plans to be found in a 1950s Cooroy garden in Queensland,
and the ways in which the seemingly female space of the wash house could
double as a man's workroom.

Freddy seems to be really interested in his home at last. We have done quite a
lot the last few months. Especially in the garden. Most of the paths are covered
with clipped lawn & the flower beds are all planted & set out as we want them.
We have quite a lot of pot plants & hanging baskets now & I have painted them
all red. There are 60 so far. Have room for about another 40. Freddy has made
a rockery under one mango tree & we have the pot plant stands under the
other. He has fitted the wash house with shelves etc. for his tools & my washing
requisites & has quite an effective work room. He has made a book shelf & tray
so far, & a very nice cage (like a house) for the canaries. Also lots of odd jobs
that have needed doing for so long. He has pulled down the fence that was
round the vegetable garden & we are making a rose garden there. The vegetable
garden will be in the old fowl house. I want an orchard planted too, but talking
hasn't done any good so far. I can plant it, but I want a really good fence to keep
the cows out.[28]

Dorothy Lamont's garden contained many of the features typically found
in Australian backyards, but her alterations suggest some of the ways in which

its style was changing: flower beds, rose gardens and rockeries are all suggestive of an emphasis on the pleasure of the garden, rather than its functional attributes.

As the style and use of the garden changed, so the performance of gender within it also altered. Use of the garden as an 'outdoor living area' shifted some of the focus of women's domestic work from within the house to outside. In her book *Australian Gardens: Their Planning and Making* (1949), Nerine Chisholm devoted a whole chapter to the Outdoor Living Room. In it she noted that this room 'should be of easy access in relation to the back entrance of the house, in order that the housewife may be saved as many steps as possible, and also be able to keep touch with arrangements indoors. If this is not the case the constant journeys into the telephone room or kitchen will be troublesome and irritating.'[29] Similarly, she noted that an outdoor barbecue would make hospitality easier for the housewife. This may have been so, but it also meant that the back garden as well as the house now needed to be kept neat and tidy. The change in living style and values that this represented is well captured by the comments of Malda Bertram, a Townsville correspondent to the National Museum of Australia's 'Backyards' project: 'Backyards weren't to eat in. Our parents were so glad to have a nice house, they didn't want to go back pioneering. They would have thought a barbeque [with flies etc.] silly when you had a nice table and chairs to use upstairs.'[30]

As outdoor entertaining became more popular in the 1950s and 1960s, we can see even more clearly the ways in which, for the woman of the house, the garden could be an extension of her domestic responsibilities: she remained the housewife in the garden, while the man became the gardener. But women's presence in the backyard or garden was by no means new. The functions of the backyard were intimately tied to the needs of the house: an area for drying clothes, chooks for eggs, vegetables for food, wood for fires. Much of the work involved in these activities had been performed by women (see Chapter 9). Malda Bertram recalls that in the backyards of her childhood in Townsville, the 'backyards & side fences & back fences were used for *talks* to neighbours. All the women stayed at home then. I didn't know one Mother who worked in Fort Street when I was a child.'[31]

The use of the garden as an area for entertaining raises the ambiguities and changes in the definition of space within the garden. It is both a public and domestic space, a borderland between the domestic hearth and the world beyond, a place where traditional understandings of gender could become blurred. Women became actively engaged with the land, and men were brought into a more intimate association with the domestic sphere. Even if this manifested itself in ensuring there were flowers for arranging inside the house, or indeed in preparing the barbecue, men's awareness of the daily needs and operations of the home could be raised. When women were actively engaged in the planning and tending of the garden, their work was less likely to be seen as simply an extension of their duties as housewife. And for women who took great pleasure in the garden, there was a clear distinction in their minds

175

between the satisfaction of gardening compared with the repetition and drudgery of housework.[32] Indeed gardening could provide women with an escape from the demands of the home, an activity from which they might derive great pleasure, and an outlet for their creativity and skill, yet one which was still seen as appropriately feminine. As Jean Duruz writes: 'In the mini landscape of the suburban garden . . . femininity could be assured and rewarded.'[33] So also, could masculinity. But for women living in a house where the garden was a male domain, it could operate as an area of exclusion, a further space over which he exercised control. As one of Ian Hoskins's interviewees recalled of her parents' lives in Daceyville:

> My mother was only allowed to hose because she used to pick the wrong things
> at the wrong time . . . I mean she loved flowers—she loved them in the house,
> though, and Dad liked them in the garden . . . He was the one who did the
> cutting because she'd have gone out and picked herself a bunch of flowers and
> it was probably the one he was going to show that week in competition.[34]

The dynamics of gender in the garden were not fixed, but a source of negotiation, contest and performance.

There were other activities performed in the garden that could also carry the inflections of gender and class. The use of the garden as an important area for parenting received increasing attention during the inter-war years as advice manuals on good mothering, such as May Gutteridge's *The Child at Home* (1934), emphasised the need to provide special areas and activities for the children: 'The backyard should provide excursion and adventure, and contact with animals, plants and people . . . The child needs to find adventure in his backyard.'[35] And so the sand pit entered the backyard, while gardening journals such as the *Garden Lover* encouraged parents to provide children with their own section of the garden for growing their own flowers and vegetables. Mae Murphy recorded in her 1944 diary the growth and development of her daughter Marie. Noting Marie's use of her new pullable horse, Mae noted that is was designed to help her 'coordinate other movement with her own, as is the swing'. Her play in the garden was carefully supervised, but toys were restricted to the simple and at hand: 'The house paddock is spacious and safe from "traps"—flowers and vegetables well shut off. Her time is divided between a path of gravel and the box of pegs and a space in front of the fowl pens'.[36] For children the garden could be a place where new worlds were created, great battles won or lost, and escapes possible. For more practical play, the side driveway could double as a cricket pitch and the wall of the garage provided a convenient place for a netball ring. Deidre O'Donnell reflected on the desires which led to the creation of their back garden in the Sydney suburb of Castlecrag in 1950:

> I wanted a safe place outside the kitchen door for the children to play. I want
> a Hill's hoist, some trees and a lawn, so we paved an area with concrete slabs,

planted a lawn with runners, put up a Hill's hoist not far from the kitchen door & enclosed it on all three sides with paling fences & bought some sandstone & made garden beds. We built ourselves a barbeque, spent some money on white outdoor furniture & proceeded to live a very different life style from the one we'd known pre-war.[37]

The growing affluence of the community was clearly reflected in back gardens.

## The Australian house and garden

Just as the garden contained expressions of class and gender, so also it reflected ideas about nationalism and the nation. When A. E. Cole published *The Bouquet: Australian Flower Gardening*, in the second decade of this century, he included several suggestions for garden designs. The most novel among these featured a lawn shaped as a map of Australia, complete with Tasmania. Gravel surrounded the lawn, and around the gravel were planted flower beds and rose borders. Cole noted of this design that 'the novelty and tastefulness of the piece repays for the trouble involved'.[38] The flower beds of course contained exotics—annuals and perennials. In spite of the lawn's shape, there was nothing 'Australian' about this garden. Its design, however—taken from a public garden in Sydney where the map had been planted with flowers rather than lawn—reflects a strong sense of national pride. The garden was being used as an expression of national identity; its post-Federation appeal suggested the triumph of the nation over the states, and proclaimed both the nationalism and citizenship of the owners. The nation, the citizen, were all reflected in one 'tasteful' garden design.

177

The vision proclaimed by this early-twentieth-century garden evokes both the present and the future of the Australian nation. But it did so in terms which remained bound by the traditions from which it grew. There was no native Australian flora in this, nor any of the other designs suggested by A. E. Cole. Indeed, according to William Elliot in *Coles Australasian Gardening and Domestic Floriculture* (1896), the natural environment of Australia provided little of use to the home gardener: 'a garden must differ, in all material qualities, from anything existing in a state of nature'. Mounds or rises were to be levelled or reduced to regular curvature. 'Should indigenous trees be planted, they should not be grouped as though they had grown up naturally, but planted singly and allowed so much space to develop that they would be at once recognised as having come under the dominion of art.'[39]

Other writers were not so dismissive of the potential of the local flora for gardens and indeed encouraged gardeners to make greater use of native plants in their gardens. Some took to advancing the benefits of native plants for the garden. In *Home and Garden Beautiful* Marcus Barlow espoused the possibilities of indigenous trees for the garden:

Australia boasts of many beautiful trees, and it is a matter of great regret that they so seldom appear in our private gardens. When designing the house, if the land available will permit, have it placed well back on the section, and you will never regret the laying out and planting of a garden which comprises a representative selection of Australian flora.[40]

Cognisant of the unique nature of Australian flora, horticulturalists consistently encouraged Australians to grow more native plants. It was not the design of the garden but its contents which were to reflect an affiliation with the environment and pride of country. Despite repeated encouragement, however, Australian gardeners were very slow on the uptake. Perhaps this is not so surprising when we consider that the very journals which printed periodic encouragement to grow more Australian flora still devoted most of their detailed discussions on the growing and cultivation of flowers to exotics, most particularly chrysanthemums, carnations, roses, sweet peas, daffodils and dahlias. There was a distinct lack of direction on what Australian plants to grow or how to grow them. S. H. Hunt in the 1930s espoused an alternative approach: rather than remove the native plants in the first place, 'Far better would it be to preserve the best specimens of native flora, then plan your garden on lines that will include them in the picture — native plants and cultivated species combining to form a picture of which you will be justly proud.'[41]

The vision of the garden advocated by those writers encouraging the use of native plants did not involve a replication of the natural environment. In the garden, such plants became tamed and controlled. They were pruned and clipped; they too became 'cultivated'. Indeed, if they were not pruned, they became, according to the *Journal of Horticulture*, 'straggly and unsightly'.[42] At this stage in the evolution of Australian gardens, when native plants were used, they were usually specimens taken and trained to fit in with a European understanding of what a garden should look like. Indeed, the European garden allowed room for exotics; incorporating unusual species within the garden was entirely within the European tradition of gardening. In Australia the ratio of exotic to native plants became reversed.

The encouragement to grow more native plants can be seen as an expression of nationalism; like the urge to establish gardens and cultivate a 'civilised' citizenship, the garden becomes a reflection of ideas about nationhood. An enthusiasm for indigenous plants reflected an awareness of and a desire to promote things distinctively Australian. But there was a notable difference between those who knew and loved native plants, and the majority of gardeners. When Reginald Edwards, the horticultural editor of the *Australian Women's Weekly and Sunday Telegraph*, published *The Australian Garden Book* in 1950 he lamented the lack of an identifiably Australian garden and bemoaned the unimaginative use of English and 'Continental' gardening styles.

Although gardening has taken a great jump forward in Australia in recent years, we are still lagging behind other countries in many respects, particularly as regards the development of a purely local gardening sense or system of design . . . The only original touch I can see we Australians have introduced to our gardens after over one hundred and fifty years of work is the bush-house, and even this leaves room for improvement.[43]

Edwards, writing at a time when Australians were becoming increasingly concerned about what was distinctive in their culture, was searching for something identifiably and proudly Australian. The garden was a form of cultural, national expression.

It was not until the 1960s, with the invention of the 'bush' and 'native' garden, that the garden was seen to proclaim something uniquely Australian and the passion for growing native plants became more widespread. At last Australians, it was felt, had come to terms with their environment enough to want to replicate it in gardens. There is a certain irony, however, in the fact that bush and native gardens became popular at a time when the style of vegetation they were meant to replicate was increasingly to be found only beyond the city limits. If we see the increased use of native plants as marking a growing confidence about Australians' place in the landscape, we might also recognise that bush gardens were only planted in the suburbs, and only a few at that, when the surrounding bush had been all but destroyed.

It is also significant that, just at the moment when garden styles were being required to reflect distinctly 'Australian aspects', the arrival of large numbers of immigrants was causing Australian gardens to diversify considerably. Each new wave of immigrants brought with them particular gardening traditions. So while the popular trend for Anglo-Australians in the 1950s was away from the functional purpose of the backyard to a place for entertaining and leisure, for Southern European immigrants, the back garden was transformed into a highly productive space, supplying vegetables and herbs for the kitchen, grapes for wine-making, and the area and facilities to make wine, cure meats, dry fruit, etc. The garden was again a site for recreating the familiar and known in an alien landscape. The Southern European garden was distinctive in its use of space, its emphasis on productivity, and the incorporation of features not seen in older Australian gardens. Significantly, just as these traditional backyards were moving away from their functional focus, immigrants were using the garden in precisely this functional, productive way, and on a scale rarely seen in Anglo gardens. As these shifts occurred, so the garden became a marker of difference where the values and styles of the dominant culture became the standard against which 'taste' was measured.

Far from being the bland, unimaginative and unrewarding sites that Boyd describes, gardens can be seen as complex spaces invested with layers of individual and cultural meanings, where ideas about nation, citizenship, gender and place can all find expression. Although the style of gardens and the plants that go in them are subject to fashion and the vagaries of climate, the creation of gardens is a crucial 'ritual of habitation'.[44] Gardens reflect an investment in the future as well as the present. As one of the key features of our suburban living, they form part of our daily experience of landscape and reveal the variety of ways in which space, place and identity can be negotiated.

1  R. Boyd, *The Australian Ugliness* (Melbourne, 1960), p. 150.
2  M. Francis and R.T. Hester Jr (eds), *The Meanings of Gardens: Idea, Place, Action* (Cambridge, Mass., 1990); G. Seddon, *Landprints: Reflections on Place and Landscape* (Melbourne, 1997).
3  G. Davison, 'The Past and Future of the Australian Suburb', in Louise Johnson (ed.), *Suburban Dreaming* (Geelong, 1994).
4  For an account of Aborigines working in a homestead garden, see Aeneas Gunn, *We of the Never Never* (1908).
5  See D. Goodman for a discussion of the ways nineteenth-century landscape painting both erased and celebrated the history of the acquisition of land: Goodman, 'Gold Fields/Golden Fields', *Australian Historical Studies*, vol. 23, April 1988.
6  *Home and Garden Beautiful*, September 1911.
7  *Ibid.*, November 1911.
8  *Ibid.*, July 1914.
9  *Australian Home Beautiful*, October 1926. Walling was evoking a particular aesthetic here. In the tradition of the English garden designer Gertrude Jekyll, Walling combined formal and informal plantings and design, mixing the rustic cottagey influence of William Morris, as did Jekyll, with the formal structures of Edward Lutyens and William Robinson: P. Watt, *Edna Walling and Her Gardens* (Melbourne, [1981] 1991), pp. 57–60.
10  A. Latreille, 'Behind the Front Fence: Gardens and Gardening', in J. O'Callaghan (ed.), *The Australian Dream* (Sydney, 1993), p. 126.
11  *Garden Gossip*, September, 1928, p. 5.
12  *Garden Lover*, April, 1925, p. 2.
13  Melbourne, 1918, p. 49.
14  *Journal of Horticulture*, December 1910, p. ix.
15  K. Reiger, *The Disenchantment of the Home* (Melbourne, 1985).
16  I. Hoskins, 'Constructing Time and Space in the Garden Suburb', in S. Ferber, C. Healy and C. McAuliffe, *Beasts of Suburbia* (Melbourne, 1994), p. 5.
17  *Homes in the Sun* (Sydney, 1945), p. 5.
18  *Yates' Seed Annual*, 1900, p. 32.
19  *Ibid.*, 1903, p. 35.
20  Letter to Mr Davidson, Town Planning Commissioner, WA Town Planning Board Archive. Acc 955, AN 93/2, Item 527/36, 1936, 'Gardening Competitions'.
21  J. Foster, 'Brunning's Australian Gardener', *Meanjin*, vol. 47, no. 3, 1988, p. 416.
22  *Australian Gardens, Their Planning and Making* (Melbourne, 1949), p. 4.
23  Sydney 1950, p. 3.
24  *Home and Garden Beautiful*, February 1913, p. 145.
25  *Garden and Home Maker of Australia*, February 1931, p. 145.
26  *Australian Home Beautiful*, January 1926, p. 46.

27  Una Falkiner's diaries are held at ML MSS, 423/1–113, Mitchell Library Collection, State Library of NSW.

28  'Wendy O'Dowd' is a pseudonym. Letter dated 5 February 1953. Denholm papers, John Oxley Library, OM 71–15/1.

29  Chisholm, *Australian Gardens*, p. 59.

30  Malda Bertram, 6 August 1992, letter to the consultant on 'The Material Culture of Backyards' project, National Museum of Australia, Public Response Folder, vol. 2.

31  *Ibid.*, 27 October 1992.

32  J. Duruz, 'Suburban Gardens: Cultural Notes', in Ferber, Healy and McAuliffe, *Beasts of Suburbia*, pp. 204–5.

33  *Ibid.*, p. 206.

34  Hoskins, 'Constructing Time and Space', p. 13.

35  Reiger, *The Disenchantment of Home*, p. 170.

36  Mae Murphy, personal diary, 13 May 1944.

37  Deidre O'Donnell, 15 February 1993, letter to the consultant on 'The Material Culture of Backyards' project, National Museum of Australia, Public Response Folder, vol. 1.

38  *The Bouquet,* c. 1910, p. 20.                                                                181

39  W. Elliot, *Coles Australasian Gardening and Domestic Floriculture* (Melbourne, 1896), pp. 10–11.

40  *Home and Garden Beautiful,* July 1914.

41  *Gardening Simplified* (Sydney, c. 1934), p. 9.

42  *Journal of Horticulture,* July 1909, p. 4.

43  Edwards, *The Australian Garden Book*, p. 1.

44  C. Moore, W. Mitchell and W. Turnbull Jr, *The Poetics of Gardens* (Cambridge, Mass., 1903), p. vii.

# Connections

## Chapter 11

*Lionel Frost*

182     A house is its owner's or occupier's space, which may be used and personalised according to individual needs and wants. How this space is created and used and how people have lived their lives within it are central themes of most of the chapters in this book. But the way in which a house is built and occupied is also affected by what happens outside the property: the things that when a house is for sale every prospective buyer looks at, but the owner cannot do anything about. This is a simple but important point. In a particular context a house may be regarded as a good investment worth renovating; in another it may be seen as a slum fit only for demolition. An unsewered inner-city house with no indoor plumbing would be seen by many people as unhealthy and lacking in privacy; but with proper sanitary connections the same house would to many people offer a desirable way of living in a lively, cosmopolitan setting. A house dismissed as being part of a bare, bland neighbourhood of identical houses may in another time be seen as part of a leafy suburb, surrounded by mature trees and gardens and other houses which have been modified with individual touches. One house may have a smooth lawn leading to a low fence and a quiet street frontage; in another context the same house may hide behind a high brick wall in an attempt to keep the sounds and smells of heavy motor traffic at bay.

    In each of these cases the housing experience has been influenced by factors which are beyond the control of individual householders. The availability of network technology shaped what type of urban living environment would be available and how successful suburban development would be. The importance to people of housing as an investment, which would retain and hopefully improve its value over time, meant that basic ideas about style and living space were conformed to and repeated. Where people could build or buy, and the type of neighbourhood in which they could live, were affected by decisions about planning and land use which had been made in the past. These exerted a lasting impact on housing. This chapter will examine two types of connections: between housing and networks of tracks, pipes, wires and asphalt, and between the city of the past and that of the present (and future). Both played a major part in determining the quality of the housing experience, in ways which no individual builder or buyer could influence.

## Connections and the nineteenth-century city

From virtually the beginning of white settlement, the building of Australian cities was dominated by a preference for suburban, rather than town, living. Inspired by the example of middle-class Britain, which was the source of most Australian immigrants, planners and settlers began laying out areas of villas and cottages which were sufficiently distant to shield families from the problems of crowding and pollution associated with town centres, yet close enough for breadwinners to commute to town workplaces each day. For most people, disposable incomes were high enough for them to afford to buy or rent a house of their own, not one shared with other families. In Britain, a private house on an elevated site, preferably one freshened by sea breezes or mountain air, was something only the elite could aspire to. In Australian cities, such suburbs were within reach of the entire middle-class; cheaper versions, with flatter, more drab terrain and smaller cottages, were available for working-class families. Few developers offered the kind of multi-family tenement buildings which pre-dominated in continental European cities. One was the block of thirty-nine apartments built in central Melbourne in 1885 by philanthropists for working-class families. The flats were affordable, roomy and well-equipped, but only a few were let.[1] Most developers were better at reading the market. Workers wanted, and were mostly able to pay for, new houses in the suburbs, even though there was plenty of accommodation close to the city.

183

The first Australian suburbs were near to town centres. When free settlers first arrived in Hobart most of them chose land not in the town centre, where the convict and military population lived, but two miles north at an area called Newtown.[2] In Sydney, civil servants who worked in town but wanted to avoid living near shops and warehouses moved to the adjacent area of Woolloomooloo.[3] The district of Carlton, directly north of Melbourne, was surveyed just after the gold rush and became 'a semi-rural retreat' for the wealthy.[4] These areas were pioneered as suburbs by generally wealthy people who walked or took private carriages to town jobs, and pre-dated the arrival of piped water, sewerage, and paved streets.

As long as plenty of open space remained, such suburbs could retain their status as havens from city crowds, noise and pollution. With low population densities, backyard cesspits could be used safely and carters could deliver fresh water in a cost-effective way. But in growing cities such a situation could not last for long. As sites close to city centres became more built-up, wealthy residents tended to sell up and move to new areas further out. In the 1840s, Sydney had a substantial number of cottages 'which stood on land which afforded room for a fruit tree or two, and there were still areas of vacant land in the most central locations'.[5] By the following decade the charms of Woolloomooloo, for one, had all but vanished. The suburb had been infilled, with cheap houses built in the backyards of the original dwellings, linked by narrow lanes between the main streets. In 1858 W. S. Jevons observed that 'these back streets originally, perhaps, intended only to afford a second back entrance to the principal houses are rapidly becoming built up by additonal smaller houses; in time they will form crowded dirty lanes, removed from the public view, difficult to drain and ventilate, and little better than closed courts'.[6] In such areas, sanitation became a pressing issue because basic, labour-intensive methods of water supply and sewage disposal could no longer be used cheaply and safely. By now the areas which offered people the chance to live in a more secluded, countri-fied setting were generally beyond walking distance and could only be reached by inconvenient journeys over poor roads. What was needed to transform areas of surrounding farmland into suburbs was the introduction of transport facilities which were faster than walking, and cheaper than private carriages.

184

The provision of transportation and sanitation infrastructure is expensive because it has to be spread over large distances and often provided specu-latively, ahead of demand. For large-scale suburban development to take place, an institutional setting must exist or be developed which allows suburban devel-opment to be subsidised by public provision of infrastructure. Society must be prepared to meet some of the cost of developing suburbs, either directly by building public transport systems, or indirectly by giving private companies the right to lay tracks on public roads. In Australia, colonial governments were much stronger than their municipal counterparts. They worked actively to restrict the power of their potential rivals by taking responsibility for several aspects of urban infrastructure and establishing new municipalities to keep local government decentralised.[7] Local government remained weak and fragmented, while colonial governments could use their greater taxing and borrowing powers to tackle urban problems. The key boosters who controlled the pace of suburban development were those who sat in parliament.

During the nineteenth century this led to a fundamental distinction between the major cities. On the one hand, the Victorian and South Australian parliaments were dominated by members who lived in the capital, were sympathetic to suburban development, and in many cases profited from it. On the other hand, the New South Wales parliament was dominated by a 'country interest' which regarded Sydney as a vast parasite. There was fear and loathing in parliament about the size of Sydney and the way it drew young people and capital away from rural areas. As a result, the city corporation was starved of funds and power.[8]

At the height of Melbourne's land boom of the 1880s, six of the eight members of cabinet were directors of building societies or mortgage com-panies.[9] During this decade parliament boldly added to the capital's suburban railway system, seemingly safe in the knowledge that railway connections automatically led to suburban building and population growth. On new lines the stations were closely spaced—usually only about 900 to 1300 yards apart—to encourage commuting. When the depression hit, parliament was considering a grandiose scheme to build further railways across uninhabited potential suburban land, which Graeme Davison has called 'a grand strategy for the conquest of urban distance'.[10] As in Adelaide and Perth, railways had been required early in Melbourne's history because of the distance between the town site and its ports. In these three cities the streets were laid out in a spacious grid which provided ample space for a convenient rail terminus. Adelaide's rail network was more modest, being made up mainly of country lines and lines to Port Adelaide and Glenelg, which passed through suburban territory. But there was an extensive system of horse-drawn trams, perfectly suited to the city's flat, straight and wide streets. Melbourne's rail system was supplemented by a private network of cable trams, said to be the largest in the world.

The provision of piped water supplies also required heavy investment, but the labour-intensive delivery of water by private carters had so quickly become expensive that it was feasible for these cities to build reservoirs and reticulation schemes (Melbourne's opened in the late 1850s, Adelaide's in the early 1860s). These were an important aid to suburbanisation, because clean piped water and large lots enabled suburbanites to rely on cheap backyard cesspits without fear of contaminating nearby wells. The cities were dangerously unhealthy, however. Scavengers dumped the contents of Adelaide's cesspits in the city's parklands. The 'city of stinks from one end to another', as a contemporary described it,[11] suffered a run of typhoid epidemics during the first half of the 1870s. Melbourne stank, too, and this and recurrent outbreaks of typhoid led to considerable concern as to the adequacy of the sanitary arrangements. In 1878, at the height of Adelaide's land boom, work began on a sewerage system which eventually served the whole metropolitan area and conveyed wastes to a distant sewage farm for treatment.[12] In 1890 the Victorian parliament created a Melbourne and Metropolitan Board of Works to build a sewerage system and operate the city's water supply.[13] Melbourne's scheme, begun in 1897, was similar in character to that of Adelaide. There were no strong rivers or tidal outlets available in which sewage could be dumped to save costs, and so the schemes were necessarily expensive. In both cities, residents accepted that they would have to pay extra to improve the quality of the urban environment, and this says much for the incomes and aspirations of the population. Charges were increased and individual ratepayers had to pay for their own connecting drains and fittings. D. T. Merrett has calculated that in Melbourne the anticipated cost of sewerage to the householder was double that of the former labour-intensive method of collection.[14]

The other needed connection for nineteenth-century suburbs was gas, for lighting, heating and cooking. In Melbourne, a private company, formed in 1878 after a merger of gas companies, had a virtual monopoly of supply. The

185

monopoly produced economies of scale and the company invested heavily to serve every suburb, to keep potential rivals from gaining a foothold. During the land boom the company had a policy of extending the network ahead of supply. At the end of the boom it was apparent that overextension of infrastructure was not the preserve of the public sector.

Even if the New South Wales parliament had been full of Sydney boosters, it would have been difficult to improve the city's public transport system: when the first railway had been built in 1855, open space was limited and there was no room for a rail terminus close to Sydney Cove.[15] Rail commuting was limited not only to those who could afford the expensive rail fares,[16] but also an additional cab or omnibus ride to the central city. The streets were narrow and irregular and therefore not suited to trams. Given the city's hilly site and nearby waterways, the temptation to save money by draining untreated wastes into Sydney Harbour was overwhelming. There was penny-pinching, too, in the provision of water.[17] Sydney used steam trams, which were cheap but hated by passengers and nearby householders, and slow horse-drawn trams to move people. Because only a small proportion of the population could afford the time and expense needed for commuting by train or ferry, most people lived close to where they worked, or near horse-bus routes. Nineteenth-century Sydney was not a place where many people could get rich by investing in suburban development.

At the end of the nineteenth century, 'home' for most Sydneysiders was a place within walking distance of Sydney Cove. The city's woeful public transport system had forced growing numbers of workers to crowd into the housing of old middle-class suburbs like Woolloomooloo and Darlinghurst, where poor sanitation turned what might have been adequate housing into slums. There was a deterioration of the physical environment 'as rapid urban growth proceeded without adequate provision of the amenities likely to preserve the quality of living and the basic health of the citizens'.[18] While almost half of Sydney's houses in 1891 were terraces, only 11 per cent of Melbourne's were.[19] In suburbs like Paddington, linked to the city by horse buses, the terraces were expensive but well built and finished. But this was one of Sydney's better suburbs. For most workers, the high cost of housing was a reflection of the shortage of housing in convenient locations.

The citizens of Melbourne and Adelaide spent a similar proportion of weekly income on housing to their Sydney counterparts. The difference was that in the two southern cities people chose to live in railway or streetcar suburbs where the new houses—nearly all of them detached or in pairs—were roomier than those of the cheaper, old neighbourhoods. In areas like Richmond and Collingwood the houses were small and rented by low-income families. But because most workers could do better than this, the pressure on the inner-city housing stock was quite mild, and there was little demolition to make way for higher-density worker housing, as happened in Britain. Melbourne kept developing new suburbs, even though there were still sites vacant in its old ones.[20] The quality of public transport connecting these suburbs with city workplaces made those choices possible. Moreover, places like Williamstown, Footscray and Port Adelaide offered considerable local employment opportunities and abundant space for worker cottages. In 1888 Melbourne's *Daily Telegraph* noted smugly that, while 'Sydney, with all its natural beauty, is huddled up and dirty, ... Melbourne reaches out like an octopus.'[21] Melbourne's comeuppance, with the collapse of its speculative land boom that year and the depression of the following decade, was severe. For years afterwards the metropolis would have excess capacity in its networks of tracks, pipes and wires.

Network technologies in these cities were distinctive in other ways. Variations in the quality of drinking water and methods of sewage disposal have been noted. The streets of Adelaide were lit by electricity—although its use for domestic and industrial purposes was still in its infancy—while Sydney's were still gaslit. Each city had various small-scale generating plants supplying some local areas. Telephones were introduced at a fairly uniform rate, with Sydney and Melbourne opening their first exchanges in the same month in 1880, and Adelaide following a few years later.[22]

Something each city had in common was that house building was dominated by a large number of small-scale builders. Builders were short of capital and depended on quick, easy sales to repay their debts. Simple, popular styles were replicated, and experiments and eccentric embellishments were out. What had sold in the past was banked on as something that would sell or let in the future. Today, Sydney's nineteenth-century suburbs look like 'the work of some big developer intent on building the maximum number of houses for the minimum cost'.[23] In reality, the builders were people of modest means who lived locally and took years to complete rows of houses on lots that they usually owned. For them, similar houses were easy to build and let.

Uniformity was also important to buyers. Research on Adelaide in the late nineteenth and early twentieth centuries has shown that people moved house at a rapid rate: most of the original home buyers in new subdivisions had sold up ten years later,[24] and so considerations of resale value would have been uppermost in buyers' minds. As a result 'there was a basic sameness about the suburban houses that subdued the mass of individual decisions and tastes . . . Hence street after street within a suburb, and suburb after suburb throughout Adelaide copied one another; as each man's private castle looked reassuringly like the private castle next door.'[25] The basic view of a house as an investment connected the decisions of thousands of small agents and blurred individuality, creating what Sam Bass Warner called 'a kind of regulation without laws'.[26]

## Connections and the twentieth-century city

At the end of the twentieth century, Australian urban life is dominated by the same five cities—the mainland state capitals—which dominated it at the end of the nineteenth century. Sydney and Melbourne remain at the apex of the urban system. Brisbane and Perth have grown very quickly, especially since the 1960s. By the end of World War II Brisbane had taken over from Adelaide as Australia's third-largest city. Each of the five cities entered the century facing important infrastructural challenges. Brisbane was hemmed in by hills and the wide but meandering Brisbane River. Its railways terminated some distance from the city centre. In Perth, an extremely low-density urban area had been staked out by railways to Fremantle and Midland Junction. Melbourne, and to a lesser extent Adelaide, had a baggy infrastructure network which would take some time to grow into. Here the task was to maintain and modernise the networks.

It was Sydney, with more inhabitants than Adelaide, Brisbane and Perth put together, and still growing fast, which needed new public investment most urgently. In 1907 Alderman J. D. Fitzgerald called it 'The Cinderella of Cities . . . temporarily in the kitchen, covered with soot and grime, slovenly and out-at-heels, bedraggled and neglected'.[27] Fitzgerald looked forward to a replan-ned, improved Sydney, 'which travellers will come from the uttermost horizons to pay homage to'. For that to happen, it needed to be recognised that the unregulated growth and inadequate infrastructure provision of the past had created problems for the present and future. With the rising fortunes of the New South Wales Labor Party (of which Fitzgerald was president in 1915–16) and mounting political pressure from other quarters, the state began to improve the urban environment.[28] This coincided with the emergence of a school of reformers and town planners in Britain, France, Germany and the United States, which was inspired by Ebenezer Howard's view that the solution to the problem of urban slums lay in rehousing the poor in new 'garden cities'—planned urban areas built in open countryside (see Chapter 8). In Australia it was generally accepted that old, rundown inner-city housing needed to be cleared away and new, spacious suburbs opened up if urban problems were to be avoided.

Accordingly, at the end of the 1890s Sydney's network of suburban tram-ways and railways was electrified and extended and a new Central Station opened in 1906. These were like the first cracks in a dam holding back an immense volume of water. By 1911 the population of Sydney's old inner areas had peaked and in the subsequent decade the population of the suburbs increased by over 300 per cent. From 1911 to 1931 Sydney's population almost doubled, from 630,000 to 1.2 million. By the time the underground rail loop was opened in 1926 and the Sydney Harbour Bridge completed in 1932, a suburban building boom was under way.[29] Suburban developers now had the connections they needed.

Similarly, during the late 1890s Brisbane extended its tramways and improved its railway system by building an underground line and moving the terminus of the southern and south-eastern lines to South Brisbane. From there, commuters could walk or take a tram over a bridge leading to the city centre. All of Brisbane's population growth from 1911 to 1921 (from 140,000 to 210,000) took place in suburbs along the new tramlines and the improved railways.[30]

These improvements were part of a general process by which the public sector became more willing to improve the quality of urban infrastructure. Public capital formation had been dominated by railway building during the nineteenth century; from 1900 to 1930 roads, bridges, water supplies, sewerage and telegraph lines took an increasing share.[31] Electricity supplies were converted to public ownership and the larger plants and long-distance transmission provided economies of scale.[32] This provided the big cities with cheap power, creating new industries, especially those producing domestic electrical appliances, and increasing household electrical use. Houses which at the start of the century seemed modern, with their piped water, gas supply, and internal toilet, were now regarded as antiquated without electrical wiring. The radio, which like electricity itself had seemed mysterious at first, was within a few years taken for granted. The rapid adoption of the telephone—during the 1920s and 1930s the number of connections per capita more than doubled[33]—changed the way people socialised, enabling them to keep in touch with wider, more geographically dispersed circles of friends.

One of the contrasts between Australian and American suburban development during the inter-war period was that mass transit systems were run down in most American cities. These systems were privately owned and city governments refused to subsidise them. As systems became obsolete, commuters began using their automobiles, driving them on roads paid for by the general taxpayer. Land that was away from mass transit routes could now be reached by cars, and road building became an important causal factor in America's rapid suburbanisation. In Australia, public transport systems were publicly owned, and significant improvements were made to them. In Melbourne, the trains were electrified, tracks duplicated, and busy level crossings eliminated. Railway patronage was about 50 per cent higher in 1928–29 than it had been ten years earlier.[34] The private tramway companies were municipalised in 1919 when their leases expired, to facilitate electrification.

The electrification of mass transit routes encouraged the development of well-defined local shopping strips within walking distance of stations and tram stops. Railways and horse-drawn or cable trams had stimulated the growth of suburban centres, but electrification accelerated the process by placing more potential customers within a reasonable travelling distance. For instance, the building of a railway to the Melbourne suburb of Hawthorn in 1861 encouraged the growth of a village near the terminus, just over the bridge crossing the Yarra River. After the line was extended in the 1880s commercial developments sprang up along the main roads leading to the new stations, and the commercial hub of the Hawthorn area shifted from Hawthorn village to the station half a mile to the west, at Glenferrie Road. Glenferrie Road, like many booming shopping strips, had department and other stores to rival those downtown, and after its tramline was electrified in 1916 potential customers could travel

189

conveniently from crosstown St Kilda, Malvern and Kew. In the inter-war period Glenferrie Road was abuzz with crowds walking from the station or tram stops to dances, the pictures, or to late-night shopping.[35] Beyond walking distance of such routes, the land remained largely undeveloped.

As Robert Fishman, writing of the similar experience of Los Angeles, points out, these local centres, though largely unplanned, conformed strongly to the ideal of the 'garden city'.[36] Suburbs and their facilities were built in a way in which people could get around easily on foot, or by hopping on public transport, and there was a marked absence of pollution and overcrowding. In every major Australian city public transport was still the crucial connection which shaped the pace and location of suburban development, with towns along the routes being separated by large areas of open countryside. At the end of World War II Melbourne still had large areas of potential suburban land which were within walking distance of fast electric trains.

In 1918–19 there was only one car for every 103 Melbourne residents. Ten years later the ratio had fallen to one car for every twelve people.[37] The growth in car ownership was rapid, but from a very low base. Few people used them to commute to work during this period. Nevertheless, the car impacted significantly on housing styles, as buyers began to demand wider lots so that cars could be parked off the street and garaged. 'Now everyone, with or without a car, began to insist on room for a drive past one side of the building.'[38] By the 1930s garages had become 'standard additions to all but the poorest houses, but there were still not enough cars in Australia to fill them. In the poorest districts two out of three garages held nothing but children's toys and gardening equipment.'[39] As a result, houses were spaced further apart, a trend strengthened by the popularity of the ubiquitous Californian bungalow, which sat broadly across its lot.

The great boom in Australian car ownership occurred after World War II. Between 1947 and 1961 the total population of the state capitals rose by two million (a 50 per cent increase).[40] Australians had more money to spend, because employment was easy to find and wages were rising; they had more things to spend it on, because protected manufacturing industries were turning out a wide range of consumer durables. New Holdens were becoming increasingly affordable. By the end of the 1950s virtually every family owned a car.

Once people began to use their cars for commuting, which enabled them to build on suburban sites far from public transport routes, a new set of urban problems quickly emerged. Cities and their suburbs were typically short of wide, good-quality roads. On many main roads, trams and parked cars got in the way. As the flow of traffic increased, so did commuting times (one of the private costs of motoring), as well as the incidence of traffic jams, accidents, and the level of pollution (the social costs of motoring). As traffic poured into city centres, retailers complained that there was nowhere for customers to park. If traffic became gridlocked, housing close to city centres and along public transport routes would become very expensive. There was a general consensus among planners, visiting American experts, and editorial writers that new, high-capacity roads were needed if getting people to work was not to become a logistical nightmare. Melburnians were warned by the press that 'without drastic measures to meet the approaching crisis, the ultimate strangulation of the city's life appears certain'.[41]

It seemed, therefore, that the car, like any other allocation of resources, was subject to diminishing returns. Australian cities seemed to be heading towards a situation in which scarce resources—road and parking space, easily accessible land, and clean air—were being exhausted, adding to the costs of city living. It has been argued by Kelley and Williamson that these diminishing returns constitute natural limits to city size, which in time slow the rate of city population growth.[42] In fact, the experience of cities all over the world shows that people have been able to adapt to the rising costs of car usage and even turn situations to their advantage. Every time people adapted successfully, it confirmed that the same strategy should be followed in the future, and provided an example for others to follow. In other words, people received positive feedback. And when thousands of individual agents received positive feedback, patterns of behaviour began to emerge.[43]

Soon after World War II Australian manufacturers took up peripheral sites where the land was cheap and there was space for large factories to achieve economies of scale. These sites were on main roads which provided easy access for trucks. The needed labour force could live close by, often in public housing, and drive to work. Downtown retailers began to consider ways to reach potential customers who were scattered over large metropolitan areas. Kenneth Myer visited the United States several times in the late 1940s and early 1950s and saw for himself how American retailers had tackled the problem. He saw new shopping malls in the suburbs, close to consumers and with ample free parking. Myer purchased 30 acres of land in Melbourne's eastern suburbs and opened a shopping mall there in 1960.[44] Chadstone was not Australia's first drive-in shopping centre, nor was Myer the first retailer to establish suburban branches. But Chadstone did transplant whole a retailing innovation which would soon dot the landscape of cities all over the developed world.

In time, clusters of factories and offices sprouted along the main roads leading to these shopping malls. These sites are normally close to desirable residential areas where company executives want to live, and also within reasonable commuting distance for most workers. When it comes to eating out, the overwhelming preference of children is for places which their parents can drive to and order without leaving the car. For governments, improving road access to these areas has been an important way of attracting business and creating jobs. For the most part the only people who can work and do business in these 'edge cities'[45] are those who drive cars, but they have reduced business costs, commuting distances, and the need to live in expensive housing close to traditional city centres.

The success of these developments has made high car usage, despite the problems it creates, indispensable to business and everyday life. Through positive feedback, businesses know that they cannot be competitive unless they

191

can make it easy for clients and customers to park nearby; people know that it would be very difficult to be without a car; and governments know that they cannot create new jobs unless they devote resources to road building. Far from suffering diminishing returns, the car has been subject to increasing returns.

The elements of what Kenneth Jackson calls 'the drive-in culture of contemporary America'[46]—motels, drive-in theatres, fast-food places, service stations, and the decentralisation of factories, shops and offices—have become features of every Australian city. In any metropolitan area in Australia, all the suburbs of recent vintage look fundamentally the same. So much of what we know of the built environment of our cities is a twentieth-century creation, much of it dating from only the past two or three decades. Most Australians live and work in areas which, in an urban sense, have virtually no history at all. A case can be made that the distinctive history of pre-automobile cities is now irrelevant to the modern experience of urban living.

## Connections between the nineteenth- and twentieth-century cities

192

Or is it? The problems that cities face today, and the ability to do anything about them, have been shaped by the way in which people attempted to solve problems in the past. In some cases, the relevant past goes all the way back to the first acts of town foundation and planning. Path dependency is all about connections between the past, present and future. It happens whenever there is a sequence of events in which choices are made about the allocation of resources, from which it is difficult or impossible to turn back. Through positive feedback, this allocation of resources exerts a lasting impact, limiting the choices that can be made in the future. In this section I want to argue that path dependency has affected Australian cities, and the housing experience, in both positive and negative ways.

In examining the history of American cities such as Los Angeles and Detroit, one can detect such a sequence of events. The relevant decisions were made for what seemed at the time to be good, logical reasons, but that was because decisions that had been made in the past had reduced the number of options. In turn, this would create problems for later generations. American cities had typically coped with the pressure of population growth in the nineteenth and early twentieth centuries by opening up suburbs: at first served by railways and ferries for the elite and later by streetcars for the middle classes and other skilled workers. Working-class suburbs developed in some cities, with houses often being self-built, close to factories and other sources of employment. By and large, though, the suburbs were linked to downtown, the major shopping and commercial area. In the inter-war period, automobile ownership soared and new subdivisions were opened up away from public transport routes. There were complaints about mass transit: streetcar companies got into financial trouble and their services became slow and overcrowded. Downtown stores relocated to the suburbs, which also became the location of new industries. More people used cars for commuting and city voters chose to build wider roads rather than subsidise mass transit. In most cities the streetcar tracks were torn up. General Motors operated a subsidiary corporation which bought up bankrupt streetcar systems in Los Angeles and over a hundred other cities and converted them to bus routes.[47] In the south and south-west, small towns that became metropolises did so without any mass transit at all. Automobile and oil companies, real estate interests, banks, construction companies and labour unions all stood to benefit from urban sprawl, and after World War II they brought political pressure to bear on the federal government to provide funding for urban freeway building. People headed to new suburbs and left the old neighbourhoods to the underclass. The old city was scarred by 'brown-fields'—abandoned sites—which discouraged investment. The flight of tax-payers left those areas deprived of vital services, such as decent schools. Downtown areas lost their major shops and built new office blocks, but in the process became generally dead and dangerous after dark. Today, most new jobs are created in the suburbs, where the edge cities are. In some of the newest suburbs, the wealthy live in gated communities.

To say the least, this is an outcome which is best avoided. By and large, Australian cities have been able to do so (as have Canadian cities). Although these cities have much in common with their American counterparts, at certain key times there has been a different sequence of events which has taken them on a different path. Variations in their histories have taken them to other equilibrium situations, where the configuration of connections between houses result in different patterns of liveability and energy consumption.

The major Australian and Canadian cities are polycentric metropolises with suburbs as dispersed and car-dependent as anywhere in the United States. Where they differ from most American cities is in the higher densities of residents and jobs in their old cores and their greater reliance on public transport. Canadian cities have only one-quarter of the mileage of urban expressway per capita of their American counterparts, and have 2.5 times the per capita public transport patronage.[48] Vancouver, like Adelaide, still has no urban expressways, though this is not through want of trying by planners and road-building lobbyists. In the 1950s, when American cities were building freeways, Toronto built a subway system. The freeways that Toronto did build stopped short of entering the old inner neighbourhoods. Even though Perth is one of the most sprawling cities in the world, its per capita gasoline consumption is less than half that of Houston, Phoenix or Detroit. In Melbourne, where the old streetcar suburbs still have streetcars, more than 20 per cent of commuters use public transport; in Los Angeles and other similar American cities, the figure is less than 10 per cent.[49] Brownfield sites are usually snapped up by investors for townhouses and warehouse shells.

Many of the things which make the experience of living in Australian cities so pleasant are the outcome of historical forces and events. As noted previously, because of its initial planning Perth needed early rail connections to its seaport, and suburbs developed along the corridor of the line to Fremantle. When

Perth reopened its suburban railways in the 1980s, the right-of-way, the built-up suburbs and the population of commuters were already in place, greatly reducing the per capita costs of refitting the system. The development of strong colonial governments in Australia meant that the residents of low-income districts never suffered poor schools and other infrastructure because of the low tax base of their local governments. The consolidation of public ownership of mass transit meant that funding for maintenance and upgrading was often forthcoming. In certain circumstances it was possible for the actions of individuals to be magnified by positive feedback into something substantial and lasting. At a time when streetcar networks all over the world were being scrapped, chairman Robert Risson of Melbourne's Tramways Board had his system's tracks set in concrete to make them more difficult to remove. In Melbourne in the late 1960s a proposal was put forward for a massive program of freeway building which would have changed forever the character of the city's inner neighbourhoods. Public protests, supported by sympathetic trade unions, prevented the freeway plan from going ahead.

At the same time, the Australian tradition of urban sprawl has exerted a lasting impact in negative ways. The sprawl of wealthy suburbs and edge cities to Sydney's north and Melbourne's south and east has placed great distances between new jobs and the generally low-income populations of the cities' western suburbs. Since the 1920s Melbourne's Board of Works has found it difficult to meet the water and sewerage needs of new suburbs. Dingle and Rasmussen write that, the board, struggling to keep up with the rapid growth of housing that followed World War II, 'was like the runner restrained by a competitor tugging at the back of his singlet'.[50] What was holding back the board, and the other providers of infrastructure, was Melbourne's history. Every new house in the south and east took the board's pipes further away from its western suburbs sewage farm at Werribee. Sydney has persisted with its nineteenth-century method of sewage disposal because it is now too late to redesign and rebuild the network at an affordable cost. Sprawl not only raises the cost of infrastructure, but often makes the cost of replacing obsolete infrastructure prohibitive.

194

## Notes

1  G. Davison, *The Rise and Fall of Marvellous Melbourne* (Melbourne, 1978), p. 141.
2  R. J. Soloman, *Urbanisation: The Evolution of an Australian Capital* (Sydney, 1976), p. 28.
3  J. Broadbent, 'The Push East: Woolloomooloo, The First Suburb', in M. Kelly (ed.), *Sydney: City of Suburbs* (Kensington, 1987).
4  'Garryowen', *The Chronicles of Early Melbourne*, 1835 to 1852 (Melbourne, 1888), p. 30.
5  S. Fitzgerald, *Sydney, 1842–1992* (Sydney, 1992), p. 28.
6  'Remarks Upon the Social Map of Sydney', 1858.

7 D. Dunstan, *Governing the Metropolis, Politics, Technology and Social Change in a Victorian City: Melbourne, 1850–1981* (Melbourne, 1984); Fitzgerald, Sydney.

8 See Fitzgerald, *Sydney*.

9 G. Davison, 'The Capital Cities', in G. Davison, J. W. McCarty and A. McLeary (eds), *Australians 1888* (Broadway, 1987), p. 223.

10 *The Rise and Fall*, p. 166.

11 Royal Commission, 'Royal Commission into the Sanitary Condition of Melbourne, Progress Report', *Victorian Parliamentary Paper*, No. 27, 1889, p. 53.

12 L. Frost, 'Nineteenth-Century Adelaide in a Global Context', *Australian Economic History Review*, vol. 31, 1991.

13 T. Dingle and C. Rasmussen, *Vital Connections: Melbourne and Its Board of Works, 1891–1991* (Melbourne, 1991).

14 'Economic Growth and Well-Being: Melbourne 1870–1914: A Comment', *Economic Record*, vol. 53, 1977.

15 L. Frost, *The New Urban Frontier: Urbanisation and City-Building in Australasia and the American West* (Sydney, 1991), pp. 76–83.

16 A. J. C. Mayne, 'Commuter Travel and Class Mobility in Sydney, 1858–88', *Australian Economic History Review*, vol. 21, 1981.

17 D. Clark ' "Worse Than Physic": Sydney's Water Supply, 1788–1888', in M. Kelly (ed.), *Nineteenth-Century Sydney: Essays in Urban History* (Sydney, 1978).

18 S. Fitzgerald, *Rising Damp: Sydney 1870–90* (Melbourne, 1987), p. 226.

19 G. Davison, 'Australia: The First Suburban Nation?', *Journal of Urban History*, vol. 22, 1995, p. 61.

20 Frost, *New Urban Frontier*, pp. 116–18.

21 *Daily Telegraph*, 26 November 1888.

22 L. Frost and T. Dingle, 'Sustaining Suburbia: An Historical Perspective on Australia's Growth', in P. Troy (ed.), *Australian Cities: Issues, Strategies and Politicies for Urban Australia in the 1990s* (Cambridge, 1995), p. 24.

23 M. Kelly, *Paddock Full of Houses: Paddington, 1840–1890* (Sydney, 1978), p. 80.

24 P. Mein Smith and L. Frost, 'Suburbia and Infant Death in Late Nineteenth- and Early Twentieth-Century Adelaide', *Urban History*, vol. 21, 1994.

25 M. Williams, *The Making of the South Australian Landscape* (London, 1974), p. 457.

26 *Streetcar Suburbs: The Process of Growth in Boston* (Cambridge, Mass., 1962), p. 117.

27 Quoted by Fitzgerald, *Rising Damp*, p. 206.

28 R. Gibbons, 'Improving Sydney 1908–1909', in J. Roe (ed.), *Twentieth-Century Sydney: Studies in Urban and Social History* (Sydney, 1980).

29 See P. Spearritt, *Sydney Since the Twenties* (Sydney, 1978).

30 Commonwealth of Australia, Census, 1911–21.

31 L. Frost and T. Dingle, 'Infrastructure, Technology and Change: An Historical Perspective' in P. Troy (ed.) *Technological Change and the City* (Sydney, 1995), p. 27.

32 N. G. Butlin, A. Barnard and J. J. Pincus, *Government and Capitalism: Public and Private Choice in Twentieth Century Australia* (Sydney, 1982), pp. 251–8.

33 Frost and Dingle, 'Sustaining Suburbia', pp. 24–50.

34 A. J. Ward, 'The Development of Melbourne in the Interwar Years', PhD thesis, Monash University, 1984, p. 231.

35  V. Peel, D. Zion and J. Yule, *A History of Hawthorn* (Melbourne, 1993), pp. 117–21.

36  'Re-Imagining Los Angeles', in M. Dear, H. E. Shockman and G. Hise (eds), *Rethinking Los Angeles* (Thousand Oaks, 1996).

37  Ward, 'The Development of Melbourne', pp. 233–4.

38  R. Boyd, *Australia's Home: Why Australians Built the Way They Did* (Harmondsworth, 1952), p. 86.

39  *Ibid.*, p. 103.

40  D. T. Merrett, 'Australian Capital Cities in the Twentieth Century', in J. W. McCarty and C. B. Schedvin (eds), *Australian Capital Cities: Historical Essays* (Sydney, 1978), p. 172.

41  Quoted by Dingle and Rasmussen, *Vital Connections*, p. 242.

42  A. C. Kelly and J. G. Williamson, *What Drives Third World City Growth? A Dynamic General Equilibrium Approach* (Princeton, 1984).

43  See W. B. Arthur, 'Positive Feedbacks in the Economy', *Scientific American*, February 1990.

44  P. Spearritt, 'I Shop, Therefore I Am' in L. C. Johnson (ed.), *Suburban Dreaming: An Interdisciplinary Approach to Australian Cities* (Geelong, 1994), pp. 133–5.

45  See J. Garreau, *Edge City: Life on the New Frontier* (New York, 1991).

46  K. T. Jackson, *Crabgrass Frontier: The Suburbanization of the United States* (New York, 1985), pp. 246–71.

47  *Ibid.*, p. 170.

48  M. A. Goldberg and J. Mercer, *The Myth of the North American City: Continentalism Challenged* (Vancouver, 1986), p. 152.

49  P. W. G. Newman and J. R. Kenworthy, *Cities and Automobile Dependence: A Sourcebook* (Aldershot, 1989), p. 36.

50  Dingle and Rasmussen, *Vital Connections*, p. 214.

## Chapter 12

# The Comfortable House

*Graham Holland*

At their most basic, houses are shelter from the elements. This was the primary      197
concern of those disembarking to establish each new settlement and those
taking up land. However, the huts they built were expedient; reasonable comfort was sought as time, money, materials and skills allowed. This chapter seeks
to show how our houses provide comfort in the Australian environment. It
begins with the climate, points out the importance of culture in defining
comfort, and looks at forms, construction methods, building regulations, and
the use of energy. It points out the importance of subdivision patterns and
shows that, although knowledge may not have been used to make the most
comfortable houses, they may still satisfy, particularly in the benign seaboard
climate in which most live.

## The climate

As Plate 12.1 shows, Australia has three major climate zones; hot humid, hot
arid, and temperate, with sub-zones of sub-tropical humid, dry warm temperate, and cool temperate. Each zone has characteristic temperature and
humidity ranges, both seasonal and daily, and patterns of prevailing winds and
rainfall, again both seasonal and daily.

   The early settlements that have become the state capitals and where most
of the population live are (except for Canberra) on the seaboard; and they are
in the relatively benign temperate zone (except for Brisbane in the sub-tropical
humid zone) compared to the early settlers' cool temperate British origins. It
is, of course, possible to experience short periods of bitter cold and searing
heat in temperate Sydney and Melbourne, but these do not detract from their
overall temperateness. Watkin Tench, who had lived in America and the West
Indies as well as his native England, concluded in the colony's first year:

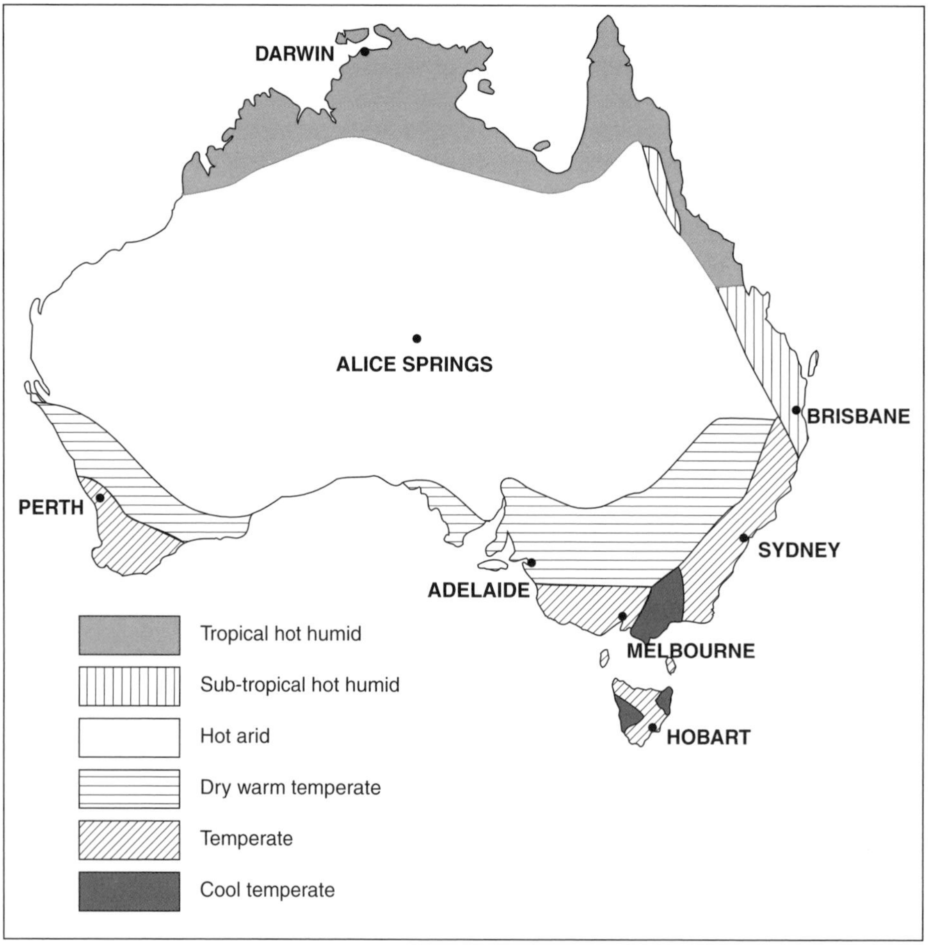

**Plate 12.1** Australian climatic zones. (Commonwealth of Australia)

> The climate is undoubtedly very desirable to live in. In summer the heats are usually moderated by the sea breeze, which sets in early, and in winter the degree of cold is so slight as to occasion no inconvenience. ... On the whole (thunderstorms in the hot months excepted) I know of not any climate equal to this I write in.[1]

In addition, each location has its unique micro-climate generated by topography, vegetation, buildings and other constructed objects, all of which affect the behaviour of buildings and the comfort of their occupants.

What is a comfortable house? Comfort encompasses temperature, noise, ventilation, lighting, and the control of intrusions such as dust, mud, water, insects and animals. It can be provided by passive means, using the fabric of the building and external objects such as other buildings, fences, and vegetation, and active means by the application of energy. However, as W. Rybczynski points out, comfort is also a cultural artifice that includes notions of privacy, ease and convenience, all of which have changed over time.[2] The evolution of ideas of comfort was influenced by changes in technology, but fundamental notions of domestic well-being did not change. A. Rapoport's seminal 1969 book showed the importance of symbolic and socio-cultural influences compared to physical functional criteria.[3]

## What are appropriate comfort levels?

It could be argued that appropriate levels of comfort are those chosen by the occupants. This could be so if the occupants had control over their environment, but in housing this has rarely been so, except for owner-builders who are in full control of design and building—although they have to compromise on cost, in many cases.[4] For the past forty years, most decisions about design and building have been made by project builders, who attempt to reflect market needs, and in turn influence those needs, but the extent to which they meet comfort needs is not clear.[5]

199

In most situations, temperature is the most important comfort factor, and will be emphasised here. A comfort zone which will suit most people can be defined in terms of dry-bulb temperature, relative humidity, air movement and radiation. Variables affect the values in each of these terms, such as level of activity, each individual's metabolic rate, clothing, acclimatisation and cultural values. Some of these variables have changed over time.

Cultural values affect standards set by statutory and semi-statutory bodies. Rapoport and Watson compared British, German and United States thermal standards for living rooms of 65, 68, and 73–75 degrees Fahrenheit (18, 20, 23–25 degrees Centigrade) and lighting levels of 150–300, 150–300 and 500–1000 lux respectively, pointing out that physical standards of such basic comfort criteria are influenced by their cultural context.[6] European recommendations for comfort in the hot humid tropics include lightweight walls and sufficient openings to provide good cross-ventilation. In contrast, a study of public housing in the hot humid Indonesian city of Surabaya found that the most favoured wall design was of fired clay bricks with relatively small openings. Almost all the respondents (95 per cent) preferred brickwork; 40 per cent gave climatic reasons such as the absorption of heat, and 30 per cent gave reasons to do with perceptions of strength and security.[7]

It is thus not desirable to define thermal comfort in narrow terms. It is preferable to design appropriately to meet appropriate ranges of dry bulb temperature, relative humidity, air movement and radiation, and to recognise cultural preferences. The Building Code of Australia (BCA) does not specify any comprehensive thermal performance criteria for dwellings; amendments for the Australian Capital Territory and Victoria specify insulation values for floors, walls and roofs, but relevant matters such as orientation and shading are considered only if a rating scheme is used to meet the code's requirements.

Noise sources affecting a dwelling's occupants and neighbours can arise within a dwelling or outside, from other dwellings or sources such as traffic, and aircraft. Acceptable levels have been hard to define and legislate for, and much still rests on perceptions of reasonable behaviour. For example, the BCA's objective is to 'to safeguard occupants from illness and loss of amenity as a result of undue sound being transmitted between adjoining dwellings'.[8] It sets standards for airborne transmission between adjoining dwellings for sounds that might be made, for example, by radios, and for structure-borne sound such as footfalls. Noise could clearly be a significant issue in higher density housing.

Some ventilation is necessary to prevent asphyxiation, and the BCA and its predecessors set out minimum areas of openings for dwellings. Most Australian dwellings have much more than the minimum, and standard construction is sufficiently 'leaky' to ensure safety. Air movement is significant for thermal comfort, increasing convective heat loss and accelerating evaporation. The cooling action of evaporation is most effective in low to medium humidity (40–50 per cent), and restricted in high humidity (85 per cent). The factors influencing comfort by air movement are sufficiently complex and subjective to defy legislation. However, most people find air movement of 0.25–0.50 metres per second is pleasant and above 1.5 metres per second annoyingly draughty.[9]

As with ventilation, most Australian houses have sufficient window area admitting enough natural light to enable most tasks to be carried out. However, this is not necessarily the case with attached dwellings, particularly those built in the nineteenth century. The BCA's objective is 'to safeguard occupants from injury, illness or loss of amenity due to (a) isolation from natural light and (b) lack of adequate artificial lighting'.[10] The natural light component is deemed to be met by windows that are not less than 10 per cent of a room's floor area, but levels of artificial lighting are not specified. The daylighting regulation has the hallmarks of a rule of thumb based on some experience, but cannot deal with other variables such as seasonal variations, external obstructions, external reflection, and glare. It is possible to predict daylight levels quantitatively by at least seven methods, and the levels are most commonly expressed as a daylight factor defined as 'the ratio of illuminance due to daylight at a point indoors on the work-plane to the simultaneous outdoor illuminance on a horizontal plane'.[11] The predictive methods could better meet the BCA's objective, but this approach has not been adopted probably because it has been assumed that it is unreasonable to expect house designers to have or obtain the expertise needed to apply it.

## Responding to the environment

As we have seen, Australia has different climatic regions, and the houses that evolved in each will be discussed separately.

The first settlements were on the seaboard. The forms and materials of the earliest houses were determined largely by the need for immediate shelter, the limited labour, tools and skills available, and knowledge of the local resources (see Chapter 3). The settlement at Port Jackson began with tents, and huts in which local timber was used as posts and beams, infilled with timber slabs or a mesh of lighter timber plastered with mud (wattle and daub). Bark, particularly from the stringybark tree, proved useful for roofing. Brick-making began in 1788, but in the early years bricks were used only for buildings of some importance, such as Government House. By the 1830s in Sydney and Melbourne, brick was the common walling for many houses, particularly those built as terraces. In contrast, when Adelaide houses progressed beyond immediate shelter, which was met as in Sydney and Melbourne, brick and stone was the predominant walling.[12] Brisbane did not develop brick houses to the same extent as Sydney and Melbourne, but used timber instead. As P. Bell points out, similar expedient responses arose in North Queensland, especially in transient mining settlements, but in spite of the presence of brickworks in some centres, such as Townsville, house building was in timber.[13]

As settlement moved inland, immediate needs were met with the same responses, and the methods required little alteration or adaptation. That is, they remained common when a new house (or more likely, hut), was needed whether in 1830 or 1870, so we can deduce that they were seen as the most appropriate.[14] For example, in the northern parts of South Australia, settled from the 1860s, stone and mud brick were used for walling, and the sparse timber was kept for roof framing.[15]

As the cities developed, brickwork became the most common walling, except in Brisbane. By the middle of the nineteenth century most building materials were available from either local or imported sources, including rough and dressed timber for structural or finishing use, slates, clay roofing tiles, corrugated iron, decorative cast iron, local and imported timber flooring, doors and windows, and various fittings. However, each city contained numerous examples of every kind of building method, from the most primitive as used in each colony's beginnings, to the most sophisticated and fashionable that local and overseas sources could offer.

Building for comfort figured little in the information available to emigrants. Writers about early Australia made little reference to the comfort of its houses. In his two-year stay in Australia, Richard Twopeny was not very impressed with the comfort of nineteenth-century houses. He observes that, although the sun's strong light and heat limit the number and size of windows, shutters were not common. However: 'Nearly every house that can afford the space has a veranda, which sometimes stretches the whole way round. The rooms are usually lofty for their size, in winter horribly cold and draughty, in summer unbearably stuffy in small houses, the science of ventilation being of recent introduction'.[16]

Joseph Elliot's detailed 1861 description of life in his modest single-storey stone cottage in North Adelaide makes few references to comfort. The narrow (4 feet) verandah on the front 'shelters the windows from the intense heat of the sun in summer weather, the frontage being to the East'. However, more protection was needed from the 'very strong and glaring' light, and two blinds and a curtain shielded the windows. Similar blinds and curtains covered the west-facing windows at the rear of the house.[17] The house may have offered enough comfort for him not to have remarked on it, and to tolerate its shortcomings.

Although the aspiration for a detached dwelling was clear from the early days of all settlements, many working-class residents lived in terrace and semi-detached houses. Though largely brick built, these forms obviously provide less opportunity for design to modify the climate: they have fewer walls available for openings, and there is likely to be a greater distance between the front and back walls, thus reducing the penetration of daylight and restricting air movement. From the 1880s in Sydney and Melbourne, the expansion of rail and tram transport enabled all classes to seize upon the possibility of detached suburbia (see Chapter 11).

Stylistic changes can also bring possible benefits to comfort. The changes in appearance from the Italianate Boom style of the 1880s to Queen Anne and Federation were dramatic, but the only potential changes to comfort might have come from the decorated verandahs, and the profusion of roof overhangs. In the 1910s, the Craftsman bungalow style found its way to Australia from the west coast of the United States, followed in the 1920s by the Californian bungalow. Both styles were characterised by more open planning, lightweight timber construction, wide eaves, covered porches, and extensive verandahs, and often had vents in the gable ends. Placed appropriately, these features could improve the thermal performance of a house.[18]

## Climate control methods

Early huts provided simple shelter and had few elements to modify the climate. The verandah has come to be regarded as one of the characteristic Australian elements of house design, for modifying climate, but even a simple verandah was not an automatic part of a basic hut, although it was the most obvious addition. The verandah was brought to the colony from many sources, including written accounts of the buildings of other colonies and former colonies, such as India (and India via England), South Africa, the West Indies, the United States, and by those who had lived in those places. P. Drew suggests that 'verandas were rare in the first two decades of settlement' and that 'Even after 1820, their construction is confined to the privileged classes.'[19] Most illustrations of early Sydney, such as Major Taylor's 'Panorama of Sydney' of 1821, show few verandahs or eave overhangs. Verandahs provided not only shade, but also shelter from rain as well as relatively cheap additional living space. They shaded the area in front of the house's wall, as well as the windows and doors in that wall. Their success in increasing comfort depended on the house's orientation, as we shall see. Many of the stylish villa verandahs were, at about 10 feet, relatively deep, indicating their usefulness as a place for relaxing and as a transition space between public and private areas. However, such verandahs also prevented the penetration of warming winter sun, and significantly reduced interior light levels. Two-storey villas with verandahs commonly had small roof overhangs and no external shading to upper windows, suggesting that reasons other than sun control were more significant. External shutters, roller blinds of bamboo canes, and tatties (screens of cloth on rollers that could be dampened to provide cooling by the evaporation of water, as in the Coolgardie safe), were not common. They would have been known to many from the same sources as the verandah, and could have provided more flexible control.

Queenslanders developed the verandah and its use into a minor art form. In sub-tropical North Queensland, early simple houses were of two side-by-side rooms similar in plan to those in most urban areas, but rapidly acquiring front and rear verandahs, with cooking and washing facilities housed separately. The sides of the house could also have verandahs, and the core rooms and verandahs were roofed with corrugated iron. Larger houses had four rooms with a corridor in the middle and similar verandah variations. Rear extensions could house cooking and washing facilities. However, the classic form of the Queensland house, from Brisbane to the north, was a symmetrical plan, usually, of four core rooms, surrounded by a relatively deep (10-foot) verandah. One of the consequences of this enclosure was to restrict cross-ventilation and reduce light levels, particularly to the core rooms, and thus increase the verandah's importance as a living space. As Plate 12.2 shows, where verandahs did not encircle the house, their location was not necessarily determined by the most appropriate orientation for sun control, but by orientation to the street, reinforcing their social and symbolic role.

Another classic Queensland characteristic is the setting of the house on timber stumps 6 to 10 feet above the ground. This had become common in North Queensland by 1880, and was becoming so in Brisbane by the same period. There is no clear evidence as to why this was adopted, but the most commonly accepted reasons are control of termites, protection from flooding, dealing with sloping sites, and to provide low-cost useable areas, but not to capture prevailing winds.[20] It is obvious that the micro-climate of suburban development would restrict wind flow similarly if all houses were low or high set.

The characteristics of houses in the hot humid north were also common in the dry warm temperate and hot arid zones. That is, they were of light-weight timber construction with similar window patterns, and had corrugated iron roofs and encircling verandahs. The miners' houses of Broken Hill are timber-framed, with walls and roofs of corrugated iron. Although such light-weight structures might be explained by the potential transience of mining

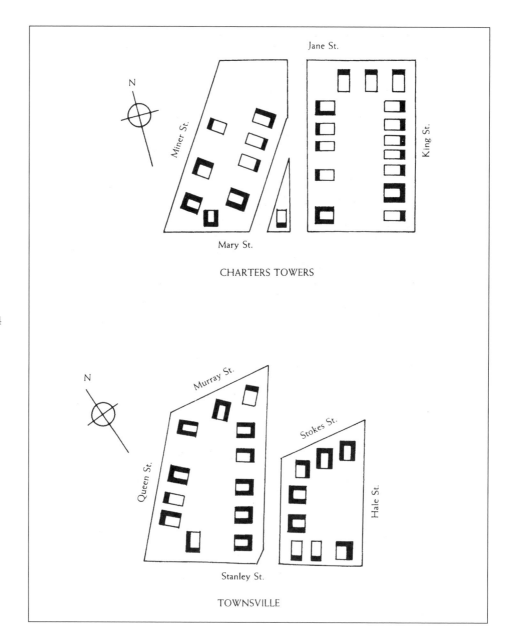

204

**Plate 12.2** Verandahs, streets and orientation. Plans of urban houses in two North Queensland cities showing the orientation of verandahs. (P. Bell, *Timber and Iron: Houses in North Queensland Mining Settlements, 1861–1920* Brisbane, 1984)

towns, Broken Hill and the houses have remained.[21] Heavyweight walls of stone or brick appear in some parts of Victoria and particularly South Australia. Lightweight walls and roof construction are not the most appropriate method for such zones, as they are less able to modify the significant diurnal temperature fluctuations. Glare and dust also reduce comfort. Shade from encircling verandahs reduces the heat load. As put to use in other regions, appropriate knowledge and experience would have been brought to Australia from, for example, India, including massive walls, small openings, courtyards, water, punkas, shutters, and tatties, all of which would, if used appropriately, be better climate modifiers than lightweight construction.

It is likely that lightweight construction was adopted because it could use readily available timber cut and assembled by relatively unskilled labour. Itinerant pit sawyers travelled the bush; steam-driven sawmills were in the cities from the late 1830s, and there were many in the bush by the 1860s. They did not require much capital to establish, and could supply the structure of floors, walls, and roofs, and floor and wall cladding.[22] Brickworks were also established in country towns, and many were able to make terracotta tiles. However, transport costs were higher for such heavy materials, and tiles were much more vulnerable to breakage on rough bush tracks than corrugated iron. Brick and stonework requires more skilled labour than timber framing, and rural Australia was always short of labour.

However, the most likely reason for the house form adopted was that it followed the British model of how a house was planned and what a house looked like. The books of advice on building did not include houses with internal courtyards.

## Using energy for heating and cooling

The coastal regions from Sydney south in most cases require heating for comfort during winter, but the fabric of the house can reduce the heating required. The performance of the fabric is influenced by the airtightness of openings and the building elements themselves, the fabric's mass, and its thermal insulation values. The expedient hut performed poorly in all aspects. The walling of masonry houses was more airtight than timber, and its greater mass moderated the diurnal temperature changes but had poor insulation values. Corrugated iron has negligible thermal mass and high conductivity and thus transfers heat quickly.

Many bush buildings, even the roughest hut, had a fireplace, but this was for cooking as well as heating. Overall, improved comfort came from active means. Until the 1930s, these were open fires burning timber or coal, after which more sophisticated enclosed solid fuel burners became available, along with electric and gas appliances. Wood, gas and electricity were also used to heat water, initially to one point, but later centrally.

205

Evaporative cooling was known to the ancient Egyptians, and was used in India. The Coolgardie safe uses the same principle, so it is not surprising that it was adapted to cool houses, particularly when electricity was available to drive fans to move air through moist filters. As the process raises the moisture content of the air, it is only suitable for dry regions. Air conditioning removes heat, but also dehumidifies air. It did not become common in buildings until the 1950s, and the first fully air-conditioned office building in Sydney dates from 1936.[23] Room air-conditioning units for domestic use became available in the 1960s, and are far more common than ducted systems. It is not possible to say to what extent the increasing use of these cooling methods is due to the need to make a poor design habitable, or to the desire for a higher standard of comfort.

## Regulation

Thermal comfort was also influenced by building regulations. The New South Wales *Building Act* of 1837 drew on the *London Building Act* (see Chapter 2); its primary purpose was fire control, requiring fire-separating party walls and the general use of incombustible materials. But it also prohibited projections beyond the street line, thus depriving the closely settled Sydney streets of window awnings, eaves and verandahs across footpaths and thus protection from the sun and rain. It was repealed in 1845 and street verandahs proliferated. Melbourne's *Building Act* of 1849 specified details of sizes and materials, with an 1859 by-law specifying corrugated iron covering. In all the major settlements footpath verandahs proliferated.[24]

Regulation applied only to the city centre. Even a suburb as relatively close to Sydney's centre as Paddington was without building regulation into the 1880s.[25] Country towns were similarly without regulation, and footpath verandahs for shops were commonplace.

Until the 1990s, for most houses regulation has had little effect on all aspects of comfort. As we have seen, except for amendments for the Australian Capital Territory and Victoria, the BCA does not have comprehensive thermal performance criteria for dwellings. The amendments' objectives are energy efficiency rather than comfort: in the Australian Capital Territory 'to facilitate the efficient use of energy in buildings' and in Victoria 'to prevent undue loss of energy from a residential building'.[26] The objectives can be met by achieving specific insulation values for floors, walls and roofs, or achieving a specified level in each state's energy rating scheme. The first method does not take orientation or size and location of openings in account; the second is more comprehensive.

These regulations do not have improved comfort as their objective, but the increased efficiency which may result is likely to increase comfort also. However, to meet the regulations will require informed design decisions, and thus comfort will rely on good design rather than regulation.

206

## Knowledge

One could be forgiven for thinking that much of the knowledge needed to create a comfortable house is common sense, based on intelligent observation. Principles derived from the application of such observation were put forward long before the rise of scientific method. Socrates and Vitruvius pointed out the virtues of appropriate orientation, shading and the location of windows for light and the moderation of cold winds. In the sixteenth century Palladio drew upon Vitruvius as well as his extensive practical experience to offer similar advice. The eighteenth and nineteenth centuries produced a number of books offering architectural advice, mostly on stylistic matters, but often containing sound practical suggestions. Emigrants to various colonies could go armed with books offering advice on building, farming, and an astonishing range of knowledge that might come in handy. However, few offered any advice on orientation, window placement, shading, verandahs or other matters that would influence comfort. Thomas Tegg's very popular *Handbook for Emigrants* of 1839 has a wealth of information on various building trade work, and included a list of tools that should be taken. He suggests taking a tent or prefabricated house, but gives no information on site or house planning or building. In his book *Two Years in New South Wales,* first published in 1827, Peter Cunningham described houses built of wattle and daub, layers of turf and stone, and how a house is built using split timber plastered with soil and cow dung and whitewashed. He did not comment on siting or orientation, but observed that a verandah cools by shading and is useful for cooling dishes of milk. His later *Hints for Australian Emigrants* has nothing on building.[27] Peter Nicholson wrote several books on architecture and building, offering much information on design and considerable details of trade work, but nothing on house design or comfort.[28]

There have been a number of professional advocates of appropriate responses to Australian climates. In his 1874 report to the South Australian parliament, the architect J. G. Knight described his modifications to prefabricated iron houses sent from Adelaide to Palmerston (Darwin) to make them more appropriate to the tropical climate, by increasing the size and number of openings to increase ventilation. After the responsibility for what became the Northern Territory was taken over by the federal government in 1911, the government housing responded to the climate with all the appropriate features: lightweight construction, shallow plans to maximise the opportunity for cross-ventilation, and verandahs and wide eaves, all of which were, by then, part of tropical housing vernacular.[29]

The architect Robert Haddon suggested a number of measures to improve comfort and thermal performance in his 1908 book *Australian Architecture.*[30] He advocates appropriate aspect, and his designs for modest houses for temperate, sub-tropical, and country areas take prevailing winds into account, those for the latter two areas have wide verandahs and shaded windows. He does not discuss window shading for 'suburban' houses in temperate climates, but his designs show awnings or shutters. Brickwork is preferred for all houses, but not for reasons of thermal mass; and the 'bush houses', implying houses of a lower standard, are of timber. He also recommends insulation and roof ventilation: 'as ceilings of attics are closer to outside roof surfaces than ordinary apartments, the roof should be covered with insulating material . . . windows secure the draught of cool prevailing winds'; 'Roof ventilation [is] by louvred gables near the ridge'; and 'closed-in roofs should be ventilated separately from apartments below them'.[31]

There is no clear evidence to show the extent to which 'intelligent observation' has informed the design of Australian houses. As we shall see, application of such observation can be limited by the planning of land subdivision.

More than intelligent observation became available after World War II. The Commonwealth Experimental Building Station was set up in 1944 on the recommendation of the Commonwealth Housing Commission. It systematically researched the performance of houses of various constructions, concentrating on thermal comfort. The results were summarised in J. W. Drysdale's *Designing Houses for Australian Climates*, which was first published at low cost in 1947, more readily available from 1952, and republished and reprinted continuously since. It was deliberately written to be accessible to all, and its observations and recommendations are set firmly in the context of local needs, industry capability, cost structures, and cultural aspirations. All that it recommends was, and is, readily achievable. Plate 12.3 is a table from Drysdale summarising its recommendations, and showing how straightforward they are. It also showed that some cherished beliefs were without foundation: for example, it exploded the myth that a house elevated on stumps is more comfortable indoors, pointing out that the coolest place in an elevated house is the space beneath it.

W. Bunning's *Homes in the Sun* was an attempt to popularise some of the main views of the Commonwealth Housing Commission's report. As executive officer, he had written much of the report, and his book included several house designs consistent with the principles in Drysdale.[32] It is not possible to say what influence it had; it is more likely that his designs published in the *Australian Women's Weekly* reached a much wider audience, as would its *Home Plans* book published in 1946. The architect-designed houses in the book are well oriented, with good opportunities for cross-ventilation, appropriate roof overhangs for shade, and much modernist emphasis on large areas of windows and the benefits of lots of natural light. As Greig has pointed out, the promotion by Robin Boyd (and his successor Neil Clerehan) of efficiency and modernity in his *Age* column and through the Small Homes Service included the application of good thermal design principles.[33] The various home magazines also supported their application.

Consideration of these principles was boosted by the energy 'crisis' of the 1970s. Domestic energy consumption had been largely the concern of the household, based on its idea of acceptable comfort and what it could afford. However, the 'crisis' focused attention on the amount of energy used by

| Element or Factor | Recommendations | | |
|---|---|---|---|
| | Hot-humid zone | Hot-arid zone | Temperate zone |
| Walls | Heavyweight construction or insulated frame construction for sunlit walls; otherwise frame construction | Heavyweight construction for living-rooms, dining-rooms, and kitchens; frame construction | Weight of construction not important, but provisions for hot-arid zone useful in districts remote from coast |
| Partitions | Frame construction adequate but heavyweight construction offers better resistance to transmission of noise | As for walls above | As for walls above |
| Roofs | Cladding and pitch to be selected primarily for weather-resistance. Roofs may be framed or of heavy-weight construction | Cladding and pitch to be selected primarily for weather-resistance. Roofs may be framed or of heavy-weight construction | Cladding and pitch to be selected primarily for weather-resistance. Roofs may be framed or of heavy-weight construction |
| Ceilings | Essential and if not insul-ated should be fixed clear of roof to permit roof space to be ventilated freely | Essential and if not insul-ated should be fixed clear of roof to permit roof space to be ventilated | Essential and if not insul-ated should be fixed clear of roof |
| Floors | Concrete on ground or sus-pended, or timber suspend-ed, as desired | Concrete on ground or sus-pened, or timber suspended, as desired. Enclose under-floor spaces, if any | Concrete on ground or sus-pended, or timber suspended, as desired. Enclose under-floor spaces, if any |
| Windows | Casements, top-hung sashes, louvres, used extensively to minimise blank walling | Casements, top-hung sashes, double-hung sashes or hori-zontal sliding, all capable of being closed tightly. | Casements, top-hung sashes, double-hung sashes or hori-zontal sliding, all capable of being closed tightly. |
| Thermal insulation | Desirable to provide at least 25 mm mineral wool or layer of reflective insulation between roof and ceiling, and in frame walls which cannot be shaded | Desirable to provide at least 25 mm mineral wool or layer of reflective insulation between roof and ceiling, and in frame walls though they be shaded | Advantageous to lay at least 25 mm mineral wool on ceil-ings, or layer of reflective in-sulation over ceiling joists of heated rooms |
| Vapour barrier | Not required, except where space is air-conditioned | Not required | Required in cool temperature regions, especially when walls and ceilings are insulated |
| Shade | Shade walls by eaves or with trellis or vegetation; shade windows with shutters or blinds, preferably externally | Shade walls by eaves or with trellis or vegetation; shade windows with shutters or blinds, preferably externally | Shade walls by eaves; ad-ditional shade optional; internal blinds adequate |
| Surface treatment | Not essential, but paint or base material should be of lightest practicable colour if wall or roof not insulated | Not essential, but paint or base material should be of lightest practicable colour if wall or roof not insulated | Surface treatments and colours of external surfaces not important, though light colours preferable if wall or roof not insulated |

209

**Plate 12.3** Drysdale's recommendations. (J. W. Drysdale, *Designing Houses for Australian Climates*, Bulletin No. 3, Commonwealth Experimental Building Station, Sydney, 1947)

the built environment, and prompted moves for greater efficiency in all its parts, including housing. This led to a flurry of research, publicity and the promotion of largely voluntary ways of reducing energy consumption, including the principles referred to above. Indeed, the greatest gains were correctly seen to be from the application of 'passive' principles (a term not used by Drysdale). Passive methods include orienting the dwelling, and using the fabric and planting to maximise the use of solar radiation, in contrast to active methods, such as increasing the efficiency of heating and cooling equipment.

It is difficult to demonstrate the degree to which these principles and their promotion have been applied in housing generally, or in the small proportion of housing designed by architects who would be expected to be familiar with them.

## Patterns of land division

As we have seen, ancient wisdom and scientific research agree that orientation and appropriate use of sun and wind are important for comfort. For houses in the temperate zones of this southern hemisphere, the optimum can be best achieved by orienting houses with their long axis east–west, with minimal openings in west-facing walls, and living areas facing north. The opportunity to achieve this depends, of course, on the pattern of land subdivision.

Most subdivision patterns begin with, or become with further subdivision, blocks of land with street frontages that are narrower than their depth, to reduce the costs of road building. Plate 12.4 shows that Sydney's early street pattern would have resulted in the frontages being oriented east–west. This can be accounted for by its topography, with the main roads following the ridges. However, Adelaide and Melbourne were not so influenced by topography and were laid out orthogonally to the cardinal compass points. Areas of North Adelaide and near the centre of Melbourne that vary from the grid do so for topographical reasons.[34] Thus some blocks may have a more useful orientation, but it is unlikely that this was the main motive for the pattern. Although the patterns of Adelaide and Melbourne were laid out long before the roads were built and development occurred, they defined the potential for optimising house orientation. The suburban subdivision plan shown in Plate 12.5 has both north–south and east–west patterns in the one area, suggesting that factors other than optimum house orientation determined the pattern. The street directories of Australian cities are a good guide to the patterns of subdivision, and observation on the ground with compass in hand of what has been built shows that optimum house orientation has not been a significant criterion.

The garden city movement represents the most persistent attempt to lay out suburbs on principles other than surveyors' often rigid geometry (see Chapter 8). The most eloquent spokesman of the British garden city movement

210

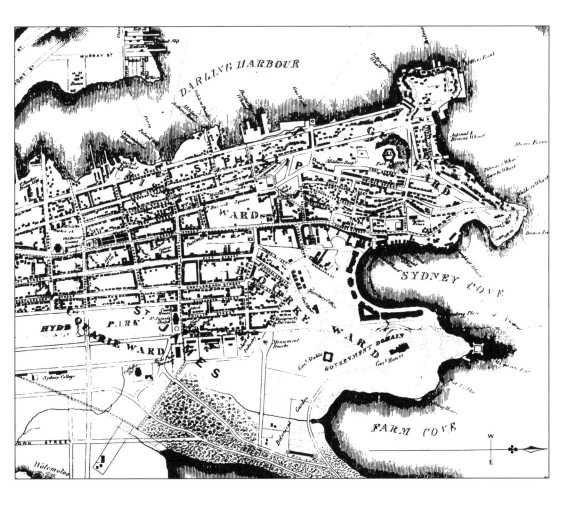

**Plate 12.4** Early Sydney. (S. Fitzgerald, *Sydney: 1842–1992*, Sydney, 1992)

was Ebenezer Howard and his book of 1898, *Garden Cities of Tomorrow*, had worldwide influence, including, not surprisingly, Australia. As R. Freestone observes:

> There was a distinctly Australian interpretation of the ideal urban environment—somewhat fuzzy but unmistakable with gum trees rather than elms, detached rather than group housing. The accent was still on spaciousness, orderliness, parks, trees: the planned community of happy homes. For most planners, and certainly the informed public, this was what the garden city ideal represented.[35]

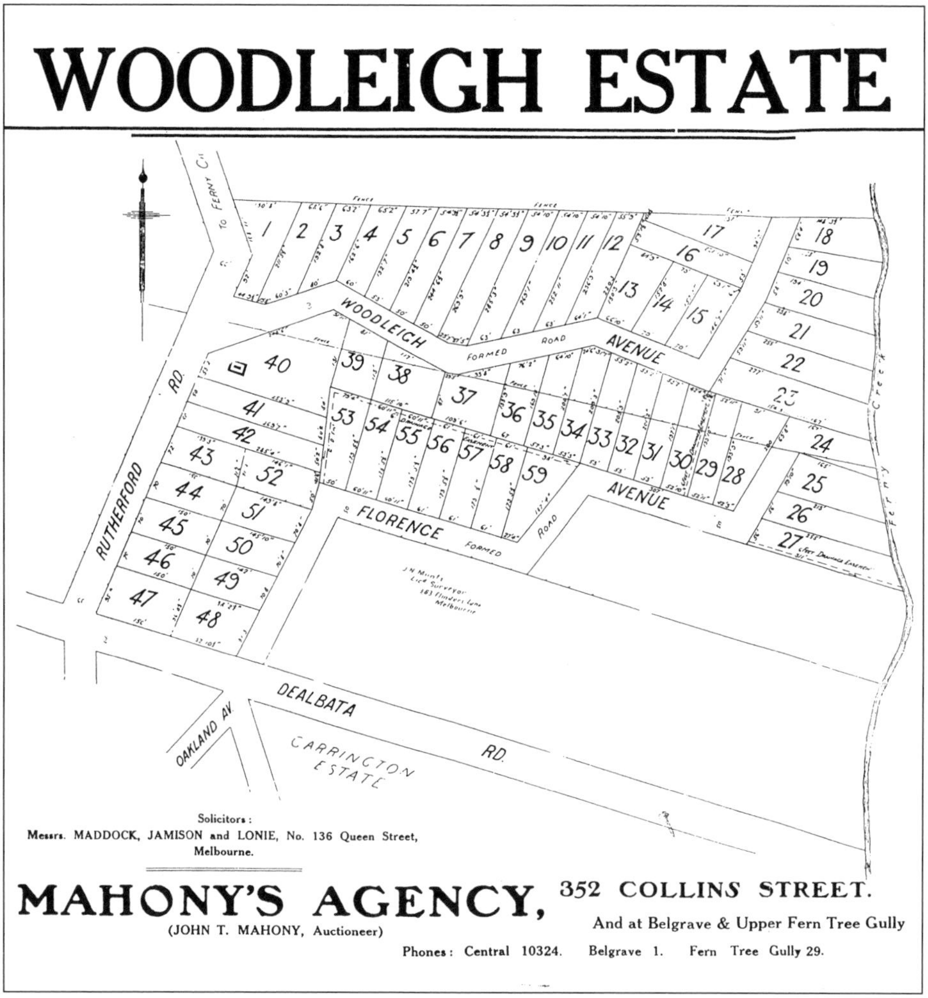

**Plate 12.5** Suburban subdivision, 1922. (J. Leeuwenburg, *The Making of Melbourne in Maps*, Sydney, 1987)

Freestone discerns several recurring themes in the promotion of the garden city ideal: a healthy, disease-free environment; reproduction of a virile race of white Australians; moral health; social stability; and a sound financial approach to urban environment. These themes were more or less expressed in developments at Haberfield (1904–14), Daceyville (1912–24), Matraville (1918–20s) (Plate 12.6) in Sydney; Novar Gardens, Allenby Gardens, and Galway Garden

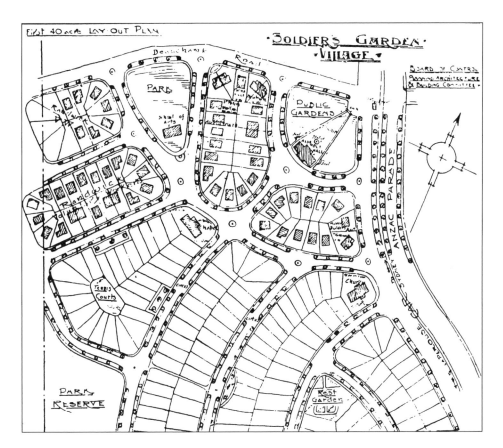

**Plate 12.6** Matraville Garden Village. (R. Freestone, *Model Communities*, Melbourne, 1989)

Suburb (1920s) in Adelaide; Sunnybank (1920s) in Brisbane; and Floreat Park (1937) in Perth. However well they demonstrate these themes, the plans show that optimum orientation for thermal comfort was no more common than in subdivisions not designed on garden city principles.

Some recent subdivisions attempt to provide layouts to improve orientation. Plate 12.7, depicting a development by the Sydney land and house developer Long Homes, shows that, on small blocks of around 400 square metres, it is possible to give some living areas solar access in winter.

Concern for appropriate patterns of land division persists with two publications sponsored by the federal government, *Australia's Guide to Good Residential Design* and *Site Planning in Australia*.[36] They link appropriate sub-

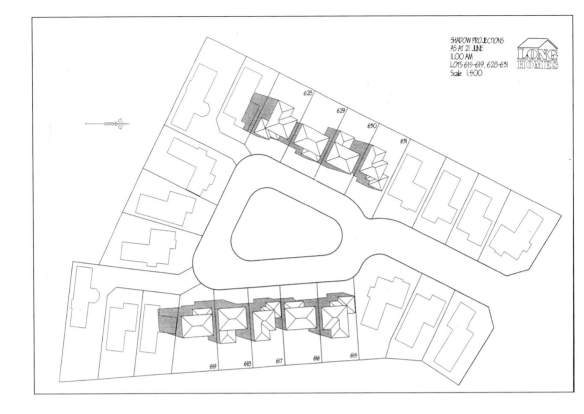

**Plate 12.7** Winter solar access. (Long Homes, Orlit Pty Ltd, Wentworthville, New South Wales)

division to urban consolidation, pointing out its benefits. It is not suggested that a particular subdivision pattern is needed to achieve these benefits, but that it makes them more readily achievable.

## Conclusion

Like most things to do with housing in Australia, it seems that comfort and its achievement combine to create a complex issue. It includes when the housing was produced and by whom; the materials available and used; the financial and technical potential to use energy; the pattern of land subdivision; and, perhaps most importantly, the attitudes and values of house owners. The verandahs of Sydney's early grand houses were as much, or more, a place of display and reception as protection from sun and rain; the placement of verandahs in

North Queensland in Plate 12.2 showed the importance of the relationship between the front of the house and the street.

The importance of the market can be further illustrated by the levels of insulation currently (1998) included in the base price of project houses offered by some of Sydney's major project builders and, based on anecdotal evidence, that of most Sydney builders. Up to about four years ago, builders included reflective aluminium foil insulation under tile roofs in the base price. This is a cost-effective way of reducing heat gain. Then a new market entrant began aggressively marketing houses that gave more floor area for the same price as its competitors by adopting a cheaper rectangular plan, reducing the quantity and quality of fittings, and omitting eaves and roof insulation. Its competitors were forced to reduce costs and prices and the omission of roof insulation was a simple step, saving about $400 without altering the houses' appearance. It appears that many buyers are aware of the costs and benefits, and many buyers of second and third homes pay extra for roof insulation.[37]

Project house plans are designed to be placed on the common sizes of blocks of land in one way, regardless of orientation. In the last twenty years living spaces are more often at the back of the house opening onto the backyard, but this is more a reflection of rising living standards because these areas are often in addition to, rather than instead of, the traditional placement at the front of the house. This makes it more likely that some living areas will receive the benefits of appropriate orientation. The moves to improve thermal efficiency through regulation and firm, government-sponsored persuasion are likely to improve comfort, but are also likely to increase the cost of housing, and do little to improve the performance of the existing housing stock.

There is little evidence to show how Australians use their housing, or to what extent they are satisfied with it in general, and even less on how comfortable they are. We know that significant amounts are spent on home improvements, but there are few indications of how much is to make the house tolerably comfortable, or to improve comfort levels, or to display wealth. For example, it can hardly be claimed that ducted air-conditioning throughout the whole house is necessary for comfort in Sydney. It has been suggested that as owner-built houses, where the owner is in full control of design and building, resemble project houses, perhaps what project builders build is what is generally wanted, including levels of comfort.[38]

215

> They don't build houses like that any more—not
> With verandahs the way they used to: wide verandahs
> Running round three sides of the place, with vines
> Growing up the posts and along the eaves—passion-
> fruit, grape, wisteria—and maiden-hair fern in pots,
> And a waterbag slung from the roof in the shade with the water
> Always cool and clean and tasting of canvas.
>
> R. F. Brissenden, *Verandahs*

I am pleased to acknowledge the research assistance of Sue Clarke in the preparation of this chapter.

1　W. Tench, *1788: Comprising a Narrative of the Expedition to Botany Bay and a Complete Account of the Settlement at Port Jackson*, ed. T. Flannery (Melbourne, 1996), p. 76.

2　*Home, A Short History of an Idea* (New York, 1987).

3　*House Form and Culture* (Englewood Cliffs, NJ, 1969).

4　G. Holland, *Emoh Ruo: Owner Building in Sydney* (Sydney, 1988).

5　G. Holland, 'Owner-building as an Expression of Popular Culture', *People and Physical Environment Research*, vol. 52, 1997.

6　A. Rapoport and N. Watson, 'Cultural Variability in Physcial Standards', *Transactions of the Bartlett Society*, vol. 6, 1967.

7　H. Sufianto and T. J. Williamson, 'Thermal Preferences of Low-Cost Housing Occupants in Surabaya, Indonesia', in A. Dawson (ed.), *Architectural Science: Its Influence on the Built Environment* (Geelong, 1994).

8　Building Code of Australia, 1996, Section 02.4.6.

9　S. Szokolay, *Environmental Science Handbook* (Lancaster, 1980).

10　Building Code of Australia, 1996, Section 02.4.4.

11　Szokolay, *Environmental Science*.

12　S. Pikusa, *The Adelaide House, 1836 to 1901* (Adelaide, 1986).

13　*Timber and Iron* (Brisbane, 1984).

14　M. Lewis, *Victorian Primitive* (Melbourne, 1977).

15　D. W. Berry and S. H. Gilbert, *Pioneer Building Techniques in South Australia* (Adelaide, 1981); H. Pearce, *Homesteads of the Stony Desert* (Adelaide, 1978).

16　R. Twopeny, *Town Life In Australia* (Ringwood, Vic., [1883] 1973).

17　J. Elliott, *Our Home in Australia* (Sydney, 1984).

18　P. Cuffley, *Australian Houses of the 20s and 30s* (Melbourne, 1989); G. Butler, *The Californian Bungalow in Australia* (Melbourne, 1992); J. Archer, *The Great Australian Dream* (Sydney, 1996).

19　*Veranda, Embracing Place* (Sydney, 1992), p. 42.

20　P. Bell, *Timber and Iron* (Brisbane, 1984).

21　G. Ashley, 'Two Centuries of the Western NSW Dwelling', in P. Freeman and J. Vulker, *The Australian Dwelling* (Canberra, 1992).

22　R. Irving, *The History and Design of the Australian House* (Melbourne, 1985); M. Lewis, 'Australian Building', work in progress, 1998.

23　H. J. Cowan and P. J. Smith, *The Heritage of Australian Buildings: An Historical Review of Australian Building Design and Construction* (Melbourne, 1998); N. P. Hunt, 'Air Conditioning of Railway House, Wynyard, Sydney', *Building*, 1998.

24　M. Freeland, *Architecture in Australia* (Melbourne, 1968); M. Lewis, *Melbourne: The City's History and Development* (Melbourne, 1995).

25　M. Kelly, *Paddock Full of Houses* (Sydney, 1978).

26　Building Code of Australia, ACT, Section 5.1; *ibid.*, Vic., Section 1.1.

27  P. Cunningham, *Two Years in New South Wales* (Sydney, 1966) and *Hints for Australian Emigrants* (London, 1841).

28  For example, *New Practical and Builder's and Workman's Companion* (London, 1822); *Builder's and Workman's (New) Director* (London, 1836); *Principles and Practice of Architecture* (London, 1841).

29  R. Allom, 'The Regional Dwelling', in Freeman and Vulker, *The Australian Dwelling*.

30  *Australian Architecture* (Melbourne, 1908).

31  *Ibid.*, pp. 48, 44.

32  W. Bunning, *Homes in the Sun* (Sydney, 1945).

33  A. Greig, *The Stuff Dreams Are Made Of* (Melbourne, 1995).

34  Lewis, *Melbourne*.

35  R. Freestone, *Model Communities* (Melbourne, 1989), p. 82.

36  Anon., *Australia's Guide to Good Residential Design* (Canberra, n.d. [circa 1996]); S. King et al., *Site Planning in Australia* (Canberra, 1996).

37  T. Keenan, Masterton Homes, Sydney, personal communication, 1998; T. Miller, Long Homes, Sydney, personal communication, 1998; R. Lemaire, A. V. Jennings, Sydney, personal communication, 1998.

38  Holland, 'Owner-building as an Expression'.

# Project Homes or Homes-as-Projects

FASHION AND UTILITY IN TWENTIETH-CENTURY AUSTRALIA

## Chapter 13

*Alastair Greig*

Most people familiar with the Australian built landscape can look upon a house and provide a rough estimate of its age, and they can often attach a label to its style. Renters and buyers in the housing market must obtain some degree of familiarity with these stylistic terms in order to discriminate among the abundance of houses advertised in weekend newspapers and weekly real estate magazines. Some rudimentary knowledge of a geographic location, socio-economic status or house style is an invaluable skill in determining whether to circle a house in the Saturday classifieds.

Like any fashion, the aesthetic value attached to a particular house style alters over time, regardless of its use-value. J. M. Richards claimed that sub-urban house styles experience a 'cycle of popularity', moving from the new-fangled, through the fashionable, the merely commonplace, the rather dowdy, the laughably old-fashioned, the out-of-date, the period piece to the museum piece.[1] The twentieth-century Australian experience suggests that approximately a generation elapses between the fashionable and the out-of-date.

Once the temporal nature of styles enters our consciousness, it remains difficult to feel secure in one's own aesthetic preferences and dislikes. Accordingly, this chapter avoids making architectural judgements on twentieth-century Australian house styles. Instead, it reveals some of the social forces that contribute to stylistic changes and explores the meanings which households attach to dwellings and the use of space. The chapter focuses on popular, rather than contrived, styles or on the ongoing search for the Australian vernacular. It remains on the plane of popular culture rather than high culture and the canons of taste.

After briefly describing changing architectural styles, I introduce two opposing analytical perspectives, both of which are useful for explaining changes in Australian house styles throughout the twentieth century—theories of mass culture and theories of popular culture. Combined, these perspectives help us appreciate the tensions that exist in cultural formation and cultural reproduction. I argue that this tension can be captured using Herbert Gans's perspectives of 'creator-orientation' and 'user-orientation'. I point out that both these apparently competing perspectives of mass culture and popular culture help highlight different aspects of the utility that social actors attach to the housing product. Houses are more than representations of historical periods. Houses themselves have histories that reflect and shape cultural change, but only through the households that dwell within and the wider social relationships they are engaged in.

## A brief overview of stylistic change

Although this chapter is concerned with Australian commentators' approach to the relationship between housing fashions and cultural change, the specific changes themselves need to be briefly identified.

There are a number of invaluable references for the history of Australian architectural styles. For instance, R. Apperly *et al.* classified post-1788 architecture into six key epochs, or 'periods'—Old Colonial, Victorian, Federation, Inter-War, Post-War and Late Twentieth Century. These six periods contain sixty-six different style characteristics although—as their style chart illustrates—in each epoch a number of styles have commingled or coexisted. While encyclopedic, their examples concentrate upon buildings designed by professional architects rather than the more popular houses which speculative and project builders have erected in the suburbs.[2]

A number of more popular texts have examined some of the generic styles referred to in Apperly *et al.* These include the Victorian Terrace, the Federation house, the Californian Bungalow, Inter-War styles and Post-War styles. C. Pickett has recently documented how most of these styles look dressed in fibro.[3]

If attention paid by Apperley *et al.* to historical variety gives a sense of perpetual motion in twentieth-century housing style, then Robin Boyd's history of the Australian home focuses more on structural continuity than historical change. This position was summed up in his famous claim that 'Australia is the small house'. However, Boyd also recognised the irrepressible nature of fashion cycles. Indeed, he believed that the small functional European country cottage fell in with the bad company of 'fashion' and 'jealousy' when it lost its way in the Australian city.[4]

Although he never committed all the stylistic detail to paper, Boyd could claim an even more discriminating eye than Apperly *et al.*, arguing that the first half of the twentieth century contained 'at least seven hundred varieties of small houses'. However, if these derivative cottages were stripped to their essence, they bore a striking resemblance to each other, there being 'no more than four or five types, within which were superficial variations like the individual contortions of a tree's branches'.[5] These plan types were the Primitive Cottage, the Bungalow, the Asymmetrical Front, the L-Shape and the Triple Front. Again, emphasising structural continuity, Boyd argued that the alterations in the plans through time merely 'resulted in differences in the external appearance of both the structure as a whole and of its component parts'.

Nevertheless, Boyd's stylistic variations became orthodoxy in classifying Australian historical fashions. These styles move from Georgian Primitive and Colonial Georgian to Gothic Revival, then on to Italianate and Boom Style before turn-of-the-century Queen Anne Revival, the inter-war Californian Bungalow, Spanish Mission and Waterfall Front and then Post-War Austerity. In his 1968 preface to *Australia's Home* he reiterated that 'in little ways the details keep changing. But the pattern seems to continue as ever.'[6]

Boyd performed an important service by stripping bare the 'small house' and revealing structural similarities. This might underestimate the cultural significance of fashion—what does stylistic difference mean? Yet, ironically, it is difficult to find an architectural historian who speculated as often and as playfully as Boyd did on the social significance of trimmings. As Geoffrey Blainey noted in his preface to the 1977 edition of *Australia's Home*, Boyd 'assumed that what the people did was more important than what was done in the name of the people', even if he did not always like what the people did and applied his wit to exposing what he saw as the pretentiousness of passing fashion. To employ the terminology introduced in the next section, while Boyd pointed out what a popular cultural history of Australian architecture could look like, his work never resolved this uneasy tension between a 'creator-orientation' and a 'user-orientation'. As Fiske *et al.* point out, his perspective on suburban style emphasised culture as mass-produced rather than popularly fashioned.[7]

## APPROACHES TO STYLISTIC CHANGE

Richards observed that the suburban villa is the 'despair of people with taste'. His remark characterises the cultural commentary on Australia as much as that on any other modern industrial society.[8] Mass housing has been seen as a reflection of mass society. Throughout this century, many cultural commentators have tended to dismiss Australian suburban dwellings as ugly, tasteless, alienating and soulless.[9] Yet, whether one condemns or celebrates the suburban built environment, one means of locating the causes of the visual effect is to use a continuum from supply factors to demand factors. Those who stress supply factors adopt a mass cultural perspective; those who emphasise demand factors adopt a perspective closer to popular culture. The former stress the role of those who produce and sell houses; the latter focus upon those who buy and consume them. The former emphasise the mass manipulation of consumers by capital and/or experts; the latter emphasise self-expression, desires and meaning.[10]

220

An example of a mass cultural perspective on the Australian suburban villa comes from Norman Day's 1976 claim that the 'standard "spec" house is the product of a marketing industry which creates trends to suit the demands which it also creates'.[11] More recently, in a controversy in *The Australian* sparked by an attack on modernism, an architect claimed that Australian mass housing 'fails abysmally' and blamed 'a conservative and complacent building industry which manipulates an ill-informed and timorous population'.[12]

Although mass and popular cultural perspectives can be analytically separated, most housing commentators throughout the century have argued that builders of speculative and project suburban houses carefully read the market, or the desires and aspirations of the consumer. This shifts the focus towards a more popular cultural perspective. For example, in 1908, Robert Haddon claimed: 'It is with the suburban villa that the greatest house-building activity will always prevail, and there good work and bad will the most commingle with the sway of popular taste, and the come and go of styles, mannerisms and modes of life.'[13] Half-a-century later, Robin Boyd echoed Haddon, claiming that:

> in the field of stylism, or fashion, most major developments were seen in the lower-middle-class bracket. In this class, most houses were designed by speculative builders, who judged carefully the tastes and desires of the average mistress . . . They instigated no fashions—this was left to experimenters and exhibitionists in upper-class homes—but they were sensitive to the fashion temper of society.[14]

This debate highlights the problems associated with extreme variants of both perspectives. Popular cultural theorists emphasise that consumers are not simply empty vessels into which the manipulating image-makers pour their hidden messages and signs. However, mass cultural theorists provide us with a timely warning against the idea of abstract, asocial, free-choosing individuals, as well as the ideology of consumer sovereignty.

Those who produce and sell commodities, and those who purchase and consume them, do not necessarily share the same objectives, meanings and orientations. Both mass and popular cultural perspectives grasp different elements of social encounters. A variety of orientations exist simultaneously in any such encounter. Herbert Gans referred to these different orientations—which correspond with mass cultural and popular cultural perspectives—as 'creator-orientation' and 'user-orientation':

> any item of culture may be evaluated from two perspectives—that of the creator and that of the user. The former views culture as existing for those who create it, rejecting any attempt to satisfy an audience: the latter looks at culture from the point of view of its users, and asks to what extent culture is meeting their wishes and needs.[15]

The next section examines explanations for the physical characteristics of houses, while the following section attempts to deepen these analyses by focusing upon the household inhabiting and shaping this space. This shift from house to household also corresponds with a shift from a more creator-oriented towards a more user-oriented approach.[16]

## Housing, style and utility

It is easier to uncover research on architectural values than on users' needs. In the mid-1980s, R. J. Holton lamented that 'the symbolic meaning of the visible features of popular homes and gardens has yet to be understood by social analysts'. This claim implicitly called for more research on the use of private space by households, such as I. Halkett's study on the use of suburban gardens.[17] However, a decade later, Graham Holland's review of cultural studies literature on housing and the built environment still found a 'remarkable dearth' in this field.[18]

This neglect of household utility is also evident in policy studies. Earlier Australian government reports—such as the 1944 Commonwealth Housing Commission report and earlier state government reports into the condition of working-class housing—devoted considerable attention to ways in which households used domestic space. In contrast, the National Housing Strategy, commissioned by the federal government in the early 1990s, paid little attention to such usage.[19]

However, over the past decade a number of attempts have been made to understand the meaning of Australian housing styles. In an innovative exploratory study of Australian popular culture, Fiske *et al.* adopted a semiotic technique of 'reading' advertisements for display homes and home magazines in order to interpret the meanings behind the popular myths of the Australian home. This methodology rejected the assumption that such cultural artefacts are mere expressions of mass cultural manipulation. Adopting a more user-oriented stance, they argued that within mass-produced style 'there is scope for the exercise of taste, and . . . taste, as a personal use of style, is where individuality is expressed within the social'.[20] Fiske *et al.* interpreted advertisements, styles and fashions as manifestations of a range of social contradictions, which household consumers must negotiate—tensions between elitism and egalitarianism, nature and culture, individuality and the social, the private and the public. Examples of such negotiations are found hidden everywhere: in builders' names, house labels, changing garden designs, floor plans, kitchens, barbecue areas and furnishings. The layers of meaning support the claim that the suburban home 'is not as simple, nor as banal, as it looks to many observers'.[21]

K. Dovey has added a comparative historical dimension to such semiotic approaches by analysing popular 'model homes' advertised in newspapers from

222

the late 1960s and the late 1980s. He argues that if advertising succeeds through its ability to tap 'a reliable experiential base' among consumers, then the promotion material for such model houses can act as a 'mirror in which a suburban subject is constructed, which at once reflects and reproduces the great Australian Dream'.[22] In this manner, we can begin to appreciate 'the social construction of the meaning of the house'. His textual analysis interprets changes in design, space zoning, division between formal and informal living space, backyards and house names as indicators of wider social changes relating to class and status, the role of women and the status of children within the household.

In an even more ambitious semiotic study, M. Lozanovska has used a post-colonial framework to deconstruct the migrant house in contemporary Australia. Her study interprets the style identified by Apperly *et al.* as 'Late Twentieth Century Immigrants' Nostalgic' as a constant threat to our ideal of multiculturalism. Noting—as did Apperly *et al.*—the disdain that 'people of taste' have towards this style, she speculated that:

> If the intention in the initial postwar policies was to have migrants fill gaps
> rather than contest space, the construction of these houses and 'enclaves'
> constitutes some sort of territorial claim that not only contests with such an
> intention but that is a constant threat to Australia's difficulty, as a nation, to
> deal with cultural difference.[23]

223

Lozanovska suggests that housing style can be a form of subaltern resistance to dominant cultural practices and discourses.

The strength of these semiotic approaches lies in their recognition of the tension between creator-orientation and user-orientation. This tension is a reflection of the distance between the 'text' and the user. As Fiske *et al.* noted: 'the Australian accent is to be found not in the texts themselves, where capitalism seems to hold unchallenged sway, but in the uses made of those texts as they are incorporated into the structures of everyday life'.[24] The cultural artefacts on display in advertisements and magazines might reveal the dreams and aspirations of readers, but this does not necessarily correspond with the use which readers and consumers make of the texts and products.

However, these semiotic perspectives have been subjected to a number of criticisms. R. Madigan and M. Munro have claimed that Fiske *et al.* overstated 'the freedom of consumers to impose their own meanings' on received artefacts.[25] A more important methodological criticism involves the gap between theoretical intention and the evidence presented. Despite their avowed concern to reveal user-meanings, the types of texts dominating their attention —magazines, display home advertisements, backyards and public housing architecture—rarely capture the users' voices. This criticism has been made by Holland, who notes that the 'meanings' uncovered owe more to the author's interpretation than those of consumers and users. Accordingly, we still 'know little about the attributes, motivations and values of those who buy houses. The fact that particular houses are bought does not mean that they meet the physical and cultural needs and wants of those who buy them.'[26]

However, despite the largely conjectural nature of this body of research, its speculative, interpretive starting point is the stuff of any good hypothesis-generating study. As Fiske *et al.* argued:

> If 'imaginative' or 'creative' are not words normally associated with a description of suburban living in Australia, that is due to the poverty of cultural analysis of the society to date and its inability to even hint at the reasons why most Australians make sense of their lives within that most maligned of environments, suburbia.[27]

Other researchers have also started to explore the meaning of the home from a more user-oriented perspective. Thorne has observed how illustrations of different types and styles of houses elicit different responses among audiences. Holland has conducted in-depth interviews with owner-builders in an attempt to understand the significance and meaning of design to this unique form of producer/consumer. S. Thompson has examined the 'private domain of domesticity' to interpret the lived experience of migrants and the nexus of household, ethnic and national power relations they are enmeshed in. Following her earlier research on the family, L. Richards has conducted interviews with households in newly subdivided estates in order to understand how they experience 'community', and has measured the gap between 'dreams and realities'. Indeed, some of the most informative insights into user meaning have been conducted on the 'suburban frontier', usually with a much broader research purpose in mind. In another interesting and innovative housing study, Geoffrey Bolton examined the evolution of a single Perth street, focusing not only upon the changing architecture, but also upon the experiences of the individuals who lived within and moved through the dwellings.[28]

Despite their diverse intentions, one similarity that these recent approaches share is a greater sensitivity to the 'meaning' of the house and to the way households understand their use of domestic styles and spaces. As this section has argued, even though semiotic studies recognise the need to move beyond creator-orientation towards user-orientation, most have retained a *methodology* which emphasises production rather than meaning, and have focused on the promotion of the physical dwelling rather than the household occupying the dwelling space. In other words, they still tend to 'fetishise' design and architecture by abstracting them from their user context.[29] To appreciate how style is used, it is also necessary to appreciate the meanings that different social agents in different situations attach to the space they confront and help shape. This involves analysing the tension between creator-orientation and user-orientation within specific domestic circumstances. From this perspective, the household will tell us as much about the meaning of style and the use of space as the house itself.

## Households, fashion and utility: The presentation of the household in everyday life

In the previous section I noted how semiotic research uses house designs as texts that reveal changing social relations. I also argued that their interpretive analysis tends to remain 'creator-oriented'. This section examines how households use space in order to negotiate a series of tensions that arise out of contemporary living: tensions between the household and the outside world; tensions within the household unit; and ideological tensions which confront each individual.

### INTIMATES AND OUTSIDERS

The dramaturgical analogy employed in this section is borrowed from E. Goffman, who presents society as a series of 'productions', in which social beings require complex communicative skills in order to maintain normality under specific circumstances and make credible their dramatic performances.[30] This analogy helps reveal a range of social tensions that face individual members of households when acting out their various roles and identities on different stages, public or private.

225

Goffman's dramaturgical analogy was extended by A. de Swaan to the study of domestic architecture and the development of intimate family relationships under modernity. The credibility of our intimate performances requires a distinction between the public 'front stage' and the more intimate 'back stage':

> Modern domestic architectural layout is such that it permits the family as a unit to withdraw behind the wings . . . and stage an appropriate performance for those outsiders who are allowed in. Equally, each grown-up family member is allotted some 'backstage area' . . . where he or she can take care of bodily grooming, prepare for acting out a suitable part in the family proceedings, or join with someone else in some exclusive activity such as parental intercourse or teenage sociability.[31]

This dramaturgical analogy can articulate a number of aspects of design and style through the language of intimacy as a functional requirement of modern households.

For instance, many commentators have observed how the distinction between front and back stages is written into design. J. D. Porteous pointed to the 'sanctity' of the threshold as the 'fundamental divide' between the space that we feel we can control, and the less predictable and more vulnerable public world. Madigan and Munro have claimed that this boundary marks the distinction between the display of socio-economic status (the front, exterior, fashion, style, taste) and utilitarian design (the back, interior, intimacy, need).[32]

These stages also appear in the semiotic approach of Fiske *et al.*, who note that, even though front gardens reveal a variety of meanings which the household wishes to convey to the public, one consistent message is that 'the house itself is private property'. Dovey has also illustrated these different 'stages' in the Australian trend towards the differentiated backyard, with a section dedicated to leisure (the 'front' of the backyard) and a screened-off utilitarian section (the 'back' of the backyard).[33]

Innovations that attempt to 'rationalise' dwelling sites, or that attempt to protect pedestrians and children from traffic, such as the Radburn design (which separates walkways from cars through rear-entry cul-de-sacs), often fail to accommodate this symbolic importance between front stages and back stages. The aspirations which Glaswegian tenement dwellers expressed for a 'door of our own'—discussed in Chapter 1—can also be interpreted as a desire to overcome the symbolic ambiguity between front and back stages evident in the architecture of the open tenement stairwell or 'close'. However, the close assumed the symbolic appearance of a threshold, or personal front stage, the higher one climbed the stairs. As my father recalls: 'Third-level tenants, although having the disadvantage of climbing sixty stairs to get to their door, had the advantage of no through-traffic passing their door and no noise from the neighbour above.' However, this feeling of greater sanctity experienced by top-floor tenants often failed to compensate for the 'added risk of severe flooding and ceiling collapse if the water piping busted and released the contents of the water storage tank that was located immediately above them'.[34] The symbolic advantage of a threshold came at the substantial cost of functional disadvantages. On the other hand, the street plans of the Queensland bungalows discussed in Chapter 12 reveal how the symbolic reference to front and back—in this case the verandah—often takes precedence over functional concerns such as siting, sun, shade and comfort.

Once we move into the interior of the home, this distinction between front and back becomes more complex. When outsiders make their entrance within domestic homes, they need to negotiate a series of stages, and must take their cue from the organisation of space. For example, Fiske *et al.* revealed the way interior layout leads or ushers the guest towards the living room, which represents not only the communal centre of the household and its withdrawal from the public but also its 'showcase'. Quips from intimates to guests such as 'Don't mind the mess' or 'You'll have to take us as you find us' are intended to convey the sense that the setting has not been arranged for the sole purpose of public display and that other more intimate scenes take place in this space.[35]

## THE BATTLE FOR INDIVIDUAL PRIVACY AMONG INTIMATES

Yet domestic space is not organised simply to keep outsiders from intruding and household intimates safe from detection. Although this household/ outsider level is scripted into domestic space and its symbolic utility, there is another level that is equally important. Continuing with Goffman's analogy, the householder/outsider script is overlain by other scripts between household intimates.[36]

This issue of individual privacy between household members has been discussed in the Australian context in Dovey's comparative historical analysis of home plans, where he notes a shift between the 1960s and the 1980s towards greater zoning of domestic space. This zoning is most marked in the spatial relations between children and parents. He argues that this shift towards more complex zoning is conceived by designers as a solution to specific social problems, 'wherein the warring generations retreat to opposite ends of the house and meet occasionally in the great room to negotiate treaties'.[37]

On the other hand, the spatial (re)zoning of the family home has been hailed by many as progress, and a welcome departure from the modernist fad of open-plan design. However, this sentiment began to be echoed in home magazines as early as the early 1960s.[38] Chapter 7 also suggested that the debate over whether to merge or divide domestic spaces has been played out numerous times in Australia's history in accordance with changing conceptions of comfort.

As we consider individual requirements for intimacy within households, rather than households' retreat from the public gaze, the demarcation between front stage and back stage develops more layers. Dovey shows that a creator-orientated approach can make important social changes more transparent through the evolution of style and space.[39] However, the focus on the creation of space still cannot capture other social tensions within households that can only be understood by looking at how users shape and understand space. The negotiation of domestic space is not left solely to designers attuned to contemporary household conflicts. To continue with the dramaturgical analogy, each household member is forced to rewrite their spatial script in innovative ways that reflect their own individual characteristics due to the relative scarcity of space.

Even though the average size of the Australian family home has been increasing over the past few decades, few households have sufficient space to dedicate to each key function and pastime pursued by their members.[40] As a result: 'Privacy in the home is something to be negotiated within the constraints of the physical space available.'[41]

One means whereby households apportion this space is through 'time zoning' of space. Time zoning, or 'time-staggered use of space', is an important, though often neglected, aspect of social relations within a family home. This form of negotiation is a reflection of the reality that 'men and women have different patterns of work' and have predictable routines.[42] As an example of the importance of such household routines, consider the problems that arise when household patterns are disrupted by unemployment, school holidays, retirement, or lengthy visits from friends or relatives. These events and interactions disrupt the routines upon which time zoning of space is negotiated.

An obvious example of time zoning is the use of the bathroom, where an individual has the right to the exclusive use of its scarce and valued facilities without intrusion, yet also without monopolising or personalising the space permanently. In the last twenty years the inclusion of the ensuite in many houses has converted the use of this valued facility from time zoning to space segregation.

Another space where household conflict often requires negotiation is the living room, especially the use of the television set and the video recorder. Parental monopoly of this space and its focal resource in the evening can be achieved either by sending children to bed (which often leads to secondary conflict) or, when the weather and season permit, by sending them to play outside for a respectable period of time. This conflict over television time zoning has gradually abated over the years for a number of reasons. Dovey noted the growing popularity of the family room between the late 1960s and the late 1980s, enhancing the zoning of space by activity.[43] Another means of conflict resolution is the purchase of additional television sets, often placed in children's bedrooms. This means of negotiating time and space has been resolved in a similar manner to the bathroom and the family room, through distributing more resources through space. Parents have been able to increase their use-time of the family room through their control of the family budget, by luring children into other parts of the home.

228

Another potential arena of conflict between parents and children in the living room occurs over its use as a play area. Although this function results in an untidiness associated with the back stage—comfort, ease and intimacy —parents also need to regularly recycle this space as the public front stage for guests and visitors. The inclusion of the rumpus room was one means of overcoming the tension between the different stages that the family room symbolises. In this manner, parents are able to dedicate a space to children that remains 'behind the scenes' and therefore unaffected by perceived public standards. The tensions that households (especially parents, being engaged in more secondary social relationships) must negotiate are those between the front stage and the back stage: on the one hand, a place to relax, feel comfortable and let down one's guard; on the other hand, a place in which members of the household can reveal what they want about themselves to the world.

Although the average Australian family house has increased in size during the twentieth century, the average household size has declined, as has the fertility rate.[44] Despite these long-term trends, the amount of energy and resources devoted to children has increased. This is reflected in the increased space devoted to children within the family home. As suggested here, this expansive colonisation by children can be interpreted as a negotiated solution for individual intimacy within the household. By supplying children with additional space and additional electronic goods, parents overcome the potential conflict over the use of scarce resources, in particular spaces, which they recycle as the household's front stage. The growing possession of domestic consumer items and expanding space might express more about evolving household relationships than about economic well-being.

It is at the level of gender relations that the need to move beyond the household-as-a-unit becomes most acute. Research in Britain by Madigan and Munro suggests that women are the most active household members in this process of negotiating space. They demonstrate that 'privacy, and by implication the home, has very different meanings for different members of the household, women, men and children, as a result of the systematic differences in their patterns of work, economic independence (or lack of it) and social expectations'.[45]

Madigan and Munro advance a range of reasons why women tend to perceive and experience the home in a manner different from men and children. Existing research suggests that these arguments also pertain to contemporary Australia. First, according to S. Watson, women tend to predominate in many low-income Australian household types. Second, despite recent changes in workforce patterns, the home still occupies a more central role in many women's lives than it does for men. Australia-wide data gathered by J. Baxter and D. Gibson revealed that 'married women, in the majority of cases still bear the brunt, if not the entirety, of domestic and parental responsibilities'. Third, at the level of consumption as well as the symbolic level of meaning, men and women experience the home differently, and attach different meanings to security, affection and comfort. Lyn Richards's research in outer suburban Melbourne revealed that 'home' means different things for men and women, and that countervailing insecurities such as high mortgage repayments often thwart the dream of security. Fourth, the intensification of socio-economic processes that encouraged greater social interdependence over the past century have also involved an ongoing process of spatial segregation between work and leisure, employment and residence. Reiger's work on the prewar evolution of the Australian family and analysis by Game and Pringle of postwar consumerism and the suburban dream reveal the extent to which gender and sexuality were spatially as well as socially constructed through the demarcation of masculine and feminine space.[46]

The salience of gender relations in the meaning of the home adds a further complexity to the dramaturgical analogy of front stage and back stage. There is clearly more to housing studies than houses. The house, the home and its meanings—whether in the form of intimacy, security, ownership, or comfort—is experienced differently by individual household members.

## STYLE, UTILITY AND HYBRIDITY

In addition to the tensions between the home as a place of personal relaxation (back stage) versus the home as a showcase meeting social expectations (front stage), Madigan and Munro have indicated two other associated tensions which contribute to the difficulties that users face in aesthetic judgement and which

229

mediate between fashion and utility. These include, first, 'the idea that consumerism is something to be rejected and to be seen as out-of-date, or old-fashioned is a personal condemnation'; and, second, 'the belief that things should be selected for utility and comfort competing with the desire for things which are new and look new'.[47] The final section of this chapter considers these contradictions and makes some observations on the discrepancy between 'grand historical styles' and actual household lifestyles. Rather than ask why styles *appear*, it examines the more user-oriented question of how styles are *picked up*.

The first observation that needs to be made is that new dwellings represent only part of the housing market, and that the majority of households make do—usually through choice—with living in and modifying the existing housing stock. Thus, the majority of houses in any era were built for households in previous generations, and these houses had different use-values and different stylistic and appeal values. Houses do not simply reflect the period in which they were built. They also have their own histories. G. Connah has pointed out that stylistic developments are far more complex than chronological sequence implies:

230

> Houses are rarely artefacts frozen in time. As the years go by they are extended, or parts of them are demolished, internal walls are removed or new ones built, windows are replaced, doors are changed, and many smaller fittings wear out and have to be replaced . . . many houses have very complex structural histories. It is not enough merely to say that a particular house is of such-and-such a style.[48]

This reinforces Bernard Smith's warning that buildings cannot be taken 'on trust' visually.[49] Many houses are demolished before their use-value has been spent, and many others are renovated beyond recognition. As W. Rybczynski notes, houses 'must survive the ravages not only of time but also of fashion'.[50]

Because the new-home market represents only a small proportion of sales, it is arguably more relevant to examine what people do with the houses they buy 'secondhand'. This is one of the neglected fields of Australian housing studies. A user-oriented perspective might look more at used houses, either from a semiotic perspective such as Fiske *et al.* or Dovey, or from a perspective of buyer preference such as Thorne.

The newspaper advertisements mentioned at the beginning of the chapter often indicate both the ravages of time and fashion, physical wear and cultural meaning. As Richards pointed out, the ravages of time can be reversed. Compare the following illustrations drawn from the *Age*: 'Aspire to Victorian Gothic' (Taradale); 'The years haven't been to kind to this wonderful grande dame of Edwardian architecture' (Caulfield North); 'Beautifully presented Edwardian family residence' (Hawthorn); 'Affordable—unrenovated Victorian style with lots of scope to improve' (Coburg); 'Authentic Californian Bungalow with charm and character' and 'Great opportunity to renovate 1940s style' (Box Hill); 'Period charm—1890s sophistication' (Caulfield South); 'Single-fronted Victorian worker's cottage' (Brunswick). Not all examples of period style have period 'charm'; some have scope to 'improve'. Not all houses are 'residences'; some are merely 'properties'. Some dwellings are ready for 'restoration', others require 'renovation'. You 'aspire' to some houses, while others are merely 'affordable'. At the top of the market, the home-hunter can find not merely a well-presented charming period piece, but a residence with its own individual name and age such as 'Avondale 1903'. Some houses are personified as 'grand dames' fallen on hard times, while others are merely 'workers'. This secondhand market can tell us as much about social change, class, status and location as the new housing market that is the focus of Fiske *et al.* and Dovey.

Furthermore, the word 'potential' in advertisements is not simply used negatively in order to lower customers' expectations of the condition of a property, but also, more positively, to suggest that the owners can shape their own dreams out of the house for sale. One's heart need not sink coming across the word 'unrenovated'—and not everyone need 'aspire' to Victorian Gothic, no matter how pleasant they find it.[51]

A second observation concerning the use of historical styles involves the value of historical 'texts'—whether visual, such as physical dwellings, or documents, such as magazines. Their use in revealing 'period style' and especially 'lifestyle' requires care and qualification. When we read through the most recent *Vogue Living*, *Australian Home Beautiful* or *Australian House and Garden*, we need to suspend disbelief to accept that the images represent how our contemporaries are living, especially the poorer among us. The same suspension of disbelief must therefore also apply to the use of such resources as historical evidence. A reading of period magazines can often uncover not only the 'essence' of a style, but also the strong 'resistance' of publics to specific fashions and styles being promoted.

Dovey explicitly qualifies his semiotic findings in this regard, conceding that the houses advertised do not necessarily live up to their creator's claims or necessarily provide an accurate picture of the consumers' life. What such approaches can do is unpack 'the form of discourse, to interpret the nature of the myth and to understand and articulate the experience with which the dweller is *asked* to identify'.[52] By 'de-naturalising' the Great Australian Dream— or 'making it strange'—we add another dimension to cultural analysis. This allows us an insight not only into what the dream and the style 'delivers' but also what it 'denies' and what it 'promises'.[53] Magazines tap into 'everyday experience', and also into the dreams and desires of readers and consumers, and the texts help illustrate this important component of our aspirations.

At any particular point of time, there is invariably a wide discrepancy between what the mass market has on offer and what people possess. A focus on the temptations of the mass market tends to overemphasise the importance of the supply side of the cultural equation rather than how households lived.

231

Few households can afford to buy all their household items at any one time and, as a consequence, an individual household is more than likely to contain an ever-changing eclectic mix of fashions.

Many households are unable to enter the new furniture market at all, and rely on hand-me-downs and secondhand household items from a previous era. Once this financial constraint is recognised, the limitation of reconstructing grand historical styles becomes more apparent. Many other households retain and display items that have an emotional value (heirlooms), regardless of contemporary style. There is a more gradualist reality to fashion and design than stylistic 'periods' can capture, and fashion lags with people's means.[54] In addition, for many, fashion sense (whether design, clothes, music or literature) often develops during particular formative years and is retained regardless of pressure from mass marketing. Stylistic hybrids are the norm, rather than the period ideal types found within magazines. Understanding this hybridity remains a challenge for Australian housing research.

As a consequence, historical analyses that focus on identifying what the mass market has to offer and what advertisers are trying to sell at a particular point of time might capture a sense of 'ideal-type' period styles, but inevitably they overemphasise what producers have on offer when determining the meaning and utility of commodities, rather than what people make do with. If we look solely at the orientations of designers, professionals and marketers, we lose sight of the tensions that help construct 'reality'. As Holmes recognised in Chapter 10, to capture this tension it is necessary to use a range of materials, from magazines, manuals and novels, through to more personal manuscripts such as autobiographies, letters, diaries and interviews. As de Swaan argues, because housing professionals appear to constrain and shape our choices, 'nothing is more obvious than to explain everything in terms of the professional's design . . .but there are latent dependencies and latent resistances that work the other way'.[55] This section has speculatively glanced in that opposite direction, employing a more user-oriented approach.

## Conclusion

As the first section of this chapter demonstrated, the classification of twentieth-century Australian architectural styles provides a rich insight into 'the visions of individual architects'. It then examined a number of semiotic approaches that have attempted to unpack the meaning of house styles as popular cultural artefacts. The value of these approaches lies in their ability to reveal the aims of producers and advertisers, as well as delving into the dreams, desires and aspirations of those who constitute 'the market'. Following Gans, I labelled these approaches creator-oriented, and contrasted them to user-oriented approaches. User-oriented approaches have focused more on communities and households and provide a more detailed picture of how consumers incorporate images, styles and products into their everyday life. An additional advantage of user-oriented approaches is their greater sensitivity to the hybridity of style as found within actual homes, rather than reconstructing images of ideal period styles.

However, the methodologies applied by both creator-oriented and user-oriented approaches help reveal different aspects of the meaning of style as a social encounter. A user-oriented perspective—focused on the household—is an appropriate means for approaching lifestyle and utility, but a creator-oriented perspective—focusing on popular cultural artefacts such as house advertisement and magazines—is an appropriate means for appreciating style and fashion. A significant proportion of the difference between the approaches can be explained away as the 'mismatch' that Holland observed between the creators' values and the users' needs.[56]

## Notes

1  *Castles on the Ground: The Anatomy of Suburbia* (London, 1973), pp. 46–7.
2  R. Apperly, R. Irving and P. Reynolds, *A Pictorial Guide to Identifying Australian Architecture* (Sydney, 1989), p. 20.
3  For the terrace house, see B. Turner, *The Australian Terrace House* (Sydney, 1995); for the Federation House, see G. Butler, *The Californian Bungalow in Australia* (Melbourne, 1992); for the Californian Bungalow, see T. Howells and M. Nicholson, *Towards the Dawn: Federation Architecture in Australia, 1890–1915* (Sydney, 1993); for inter-war styles, see P. Cuffley, *Australian Houses of the '20s and '30s* (Melbourne, 1989); for postwar styles, see P. Cuffley, *Australian Houses of the Forties and Fifties* (Melbourne, 1993) and J. O'Callaghan (ed.), *The Australian Dream: Design of the Fifties* (Sydney, 1993); and for fibros, see C. Pickett, *The Fibro Frontier: A Different History of Australian Architecture* (Sydney, 1997).
4  *Australia's Home: Its Origins, Builders and Occupiers* (Melbourne, 1991).
5  *Ibid.*, pp. 7–8.
6  *Ibid.*, p. xviii.
7  J. Fiske, B. Hodge and G. Turner, *Myths of Oz: Reading Australian Popular Culture* (Sydney, 1987), p. 45.
8  Richards, *The Castles on the Ground*, p. 15.
9  See A. Gilbert, 'The Roots of Anti-Suburbanism in Australia', in S. L. Goldberg and F. B. Smith (eds), *Australian Cultural History* (Cambridge, 1988); and T. Rowse, 'Heaven and a Hills Hoist: Australian Critics on Suburbia', in *Meanjin Quarterly*, vol. 37, no. 1, 1978.
10  See R. Madigan and M. Munro, ' "House Beautiful": Style and Consumption in the Home', *Sociology*, vol. 30, no. 1, February 1996.
11  Quoted in J. Archer, *The Great Australian Dream: The History of the Australian House* (Sydney, 1996), p. 227.
12  *The Australian*, 2 February 1998.
13  Quoted in Archer, *The Great Australian Dream*, p. 140.

14 *Australia's Home*, p. 12. More recently, G. Holland claimed that 'the extent to which these houses can be an expression of popular culture is limited' due to the control which builders exert over the design and construction process. Holland argued that for housing to be a more accurate expression of popular culture, the divide between production and consumption needs to be minimised. Owner-building is therefore the quintessential expression of popular culture. However, noting the difficulties distinguishing owner-built from speculative and project houses, he also concluded that 'project builders are reading the prevailing culture well'; see 'Owner Building as an Expression of Popular Culture', *People and Physical Environment Research*, vol. 52, 1997, pp. 24–6. R. Thorne has adopted a similar position on the relationship between producer and consumer; see 'Housing as "Home" in the Australian Context', *People and Physical Environment Research*, vol. 26, April 1991.

15 *Culture and High Culture: An Analysis and Evaluation of Taste* (New York, 1974), p. 62.

16 This literature I engage with tends to restrict its universe of discourse to 'the modern family home' or 'the dream home', and tends to work on the assumption that it is inhabited by a two-generation nuclear family. Therefore, the findings and speculations in the remainder of this paper must take this qualification into consideration.

17 See R. J. Holton, 'Twentieth Century South Australia: From a Patrician to a Plebeian View', in E. Richards (ed.), *The Flinders History of South Australia* (Adelaide, 1986), p. 579; and I. Halkett, *The Quarter Acre Block* (Canberra, 1976).

18 'Owner Building as an Expression of Popular Culture', p. 20.

19 S. Thompson noted that, despite the breadth of its scope, 'the Strategy ultimately pays very little attention to the meanings which people imbue their lived spaces and the significance of this for housing policy'; see 'Home: A Window on the Human Face of Planning', in R. Freestone (ed.), *Spirited Cities: Urban Planning, Traffic and Environmental Management in the Nineties* (Sydney, 1993), p. 151. This observation is not confined to Australia. R. Madigan and M. Munro have levelled a similar criticism at contemporary British housing policy: 'Gender, House and "Home": Social Meanings and Domestic Architecture in Britain', *Journal of Architectural and Planning Research*, vol. 8, no. 2, 1991, p. 127.

20 Fiske *et al.*, *Myths of Oz*, p. 34.

21 *Ibid.*, p. 45.

22 K. Dovey, 'Dreams on Display: Suburban Ideology in the Model Home', in S. Ferber, C. Healy and C. McAuliffe (eds), *Beasts of Suburbia: Reinterpreting Cultures in Australian Suburbs* (Melbourne, 1994), pp. 128, 146–7.

23 M. Lozanovska, 'Abjection and Architecture: The Migrant House in Multicultural Australia', in G. B. Nalbantoglu and Wong Chong Thai (eds), *Postcolonial Space(s)* (New York, 1997), pp. 106–7.

24 *Myths of Oz*, p. 41.

25 ' "House Beautiful" ', p. 43.

26 Holland, 'Owner Building as an Expression of Popular Culture', pp. 21, 26. Thorne's critique of semiotic approaches arrives at a similar conclusion: 'there

has been considerable "reading" and "deciphering" ' of the signs and symbols produced by house builders ... S*uch readings may be correct but they are interpretations of visual evidence without confirmation from the home-owners themselves* . . . Obviously, the visual qualities are important to home-builders and purchasers, but what is their meaning to these people?' (my emphasis), 'Housing as "Home" in the Australian Context', p. 59.

27  *Myths of Oz*, p. 52.

28  See G. Holland, *Emoh Ruo: Owner Building in Sydney* (Sydney, 1988); S. Thompson, 'Suburbs of Opportunity: The Power of Home for Migrant Women', in K. Gibson and S. Watson (eds), *Metropolis Now: Planning and the Urban in Contemporary Australia* (Sydney, 1994); L. Richards, *Nobody's Home: Dreams and Realities in a New Suburb* (Melbourne, 1990); B. Davison and G. Davison, 'Suburban Pioneers', in G. Davison, T. Dingle and S. O'Hanlon (eds), *The Cream Brick Frontier: Histories of Australian Suburbia*, Monash Publications in History No. 19 (Melbourne, 1995); M. Peel, *Good Times, Hard Times: The Past and the Future in Elizabeth* (Melbourne, 1995); D. Powell, *Out West: Perceptions of Sydney's Western Suburbs* (Sydney, 1993); G. Bolton, *Daphne Street: The Biography of an Australian Community* (Fremantle, 1997); Thorne, 'Housing as "Home" '.

29  See P. Dickens, 'Architecture as Commodity Fetishism: Some Cautionary Comments on "Green Design" ', *Housing Studies*, vol. 8, no. 2, 1993.

235

30  *The Presentation of Self in Everyday Life* (London, 1974).

31  A. de Swaan, *The Management of Normality: Critical Essays in Health and Welfare* (London, 1990), p. 190.

32  See J. D. Porteous, 'Home: The Territorial Core', *Geographical Review*, vol. 66, no. 4, 1976; and Madigan and Munro, 'Gender, House and "Home" '. S. Muthesius posited a positive relationship between socio-economic status and the differentiation between front and back regions. In other words, as a household gains higher socio-economic status, the more pronounced becomes the visible distinction between the formal front and the more informal and intimate back: *The English Terraced House* (London, 1992). See also P. Spearritt, *Sydney Since the Twenties* (Sydney, 1978), p. 202.

33  Fiske *et al.*, *Myths of Oz*, p. 34; Dovey, 'Dreams on Display', pp. 135–7.

34  R. J. Greig, 'Life in a Glasgow Tenement', Unpublished manuscript prepared for author, 1997, pp. 1–2.

35  See Fiske *et al.*, *Myths of Oz*, p. 33; de Swaan, *The Management of Normality*.

36  As M. Munro and R. Madigan point out: 'The home is indeed generally valued as a "back region" . . . a collective retreat from public life. The home in this case is seen as a place where outsiders can be excluded . . . However, the notion of individual privacy has received much less attention from analysts of the home': 'Privacy in the Private Sphere', *Housing Studies*, vol. 8, no. 1, 1993.

37  K. Dovey, 'Model Houses and Housing in Australia', *Housing Studies*, vol. 7, no. 3, 1992, p. 182. This relationship between modern design and 'intergenerational warfare' was also used as a metaphor by Mark Davis to introduce his book Ganglands, which argues that the 'babyboomer generation' (the parents) are monopolising contemporary cultural space and are marginalising the so-called

'generation X' (the children): *Gangland: Cultural Elites and the New Generationalism* (Sydney, 1997). While Davis sees these shifts in design as a reflection of intergenerational warfare, Dovey sees them as an attempted solution or negotiation.

38  See Archer, *The Great Australian Dream*, p. 206.

39  'Dreams on Display'.

40  P. N. Troy, *The Perils of Urban Consolidation: A Discussion of Australian Housing and Urban Development Policies* (Sydney, 1996).

41  Munro and Madigan, 'Privacy in the Private Sphere', p. 41.

42  *Ibid.*

43  *Ibid.*, pp. 133–5.

44  Troy, *The Perils of Urban Consolidation*, p. 14; G. McNicholl, 'Are Australian Families Like Others?', in F. G. Castles (ed.), *Australia Compared: People, Policies and Politics* (Sydney, 1991), p. 62.

45  Munro and Madigan, 'Privacy in the Private Sphere', p. 41.

46  S. Watson, *Accommodating Inequality: Gender and Housing* (Sydney, 1988); J. Baxter, and D. Gibson, *Double Take: The Links Between Paid and Unpaid Work* (Canberra, 1990), p. 93; Richards, *Nobody's Home*; K. Reiger, *The Disenchantment of the Home: Modernising the Australian Family, 1880–1940* (Melbourne, 1985); A. Game and R. Pringle, 'Sexuality and the Suburban Dream', *Australian and New Zealand Journal of Sociology*, vol. 15, no. 2, 1979.

47  Madigan and Munro, ' "House Beautiful" ', p. 55.

48  G. Connah, *The Archaeology of Australia's History* (Cambridge, 1993), p. 77.

49  *The Critic as Advocate: Selected Essays, 1949–1988* (Melbourne, 1989); review article originally published in 1969.

50  *Most Beautiful House in the World* (New York, 1990), p. 6.

51  Another example of the value in studying the secondhand market is in the popularity through time of 'transformation-job' stories in home magazines. These stories help identify first, what is considered 'old-fashioned' at a particular historical juncture; and second, how the 'transformation job' accords with new fashions, styles and changing social relations; see A. W. Greig, *The Stuff Dreams Are Made Of: Housing Provision in Australia, 1945–1960* (Melbourne, 1995), ch. 9.

52  Dovey, 'Dreams on Display', p. 128 (my emphasis).

53  See A. Colquhoun, 'The Concept of Regionalism', in Nalbantoglu and Wong (eds), *Postcolonial Space(s)*, p. 18; Dovey, 'Dreams on Display', p. 147.

54  Madigan and Munro, ' "House Beautiful" '.

55  *The Management of Normality*, p. 2.

56  'Owner Building as an Expression of Popular Culture', p. 21.

## Chapter 14

# Paying for It All

*David Merrett*

How did European Australians pay for their houses? Home ownership rates of around 70 per cent from the 1960s indicate that most Australian households have been able to find the money. The plethora of advertisements for home loans in the late 1990s suggests the answer to that question. Any person wishing to buy a new house or an existing property goes to one of the many banks or mortgage originators who are actively seeking their business. Access to the housing market is by way of borrowing. The fact that women were less likely to qualify for a loan than men,[1] or that a sizeable 'deposit gap' emerged in the 1980s when house prices rose faster than incomes,[2] has not weakened the perception that there was a direct causal relationship between the supply of loans for housing and the ability of Australians to realise that demand.

This chapter explores how Australian owners of homes, both owner-occupiers and landlords, found the money to buy their properties during the two centuries of European settlement. At an aggregate level and over the very long term, the required money was forthcoming. Australians have been well housed. Population growth was unusually high compared to economies with comparable per capita incomes[3] yet the housing stock grew at much the same pace. Moreover, measures such as the number of persons per room, the material of the outer walls, and fixtures and fittings all indicate that the size and quality of new houses rose steadily over time.[4] However, the purchase of a house whose average price was a large multiple of average annual incomes has been beyond the means of many Australians.[5] Those who could afford to buy had a number of options. First, many buyers went into debt. A range of financial institutions such as building societies, trading and savings banks, insurance companies and others made loans to those wishing to construct a new home or to buy an existing house or apartment. Second, some buyers borrowed smaller amounts and for shorter periods from other sources such as the vendors, solicitors' trust funds, money lenders or financial agents, or friends and relatives. Third, a fortunate minority could pay the purchase price at the time of sale from their own wealth.

Information about the choices made by past generations of purchasers is elusive. The period after World War II is examined in the second section of the chapter. It starts with Hill's study of housing finance in the postwar decade[6] and continues with an examination of the comprehensive official data from the 1970s about the lending by financial institutions for the construction of new houses and purchases of existing houses. These data produce the surprising result that lending by the principal financial institutions financed just over one-half of the houses built in Australia in the ten years up to 1956, and a similar ratio between 1971 and 1991. The chapter then reviews the evolution of those financial institutions that made loans to house buyers from the mid-nineteenth century up to World War II. An examination of the value of loans made by trading banks, building societies, savings banks and insurance companies and the like suggests that in the nineteenth century and the first part of twentieth, the pool of loan funds available to house buyers fell short of the value of new construction by an even wider margin than in the fifty years after World War II. The fourth section speculates about the extent of direct purchase and borrowing from sources other than the large specialist financiers. The chapter concludes that most Australian paid for their houses without recourse to a loan from a building society, bank or insurance company. Up to World War II the wealthy bought houses from their savings or liquidated other assets, or were able to satisfy the credit requirements of a small and unsophisticated financial market. Those in the middle struggled to borrow or, at the margin, dealt with other types of creditors to supplement their savings. Some built their own homes. The poor rented. That situation altered substantially only after 1945, for reasons that will be discussed below, allowing a much larger proportion of prospective purchasers to have access to the market for home loans.

## Building, buying and paying for it, 1945–1955

Malcolm Hill's seminal study of housing finance from 1945 to 1956 provides an appropriate launching pad for a study of 'paying for it'.[7] Hill trawled through a wide range of sources relating to both pre-eminent and fringe institutions, making a number of estimates and assumptions, which enabled him to calculate the amount of new lending for housing by a complete range of financial institutions, the amount of loans outstanding, and the number of houses constructed in each year with loans from these institutions. His study provided, for the first time, a clear picture of the importance of the many types of institutions who made loans for housing, the aggregate amount of lending done in any year, and the proportion of new housing financed by these institutions.

The results are noteworthy in a number of respects. First, financial institutions played an important role in facilitating the 'paying for it' by many house buyers. The total amount of lending for housing by financial institutions identified by Hill,[8] including War Service Homes and state government housing authorities, over the years 1947 to 1954 approximated a little over 80 per cent of the Commonwealth Statistician's estimates of the value of both new dwellings completed and of gross residential capital formation.[9] However, that figure greatly overstates the role of lending in 'paying for it' for the following reasons. It should be noted that not all of the lending identified by Hill was applied to the construction of new dwellings. An unknown proportion of it was used to pay for the land on which the new dwellings were built. More importantly, institutions also lent to purchasers of existing dwellings. Furthermore, those borrowing for a new house had to find some of the equity as a deposit because institutional lenders advanced considerably less than 100 per cent of their valuation of the property, including its site value. The size of this 'deposit gap' was widened further as the total amount lent was capped by the borrower's income: repayments could not exceed around 30 per cent of pre-tax earnings over twenty-five years.[10]

We are on firmer ground if we compare the number of loans made for new houses by institutional lenders. Hill's data shown in Table 14.1 shows that lending for new building financed a little more than a half of the increase in housing starts over the years 1946 to 1956.[11] Furthermore, the value of these loans was the equivalent of 42 per cent of the expected value of all houses being built.[12] Only a half of the advances made for housing were directed to new houses.[13]

Funds for housing came from a wide variety of institutions. The banks were the major providers, with the trading banks, savings banks and other cheque-paying banks making 40 per cent of all loans from 1946 to 1956.[14] The savings banks emerged as the most important source of funds from the end of the war up to the early 1970s, with their share of outstanding loans rising from 16 to 31 per cent.[15] The greater part of the increase came after the opening of savings bank subsidiaries by the private trading banks in the latter part of the 1950s. Building societies were another major source of housing finance: their share of outstanding loans rose from 21 per cent in 1945 to 32 per cent in 1972.[16] The growth in the importance of building societies came initially from terminating rather than permanent societies. They became important conduits of state funding to housing under the 1956 Commonwealth–State Housing Agreement, which provided nearly half of their funds. The rest came largely from loans by banks, particularly the government-owned Commonwealth Bank of Australia.[17] Permanent building societies also grew apace by capitalising on their ability to offer higher returns to their depositors than the regulated banks, offering the security of an implied guarantee by state governments, and by taking advantage of the introduction of mortgage insurance in 1965 to offer higher loan-to-valuation ratios.[18] By 1969 the permanent societies' outstanding loans were larger than those of the terminating societies. Mortgage lending by life offices declined in relative importance over the long term.[19]

**Table 14.1** Loans for new houses as proportion of all new houses by number and volume, 1946–1956

| Lender | No. of loans | % all houses commenced | Value of loans ($m) | % value of all houses commenced |
|---|---|---|---|---|
| Building societies | 113,240 | 16.0 | 364.4 | 12.4 |
| War Service Homes | 69,570 | 9.8 | 272.6 | 9.3 |
| Government housing authority | 22,810 | 3.2 | 73.4 | 2.5 |
| Savings banks | 59,290 | 8.4 | 176.1 | 6.0 |
| Life offices | 23,460 | 3.3 | 98.7 | 3.4 |
| Trading banks | 76,690 | 10.8 | 183.1 | 6.2 |
| Other cheque-paying banks | 17,250 | 2.4 | 42.2 | 1.6 |
| Friendly societies | 9,840 | 1.4 | 22.8 | 0.8 |
| Total | 392,150 | 55.3 | 1,237.5 | 42.1 |

*Source:* M. R. Hill, *Housing Finance in Australia, 1945–1956* (Melbourne, 1959), tables 44, 46, pp. 134, 136.

240  The government, however, was an important direct provider of funds through defence housing and the activities of state housing authorities. Together those two avenues provided 22 per cent of all housing advances, and 13 per cent of the loans made for new homes, from 1946 up to 1956.[20] Moreover, new houses provided by governments for low-cost rental accommodation made up nearly one-fifth of the construction of new houses over that same period.[21] The provision of housing loans for ex-servicemen and women through War Service Homes was extended from the mid-1970s to include serving personnel. The outstanding housing loans of the Defence Service Homes Commission were twice those of life offices. Its portfolio of 127,000 housing loans was sold to Westpac in 1989.[22] Other government housing authorities that provided houses for sale as well as rental from the mid-1950s still accounted for 10 per cent of all outstanding loans for housing in 1972.[23]

  The flow of funds from financial institutions for housing in the quarter of a century after the end of the war suggests that only a half of those purchasing a new dwelling did so by going into debt with a mainstream institutional lender. Many buyers of existing dwellings were also able to buy loans from those institutions. A subsequent study by Hill explores the amount of equity held by home owners in the early 1970s. The estimated 4.2 million units of housing in Australia in 1973 consisted of 3.5 million houses, 600,000 flats and home units, and another 100,000 'other' private dwellings. Of this stock, 70 per cent of private dwellings were owner-occupied; 8 per cent were occupied by tenants of government housing authorities and departments; and roughly 20 per cent were occupied by tenants of private landlords. The estimated market value of this stock was $40 billion for the owner-occupied houses, or $12,500 each, and $10 billion for private landlords. The value of all outstanding housing loans by

**Table 14.2** Institutional lenders' share of financing new houses by number and value, 1954–1991

| Period | Census change in private dwellings (000s) | Lending by institutions for new dwellings | | Gross fixed capital expenditure dwellings ($m) | Lending by institutions for new dwellings | |
|---|---|---|---|---|---|---|
| | | number (000s) | % | | value ($m) | % |
| 1954–61 | 439 | 171 | 39.0 | 4,133 | 774 | 18.7 |
| 1961–66 | 370 | 167 | 45.1 | 4,503 | 1,034 | 23.0 |
| 1966–71 | 381 | 239 | 62.7 | 7,399 | 1,941 | 26.3 |
| 1971–76 | 607 | 367* | 60.5 | 14,940 | 4,736* | 31.7 |
| 1976–81 | 998 | 413 | 41.4 | 30,820 | 9,991 | 32.4 |
| 1981–86 | 613 | 355 | 57.9 | 47,117 | 12,557 | 26.6 |
| 1986–91 | 608 | 400 | 65.8 | 76,781 | 2,141 | 28.8 |
| Total | 4,016 | 2,112 | 52.6 | 185,693 | 53,174 | 28.6 |

*Notes:* *No data for 1975/76. Estimated as average of other years in inter-censal period.
*Source:* Census.
   Forster, 1996, tables 3.3, 5.1, pp. 118, 214–15.

financial institutions in that year was roughly $10 billion, or a quarter of the value of owner-occupied housing and one-fifth of that of the private housing stock. Hill concludes, after carefully adjusting the census data relating to 'owner occupiers' and 'purchaser by instalments', that about half of the housing stock was being purchased with the assistance of loans. The outstanding debt was about half of the market value.[24]

Data collected by the Australian Bureau of Statistics (ABS) and the Reserve Bank of Australia indicate the contribution made by the advances of lending institutions to the construction of new dwellings from the early 1950s up to the present. The results are shown in Table 14.2.

All the data have been converted to inter-censal periods. Changes in the stock of private dwellings and the summed value of the ABS estimate of gross fixed capital expenditure on dwellings provide a measure of the growth of the units of housing stock and its cost. These data can be compared to the amount lent by financial institutions and the number of dwellings that those loans financed. Although the latter data should be treated with caution—the series relating to financial institutions in particular have not had consistent coverage over the whole period under consideration[25]—the role of financial institutions in financing new housing construction over these years was similar to that in the decade after the war. In the broadest terms, the number of new dwellings constructed with the assistance of loans made up a little more than half of the increase in dwellings between 1954 and 1991. Moreover, the amount lent by these financial institutions was less than 30 per cent of the ABS calculation of the value of dwelling construction during the same period.

How important were trades in the existing housing stock, and to what extent were these financed by lending institutions? We know of no reliable data that provide an answer to the first part of the question. Some feel for this issue can be gained by comparing the number of loans made by financial institutions for the construction of new houses and the purchase of existing ones. Hill's statistics suggest that the value of loans for the purchase of new houses was matched by loans for established houses from 1946 to 1956.[26] Loans for the purchase of existing houses outnumbered those for the construction of new houses by a factor of two to one from the late 1960s until the mid-1990s.[27] As we have no reason to believe that the purchaser of a newly constructed house is any less wealthy or creditworthy than the purchaser of an established house, it seems reasonable to assume that lending institutions financed the same proportion of trades in the secondary housing market as they did in the market for new homes, that is around one-half.

That so many purchasers appear to have built or bought their homes without recourse to a loan from a bank, a building society or another financial institution since 1945 is puzzling. The modest role of lending institutions is all the more surprising in view of government policies towards the finance sector to encourage house buying.[28] Part of the answer lies in the evolution of the financial system since the war. Although the total assets held on the balance sheets of deposit taking institutions rose faster than gross domestic product, particularly during the 1970s and 1980s, the growth of housing loans did not expand as quickly. Building societies and savings banks were the principal lenders. The ability of each to increase its lending was constrained in different ways. Building societies could offer unregulated market rates to raise funds, but they did not take full advantage of that freedom. The permanent societies raised the bulk of their funds through the sale of shares, and the terminating societies relied on funds provided by governments or other financial institutions.[29] The growth of their balance sheets was checked further by the characteristics of the industry. There were many small societies serving limited regional markets. It was not until the 1980s that a rationalisation took place, with larger societies emerging from a series of mergers. A number of the biggest, whose distribution networks extended across several states, converted to savings banks.[30]

Savings banks, on the other hand, were also constrained in their ability to lend for housing. First, the capping of interest rates on savings bank deposits, from the 1940s until the early 1980s, limited their ability to attract funds.[31] Second, from their beginnings in the early nineteenth century, governments had used deposits collected by savings banks to make loans to colonial treasuries and to buy government securities. Such practices continued into the new century. Additional mortgage loans by savings banks made up only 17 per cent of the increase in their assets between 1901 and 1931, the prewar peak in home lending.[32] Governments continued to use savings banks as a captive market for their securities after World War II. Consequently, advances for housing comprised less than 20 per cent of savings bank assets as late as 1960.

It was only in the mid-1970s that housing loans finally outstripped government securities as the most important item on the asset side of the balance sheet when their share rose above one-third. A relaxation of mandatory asset ratios as part of deregulation of the financial system had a liberating effect on the capacity of savings banks to increase their lending for home purchasers. By the latter half of the 1980s that share had risen to around 55 per cent of their assets.[33]

It was only after deregulation of the financial system in the 1980s that those seeking housing loans faced a greater choice of lending institutions, loan products and terms. Previously many borrowers were excluded from the market because they could not meet the credit conditions of the dominant lenders or had to seek supplementary funds from more expensive alternative sources. The emergence of mortgage originators, funding their loan books through wholesale money markets, has reduced the real cost of borrowing. Access to the market for mortgage loans has increased dramatically as the number of housing loans made has risen at more than twice the growth of population from 1977 to 1996.[34]

## The emergence of a market for house loans, 1788–1970

### FROM THE BEGINNINGS TO THE 1870s

Australia's financial system was primitive before the 1830s. Trading banks quickly established themselves as the dominant financial institutions and remained so for the next century and three-quarters. Wool, gold and the import trade catapulted their business past that of the much smaller savings banks and life offices. The trading banks' business was skewed towards providing short-term credits and trade-related financing and foreign exchange services.

Trading banks were reluctant to provide loans for housing before the 1860s because of uncertainties about the property rights relating to title of real property. A voluntary deed registration system, established in 1851, was replaced by the more effective Torrens system in the late 1850s and early 1860s; it provided cheaper and more accurate information about the state of title, and gave greater legal certainties about claims of all parties.

The Anglo-Australian banks, in particular, were reluctant to make mortgage loans that were the principal lending instrument used for real property. Bankers held this aversion for a variety of reasons. First, the Colonial Banking Regulations of 1840 and 1846 issued by the British Treasury included prohibitions against direct lending on land because it was perceived as an illiquid asset that could lock up a bank's funds. Australian bankers reluctantly engaged in mortgage lending to pastoralists only in the 1860s when pastoral companies challenged the banks' lucrative relationship with the wool industry. This new form of mortgage lending became more widespread as responsibility for banking supervision passed from Britain to the Australian colonies in the

1870s.[35] However, the weight of British banking principles continued to deter trading banks from lending for house construction or acquisition before the 1870s. Second, banks faced higher transaction costs in securing assets by mortgage because the legal uncertainties associated with this type of security were higher than those associated with lending against goods in transit.[36]

## THE 1870s AND 1880s

The 'long boom' in the economy from the 1860s onwards generated sustained increases in real per capita incomes. Despite the merits of the claim that Australia was a 'working man's paradise' it is clear that the average cost of construction of a new dwelling, excluding the site value, was a large multiple of average wages. Before the onset of the 1890s depression, the average cost of construction of new dwellings during the decade from 1881 to 1891 was five times the average annual wages paid to workers in manufacturing in Victoria and New South Wales.[37] Young adults, newly married and recent entrants to the workforce, without accumulated savings, faced an almost insurmountable burden when they were attempting to purchase a new or existing house. We might expect that a significant proportion of buyers in the housing market needed access to loans.

Their ability to borrow rose sharply in the late nineteenth century as the assets of financial institutions outstripped the growth of gross domestic product. The sustained growth of the Australian population and economy stimulated important new developments in the financial system. A strong inflow of British funds increased the credit base. A construction boom driven by the need for public sector infrastructure, the requirements of the expanding pastoral industry, and the demand for housing from a rapidly growing population, all reshaped the finance industry.[38] The number of trading banks rose between 1870 and 1890. Property development and the real estate market provided rich pickings for a host of new institutions—building societies, land investment and mortgage companies, and savings banks—all of whom lent on mortgages.[39]

Innovation in the finance industry provided a larger pool of funds available to house buyers. The share of total assets held by financial institutions other than trading banks rose from 6 per cent in 1861 to more than one-third by 1891. Savings banks and building societies accounted for 17 per cent of the total at that later date.[40] How much of this increased lending capacity was directed towards housing? This question cannot be answered with any precision because two potentially important lenders, trading banks and life offices, did not distinguish how much of their advances or mortgages was for residential investments. Guesstimates must suffice in lieu of hard data, as trading banks did not provide information about the purposes for which they made loans until 1948. Some clues exist. Information provided by trading banks to the Royal Commission into Money and Banking in the 1930s about

**Table 14.3** Loans for new housing by financial institutions as proportion of value of new construction, 1861–1947

| Period | Estimated expenditure on new dwellings ($m) | Increase trading bank loans ($m) | Increase savings bank loans ($m) | Increase building society assets ($m) | Increase life office mortgages ($m) | Total loans ($m) | Loans as % of expenditure |
|---|---|---|---|---|---|---|---|
| 1861–71 | 54.7 | 0.8 | 0.6 | – | – | 1.4 | 2.6 |
| 1871–81 | 80.5 | 2.9 | 2.1 | 5.6 | – | 10.6 | 13.2 |
| 1881–91 | 169.3 | 6.7 | 6.0 | 42.4 | – | 55.1 | 32.5 |
| 1891–1901 | 70.1 | –3.2 | 0.4 | –40.0 | 3.4 | –39.4 | – |
| 1901–11 | 138.1 | 1.6 | 4.0 | 2.0 | 5.0 | 12.6 | 9.1 |
| 1911–21 | 256.6 | 6.8 | 12.6 | 5.0 | –0.6 | 23.8 | 9.3 |
| 1921–33 | 645.0 | 3.8 | 43.6 | 11.0 | 13.0 | 71.4 | 11.1 |
| 1933–47 | 530.0 | 9.0 | –29.0 | 33.0 | 12.6 | 25.6 | 4.8 |

*Notes:* Trading bank housing loans estimated as 4 per cent of total advances. Savings banks increase in mortgage loans up to 1947, after which increase in Commonwealth Savings Bank's total loans are included. Credit foncier loans included with State Bank of Victoria data. Life office mortgage lending for housing estimated as one-third of mortgages within Australia.

*Sources:* N. G. Butlin, *Australian Domestic Product, Investment and Foreign Borrowing, 1861–1938/9* (Cambridge, 1962), table 5, pp. 18–19; N. G. Butlin, *Investment in Australian Economic Development, 1861–1900* (Cambridge, 1964), App. II, p. 454; S. J. Butlin, A. R. Hall and R. C. White, *Australian Banking and Monetary Statistics, 1817–1945* (Reserve Bank, Sydney, 1971), tables 1, 531, pp. 112–15, 501–4; R. C. White, *Australian Banking and Monetary Statistics, 1945–1970* (Reserve Bank, Sydney, 1973), tables 12, 67, 68, 70, pp. 151, 500–3; *Australian Insurance and Banking Record* (Sydney, 1882); D. Pope, *Australian Money and Banking Statistics* (Canberra, 1986), table 1; Commonwealth Bureau of Census and Statistics, *Finance Bulletins* (Canberra, annual).

their loans indicated that advances for 'building' made up only about 4 per cent of the total outstanding from 1927 to 1935.[41] Applying this ratio of 4 per cent and Hill's estimate that one-third of life offices' mortgages were for house purchase[42] allows a calculation of the amount lent in earlier years that is shown in Table 14.3. The modest role of the trading banks and life offices is consistent with Butlin's observation that 'ordinary commercial banks and life offices seem to have had a fluctuating interest in building finance, both indirectly through advances to building societies and directly through loans to individual clients'.[43]

The contribution made by trading and savings banks, and life offices, to housing loans was modest in comparison to that of the building societies. Butlin argued that advances by Victorian building societies between 1874 and 1891 were equal in value to two-thirds of new residential investment in that colony.[44] However, Table 14.3 shows that the important role of building societies in Melbourne's building boom of the 1880s was not repeated on a national scale. Lending by all institutions increased from 3 to 13 to 33 per cent of the expenditure on residential construction during the 1860s, 1870s and 1880s. The providers of loans, although more forthcoming than in earlier years, must have left many prospective purchasers unsatisfied.

## 1890s TO WORLD WAR II

The collapse of the property boom at the end of the 1880s and the subsequent bank crashes had a profound effect on the structure and behaviour of the financial system.[45] Those institutions most closely associated with urban property development and speculation were swept away. The number of building societies, and the assets of those survivors, fell precipitously. Trading banks struggled to make good losses incurred in the 1890s. Chastened depositors sought the safer waters of government-guaranteed savings banks and the whole-of-life and industrial policies offered by life offices. The assets of these two types of institutions rose from 12 per cent of the total for all financial institutions in 1891 to 39 per cent in 1939.[46] Trading banks, though losing market share, remained the most important segment of the finance industry in terms of assets.

246

Residential construction proceeded apace from 1891 to 1933 as a further 844,000 dwellings were recorded at the censuses. How did the finance institutions respond to the demands for loans by house purchasers? The estimates in Table 14.3 suggest that the value of aggregate outstanding loans fell in the 1890s as building societies collapsed. Savings banks emerged as the most important provider of housing loans. However, the combined housing loans of all banks, building societies and life offices from 1901 until 1933 was only about 10 per cent of expenditure on residential construction. The share fell sharply during the depression and war, primarily as savings banks curtailed house lending and amassed government securities.

These figures imply that lending by financial institutions played little part in funding the construction of new homes, the acquisition of the sites on which these houses were to be built, or the purchase of existing housing stock. Is the funding 'gap' shown in Table 14.3 so great as to make the estimates implausible? A litmus test can be applied to ascertain whether the results have a degree of validity. Let us suppose, even more implausibly, that all trading bank loans and all the mortgage lending by life offices[47] were made for housing purposes. Would 'demand' have been satisfied? A recalculation of the amount lent applying 100 per cent of trading loans and life office mortgages shows that only 43 per cent of the cost of residential construction between 1901 and 1947 would have been 'paid' for by loans from financial institutions. It seems that a pessimistic view of the relatively small contribution made by financial institutions is warranted.

Such a conclusion is at odds with that presented by R. Murray and K. White in their recent history of the State Bank of Victoria.[48] The bank made many mortgage loans. Unfortunately these were of little use to people of low net worth who sought to enter the housing market: the minimum loan was for £1000, the term of the loan was restricted to three years, and the maximum loan was no more than three-fifths of the bank's valuation of the property.[49] However, most of the bank's lending for houses from 1911 onwards was through its Credit Foncier department. The scope of that department was widened in 1917 to include loans to returned soldiers, and from 1921 to making housing loans available to persons on low incomes. The bank was also involved in making advances for houses constructed or purchased under the *War Service Homes Act*. Loans made by the Credit Foncier department led to the construction of 19,000 new dwellings from 1921 until 1933, with an additional 3800 dwellings constructed under the *War Service Homes Act*.[50] By way of contrast, the number of dwellings in Victoria rose by 104,000 between the census of 1921 and 1933, while the number of dwellings in Melbourne and its suburbs increased by 71,463. The amount of construction financed by loans by the State Bank was the equivalent of about one-third of new houses in Melbourne, or 22 per cent of those built in the state between the census dates. Although these figures are impressive, the estimates in Table 14.3 make it plain that they were the exception rather than the rule. No other savings bank took such an active role in lending for housing. Only the State Savings Bank of South Australia operated a credit foncier before World War II.[51]

## Going it alone

The review of the estimates of the contribution made to 'paying for it' by lending institutions during the period since European settlement suggests that a majority of house buyers had to find all or most of the purchase price from other sources. This statement is more likely to be true in some periods rather than others. The 1880s, 1920s and post-1945 period were times when access to housing loans was markedly higher than in earlier and intervening years.

What alternative sources of funds were available? Purchasers who did not have recourse to lending institutions could have 'paid for it' by accumulating sufficient wealth to buy the property outright. Such a strategy was more feasible for the old and the rich seeking to buy a cheap house than for the young or the poor who hankered after a mansion. How many individuals or families fell into this former category we cannot know.

Transfers of wealth between generations could have been an important source of access to housing. For instance, in 1915 nearly 4500 estates were passed through probate in Victoria with a net value of nearly $18 million. The value of real property in these estates was valued at nearly $9 million dollars,[52] or nearly three times the value of new residential construction within Victoria in 1914–15.[53] These fragmentary data remind us that inheritance changed the life chances of the beneficiaries. Receiving a nest egg loosened financial bonds.

Often, it might be assumed, real property was passed directly to heirs in the next generation, especially to sons carrying on the family farm or to spinster daughters who had looked after their parents in old age.

Family networks provided another source of funds to those wishing to enter the housing market. Gifts by parents, or 'soft' loans from more prosperous kin, gave a start to young married couples. Landlords had the capacity to provide rent-free accommodation to relatives that would help them save for a deposit for their own home or scrape together the purchase price. Little is known about the identity of Australia's private sector landlords. Drawing data from a pioneering study, it is possible to guesstimate that there may have been as many as 100,000 landlords in the capital cities in 1911.[54] Families 'doubled up' not only in time of economic hardship but also to provide a rent subsidy to kith and kin. Living with parents and boarding were staging posts for many entrants into the Adelaide housing market in the 1970s.[55]

Self-financing was likely to be an important way of creating equity in a home. Owner-builders, buying cheap land on the fringes of the city, could stretch out the process of construction to match their cash flow. This was a widely used method in times of extreme housing shortage such as the 1860s,[56] and again after World War II when about one-quarter of new houses were owner-built (see Chapter 4). It would also have been widely used in rural communities and in the building of the weekender cottages that became increasingly popular after World War II.

Direct financing is likely to have been the most important source of funding. Many purchasers borrowed from sources other than the institutional lenders discussed above. The *Australasian Insurance and Banking Record*, commenting on the prosperity of Melbourne's building trade during 1881, noted that 'this money, however, is not obtained from building societies. Owing to the cheapness of money, borrowers can go into the open market and negotiate loans on fixed mortgages.'[57] Country storekeepers were important providers of credit to their customers. Clergymen made investments on behalf of their parishioners. However, solicitors and real estate agents were the primary source of private mortgage funds. In the inter-war years Sands & McDougall's Melbourne directories listed a number of 'financial agents' who were also real estate agents.[58] Many of the money lenders licensed in Australian states took mortgages on real estate with interest rates capped at 48 per cent per annum.[59] Vendors lent on mortgage to the purchaser. Some scattered data on the importance of mortgage lending by non-institutional lenders are available for the 1950s through to the 1970s. The Victorian government published statistics on the lodgement of mortgages on real estate by type of lender from 1955 until 1978. Over that time non-institutional lenders, most of whom were individuals, averaged between 40 and 50 per cent of all the mortgages registered by number, and from one-quarter to one-half by value.[60] Data collected for the Australian Financial System Inquiry in early 1980 suggested that solicitors' trust funds and mortgage brokers had made loans for housing of $5 billion. It was noted that the demand for this type of financing rose during periods of financial stringency when funds from institutional lenders dried up.[61]

## Conclusion

This chapter raises more questions than it can answer. It attempted to estimate the contribution made by lending institutions to financing the construction of new houses and the buying of dwellings from the existing stock. We can have a greater degree of confidence in the post-1945 data than in earlier periods. Since World War II about one-half of new dwellings have been financed by loans by banks and other financial institutions. This is a counter-intuitive result, given the dramatic expansion of the capacity of the financial system to make loans over this period. It is also at odds with the increased propensity of postwar governments to make policies designed to promote the supply of housing and to implement policies designed to increase the ability of new entrants and low-income earners to enter the housing market.[62] The calculations of the contribution made by institutional lenders to new dwelling construction in the second half of the nineteenth and first half of the twentieth centuries clearly indicate that most of new houses, at least, were 'paid for' by means other than loans from mainstream lending institutions.

Are the results feasible? What part of the lending 'gap' is accounted for by under-reporting of lending for housing by trading banks and life offices or fringe institutions such as friendly societies or credit co-operatives before Hill's exhaustive study (1959) and the more comprehensive data provided by the Reserve Bank from the mid-1970s? Could inheritances and other forms of intra-family transfers, the activities of owner-builders and types of direct financing identified above have filled this gap? Unfortunately, the valuable micro studies of house purchases done in the 1970s provide little evidence about these various types of financing.[63]

The issue of owner-occupancy is explored in more detail in Chapter 15. It needs to be mentioned briefly here. Although not all who rent do so from necessity, most of those renting in Melbourne, Sydney and Adelaide in the early 1990s said that they did so because they could not afford to buy.[64] Perhaps we can regard tenancy rates as a proxy for the degree of difficulty in putting together the funds from any source to buy. Whereas the high rates of owner-occupation since World War II have attracted much attention, a revisionist perspective is appropriate. It was not until the 1920s that half of the private dwellings in the capital cities were owner-occupied. Estimates of ownership rates in 1891, which should capture the influence of building societies' loans in the preceding decades, indicate that only 30 of per cent of private dwellings in a sample of Sydney's suburbs, and 40 per cent of those in Melbourne, were owner-occupied.[65] Little more than one-third of the houses built in Sydney between 1871 and 1891 were occupied by their owners.[66] Higher land prices in the capital cities held the owner-occupier ratio lower in metropolitan areas than in other urban or rural areas.[67] It was not until after World War II that ownership rates in metropolitan areas rose to match those in other parts of Australia, and that the overall ratio of home ownership rose sharply before peaking in 1966.[68] Before 1939 house building and buying was the preserve of the wealthy and a large number of private landlords who were making a commercial investment. Governments became important providers of housing first to war veterans and later to low-income earners. The sharp rise in owner-occupation in the twenty years after the war probably owed more to full employment, rising real incomes and dual-income families than to the expanded activities of financial institutions making loans for houses.

Loans from institutional lenders to those buying houses were a far more important source of funds after World War II than in the preceding one hundred years. The limited pool of mortgage loans to real estate reflected the character of the financial system. In many respects Australia possessed an immature set of financial institutions before the 1950s. Deposits in savings banks and building societies, friendly societies, credit co-operatives, and the weekly payments towards the 'industrial' policies sold by the life offices, provided a repository for savings, especially of the thrifty poor, that were invested in government securities rather than being available for housing. Trading banks and life offices lent primarily to the well-to-do before 1939. Loans for house purchase formed only a small part of the business of these important institutions. It was not until after World War II that Australia began to experience a 'democratisation of credit',[69] when individuals of limited means could borrow. Finance companies liberated working-class Australians from the tyranny of bankers by providing 'personal loans' that made possible the boom in consumer durables of the 1950s and 1960s.[70] The trading banks became seriously interested in housing loans only after their entry into the savings bank market in the 1950s. However, that early promise of a relaxation of credit availability took several decades to be realised. It was not until the 1980s and financial deregulation that household indebtedness rose to unprecedented levels.[71] Borrowing to 'pay for it' has never been easier than in the 1990s.

250

**Notes**

1  S. Watson and C. Helliwell, 'Home Ownership—Are Women Excluded?',
   *The Australian Quarterly*, Autumn–Winter, 1985.
2  T. Burke, 'Housing Affordability and the Decline in Home Ownership—Myth
   or Reality?', in B. Judd (ed.), *Housing Affordability* (Red Hill, 1987); J. Yates,
   'Housing Affordability—an Economic Perspective', in *ibid.*; M. Neutze, 'Housing
   Affordability in Australia', in *ibid.*; M. Neutze and H. Kendig, 'Achievement of
   Home Ownership amongst Post-war Australian cohorts', URU Working Paper
   No. 16 (Canberra, 1989); S. C. Bourassa, 'The Impacts of Borrowing Constraints
   on Home-ownership in Australia', *Urban Studies*, vol. 32, no. 7, 1995.
3  A. Maddison, *Explaining the Economic Performance of Nations, 1820–1989*
   (Canberra, 1993).
4  R. Jackson and H. Bridge, 'Housing', in W. Vamplew (ed.), *Australians: Historical
   Statistics* (Broadway, 1987); G. D. Snooks, *Portrait of the Family with the Total Economy*
   (Cambridge, 1994); R. A. Carter, 'Housing Policy in the 1970s' in R. B. Scotton

and H. Ferber (eds), *Public Expenditures and Social Policy in Australia: Volume II* (Melbourne, 1980).

5 There is no single measure of the 'cost' of housing relative to income that covers the entire period under consideration. N. G. Butlin provides data on construction costs per room from 1861 to 1939: *Australian Domestic Product, Investment and Foreign Borrowing, 1861–1938/39* (Cambridge, 1962). A crude estimate of the 'cost' of a new dwelling can be derived by dividing the increase in the number of dwellings from census to census by the accumulated gross residential capital formation from 1861 to 1933. Official estimates of the value of completed dwellings are available from 1946: R. A. Foster, *Australian Economic Statistics, 1949–50 to 1994–95* (Sydney, 1996). We lack any continuous or reliable data on house prices over the longer term, although estimates of real prices in capital cities are available for the 1980s: S. C. Bourassa and P. H. Hendershott, 'Australian Capital City Real House Prices, 1979–1993', *Australian Economic Review,* 3rd Quarter, 1995, pp. 16–25. The only accurate historical series of house prices is available for Sydney from 1925 to 1970: P. Abelson, 'House and Land Prices in Sydney: 1925 to 1970', *Urban Studies,* vol. 22, 1985, pp. 521–34. House rents can be used as a proxy for house prices from the 1860s up to the 1930s. They are less useful as a signal of market prices from that date as government controls from the 1930s into the 1950s introduce an element of distortion into the series. Wage data was employed as a proxy for incomes: G. Withers, T. Endres and L. Perry, *Australian Historical Statistics: Labour Statistics* (Canberra, 1985), pp. 162–3, 156–7. The various series suggest that the cost of new housing, excluding the cost of land, was approximately five times average wages in manufacturing from the 1860s until 1947. The ratio was three to one from 1947 until 1981. What about the price of a dwelling plus land relative to incomes? The official statistics of rents for houses in Melbourne (Butlin, *Australian Domestic Product,* Table 134, p. 239) indicates that rents were approximately one-third of minimum average weekly award rates for males from 1911 to 1933 (Withers *et al., Australian Historical Statistics,* pp. 140–1). The average price of a large sample of Sydney houses was nearly four and a half times annual earnings in manufacturing from 1933 to 1970 (*ibid.,* pp. 156–7; Abelson, 'House and Land Prices in Sydney', Table 1, p. 523).

6 M. R. Hill, *Housing Finance in Australia, 1945–1956* (Melbourne, 1959).

7 *Ibid.*

8 *Ibid.,* Table 39, p. 128.

9 Jackson and Bridge, 'Housing', pp. 356, 360.

10 See M. R. Hill, 'Housing Finance Institutions' in R. R. Hirst and R. H. Wallace (eds), *The Australian Capital Market* (Melbourne, 1974).

11 Hill, *Housing Finance,* Tables 44, 45.

12 *Ibid.,* Table 46.

13 *Ibid.,* Table 39 and 46.

14 *Ibid.,* Table 39.

15 *Ibid.,* Table 39; Hill, 'Housing Finance Institutions', Table 8. 1.

16  Hill, *Housing Finance*, Table 39; Hill, 'Housing Finance Institutions', Table 8.1.
17  Hill, 'Housing Finance Institutions', pp. 340–1.
18  K. P. O'Brien, 'The Thrift Institutions', in M. K. Lewis and R. H. Wallace (eds), *The Australian Financial System* (South Melbourne, 1993), pp. 92–3.
19  Hill, 'Housing Finance Institutions', Table 8. 1.
20  Hill, *Housing Finance*, Tables 39, 46.
21  *Ibid.*, Table 45.
22  Westpac Banking Corporation, *Annual Report*, 1989.
23  Hill, 'Housing Finance Institutions', Table 8.1.
24  *Ibid.*, 1974, pp. 350–2.
25  Foster, *Australian Economic Statistics*, Table 3. 3, pp. 118–19, note (a).
26  Hill, *Housing Finance*, Tables 39, 46.
27  Foster, *Australian Economic Statistics*, Table 3.3, pp. 118–19.
28  G. A. Wood, 'Housing Finance and Subsidy Systems in Australia', *Urban Studies*, vol. 27, no. 6, 1990.
29  Hill, 'Housing Finance Institutions'.
30  O'Brien, 'The Thrift Institutions', Table 4. 3, pp. 90–5.
31  *Australian Financial System: Final Report* (Canberra, 1981), pp. 636–40; J. O. N. Perkins, *The Deregulation of the Australian Financial System* (Melbourne, 1989), pp. 38–45.
32  S. J. Butlin, A. R. Hall and R. C. White, *Australian Banking and Monetary Statistics, 1817–1945* (Sydney, 1971), Table 5. 3(ii), pp. 503–4.
33  Foster, *Australian Economic Statistics*, Table 3.9, p. 137.
34  *Financial System Inquiry Final Report* (Canberra, 1997), pp. 623–5.
35  S. J. Butlin, *Foundations of the Australian Monetary System, 1788–1851* (Sydney, 1954); S. J. Butlin, *Australia and New Zealand Bank: The Bank of Australasia and the Union Bank of Australia Limited, 1828–1851* (London, 1961), pp. 212–14, 249; S. J. Butlin, *The Australian Monetary System, 1851 to 1914* (Sydney, 1986), pp. 89–93.
36  F. E. Perry, *Law and Practice Relating to Banking* (Harmondsworth, 1972), pp. 181–4.
37  P. G. Macarthy, 'Wages in Australia, 1891 to 1914', *Australian Economic History Review*, vol. 10, no. 1, 1970; Butlin, *Australian Domestic Product*; Jackson and Bridge, 'Housing'.
38  N. G. Butlin, *Investment in Australian Economic Development, 1861–1900* (Cambridge, 1964).
39  Butlin, *The Australian Monetary System.*
40  D. Pope, *Australian Money and Banking Statistics* (Canberra, 1986), Table 1.
41  Royal Commission into Monetary and Banking, Systems in Australia (*Commonwealth Parliamentary Papers*, vol. 5, 1937, paper no. 74), Table 10, p. 314; cf. Hill, Housing Finance, p. 100.
42  Hill, *Housing Finance*, p. 96, n. 3.
43  Butlin, *Investment in Australian Economic Development*, p. 245.
44  *Ibid.*, Table 59, p. 265.

45  D. T. Merrett, 'Australian Banking Practice and the Crisis of 1893', *Australian Economic History Review*, vol. 29, no. 1, 1989; *The 1893 Bank Crashes and Monetary Aggregates* (Sydney, 1993).

46  Pope, *Australian Money*.

47  Cf. P. C. Wickens, *The City Mutual Story* (Sydney, 1978), chs, 8, 12 and 16.

48  *A Bank for the People* (North Melbourne, 1992), chs 17–19.

49  State Bank of Victoria, *Annual Reports*.

50  *Ibid.*, 1921–33; A. Cooch, *The State Savings Bank of Victoria* (Melbourne, 1934), p. 161.

51  Royal Commission into Monetary and Banking Systems in Australia, 1937, pp. 130–6.

52  Victoria, *Statistical Register 1916, Part II, Law, Crime etc.*, Papers presented to Parliament, Session 1917, vol 2.

53  Butlin, *Australian Domestic Product*, Table 201, p. 331. Figures have been converted to dollars.

54  A. E. Dingle and D. T. Merrett, 'Landlords in Suburban Melbourne, 1891–1911', *Australian Economic History Review*, vol. 17, no. 1, 1977; Jackson and Bridge, 'Housing'.

55  H. Kendig, *Buying and Renting* (Canberra, 1981), Figs 5. 2 and 5. 3, p. 81.

56  Butlin, *Investment in Australian Economic Development*.

57  *Australasian Insurance and Banking Record* (Melbourne, 1881), p. 343.

58  Sands & McDougall's *Melbourne and Suburban Directories* (Melbourne, various dates).

59  C. L. Pannam, *The Law of Money Lenders in Australia and New Zealand* (Sydney, 1965).

60  Hill, *Housing Finance*, Table 38; *Victorian Year Book*.

61  *Australian Financial System: Final Report*, p. 642, n. 19.

62  Carter, 'Housing Policy in the 1970s'.

63  H. Kendig, *Buying and Renting; The Cost of Housing* (Canberra, 1978).

64  P. Waxman and D. Lenard, *Investing in Residential Property* (North Brighton, 1994), Table 1. 4, p. 18.

65  R. V. Jackson, 'Owner-Occupation of Housing in Sydney, 1871 to 1891', *Australian Economic History Review*, vol. 10, no. 2, 1970; Dingle and Merrett, 'Landlords in Suburban Melbourne'.

66  Jackson, 'Owner-Occupation of Housing in Sydney', p. 143.

67  P. Abelson, 'House and Land Prices in Sydney from 1931 to 1989', *Urban Studies*, vol. 34, no. 9, 1997; Jackson and Bridge, 'Housing'.

68  Jackson and Bridge, 'Housing', Table HS 142–159, p. 353.

69  J. Grant, *Money of the Mind* (New York, 1992).

70  G. Whitwell, *Making the Market* (North Fitzroy, 1989).

71  Foster, *Australian Economic Statistics*, Table 5. 5b, p. 235.

253

# Home Ownership and the Illusion
# of Egalitarianism

## Chapter 15

*Blair Badcock*

From the vantage point of the munificence of home ownership following World War II, most Australians regard their housing system as a very fair one. Estimates suggest that during Australia's 'Golden Age' of home ownership, which spanned the 1950s, 1960s, and 1970s, almost 90 per cent of all households had a taste of owning at some stage of their lives.[1] Because the experience of home owning is so widespread, it is natural to assume that well-nigh everyone is still able to enjoy its benefits.

One of life's milestones is marked symbolically with the handing over of the keys to the first home that a family can really call their own—even if the bank does hold the mortgage for years after. For the first couple of generations after World War II this has been 'The stuff dreams are made of'.[2] Home ownership was not an unreasonable expectation for most Australians during the 1960s and 1970s, and it was this promise that helped to give substance to their sense that the society in which they were growing up was reasonably fair-minded in terms of opportunity and outcomes. More than half of Australia's city building took place during these decades and it was the physical production of equally modest homes on similarly sized building blocks in the suburbs that helped give additional credence at the time to this sense of good access and tolerably fair shares of housing.[3] In this way the suburban bungalow, with its generous backyard, came to occupy pride of place in popular versions of the good society.[4]

This consensus that Australians as a whole have been well served by a property system dominated by owner-occupation does not rest on sentiment alone. As it turned out, buying a home proved to be much more than just a means of 'getting ahead' for postwar generations. As stakeholders in the property system, and approaching retirement, these home owners have typically reaped the rewards of asset inflation through the 1970s and 1980s in the form of a 'wealth dividend'. On top of the equity steadily built up in the process of paying off the mortgage, they also profited from windfall capital gains as a result of the appreciation in house prices over time. Because wealth accumulation within owner-occupation has been so broadly based over the last few decades, on the face of it everyone seemed to be winners. Thus this sense among home owners of receiving a share of the wealth generated from buying and selling the family home is a further source of affirmation, if one was needed, that the Australian housing system works well and is equitable.

This view is also held by a number of expert commentators. They argue that as one of the pillars of our system of social distribution, the distinctive mode of housing provision that has been developed by Australian governments since the early 1950s has made an important contribution to the 'relatively egalitarian society' that Australia had become by the end of the 1980s.[5]

This chapter looks critically at the nature of home ownership in Australia, and in particular the underlying premise—so widespread as to be almost taken for granted—that the housing system has worked equally well for the majority of Australians. This belief in the inherent superiority of owner-occupation as a tenure is grounded in two assumptions: first, that the favoured form of housing provision in Australia is one of the defining traits of a genuinely egalitarian society; and second, that full participation as citizens is bound up to some extent with the property rights enshrined in home ownership. In the process of tracing the rise of owner-occupation the reasons for this become clearer, including the cultivation of the Great Australian Dream and the determination with which Australians pursue home ownership. The emphasis will be upon the two to three decades after World War II, which increasingly appear as Australia's Golden Age of home ownership.

In the next part of the chapter, attention turns to the presumption of fair shares of housing. What shares do different households get according to their employment, class, gender, age, and ethnic background? How well are the housing needs of these different households catered for in terms of tenure, costs, amount, condition, and location of their housing? Who misses out on home ownership, and are they disadvantaged as a result? And, given the way in which owner-occupation at around 70 per cent of all households so dominates the tenure mix in Australia, just how varied is the experience of home owners with respect to wealth accumulation? How evenly are the benefits of home ownership distributed amongst home buyers?

One of the implications behind these questions is that the kind of housing that society gets is ultimately a matter of public choice. When judged in terms of fairness, then, how does Australian society with such a large owner-occupied sector, and as one of the leading 'property-owning democracies',[6] compare with countries with different tenure systems—in particular, the Western European countries with much larger social housing sectors? Here we weigh up the views of various commentators who have given consideration to this question: on one side, Travers and Richardson, and Castles, and on the other, Kemeny. In between are people like Paris and Yates who, although acknowledging that a majority of Australians currently enjoy enviable housing standards and the fruits of wealth accumulation, are nonetheless perturbed by economic and social developments in the 1990s that contain the seeds of widening housing disparities.[7]

This raises the possibility that by the 1990s Australia had reached a crossroad in housing provision. Although governments and housing industry interest groups seem as intent as ever to promote and extend owner-occupation, and the desire amongst ordinary Australians to eventually own their home is undiminished, there are definite signs that some of the lustre has rubbed off the Great Australian Dream. These signs in the 1990s relate to several factors: the difficulty of knowing what the future holds in the job market, and to what extent compulsory superannuation contributions will restrict the options of prospective buyers on lower incomes; the rejection by increasing numbers of young adults of the suburban idyll; the deferral of home purchase by graduates with student loans to repay; reduced confidence in the ability of housing assets to out-perform other investments in the longer term; and a growing fear that policy reversals could render home ownership less secure in old age.

The chapter concludes with a final reflection on the place of home ownership in a fairer society.

## The rise of home ownership

Historically, Australia has been at the forefront in expanding home ownership. At the beginning of the twentieth century the level at least matched those reported in the United States and Canada, and certainly overshadowed that for England and Wales. At the time of the Commonwealth Census of 1911, when an overall home ownership rate of just on 50 per cent was recorded (Table 15.1), the corresponding figure was 46 per cent for the United States, and 45 per cent and 35 per cent respectively for Canadian and United States urban centres.[8] The economic historian N. G. Butlin notes approvingly that, even by this stage, Australian families were often able to live in their own modest cottage with a back yard.[9]

Flats were never regarded as 'the ideal home for the average Australian',[10] and Sydney and Melbourne never possessed the cramped tenement housing or the residential densities found in the inner neighbourhoods of big nineteenth-century cities in Europe and North America. At the same time rental housing investment never became as concentrated in the hands of slum landlords, feudal estates, or institutional landlords as in Britain or Europe, or the United States for that matter.

Yet national estimates tend to obscure evidence of variations in housing conditions and patterns of ownership between farming communities and the cities, and from suburb to suburb in the decades either side of 1900. By 1911 half the urban population was concentrated in just two cities, Sydney and Melbourne. But due to the local differences, economic downturn in the 1890s saw the respective rates of home ownership in Sydney and Melbourne shift from 28 and 41 per cent in 1891 to 31 and 35 per cent in 1911.[11]

Home ownership picked up again during the 1920s due to a felicitous 'conjunction of public policy and private profit seeking'.[12] Before World War I, finance was obtained from the banks, building societies and small-scale private lenders (see Chapter 14). When the New South Wales government granted its Savings Bank permission to advance home finance in 1912, this quickly caught on in the other states as well. Then immediately after the war, the Commonwealth made home loans available to ex-servicemen. Although more than 12,000 War Service Homes were financed in this way across Australia in 1918–19, the effect on the overall rate of ownership was only marginal.[13] But it seems that much of the decade's gains in the 1920s were lost in the early years of the Great Depression since, at the 1933 Census, the rate of home ownership had barely changed since 1921 (Table 15.1). It then sat around 52 or 53 per cent until after World War II.

During the twenty-five years after World War II, full employment, real wage gains, and government housing programs ensured that home ownership levels expanded in line with a fairer distribution of earnings for Australian workers. Typically, a family could pay off the mortgage on a suburban bungalow from the earnings of the main breadwinner, leaving the wife at home as nest-builder and child-rearer.[14] Near-to-full employment, combined with the guarantee of high minimum wages (the bounty of centralised wage-fixing), gave home buyers the confidence to enter into the long-term financial commitment of a mortgage. Once the downturn in the early 1960s was behind them, even tradesmen working full time, earning award rates plus skill-based margins and a bit of overtime, could generally manage the repayments, the furniture bill, and maybe a car on hire purchase.[15]

Nevertheless, the rapid climb of ownership levels to the 70 per cent mark by the beginning of the 1960s belies the extent of the housing backlog and associated housing stress after the war.[16] A government report put the housing shortfall at about 300,000 dwellings in the mid-1940s.[17] Not surprisingly, then, the Census in 1947 discovered that over 10 per cent of households were 'sharing', while over 80,000 people were counted 'sleeping out'.[18]

By 1950, and throughout the next decade or so, Australia, along with New Zealand, was constructing more housing for owner-occupation than any other industrialised country.[19] Where does the credit lie for this? This has been an open question amongst housing commentators for some time. Kemeny, for example, accuses the Commonwealth and states during the Menzies era of promoting the tenure in an 'aggressively interventionist' way.[20] In his view, the political promotion of home ownership by governments and the elaboration of an ideology to support this end has been decisive.

Certainly the War Service Homes scheme helped returning soldiers with advice and finance. 'By 1962 war-service homes agencies had assisted in the purchase and construction of nearly 72,000 homes in New South Wales, over half of which had been financed since 1956'.[21] Amendments to the

257

**Table 15.1** Major tenure categories (percentage of occupied private dwellings), 1911–1996

| | 1911 | 1921 | 1933 | 1947 | 1954 | 1961 | 1966 | 1971 | 1976 | 1981 | 1986 | 1991 | 1996 |
|---|---|---|---|---|---|---|---|---|---|---|---|---|---|
| Owner or purchaser | 49.4 | 52.4 | 52.6 | 53.4 | 63.3 | 70.3 | 71.4 | 68.8 | 68.4 | 70.1 | 69.1 | 67.3 | 67.8 |
| Tenant | 45.2 | 40.6 | 40.8 | 44.0 | 34.3 | 27.6 | 26.7 | 27.9 | 25.9 | 25.7 | 25.7 | 26.6 | 27.5 |
| Government | n.a. | n.a. | n.a. | n.a. | 4.3 | 4.2 | 5.2 | 5.6 | 5.2 | 5.1 | 5.4 | 5.7 | 5.2 |
| Private and other | n.a. | n.a. | n.a. | n.a. | 30.0 | 23.3 | 21.5 | 22.3 | 20.7 | 20.6 | 20.3 | 20.9 | 22.3 |
| Rent-free and unspecified | 5.4 | 7.0 | 6.6 | 2.6 | 2.4 | 2.2 | 1.9 | 3.3 | 5.8 | 4.2 | 5.2 | 6.1 | 4.7 |

*Note*: 'Private dwellings' excludes caravans, institutional accommodation, and hotels; 'government' refers to housing authority dwellings. n.a. = not available.

*Sources*: Statistics for 1911–33 from Bourassa *et al.*, 'The Limits of Housing Policy', *Housing Studies*, 10(1), Table 1, p. 85; for 1996, from ABS, *Census of Population and Housing*, 1996, Table B25, Community Profile tabulations.

Commonwealth–State Housing Agreement in 1956 diverted its funds to a Home Builders Account in support of low-income home buyers, and also paved the way for the sale of public rental stock constructed with program funds into owner-occupation. Between 1945/46 and 1968/69 almost 90,000 of these dwellings were sold Australia-wide, with New South Wales and Victoria accounting for nearly two-thirds of the total.[22] But significantly, less than 5 per cent of government-owned dwellings had been sold by 1954/55, which marks the end of a period in which home ownership rates accelerated more rapidly than in any other intercensal period (Table 15.1).

More careful consideration of contemporary accounts of conditions at the time suggest that there were other, equally important, underlying factors at work during the 1950s and 1960s that helped to 'push Australia towards a more monotenural society'.[23] Although it was certainly not the intent, the continuation of rent control after the war actually deterred new investment in rental accommodation and led to serious neglect of maintenance.[24] One option for sitting tenants was to buy the nineteenth-century terrace house from the landlord, who, unable to get vacant possession, had little choice but to sell at a reduced price. This is how many overseas migrants acquired their first home in Australia. In the decade or so after the war, about 90,000 privately rented houses were sold off by landlords, or about one-sixth of the private rental stock.[25]

Another possibility for young couples in desperate need of shelter and unable to find a place to rent was to move to a block on the edge of the city and begin to build their own home. Up to one-third of all dwellings during the 1950s were built by owner-builders who first bought the land, and then built the house bit by bit as savings and availability of scarce building materials allowed (see Chapter 4). G. C. Bethune estimates that, all told, the effects of rent control probably account for about 8 per cent of the increase in owner-occupation between 1947 and 1961.[26]

Lastly, as Bourassa *et al.* argue, the fact that home ownership rates have not climbed any further since peaking in the first half of the 1960s (Table 15.1) is a further reason for questioning Kemeny's undue stress upon state sponsorship of the tenure.

> In spite of continued government support for owner occupancy reflected in low and controlled mortgage interest rates, capital grant schemes, new mortgage instruments to cushion repayments, and exclusion from income taxes, successive Commonwealth and state governments have had to struggle to maintain owner occupancy at or near 70 per cent.[27]

## Australian housing: Fair shares?

The intuitive sense that somehow Australia is a more equal society than others because so many Australians share the material benefits of home ownership is partly true: Australian housing standards do compare more than favourably with the rest of the world. In his 1974 Boyer Lectures, Hugh Stretton claimed that those Australians who owned a quarter-acre block enjoyed housing that was the envy of the world.[28] Similarly, the audit of the housing system undertaken by the National Housing Strategy at the beginning of the 1990s determined that Australia now has an adequate stock of dwellings to meet its medium-term needs.[29] This implies that if there is a 'housing problem' it is one of distribution, and it is unlikely to be resolved in the near future given the strict limits on government spending in the 1990s.

By the same token, investment in rental housing has never been especially concentrated in the hands of a few.[30] A survey of rental investors in the mid-1990s found that only 6 per cent of the adult population owns rental property; of these, four-fifths own only the one dwelling, versus the 4 per cent with five or more.[31] According to the survey, these are overwhelmingly small-time property investors with median incomes in a range, at the time, between $25,000–$30,000—only 20 per cent of them received over $50,000 a year. This pattern is likely to become even more broadly based in the future as retirees convert termination payments and savings into rental income.

Nevertheless, if Stretton was implying that most Australians enjoyed enviable housing standards and some portion of housing wealth, he did not overlook the distributional blemishes of our housing system. Although attacked for defending 'a housing policy for the middle classes',[32] he has repeatedly drawn attention to inequities: the tendency for Australians in the upper segment of the market to over-consume housing; the insufficient consideration given to the housing needs of women and children; the way housing markets deny some poor households access to services in Australian cities — especially families allocated to public housing in the outer suburbs.[33] And more recently, with the push by governments to increase urban densities, Stretton, along with Troy, has drawn attention to the possibility that the poor will end up with the 'landless housing'.[34]

Who does this leave out then, and in what sense are they second-class citizens because they are denied access to housing with the same standards and security of tenure that the rest of us enjoy? Systemic differences are apparent between the main tenures, and there are less obvious variations within the owner-occupied housing sector. In most cases they can be traced back to the disparities that exist between market earnings, and whether or not the household as an economic unit draws upon more than one income. In Sydney and Melbourne, a one-income household must receive well above average earnings to achieve home ownership.

Judith Yates shows that the growing inequality in earnings at the household level in Australia has resulted in a corresponding increase in the home ownership differential between the lowest and highest income quintiles of almost ten percentage points between 1975 and 1994.[35] This is due almost entirely to the falling rate of ownership among households in the bottom one-fifth of the income scale: although the home ownership rate remained steady at about 80 per cent for the highest quintile, it fell away from 69.5 per cent in 1975 to 61.5 per cent in 1994 for wage earners making up the lowest quintile.[36] This has taken place against a backdrop of an ageing population and a trend to smaller households over the last twenty-five years or so. Partly as a result, home purchase rates among the under-thirties have slightly declined right across the income spectrum, while outright ownership rates among those aged over forty-five climbed in every income quintile between 1982 and 1995, according to Yates.[37] At the same time it is apparent that these lower rates of purchase among younger households are being offset to some extent in the top two quintiles by the inter-generational transfer of housing wealth. Thus inheritance is helping some fortunate households with very good earning potential to possess a fully paid-off home at an early stage of their working lives.

When the access of different types of households to the respective tenures is set against their relative preponderance within the general population, the limiting effect of a single, possibly statutory, income is clear. The 22 per cent of persons living alone and the 9 per cent of single-parent families disproportionately miss out on owning their own homes. Only 6 per cent of households headed by a lone parent own or are buying. And although more of the householders living by themselves become owners towards the end of their lives as properties are transferred to widows or widowers (24 per cent), far fewer are ever buyers (11.6 per cent).[38]

Not surprisingly, this disparity in access between one-income and two-income households also carries over into home ownership, where it acts to segment the owner-occupied housing market. With a higher combined income, 48 per cent of married couples buying their first home in 1988/90 were able to borrow $60,000 or more, compared with just 25 per cent of lone parents and 41 per cent of singles.[39] Significantly, among married couples, those without children were twice as likely in 1988/90 (37.5 per cent) to have combined earnings in excess of $55,000 as couples with dependent children (18 per cent). These income differentials, therefore, have a crucial bearing, not only on the type and quality of housing that households can afford to buy, but also on where they can afford to live, both within the state capitals and also within the Australian countryside.[40]

The background and date of arrival of postwar migrants has also dictated access to home ownership. Remarkably, those migrating from Europe in time to participate in the postwar prosperity currently enjoy higher levels of outright ownership (51.8 per cent) than their Australian-born counterparts (41.6 per cent). By contrast, much higher proportions of the recent migrant intake from countries in South-East Asia (41.7 per cent), North-East Asia (41.9 per cent), and South and Central America (49 per cent) remain trapped in the rental sector simply because of the shortage of secure employment in the 1980s and 1990s. Thus in 1988/90 the disparity in home ownership rates between the respective birthplace groups was as follows: Australia, 71.2 per cent; Europe and the USSR, 77.8 per cent; South-East Asia, 56.6 per cent; North-East Asia, 54.9 per cent; South and Central America, 51 per cent.[41]

This difference between owning and renting for most Australians holds the key to whether or not they will acquire much wealth in their lifetime. In the

261

case of tenants, rent represents money down the drain. Owner-buyers, on the other hand, are increasing their equity in a fixed asset that they will eventually own outright. Besides, the principal place of residence is a tax-privileged asset. The imputed rental income, capital gains, and housing inheritance from owner-occupied property are generally exempt from taxes or duties in Australia. Thus the tax revenue forgone by the federal government benefits home owners at the expense of tenants. J. Flood estimates that in 1990/91, the flow of subsidies to each housing tenure in Australia was as follows: public tenants, $1.04 billion; private tenants, $1.19 billion; home buyers, $1.64 billion; and, outright owners, $4.65 billion.[42] For these reasons home ownership is the dominant source of privately acquired wealth in Australia, which makes it all the more inequitable for those Australians in rental housing who miss out. Until the spread of share ownership in the 1990s, housing wealth as a share of all private wealth in Australia hovered between 60 and 65 per cent.

Beyond that, with such an extensive owner-occupied sector in Australia, home ownership can lead to widely divergent outcomes with respect to capital accumulation, or the amassing of housing wealth in the course of a lifetime. This usually depends upon when home owners bought their housing in relation to the property cycle, and in which suburb of which particular city they purchased their several homes.[43] The dominant experience throughout the decades synonymous with the Golden Age of home ownership was one of real accumulation, but not all home owners automatically stood to gain. In real terms, house price appreciation in some outer suburbs has lagged well behind the inner city during the 1980s and 1990s.[44] In fact, in some of the outermost suburbs of Sydney, Melbourne, Brisbane, and Adelaide, house prices failed to keep pace with inflation, so that homes lost value in real terms. By contrast, home owners in the inner city and nearby suburbs have all benefited financially from the strengthening housing market as middle-class renovators and townhouse developers have bid up local property values.[45]

There is also evidence to suggest that the flow of capital accumulation within the housing market tends to reinforce the systematic disadvantage encountered in the labour market with respect to job access and earnings, and that the inter-generational transmission of housing wealth is not doing much to break down the existing class structure within Australian society.[46] Therefore Australians need to realise that, under certain market conditions, owner-occupation can generate inequities in income and wealth. Of course, those households unable to buy their own home missed out altogether on the opportunity to capture the 'wealth dividend' that accompanied property inflation throughout the 1970s and 1980s.

## Does mass home ownership make Australia more egalitarian?

The idea that owner-occupation is one of the pillars upon which an egalitarian society is built remains strongly implanted in the popular consciousness of the postwar generation of Australians. It also finds support among academics like

Travers and Richardson.[47] They base their depiction of Australia as a 'relatively egalitarian society' upon four factors that are also believed to hold the key to the future: employment; the social security (or income maintenance) system; home ownership; the communal provision of other goods and services.

Kemeny has always disagreed with this assessment.[48] He says it should not be taken for granted that Australia is a more equal society than others just because we have one of the highest levels of home ownership in the world. In his view, political sponsorship has been backed up by such persuasive ideology in support of property ownership that few Australians ever stop to consider the possibilities offered by other tenure systems. What is not widely appreciated is that, despite such high levels of home ownership, property-owning democracies like Australia, the United States, Britain, Canada, and New Zealand, have fallen behind a group of countries in Western Europe with much lower overall home ownership rates and yet greater prosperity. Besides, in countries like the Netherlands, Norway, Austria, Switzerland, Sweden and Germany, the systems of income maintenance and social security are more broadly based, suggesting that it is wrong-headed to automatically equate high levels of home ownership with a fairer society.

A further perspective is offered by Castles, who maintains that this is to overlook the implicit trade-off between owner-occupation and welfare expenditure that has operated in Australia since the 1950s. He attempts to show that the tax expenditures forgone by government in support of owner-occupation, and the horizontal redistribution that occurs during a lifetime of home ownership in Australia, make up in retirement for 'the seeming lack of generosity of Australia's means-tested and flat-rate benefits system'.[49] Thus Castles sees the financial assistance made available to home buyers by successive postwar governments in Australia as part of the social bargain with workers. This is all very well, of course, but it leaves those in the rental sector out of this particular equation. These represent the spectrum of views, then, about the fairness of housing provision in Australia, and the extent to which home ownership both mirrors and helps to determine the structure of society.

263

## Owner-occupation and the egalitarian vision in the 1990s

Having reached almost 72 per cent in the mid-1960s, and remained more or less static since, home ownership is becoming increasingly difficult to sustain at this level. Housing industry analysts are perplexed by the decline in home ownership rates amongst households who have traditionally formed the majority of first-home buyers. The proportion of households buying, as opposed to owning outright, fell from 36 per cent in 1976 to 28 per cent in 1994.[50] Undoubtedly more home buyers paid off their mortgage in the interim, but this was not sufficiently offset by the numbers purchasing a first home. As yet there is no sign that this trend has stabilised; and as might be expected, the corresponding increase in the proportion of 25–34-year-olds renting—up from 36 per cent in 1976 to 43 per cent in 1994—is placing mounting pressure on the private rental sector.

The Australian Life Course Survey conducted by the Institute of Family Studies in the final part of 1996 helps to throw some light on declining entry to home ownership. Of those home owners in the survey who bought in the second half of the 1950s, just on two-thirds had achieved their 'dream' by twenty-six years of age; whereas only one-third of those home owners who bought between 1990 and 1996 managed to do so by the same age.[51]

Does this mean that the 1990s is becoming a watershed decade with respect to the Great Australian Dream? Are some young adults opting to delay the purchase of their first home in the 1990s? And are there barriers to entry that stand to lock increasing numbers of younger people out of home ownership altogether? Again, evidence from the Australian Life Course Survey suggests that low-skilled and low-paid people are increasingly unlikely to ever own a home if they have not bought by the time they reach the age of thirty-five years.[52]

A variety of complex reasons have been advanced to explain the dramatic decline in the purchase rate. Perversely, this has happened even though housing for first-time buyers became more affordable in the 1990s. Never-theless, to begin with, Malone estimates that the absolute size of the key household-forming cohort—20–34-year-olds—fell by about two-thirds when the annual additions recorded during the years 1981–91 are compared with 1991–95.[53] Second, this current generation appears to have postponed entry into home ownership partly because more of them are staying at home while they complete their studies, and partly because of competing claims on their savings: student loans, health insurance, and the compulsory superannuation levy. About one-third of the age cohort from which most first-home buyers are drawn are going on to tertiary studies, leaving them to repay their student loans when they would normally be saving for a home deposit.

Third, technological and structural pressures for change in the economy over the last couple of decades are indirectly having a major impact upon the housing options of young Australians. With not enough jobs to go round, underqualified young people are precluded from paid work altogether and face a grim time in the housing market. Also, greater numbers of tertiary students are going on to graduate studies to increase their competitiveness in the job market. Although this undoubtedly boosts the earnings of some entrants to the workforce, permanent full-time employment is on the decline and potential young home buyers now face the prospect of short-term contracts and much greater geographical mobility. According to estimates prepared by the (former) Department of Social Security, 'around one in five Australian employees work variable hours and do not have security of employment or leave entitlements'.[54]

Thus the phenomenon of fewer first-time owners lies not so much with the availability of home finance, but with the unknowable risks that workers now face in a deregulated labour market. Although financial deregulation and the competition from mortgage originators have undoubtedly led to the most affordable housing in a generation, households that are stretched to the limit when they buy become the first casualties in a downturn:

Risks of unemployment as a result of restructuring are borne primarily by the low skilled; risks inherent in cyclical collapses of housing markets are borne by those who are forced to sell because they do not have sufficient resources to wait for recovery; risks of increased interest impinge most heavily on those on the margin of home purchase.[55]

As the unprecedented tightening of interest rates emphasised in the late 1980s, home ownership can quickly become a millstone for some low-income buyers if economic events turn against them.

## The place of home ownership in a fairer society

The way the housing system has been developed by successive postwar governments in this country presents Australians with a somewhat paradoxical outcome. By international standards the majority of the community is well-housed, except that the high level of owner-occupation achieved has not ensured a higher standard of living, or the fairest distribution of income and wealth across the community. Although home owners are undoubtedly well served by the present housing system if allowance is made for the vagaries of the property market, the same cannot be said for many tenants.[56] 265

In the 1990s, at a time when poorly skilled workers were most vulnerable to workplace restructuring, Australian governments sought to redirect a significant share of the meagre housing assistance that formerly went to the public housing sector into increased rental assistance for private tenants. Consequently, state housing authorities are under pressure to sell off public rental stock and transfer tenants from the one tenure that offers needy households the greatest long-term security. Although this redistribution is justified on the grounds that it will achieve greater equity within the rental sector between public tenants and private tenants, it makes absolutely no demands on owner-occupiers, who continue to enjoy significant tax breaks.[57]

Paradoxically, if Australians are to retrieve the essence of the values that they believe owner-occupation has traditionally embodied, the long-standing obsession with home ownership will need to be tempered. This means coming to the realisation that in order for the minority to be as soundly and securely housed as the majority of households that are buying or own their own home, governments will have to develop alternative institutional arrangements and resourcing for housing provision.

Will some of the anticipated directions in national housing policy—community housing, shared equity, housing allowances for tenants to optimise tenure and locational choice—address these issues sufficiently to offset the polarising tendencies in the labour market over the next two decades? With the present political mood of the community, this seems unlikely. Part of the larger paradox is that property ownership is now so broadly based in societies like the United States, Britain, and Australia that it has given rise to a 'culture of contentment' amongst middle-class voters,[58] and with it the abandonment of the postwar commitment to building a fairer society. The middle classes continue to reap the benefits of home ownership,[59] which helps to sustain the illusion that it is accessible to all 'ordinary' Australians like themselves. It is this, more than anything else, that contributes to the perpetuation of the illusion of egalitarianism in the political consciousness.

**Notes**

1  M. Neutze and H. Kendig, 'Achievement of Home Ownership among Post-war Australian Cohorts', *Housing Studies*, vol. 6, 1991.

2  A. Greig, *The Stuff Dreams Are Made Of* (Melbourne, 1995).

3  M. Neutze, *Urban Development in Australia* (Sydney, 1977).

4  D. Horne, *The Lucky Country* (Sydney, 1968).

5  P. Travers and S. Richardson, *Living Decently* (Melbourne, 1993); F. G. Castles, 'The Really Big Trade-off', paper presented at the eighth national conference of the Australian Population Association, Adelaide, 3–6 December 1996.

6  M. Daunton, *A Property-owning Democracy?* (London, 1987).

7  Travers and Richardson, *Living Decently*; Castles, 'The Really Big Trade-off'; J. Kemeny, *The Great Australian Nightmare* (Melbourne, 1983); C. Paris, *Housing Australia* (Melbourne, 1993); J. Yates, 'Changing Directions in Australian Housing Policies', *Housing Studies*, vol. 12, 1997.

8  C. Harris and C. Hamnett, 'The Myth of the Promised Land', *Annals of the Association of American Geographers*, vol. 77, 1987, Table 1, p. 177.

9  *Investment in Australian Economic Development, 1861–1900* (Cambridge, 1964), pp. 211–12.

10  T. Kass, 'Cheaper than Rent', in M. Kelly (ed.), *Sydney: City of Suburbs* (Kensington, 1987).

11  R. V. Jackson, 'Owner-occupation of Houses in Sydney, 1871 to 1891', *Australian Economic History Review*, vol. 10, 1970; A. E. Dingle and D. T. Merrett, 'Home Owners and Tenants in Melbourne, 1891–1911', *Australian Economic History Review*, vol. 12, 1972.

12  Kass, 'Cheaper than Rent', p. 84.

13  S. C. Bourassa, A. W. Greig and P. N. Troy, 'The Limits of Housing Policy', *Housing Studies*, vol. 10, 1995, p. 85.

14  C. Allport, 'Women and Suburban Housing', in P. Williams (ed.), *Social Processes and the City* (Sydney, 1983).

15  M. Peel, *Good Times, Hard Times* (Melbourne, 1995), p. 96.

16  Greig, *The Stuff Dreams Are Made Of*, pp. 97–120.

17  Commonwealth Housing Commission, *Final Report*, 1944, p. 8–11.

18  Greig, *The Stuff Dreams Are Made Of*, p. 36.

19  ANZ, *Australian Housing Survey* (Melbourne, 1954).

20  Kemeny, *The Great Australian Nightmare*, p. 22.

21  C. Allport, 'Castles of Security', in Kelly (ed.), *Sydney: City of Suburbs*, p. 99.

22  M. A. Jones, *Housing and Poverty in Australia* (Melbourne, 1972).
23  Greig, *The Stuff Dreams Are Made Of*, p. 118.
24  Kass, 'Cheaper than Rent', p. 89.
25  M. R. Hill, *Housing Finance in Australia, 1945–1956* (Melbourne, 1959), pp. 6–7.
26  'Home Ownership in Australian Capital Cities with Particular Reference to Melbourne and Sydney', PhD thesis, Australian National University, p. 166.
27  Bourassa, Greig and Troy, 'The Limits of Housing Policy', p. 87; Kemeny, *The Great Australian Nightmare.*
28  *Housing and Government* (Adelaide, 1974), p. 7.
29  National Housing Strategy, *Australian Housing: The Demographic, Economic and Social Environment* (Canberra, 1991).
30  C. Paris, *Affordable and Available Housing* (Canberra, 1984).
31  Australian Bureau of Statistics, *Investors in Rental Dwellings* (Canberra).
32  J. Paterson, 'Home Owning, Home Renting and Income Redistribution', *Australian Quarterly*, vol. 47, 1975.
33  B. Cass, *The Housing Needs of Women and Children* (Canberra, 1991).
34  H. Stretton, *Political Essays* (Melbourne, 1987); P. N. Troy, *The Perils of Urban Consolidation* (Sydney, 1996).
35  *Trends in Home Ownership* (Sydney, 1998).                                    267
36  *Ibid.*, pp. 18–23.
37  *Ibid.*, pp. 29–31.
38  Australian Bureau of Statistics, *Housing: A Statistical Overview* (Canberra, 1996), p. 35.
39  Australian Bureau of Statistics, *First Home Buyers Australia 1988 to 1990* (Canberra), p. 12.
40  B. A. Badcock, *Unfairly Structured Cities* (Oxford, 1984), pp. 182–9; A. Beer, A. Bolam, and A. Maude, *Beyond the Capitals* (Canberra, 1994).
41  Australian Bureau of Statistics, *First Home Buyers Australia*, p. 7.
42  J. Flood, 'Housing Subsidies, 1990–91', paper presented at the conference of the Institute of Australian Geographers, Monash University, 1993.
43  B. A. Badcock, 'Homeownership and the Accumulation of Real Wealth', *Environment and Planning D*, vol. 7, 1989; B. A. Badcock, 'Urban and Regional Restructuring and Spatial Transfers of Housing Wealth', *Progress in Human Geography*, vol. 18, 1994; A. Beer, 'Owner-occupation and Profit', PhD thesis, Australian National University, 1989.
44  P. Abelson, 'House and Land Prices in Sydney from 1931 to 1989', *Urban Studies*, vol. 34, 1997; C. Maher, 'Housing Prices and Geographical Scale', *Urban Studies*, vol. 31, 1994.
45  B. A. Badcock and M. A. Browett, 'Adelaide's "Heart Transplant", 1970–88: 3. The Deployment in the Renovation and Redevelopment Submarkets', *Environment and Planning A*, vol. 24, 1992.
46  B. A. Badcock, ' "Snakes or ladders"?', *International Journal of Urban and Regional Research*, vol. 18, 1994; A. Burbidge, 'Capital Gains, Homeownership and Economic Inequality', *Housing Studies*, vol. 15, forthcoming.
47  *Living Decently*, pp. 200–23.

48  *The Great Australian Nightmare.*
49  Castles, 'The Really Big Trade–off', p. 3.
50  Australian Bureau of Statistics, *Housing: A Statistical Overview*, p. 14.
51  I. Winter and W. Stone, 'Social Polarisation and Housing Careers. Exploring the Interrelationship of Labour and Housing Markets in Australia' (Melbourne, 1998), p. 15.
52  Winter and Stone, 'Social Polarisation and Housing Careers', p. 15.
53  P. Malone, 'Emerging Housing Trends to the Next Millennium', paper presented at the eighth national conference of the Australian Population Association, Adelaide, 3–6 December 1996, p. 8.
54  A. Harding, *The Suffering Middle* (Canberra, 1997), p. 3.
55  Yates, 'Changing Directions in Australian Housing Policies', p. 277.
56  T. Dalton and C. Maher, 'Private Renting: Changing Context and Policy Directions', *Just Policy*, vol. 7, 1996.
57  Yates, 'Changing Directions in Australian Housing Policies', p. 277.
58  J. K. Galbraith, *The Culture of Contentment* (London, 1992).
59  P. N. Troy, 'The Benefits of Owner-occupation', Working Paper No. 29, Urban Research Program, Australian National University (Canberra, 1991).

## Chapter 16

# Between the Houses

*Mark Peel*

## Stories of neighbouring and community                                             269

If there is a generally held commonsense view about the Australian city, it goes something like this: there has been and continues to be a 'decline' of local community, compared to some time in the past when people knew their neighbours and looked out for each other. Women mostly stayed at home; they dropped in for a cuppa and a chat, and would do a bit of shopping for you if your kids were sick or the electrician was coming. Children played safely in a protective world of watchful neighbours. Men, home from the duties of their day, relinquished the comforts of the armchair long enough to share a beer with next door, make sure Saturday's junior football was organised, or—in the 'better' suburbs—attend a Rotary meeting or the local Lions Club. Then this kind of neighbourhood began to erode. People grew less friendly and less neighbourly. Maybe it was cars, or television, or married women who went to work. Nowadays it is all drawn blinds and high fences, people you don't see much, neighbours without names in communities without spirit.

This story is repeated in most industrialised societies. American historian Thomas Bender has shown how 'successive breakdowns' of community dominate the narrative of America's past; as he suggests, 'Statements about community assume a very definite past . . . In the past, there was community; in the present it has been (or is being) lost'.[1] The story is supported by some historians, sociologists and experts, and journalists can almost always find someone to endorse it. Yet it is, as Bender notes, a 'rather closed logic of social explanation . . . which effectively defeats historical curiosity'.[2] Certainly, if curiosity overcomes prior conviction, the evidence for a general and inexorable decline in neighbouring activity or community is not compelling. The nature and extent of social connections between households certainly vary over time and between places. Within the life-cycle of one family or one household, relations with neighbours can change dramatically. Frequent interaction—borrowing tools or sugar or milk, helping with the garden, minding next-door's children, taking part in local community organisations and events, and so on—seems to depend upon most people in the same place sharing a similar experience or life-stage. At the same time, apparently anonymous suburban streets come to life during a crisis or a celebration, revealing local connections that are hard to see from the outside. And it seems that most people living in the suburbs of the 1990s are not convinced that theirs is a world of self-absorbed isolation; a study of Melbourne's Berwick, for instance, found that most residents 'had a strong sense of the neighbourliness of their area . . . [and the] sense of isolation sometimes commented upon in regard to outer suburban areas was not very much in evidence'.[3] As Lyn Richards insists, representations of 'soulless suburbia' too readily assume that everyone shares the same experiences and the same ideas. They help little in explaining real lives in real places.[4]

Neighbourhood life has certainly changed during the twentieth century, largely because more people in the past lived in situations where localised support, exchange and interaction were an important facet of getting by. Rather than assuming that one universal experience—neighbourhood community—has been replaced by another—suburban isolation—however, it is important to examine what creates, sustains or diminishes particular forms of neighbourhood community in particular places and times.

Neighbourhoods are built from imagined as well as actual connections. While some studies attempt to quantify the frequency of interactions by counting the number of times different people attend community events or join clubs, most of our evidence about neighbouring in Australia comes from stories, largely oral histories. These stories record not a simple or straightforward decline of interactions between households, but different versions of a persistently tense relationship between neighbourliness and distance, community and privacy. In general, they focus on the achievement of privacy in a 'real home', as well as the ambivalent consequences of more and more Australians being able to fulfil that dream, mostly in the suburbs of the larger cities. The family home on a private block did not destroy community, but it has had implications for people's real and imagined connections with others. To paraphrase Richards, we do not have to satirise or reject people's desire for a home, family and privacy in order to ask about the price they—and we—pay for their dreams.[5]

## Making neighbours

The story of declining neighbourliness tends to be generalised across place and time. The contention that neighbourhoods 'as we knew them' have disappeared is, in one sense, true, because major changes in the way most people carry out their everyday activities have had a significant impact on the nature of local life. If people once walked, but now drive, their most frequent social contacts are less likely to be local. Small local shops are bypassed for larger supermarkets and malls with little connection to neighbourhoods. A much higher proportion of married women, and especially mothers, work outside the home. A greater share of leisure time is likely to be spent indoors—listening to the radio in the 1920s and 1930s or watching television from the 1950s—rather than in public places like cinemas, clubs or hotels. With higher and more secure incomes during the boom that followed World War II, more people could afford houses large enough to accommodate play, social activities and entertaining. Children are particularly adept at figuratively (and sometimes literally) breaking down fences between households; there are fewer children around than in the 1950s and 1960s, and fewer reasons for neighbours to interact because of them. Telephones mean that more people can talk with and seek support from family members and friends rather than relying upon neighbours. More children go to schools outside the local area and must be driven or take public transport. And in the future, with electronic transfer, video shopping, email and internet, some people will spend more time in 'virtual communities' than in real ones.

Yet neighbourhoods have never been static, nor is there some inexorable common history of community giving way to isolation. Local connections have not diminished for all people in all places in the same way and at the same time. If the patterns described above are relatively common, the best conclusion is that, over time, most people have reduced their need and their opportunity to rely upon the services and people of a close-at-hand, everyday world. In other words, the conditions which seem to generate high levels of neighbourly interaction—what might be called the triggers for closer connections between households—are less compelling for most people at the end of the twentieth century than they were sixty or seventy years ago, though they will continue to play a part at some stage of most people's lives.

Studies of those triggers show that some events and conditions generally lead to more intense interaction between neighbours and to the more or less temporary creation of a sense of community. Shared space is obviously important, but just as important is shared time, especially the assumption that most if not all of the people around you are engaged in the same tasks and are 'in the same boat'. Most suburbs go through a pioneer phase, when everyone in a street or on a small estate is engaged in the same activities: moving in, starting a garden, finding creches or schools. Neighbours share common tasks, or collectively solve problems like child-minding, because they are, for a time, drawn together by common needs for which there may not yet be formal or private solutions. Young children, in particular, pull people closer, even across potential barriers such as different language and different cultural background; as children age, their activities—sport, music, parties—tend to take place further and further afield.[6]

The story of a shared new start is particularly intense in the new suburbs of the 1950s and 1960s, especially when the residents were also recent migrants

271

or moved quickly—sometimes over one weekend—into raw new estates. The first residents of suburbs like Elizabeth, in Adelaide, talk fondly of 'pioneer days': everybody had children, nobody had money, you made your own fun and got to know your neighbours.[7] Yet, as Lois Bryson and Faith Thompson found in 'Newtown', the pioneer period is relatively short: after a couple of years, it is replaced by a more discriminating pattern, and people tend to see only particular friends.[8] As Richards asserts, being present during the pioneer period might encourage interaction, but it does not guarantee it, especially for people who have no children and whose children are older, or for women who are working outside the home.[9]

The various studies of interaction in Australian cities and towns show that neighbourliness and community spirit rest largely on shared needs and interests, and on the extent to which people must or wish to meet those needs collectively rather than privately. Certainly, if high levels of interaction, identification and mutual assistance persist beyond the pioneer stage or a shared crisis, the most common explanation is not shared space, but a shared conviction that real neighbourliness (as opposed to a vague commitment to being neighbourly) is a good option for getting by. This is not to say that neighbouring is merely a mercenary assessment of costs and benefits, because loyalties, friendships and traditions persevere. A good number of people actively enjoy their neighbourhood, and participate in community events, churches, local clubs and service organisations. And we know that most people place a high value on the simple signals of greeting a neighbour, helping out in times of need, being friendly. But more intense neighbouring seems to occur—or at least persist—only among people who have, on balance, most to lose from its absence.

Active or strong neighbourhoods can also reflect isolation, immobility, shared problems, or some form of threat. In the almost 'hyperactive' rural community of 'Smalltown', for instance, it is distance and isolation which 'leave Smalltownites with little choice but to find solutions to many of their daily material and social needs in their immediate neighbourhood'.[10] Earlier studies of country towns also concluded that, although they were 'essentially neighbourly', their sense of community was based to a large extent on an 'anxiety and frustration springing from economic insecurity', and often masked powerful tensions between competition and co-operation.[11]

Age and infirmity, or the absence or breaking of family ties, also increases the likelihood that people will seek out and attempt to guarantee reciprocal ties with neighbours.[12] A high proportion of neighbours remaining in the same place for many years might also generate a sense of togetherness and shared needs. Lack of resources has a similar effect: in the inner suburbs of the 1920s and 1930s, or the poorly serviced outer suburbs of the 1950s and 1960s, there were few telephones and few cars, and people needed neighbours in the event of medical emergencies and other crises. And that same lack of resources, and the identification of certain places as 'slums' or 'bad areas', helps manufacture community spirit in another way. A proud insistence on neighbourliness is often a response to stigma and misconception.[13] In Melbourne's Richmond, 'If you were considered to "belong" to Richmond you were a somebody: you had an identity and a role that helped mitigate your insignificance in the eyes of the outside world.'[14] In working-class suburbs like Sydney's Mount Druitt or Brisbane's Inala, where resistance to outside perceptions remains the strongest anchor of local identity in the 1990s, community spirit is a statement of defiant togetherness that has real implications not just for the stories people tell about their place, but for how they act towards neighbours and strangers.[15]

Intensive forms of neighbourhood and community life are functions of spatially and historically specific circumstances. In the 1920s and 1930s, for instance, leisure often brought people together because popular entertainment remained largely local.[16] People visited the local picture house, barracked for the local team, and walked to dances at the church hall. Indeed, this may have created a much more vibrant local street culture in some suburbs than was evident in the 1890s.[17] In other places, then and now, including small towns or communities of migrants, highly localised business ties, credit and debt relationships, and job opportunities reinforce an assumption that local people are an important source of help, while also encouraging neighbourly behaviour as a means of gaining and keeping reputation and being known as trustworthy.

Neighbourhood and community ties can also rest on perceptions of threat and a need to band together against enemies. Since the 1970s, the verbal and practical signs of community are often visible in defensive actions: articulating a 'community interest' against further development, safeguarding local heritage, joining local surveillance systems such as Neighbourhood Watch, protesting against unwanted facilities such as waste dumps or prisons, or defending 'local values' against threatening newcomers, be they yuppies moving into inner Sydney warehouses or public housing tenants moving into new suburbs.

Neighbouring and local identity have always registered exclusion as much as inclusion, and much of the daily work which constitutes neighbourhood interaction revolves around the need to be vigilant and protective rather than welcoming. Nor is this only a matter of organised community protest; everyday relations between households are shaped just as much around the need for certainty and harmony. As Richards suggests, neighbouring, especially in the first instance, 'is a fact-gathering exercise'; the routines into which most people then settle rest on the assertion and assurance of common values.[18] It is not always important to know the neighbours intimately, but it is important to know *about* them and to be able to rely upon them remaining neighbourly. Bad neighbours can be subjected to a variety of sanctions, from malicious talk and shaming to the calling in of outside authorities like the police. So neighbouring often means controlling and managing the spaces between the houses, perhaps by attempting to ensure common adherence to neighbourhood standards of home maintenance, children's behaviour, or garden upkeep. In Jean Martin's 1960s studies of suburban communities, for instance, good neighbours were described as those whose habits confirmed rather than undermined your own 'family style'.[19]

273

These patterns are complicated within any particular neighbourhood by the networks laid down over time by different groups of residents. A group of people who move in at the same time may establish a strong sense of neighbourliness which, over the years, excludes newcomers. In one street, there may be two quite different communities: one of older residents who have known each other for years, another of recently arrived people, perhaps sharing another language and another culture and relying on each other for support. Particular events—campaigning for a bus service, or raising money for a child care-centre—might generate alliances and a sense of commitment to nearby others, but it can also create a leadership group that is closed to those who do not agree or to those who come later.[20] The traces and legacies of these temporary ties are evident in every neighbourhood. In any event, even well-established local ties are unlikely to encompass every person's social and cultural world. Friendly neighbours go to different churches, and members of the same community organisations might have markedly different political allegiances.

An assessment of neighbouring over time must also include the balance of responsibility within households for the performance of neighbourliness. These responsibilities tend to differ according to age and especially to gender, though different social and cultural groups add their own inflections. In most cases, women assume primary responsibility for the everyday relationships. They are the 'fact gatherers' who maintain and manage neighbourly interaction. For women who do not work outside the home, especially if they have young children, neighbours continue to be an important source of immediate help and friendship, and perhaps of distraction from the hard routines of washing, cleaning, cooking and shopping. Because women are still more likely to be at home, they use—and need—neighbours more often. Yet their relations with neighbours also change over time, especially as children grow, go to school and eventually leave home.

Most studies of neighbouring and community show that men are more likely to engage only in sporadic forms of neighbouring (sharing tools or mechanical expertise, perhaps), and expect wives to deal with the neighbours as part of their domestic duties. Men's neighbouring has little to do with their work, while women's neighbouring is considered to be a part of theirs. Men's community activities take them beyond the street, into more formal organisations and clubs, as Geoffrey Bolton remembers:

> Gradually we got to know our neighbours, and, by processes which escaped me at the time and are still to a large extent mystifying, my mother established networks and boundaries with them. My father had very little to do with the process. He had few close friends, finding sufficiency in home, work and increasing involvement with the local Anglican church . . . Although a number of Daphne Street men belonged to lodges and a few to trade unions, these activities did nothing to knit the street together as a community because they happened in various places elsewhere.[21]

The most easily generalised expectation is that women make homes and neighbourhoods, while men are primarily workers and—sometimes—members and leaders of larger community organisations and clubs.[22]

There are variations, of course. In working-class neighbourhoods, for instance, women—and especially mothers—seem more likely to manage both everyday neighbouring and the wider network of small-scale institutions; Janet McCalman's description of Richmond as 'essentially a feminine community in the street [while] men were bonded through the pubs and at work' represents a widely shared experience in the first half of the century.[23] Studies of working-class neighbourhoods in the 1950s, 1960s and 1970s show a similar pattern of wives acting as the key 'connectors', 'guardians' and 'internal caretakers'; husbands did little neighbouring, and participated most often in sex-segregated sporting, union or work-based friendship groups.[24] In four 'disadvantaged' suburbs studied in the 1990s, female workers and residents also did most of the work in institutions such as the neighbourhood house and were usually most vocal and influential in local activist groups. Indeed, the public world of these suburbs was mostly female, because government-funded community initiatives had helped draw a more localised and female-dominated neighbourhood and street life into more formal activism.[25]

Most studies of middle-class suburbs, on the other hand, show their 'community' to be focused in more formal organisations such as progress associations, church groups or business and sporting clubs, or local government.[26] Churches, especially their youth clubs, were also important in working-class areas, but the local church was perhaps the most vital social cement in the comfortable suburbs, and its influence remained strong throughout the 1950s.[27] Localised neighbouring, which remains a largely female activity, is less important than in working-class areas, while women's more restricted roles in formal organisations means they have a lower public profile in community life. However, as Kerry James points out, middle-class women are neither absent from nor powerless within formal community organisations; instead, they tend to act as 'amateur manipulators' of the system, exercising considerable power while maintaining both the image and the identity of 'conventionally proper wives and mothers'.[28]

This association between femininity and the 'close-by' neighbouring of conversation, vigilance and sharing is strong enough in people's minds to provide a ready-made explanation for the supposed decline of neighbourhood life: because more women work outside the home, their attention to neighbouring suffers, and local life withers. Yet a survey of neighbourhood and community life in Australia during the twentieth century suggests that there is no simple, straightforward and generalised decline, whether or not it was 'caused' by married women going to work. The intensity and depth of neighbouring and community has always varied between different places, and within each place, it has waxed and waned over time. The most intense and persistent forms of neighbouring and community participation have emerged where the great majority of local people share a similar life-stage, similar needs and goals, and a similar lack of viable alternatives; where physical or social isolation or immobility increase the practical and emotional importance of local ties; or where a mostly defensive togetherness arises in response to stigma, unwanted change or threats to local values. What can be asserted with some confidence is that, while most people still assert the importance of having good neighbours, carry on a low-key exchange of greetings and would help if really needed, relatively fewer people now depend upon that local world of friendship and support which once met a far larger share of basic needs.

## Stories of community and privacy

If it is better to talk about changing and not declining neighbourhoods, it is nonetheless true that the connections between most Australian households are now different. This is not because people no longer value—or say they value—neighbourliness. Nor is it because, at some undefined time in the past, most people rejected community and chose isolation. Desires for privacy, autonomy and self-sufficiency have always caused difficulties in neighbouring relation-ships which are, as Jean Martin observed, 'always in danger of getting out of hand'.[29] Whatever the limitations of being your own 'master'—for women or the poor, for instance—it has been a widely shared aspiration in the modern world. And it is an aspiration in which paramount symbolic and practical importance rests in having your own space, a 'room of one's own', which is shared only with intimates. Changing connections between Australian house-holds measure the extent to which, in the last half of the twentieth century, more people have fulfilled that aspiration through the possession of a self-contained, and preferably new, house on a suburban estate. The apparent decline of neighbouring is a product not of changing aspirations, but of their increasing realisation.

In part, most studies show that neighbourliness and community spirit have declined because they are based on first-hand testimonies and stories. People turn places into neighbourhoods in their memories, and the stories they tell are tactical, showing how things came to be the way they are.[30] This does not mean that what they say about neighbouring is untrue, or a 'nostalgia' which can only be overcome by rigorous investigation. Rather, it means being aware of what is said and what is not said, and of how we actively shape our life stories to show change and significance: we recreate the past as different from the present, most often by stressing loss or gain. In his study of a Perth suburban street, for example, Bolton recognises that his memories of a highly stable neighbourhood rest partly on what he has forgotten, or did not bring into his story. We also tend to remember the past as if things in that world never changed; as Bolton says, 'in old age an individual looks back on childhood as experienced in a stable landscape'.[31] Many of the stories about a lost sense of community share this insistence on a past in which there was less change, less pressure, and fewer differences.

When people talk about neighbouring—to a friend or to a researcher with a clipboard—they are also talking not just about direct experiences but also about expectations. Neighbourliness, or its absence, can be a metaphor for the superiority of a particular way of life. Self-consciously good neighbours tell stories about how it was better in the old days when 'everyone knew each other'. For the people of rural Smalltown, who idealise a place 'without secrets' where 'pretence and masquerade cannot be sustained', the simplifying general-isation that 'city people keep to themselves' is a crucial social cement.[32] In Smalltown and elsewhere, everyone can agree that people nowadays are too busy, too preoccupied, too self-centred, that people just aren't as friendly any more, and things aren't what they used to be.

These stories are not false. But they are more complex than they might first appear. In the intricate varieties of changes and decisions that they encompass, there are always traces of another story, a story about privacy, family and the importance of controlling your own destiny. In this story, people talk about investing everything they have in a dream of autonomy, self-sufficiency and freedom, and about enjoying the good life they have created. Maintaining this good life turns on the 'careful protection of a precious and precarious investment', a separate home which makes privacy possible.[33] Stories about neighbouring are often about how it was different in the beginning, how people were friendlier and more ready to help. But they are also structured by an opposition between good and bad neighbours in which metaphors for intru-sion—especially 'living in each other's pockets'—play a crucial role. Good neighbours maintain their distance; they don't intrude, and they don't allow their noises or smells or children to invade other people's homes. Good neigh-bours see what they are meant to see and know what they are intended to know.

As Lyn Richards suggests, the most common dream expressed in these stories is a dream of privacy. And privacy serves as a shorthand for other crucial achievements: autonomy, freedom from interference, the capacity to look after yourself and not rely on others, the ability to be who you want to be. It registers something which is 'ours', a security of self-possession and self-reliance. Home is an 'affective edifice', the experience of and the aspiration for familiarity, security and togetherness.[34] Home is a project for privacy. It describes that place where the mask can be taken off and the 'good' clothes exchanged for the comfortable ones. Coming home means closing the door on a world where you always perform to other people's expectations (see Chapter 13). It is a place in which to waste time, not spend it wisely, a place to drop things rather than put them away, a place where disorder can be satisfying and pleasurable. For all the ironic acknowledgement that what is 'ours' really belongs to the bank or the finance company, there is a powerful sense that without a home —without privacy or a place where you can be yourself— you can never be 'really free'.

In their stories, people describe the achievement of privacy and autonomy as a struggle in which long-term benefits finally outweigh short-term costs. There is pressure on men to keep the good job and the steady income, and

277

pressure on women to work before and sometimes after having children. To become homes, houses might need a lot of work: gardening, shelves, cupboards, and other additions to the relatively spartan shell most people can afford. As described in Chapter 4, thousands of these private projects were built by their owners on weekends. In the new suburbs of the 1920s, or the 1950s, or the 1990s, 'home' might mean bare boards and no furniture, at least for a few years. Yet it is, the stories agree, worth it in the end.

Many different people—public and private tenants in new outer suburbs as well as home buyers—talk about achieving privacy. And if some of the 'good old days' were more neighbourly, others were marked by people coming too close. They painstakingly record the problems of shared space, especially shared laundries, toilets, bathrooms and kitchens. They talk about beds shared and rooms divided by curtains. They describe the insecurities of renting from fickle landlords, and the discomforts of life shared with in-laws and parents. In working-class suburbs like Melbourne's Fitzroy, close-by living could mean help when it was needed, but it also meant 'you were always being looked at. You were always being examined . . . You couldn't have an argument without everyone else hearing.'[35] The warm memories of togetherness that Richmond people shared with Janet McCalman also registered the perils of local regard and reputation: 'the rich community life of Richmond inevitably limited privacy—just one slip from respectability and everyone knew about it'.[36] The people of Sydney's Green Valley, studied by T. Brennan in 1966, were excited not just by a new home but by their *own* home; their most common phrase was 'having a house to ourselves'.[37] British, German and Dutch migrants in the outer Adelaide suburb of Elizabeth talk about backyards, a private bathroom, even 'your own laundry trough' in their accounts of moving in during the 1950s and 1960s.[38] Diane Powell heard similar stories in Green Valley during the 1980s, especially the pleasure of a 'new kitchen, new stove, new bathroom'.[39] Renters and buyers of small Housing Commission houses shared a sense of achieved privacy and comfort and, perhaps most important of all, they associated their own home with being in charge, with making their own decisions about the future and running their own lives.[40]

The freedom and privacy of the home is also linked strongly with family life and children: for most people, especially women, this is not a place for individual solitude. Yet, as Lesley Johnson suggests, for a good many women in the 1940s and 1950s, 'home was not a place to withdraw into, but a place to be created . . . Their modernity was about actively creating a place called home, securing a future for their children.'[41] A private home—symbolised as a separate house with a garden and a backyard—was the best place, and perhaps the only place, in which women could fulfil their aspirations as good mothers and creators of a 'good family life'. Richards found that her Green Views respondents espoused similar ideas about the 'proper paths' of men's and women's lives: men and women largely shared a commitment to the traditional dream of togetherness, security and children.[42] And so it remains in the new suburbs of the 1980s and 1990s: 'those purchasing in Berwick were looking for a good

278

place to bring up young children and they see themselves as having satisfied that aim'.[43]

This achievement of private spaces for personal and family life is part of a much larger—and often underestimated—story about ordinary Australian life in the twentieth century. It is a story, largely written into history through community studies and oral testimony, in which people record how they struggled to fulfil a vital aspiration: control over their own destinies. It is a story about self-reliance and autonomy, in which higher living standards—especially through the achievement of a more secure income—have been translated into more privacy and into more individual, convenient and autonomous ways of 'getting by' and maybe even enjoying life: a car, an automatic washing machine, a television set. And it is a story which tends to symbolise those desires in the possession of a private home, a place of your own. There are other themes in the story, especially people's increasing ability to rely upon publicly provided welfare rather than the charity of neighbours or the complications of family money. And there are other inflections: for some, the story is more about the ability to choose to be alone, to change, to reinvent yourself and become something you could not be in a place where everyone already knows who you are. If some observers have seen anonymity in the city streets, those walking them have often described the pleasures of liberation and self-invention. If critics have seen isolation in the suburbs, those living there most often speak of achievement, of a sense of control and of freedom.

279

Of course, the dream is also manufactured. A current radio advertisement for cheap homes on Melbourne's urban fringe beckons those who are 'tired of waking up in a shoebox wrapped in the smell of the neighbours' breakfast'. In the 1920s, or the 1950s, or the 1980s, advertisements for 'your own home' usually depicted houses in a kind of splendid isolation, stick-figure children playing on 'their own lawn', your car parked in your driveway, hardly a hint that your house might be surrounded by others.[44] In the heavy-handed world of marketing this dream, neighbours were and are rarely present except as part of an assumed background, a 'quiet family community' in which to build your own family's future.

The identification of privacy with a private home is also the product of the building, planning, selling and designing decisions traced elsewhere in this book. Desires and aspirations are pursued in a world where other people and larger institutions make the decisions about how, when and where dreams might be realised. The dream is sought and lived in the structures and possibilities afforded by a particular organisation of technology and decision-making. In the last half of the twentieth century, and especially in Australia, a 'real' home means a home you own. Governments, banks and housing builders have enthusiastically endorsed the supposedly natural desire for home ownership and helped make it the most desirable option.

Some critics have derided this desire for a home, for a private place, as some creature of official policy, or as the product of an ideology which is somehow beyond the comprehension of the people whose lives it determines.

A more fruitful assessment, as Richards argues, is to accept the power of this dream yet to insist that it creates both satisfactions and problems.[45] The dream, in other words, has a price. It has particular consequences for women who 'carry the contradictions of dream', including the fact that if working for wages secures privacy, it also undermines the very neighbourhood community of which people imagine themselves to be part.[46] We need to acknowledge the dream, but also examine 'what it delivers and what it denies'.[47]

## Making good neighbours

The pursuit of private space and a more private life has consequences for the world between the houses. Although it does not simply replace neighbourliness with isolation, it does mean greater distance and respect for privacy, and it creates a powerful check upon interfering. It can mean more loneliness. In a world of private places and rooms of our own, public places can become deserted and dangerous, especially for the people who cannot afford private housing or private transport or private security. There are people who still need close-by friendship and care, and find little of either among their neighbours. As McCalman found among those who had left 'Struggletown', 'from the safety and loneliness of the suburbs, many escapees began to mourn a world we have lost'.[48] And there are also people for whom the only safe place is outside, not inside, the home. Privacy can create places of torment and danger, places too safe from prying eyes.

During the twentieth century, urban planners and architects, and the governments that regulate and service the cities, have inconsistently endeavoured to balance their endorsement of separated private living with their own desire for order, regularity, and rational development. Following behind the rapidly advancing suburban frontier, governments and public authorities have tried to ameliorate the consequences of inadequate planning that allowed developers to build houses and subdivisions without sewers or schools or shops. Yet attempts to enforce public responsibilities on private developers have had only limited success in convincing them that 'best practice' might mean something more than making large amounts of money as quickly as possible.

Australia's urban history is also punctuated, however, by attempts to plan and build neighbourhood communities, and each burst of reformist activity has brought with it a characteristic form of development. During and after World War I, this was the garden suburbs—Daceyville, Darra or Colonel Light Gardens—in which the benefits of rational planning would include the victory of decent family life over the back-lane sociability of inner-suburban slums (see Chapter 8). In that sense, the garden suburb aimed to overcome the wrong kind of neighbourliness rather than its absence.[49]

In the 1930s and 1940s, planners, housing reformers and health officials became activists against isolation as well as slums. Identifying a breakdown in neighbourhood life, and a loss of communal spirit, they explored the prospects for engineering neighbourhood community—and active citizenship—through better town planning, neighbourhood units, community centres, root-and-branch rebuilding of entire suburbs like Richmond, the development of planned public housing estates, and even the temporary provision of 'decanting areas' in which those mired in the habits of the slums might receive training in the domestic arts.[50] Those public housing estates were themselves the focus of 1960s and 1970s community and neighbourhood development strategies, as investigators like Brennan identified a dearth of 'local leaders' in suburbs like Green Valley and Mount Druitt.[51] Drawing on the insights of researchers such as Lois Bryson and Faith Thompson, others pioneered and developed a more participatory, locally based form of community and neighbourhood planning, which endeavoured to allow communities the power to define their own needs and to recognise the tremendous energy and resourcefulness which already existed, especially in so-called disadvantaged suburbs.[52]

In the 1990s, showcase developments also pay specific attention to the 'architecture of community'; planning rubrics like the new urbanism demand attention to streetscapes and the provision of public space, 'urban villages' promise 'rich neighbourhood life', and redevelopment schemes propose to 'revitalise' and 'resuscitate' tired public housing estates into 'vibrant communities'.[53] Like the garden cities and neighbourhood units before them, these estates promise to create 'the kinds of communities we need in cities' and 'the kind of local feeling and interaction associated with centuries of tradition in villages'.[54]

281

All of these different projects attempted to take account of the social world around each home, of the space between the houses. They tended to affect only those most easily reached by public authorities—tenants, the poor, the 'slum' dwellers—and they were sometimes offensive in their patronising attitude to those they claimed to be helping. Some demolition and slum-removal schemes arguably destroyed some communities in order to create new ones, and the implication that middle-class suburbs possessed the community apparently lacking in working-class areas was more a matter of faith than evidence. Nor is it always clear how good planning by itself was supposed to overcome economic misery, entrenched disadvantage, or a lack of neighbourhood interaction.

There was also, at least among some reformers and planners, some distrust of ordinary lives and ordinary dreams. In the 1940s, as the private home was extolled for its benefits, and as rooms and spaces were organised to foster respectable family life, it was also distrusted for its potential secrecy and the possibility that in those unseen rooms, 'slum habits' might simply re-emerge. The urban village advocates of the 1990s, on the other hand, seem convinced that if people want to stay in their houses, they must be lonely and unfulfilled. Understandings of the balance between privacy and neighbourliness remain rather clumsy; this might be less of a problem were it not that the people most easily forced to sacrifice private space for the uncertain benefits of 'rich community life' are almost always those who lack the means to purchase the secluded alternative.

Yet attempts to plan and sustain neighbourhoods should not be judged simply by such shortcomings. There is every reason to keep insisting that the builders and developers of Australian housing should design streets and neighbourhoods in ways which allow for interaction and engagement, and that governments should acknowledge—and retain—the responsibility to provide spaces and institutions which can be shared and used collectively. The objective is better planning, not less planning. There are already too many examples of poor designs which make neighbourliness and a sense of community more difficult to sustain, which undermine rather than encourage identification, and which build divisions rather than connections. Good design follows and confirms the paths which people take between the houses, provides safe places for play and conversation, mixes together different forms of housing, makes it as easy for the least mobile to reach the shops and the community centre as it is for the most mobile to reach the freeway. Builders and developers can and should take account of the architecture of community. They should design and build living spaces in which people can carry out their desires for community activity and neighbourliness. They might also build in ways which allow for transitions, for the conversion of shared facilities to new uses as people age, move on, and are replaced.[55]

But the history of Australian housing also suggests due regard for the architecture of privacy. The determination to achieve a private space—especially for family life—seems unyielding. Fulfilling that desire need not mean home ownership, and nor is it possible only in a separated, detached house. But housing and planning policies that ignore the desires for control, autonomy and security that are currently symbolised by the detached home will simply be undermined by anybody who has the financial means to avoid them. Inadequate, poorly designed homes which provide little privacy, and little protection from noise or interference, will be the fate of the poor and the young. Reducing the space between the houses, forcing people to see and hear and smell each other, and insisting that they sacrifice backyards for the uncertainties of common space is more likely to generate conflict, retreat and isolation than community spirit. If good neighbourhoods have places in which people can come together, they must also preserve people's ability to remain apart.

The real problem posed by the achievement and enjoyment of private spaces is not the death of neighbourhoods or the decline of local feeling. More important is the fact that some people are paying a high price for their dream, and are suffering poverty and isolation and anxiety because the only way to live their dream forces them to sacrifice everything in the here and now for the uncertain guarantees of a better tomorrow. The point might be to diversify the ways in which privacy and autonomy can be achieved, not reject the desires themselves.[56] Perhaps most important, the emphasis on self-reliance, on the individual purchase and ownership of a private space, hides the fact that privacy and autonomy are only achieved—by most people and at most times—because of the significant support provided by strangers. The self-reliance and self-sufficiency of the great majority of family households is crucially dependent not just upon secure and adequate income—itself a more precarious proposition in the late twentieth century—but also upon all of those services and infrastructures that are provided in common and that cannot be easily afforded alone.

The portrayal of the home, in political rhetoric, in advertising, and in the self-perceptions of many home owners, as something earned and as something to be protected, can sometimes blind individuals to the range of shared connections and commonly provided resources that they make use of in achieving their 'self-sufficiency'. If a secure, private place is an essential part of our conception of the good life—and the evidence suggests that it is—then that good life will remain possible for most of us only insofar as we continue to provide those public resources which allow most people to construct and enjoy their private worlds. Sovereign consumers, pursuing their desires, each with no regard for the impact of their decisions on others, living free of regulations, plans and obligations and looking out for number one: that is a 'society' which even the very rich might find uncomfortable before too long.

The real problem of the dream of privacy is not the desire to look out for your own and control your own destiny. Nor is it that, in fulfilling that dream, most people choose to live in separate homes with only occasional connections to the wider social world. The problem comes from the assumption that, having achieved their dream, each person can retreat into a world where they recognise obligations only to those who share that private realm. The creation of good neighbourhoods, indeed of good societies, depends on more than the hustle and bustle of the community centre or the friendly exchanges in the street or between the houses. It depends also on the care we take of strangers we cannot see and cannot know, the balance we strike between private and public fortunes, and our ability to be 'good neighbours' for those people with whom we will never actually share a fence.

283

## Notes

1  *Community and Social Change in America* (Baltimore, 1982), p. 4.

2  *Ibid.*, p. 5.

3  Peter Macdonald (ed.), *The Australian Living Standards Study. Berwick Report. Part 1: The Household Survey* (Melbourne, 1993), p. 462.

4  *Nobody's Home: Dreams and Realities in a New Suburb* (Melbourne, 1990), pp. 178–80.

5  'Suburbia: Domestic Dreaming', in Louise C. Johnson (ed.), *Suburban Dreaming: An Interdisciplinary Approach to Australian Cities* (Geelong, 1994), pp. 114–28, 125.

6  Lois Bryson and Faith Thompson, *An Australian Newtown: Life and Leadership in a Working Class Suburb* (Melbourne, 1972), pp. 118–22.

7  See, for instance, Linda Allery (comp.), *Elizabeth: From Dusty Plains to Royal Names* (Elizabeth, 1996). These stories are also described in Diane Powell, *Out West:*

*Perceptions of Sydney's Western Suburbs* (Sydney, 1993), pp. 76–81 and Mark Peel, *Good Times, Hard Times: The Past and the Future in Elizabeth* (Melbourne, 1995), pp. 116–20.

8  *An Australian Newtown*, p. 117.

9  'Suburbia: Domestic Dreaming', p. 124.

10  Ken Dempsey, *Smalltown: A Study of Social Inequality, Cohesion and Belonging* (Melbourne, 1990), p. 3.

11  A. J. and J. J. McIntyre, *Country Towns of Victoria: A Social Survey* (Melbourne, 1944), p. 271.

12  T. Brennan, *New Community: Problems and Policies* (Sydney, 1973), pp. 135–41; Powell, *Out West*, pp. 81–5.

13  Shirley Fitzgerald, *Chippendale: Beneath the Factory Wall* (Sydney, 1991), pp. 71–2; Tony Birch, 'The Battle for Spatial Control in Fitzroy', in Sarah Ferber, Chris Healy and Chris McAuliffe (eds), *Beasts of Suburbia: Reinterpreting Cultures in Australian Suburbs* (Melbourne, 1994), pp. 18–34; K. Spillman, *Identity Prized: A History of Subiaco* (Perth, 1985).

14  Janet McCalman, *Struggletown: Public and Private Life in Richmond, 1900–1965* (Melbourne, 1984), p. 265.

15  Dempsey, *Smalltown*, pp. 30–41; Powell, *Out West*, pp. 154–9; Mark Peel, 'The Ends of the Earth: Inala and Mount Druitt', in Tim Bonyhady and Tom Griffiths (eds), *Landscape and Language* (forthcoming).

16  McCalman, *Struggletown*, pp. 138–42.

17  A. Franklin, 'Working-Class Privatism', *Environment and Planning D*, vol. 7, 1989, pp. 93–113.

18  *Nobody's Home*, p. 266.

19  'Suburbia: Community and Network', in A. F. Davies and S. Encel (eds), *Australian Society: A Sociological Introduction*, 2nd edn (Melbourne, 1970), pp. 301–39.

20  Mark Peel, 'From the City for the Future to a Suburb with a Past: Memories of Elizabeth', in Kate Darian-Smith and Paula Hamilton (eds), *Memory and History in Twentieth-Century Australia* (Melbourne, 1994), pp. 210–28.

21  Geoffrey Bolton, *Daphne Street* (Perth, 1997), pp. 98–9.

22  Dempsey, *Smalltown*, pp. 274–95; Richards, *Nobody's Home*, pp. 148–57.

23  *Struggletown*, p. 184.

24  Bryson and Thompson, *An Australian Newtown*, pp. 109–26; Claire Williams, *Open Cut: The Working Class in an Australian Mining Town* (Sydney, 1981), pp. 136–46; Charles MacMahon, 'Participation in Voluntary Associations on a Working Class Housing Estate', *Australian and New Zealand Journal of Sociology*, vol. 10, 1974, pp. 177–83.

25  Mark Peel, 'Making a Place: Women in the "Workers' City"', *Australian Historical Studies*, vol. 26, 1994, pp. 19–38.

26  Martin, 'Suburbia: Community and Network', pp. 319–30; Dempsey, *Smalltown*, pp. 188–211.

27  McCalman, *Struggletown*, pp. 133–5; David Hilliard, 'Church, Family and Sexuality in Australia in the 1950s', in John Murphy and Judith Smart (eds), *The Forgotten*

*Fifties: Aspects of Australian Society and Culture in the 1950s* (Melbourne, 1997), pp. 133–46; Janet McCalman, *Journeyings: The Biography of a Middle-Class Generation, 1920–1990* (Melbourne, 1994), pp. 235–8.

28  'Public or Private: Participation by Women in a Country Town', in Margaret Bowman (ed.), *Beyond the City: Case Studies in Community Structure and Development* (Melbourne, 1981), p. 112.

29  'Suburbia: Community and Network', p. 315.

30  Vincent Berdoulay, 'Place, Meaning and Discourse in French-Language Geography', in John A. Agnew and James S. Duncan (eds), *The Power of Place: Bringing Together Geographical and Sociological Imaginations* (Boston, 1989), pp. 124–39.

31  *Daphne Street*, p. 13.

32  Dempsey, *Smalltown*, pp. 32, 36.

33  Richards, *Nobody's Home*, p. 235.

34  Ghassan Hage, 'At Home in the Entrails of the West', in Helen Grace *et al.*, *Home/World: Space Community and Marginality in Sydney's West* (Sydney, 1997), pp. 101–4.

35  Birch, 'The Battle for Spatial Control in Fitzroy', p. 30.

36  *Struggletown*, p. 130.

37  *New Community*, pp. 124–6.

38  Peel, *Good Times, Hard Times*, pp. 108–11.

39  *Out West*, p. 79.

40  Bronwyn Hanna, 'Green Valley: Sameness and Difference in Suburbia', *West*, vol. 3, no. 1, 1991, pp. 6–13.

41  ' "As Housewives We Are Worms": Women, Modernity and the Home Question', *Cultural Studies*, vol. 10, 1996, p. 453.

42  *Nobody's Home*, p. 157; see also M. Munro and R. Madigan, 'Privacy in the Private Sphere', *Housing Studies*, vol. 8, 1993.

43  McDonald (ed.), *Berwick Report*, p. 458.

44  Kim Dovey, 'Dreams on Display: Suburban Ideology in the Model Home', in Ferber, Healy and McAuliffe (eds), *Beasts of Suburbia*, pp. 127–47; Alastair Greig, *The Stuff Dreams Are Made Of* (Melbourne, 1995), pp. 157–86; R. Thorne, 'Housing as "Home" in the Australian Context', *People and Physical Environment Research*, vol. 26, 1991.

45  'Suburbia: Domestic Dreaming'.

46  Richards, *Nobody's Home*, pp. 135–9.

47  Dovey, 'Dreams on Display', p. 147.

48  *Struggletown*, p. 296.

49  Ian Hoskins, 'Constructing Time and Space in the Garden Suburb', in Ferber, Healy and McAuliffe (eds), *Beasts of Suburbia*, pp. 1–17.

50  Peel, *Good Times, Hard Times*, pp. 19–28; Kereen Reiger, *The Disenchantment of the Home: Modernizing the Australian Family, 1880–1940* (Melbourne, 1985), pp. 32–55; Birch, 'The Battle for Spatial Control in Fitzroy', pp. 20–5.

51  *New Community*, p. 119.

52  Bryson and Thompson, *An Australian Newtown*, pp. 299–312; Peel, *Good Times, Hard Times*, pp. 176–82; Judith Healy, 'The Resurgence of Community Centres', *Australian Journal of Social Issues*, vol. 24, 1989, pp. 285–302.

53  Mark Peel, 'The Urban Debate: From "Los Angeles" to the "Urban Village" ', in Patrick Troy (ed.), *Australian Cities: Issues, Strategies and Policies for Urban Australia in the 1990s* (Cambridge, 1995), pp. 39–64.
54  Peter Newman and Jeff Kenworthy, 'Transit-Oriented Urban Villages: Design Solution for the 90s', *Urban Futures Journal*, vol. 2, 1992, p. 50.
55  Hugh Stretton, *Ideas for Australian Cities*, 3rd edn (Sydney, 1989), pp. xlvi–xlix.
56  Johnson, ' "As Housewives We Are Worms" '.

**Chapter 17**   A HISTORICAL OVERVIEW OF AUSTRALIAN HOMELESSNESS

*Clem Lloyd*

Poor naked wretches, wheresoever you are,
That bide the pelting of this pitiless storm,
How shall your houseless heads and unfed sides,
Your looped and window'd raggedness, defend you
From seasons such as these?

KING LEAR, ACT 3, SCENE 4

Lear's ranting against the storm can be interpreted as a parable of the state's failures to shelter its poorer citizens, whether Anglo-Saxon, Tudor or contemporary. In a sense, this is true. Yet even the vagrant Lear found respite in a stone hovel whose 'poor naked wretches' turned him away, but were forced to show 'scanted courtesy'. The storm scene, however, is more a representation of vagabondage, the consequences of a pitiless public policy which ejected entire populations onto the roads. *Vagabondage* and *vagrancy* have similar connotations of shiftlessness, lacking fixed habitation, drifting to and fro, straggling, itinerant. Vagabonds, however, have some aura of romantic glamour (Vagabond Kings, Gypsy Barons, roving pirates). *Vagrancy* conveys personal fecklessness much more bluntly, although there is no linguistic reason why it should be so.

Christopher Hill reminds us that vagabondage has a lengthy history: 'The catastrophe of the Black Death [in the 14th Century] was followed by a century of declining population. There was a shortage of labour, land was unoccupied, and so a splendid opportunity was offered to serfs to liberate themselves by running away and settling elsewhere on uncultivated land.'[1]

These gusts of freedom, however, were short-lived. In 1495, a statute confined beggars who could not work to their last domicile. The Reformation expelled religious orders from their monastic havens onto milling roads. *Vagabond Acts* were passed which further leashed the right to wander, and roving religious sects, such as the Flagellants, and strolling players (possibly including Shakespeare), were deemed vagabonds. Enclosing, and then eliminating, the 'commons' land' led to serfdom and wage labour entrenched by law. Those wandering too far were flogged back to accustomed abodes. Parish workhouses regulated by Poor Laws survived in British society until the late

287

nineteenth century. The Poor Law and its processes were the crude solvents for vagrancy.

If vagrancy was the embodiment of homelessness in Britain over several centuries, it was not transmitted systemically to the British colonies. There, the basic task was creating a new housing stock suitable for British settlement. The first 150 years of colonial administration in North America turned societies inwards on their own resources. The homeless sheltered with families who were reimbursed by the town overseers, who perceived them charitably as unstigmatised wards of the community. From the mid-eighteenth century, however, economic growth with its inevitable recessions produced more poverty. As relief costs rose, American communities gradually adopted the English model, introducing laws compelling vagrants to move on, or, if able-bodied, to labour in communal workhouses. Vagrancy laws excluded indigent strangers and returned them to communities of origin for shelter and sustenance. Earlier tolerance for vagrancy that was founded on circumstances beyond individual control was supplanted by notions, reinforced by law, of transients as deviants. Charles Hoch argues that in colonial America, the conceptualisation of poverty as immoral arose among prosperous reformers wanting to replace informal institutional relief with the communal workhouse.[2] An example was the Bettering House in Philadelphia, whose ethos asserted that organised relief encouraged 'self-chosen' indolence by the poor: 'Although an economic and social failure that neither reformed the poor nor reduced the costs of relief, the Bettering House did (along with other such workhouse experiments) give institutional form to a new signpost for the homeless poor—the shameful vagrant.'[3]

From the mid-eighteenth century, homelessness intertwined with the economic cycle, increasing as the economy languished and declining with returning prosperity, generating community perceptions of homelessness as deviant. Accordingly, Hoch organised his interpretation of evolving homelessness in America around three sequential processes: tramping, deviant, victim.

Linking these factors with fluctuating economic cycles, Hoch builds a plausible explanatory model of American homelessness from the colonial homelessness of the early seventeenth century to the contemporary 'New Homelessness'. Australian homelessness has significant differences, but Hoch's lucid model provides an accessible tool for analysis.

White settlement of Australia and expansion of its dwelling stock has not been impeded by major famine, epidemic or invasion of territory. Similar upheavals in other continents, however, have had important subsidiary impacts on Australian housing. Australian settlement, of course, was an indirect consequence of the American Revolution and movement of convicts from Britain. The population displacement and homelessness caused by the Irish potato famine of the mid-1840s increased the Australian population and housing demand for at least a decade after it peaked. Both world wars were followed by sustained pressures on Australia's housing demand as demobilisation progressed. The economic and social stress of coping with shortfalls in supply were accentuated by flawed soldier settlement schemes. In the late 1930s, increasing numbers of European refugees aggravated housing stress flowing from the Great Depression. Structural readjustment of housing stock, and markets after World War II, together with a vast immigration program, caused housing shortages and homelessness. Recurrent natural disasters of fire, flood and tempest destroyed valuable housing stock, but the combination of public assistance and private insurance mostly sufficed for restoration.

Because Australian homelessness has not been marked by dislocation of settlement patterns and dwelling occupation, has it been a relatively benign phenomenon? Certainly, the overall impact of lack of shelter has been mostly localised and intensive rather than national and widely diffused. But much remains to be explored; much remains to be explained about Australian homelessness. In an overview of Australian social welfare history in 1987, Brian Dickey concluded that a history of the poor in Australia was out of reach until more research was done.[4] So also is a history of homelessness in relation to poverty.

## Vagrant or destitute?

Conventional British processes of the Poor Law and the workhouse did not emerge in Australia as they had done belatedly in North America. Why not? Probably because in Australia's convict system, social control was assured until at least the 1830s. An absolute autocracy running a penal colony with the gallows and the lash did not require the relative subtleties of the Poor Law and the workhouse. With the government controlling coastal shipping and few road systems, traditional vagrancy was minimal. Absconding convicts were quickly recaptured in most cases, and harsh punishment discouraged unauthorised movement. Vagrancy and pauperism were readily confined to the population centres, where they could be dealt with either by the law or by rudimentary benevolent societies.

Dickey concludes that the 'full panoply of the English poor law' did not emerge in Australia because the British system itself changed extensively in the mid-1830s. This made it more difficult for the poor to gain 'indoor relief' whose staple was shelter. (Supplying sustenance and tools of trade was deemed 'outdoor relief'.) British work tests became more stringent, and the individual parish workhouses were consolidated into larger asylums for the destitute poor. The Australian authorities may have been deterred by these changes from accepting a statutory obligation to assist vagrants and the destitute:

> Often enough, the prospect of a poor law [in the Australian colonies] was held up to the public as a potential disaster because of the implied admission that conditions were therefore no better than those in England. In truth the main reason for the hostility to the approach in the colony lay more in the convenience of drawing funds from Britain rather than from the pockets of

local wealth. . . . In effect, the community was content that the costs were borne elsewhere (largely in London) and that a few devoted unpaid individuals were willing to administer it, while the poor were kept in subjection and out of sight with no acknowledged rights to assistance.[5]

In his copious survey of Australia's colonial practice and customs in the early 1870s, the British novelist Anthony Trollope concluded with accustomed dogmatism that there were no poorhouses in the colonies. The poorhouse, workhouse or union were peculiarly British and Irish, ensuring that men, women and children who could not, or would not, work were housed, fed and clothed at the public expense. It did not follow that because there were no poorhouses in Australia, there were no poor or that such poor should not be relieved: 'That which [the British] do by means of our parish unions, is done in Australia by benevolent asylums and hospitals. Both the hospitals and the benevolent society are supported chiefly from the [public] revenue.'[6]

...
Reliance on public funds largely emanating from the Crown in London, rather than raising private funds to alleviate destitution, was particularly attractive in New South Wales. Although the foundation of relief had been private charity, by the late 1830s benevolent and relief societies were largely funded by the Crown. In May 1813 the Benevolent Society of New South Wales was formed; among its objectives were 'to relieve the poor, the distressed the aged, and the infirm, and thereby to discountenance, as much as possible, mendacity and *vagrancy*, and to encourage industrious habits among the indigent poor as well as to afford them religious consolation in their distress'.[7]

The society collected charitable donations of some £102 sterling in its first year of operation. According to its first report in 1814, fifty-two cases were relieved in the early months of operation. In the second year donations increased to about £160 but already spending was running in excess of revenue. The number of 'Objects' relieved had risen to ninety-three:

> Many of these Objects have been assisted the entire of last year, and few less than three months; yet the average amount of relief has not been more than £1 15s 2d to each person; a proof, the [Committee trust] of their strict regard to economy in the distribution of the alms entrusted to their care . . . After 20 months weekly investigation of the state of the sick Poor of this small Town, they have become personally known to about 150 poor objects, and hear of many of their destitute connections; and, they trust, have acquired such experience as will, in a great measure if not entirely secure them from imposition.[8]

The terms 'poor objects' and 'sick poor' seem largely interchangeable, giving an inanimate detachment to destitution. Although 'objects' smacks more of fixtures than human flesh and blood, usages have changed since the early nineteenth century, and the society's reports are earnest and concerned. The society felt strongly that the peculiar structure of colonial New South Wales

290

was the principal source of super-abundant aged and destitute: 'of aged, because many are annually brought into it, in addition to those we have among us; of destitute, because the people are improvident'.[9]

The records suggest that the 'objects' relieved by the society were more the sick than the improvident poor:

> 4. a young woman, paralytic, deprived of Speech and Motion. [Given tea and a shift for five months until she died.] . . .
> 7. Man with a bad Cancer, which has consumed his face, eyes, mouth, palate, and nearly both eyes. [His rent was paid and he was given clothing, tea, arrowroot and bread for twelve months until he died.] . . .
> 9. . . . An old helpless man aged 85. [Given tea, bread, blankets and one bottle of wine.][10]

For those able to work, the benevolent and relief societies provided outdoor rather than indoor relief—food and implements, such as shovels and wheelbarrows, rather than shelter. This outdoor relief, however, had an indirect impact on homelessness because it diverted household needs from food, clothing and remunerative tools to accommodation. Also, income from work provided by tools made shelter more accessible.

The work of the Benevolent Society was taken up enthusiastically by Governor Lachlan Macquarie, and a distinctive mode of destitution relief began to emerge. Destitution asylums were funded and built by the colonial administrations, with private charities playing an important but supplementary role. For example, the asylum that Macquarie built in 1821 at government expense was administered largely by the Benevolent Society of New South Wales. According to Dickey, Macquarie used the English Poor Law to justify the venture, although no work test was applied. The asylum provided a refuge for destitute people absolutely without shelter, 'men, women and children as need demanded and space permitted'.[11] The admission figures for the Sydney asylum suggest that, while many residents were the chronically ill, alcoholics, and disabled, there were also transients, the temporarily homeless, whether arriving destitute in the colony or falling into abject poverty after arrival. Another specific function of some relief societies was to provide shelter and food for ageing convicts.

This mixed model was not achieved without resistance. In Tasmania, Governor George Arthur declined to succour the destitute from the public purse by building asylums, but insisted that relief should be funded from private charity. By the mid-1850s, however, the dual pattern of government buildings and private charity had been firmly established in Tasmania. The Sydney asylum eventually passed under government control, moving to Hyde Park and serving as a model for an institutional system administered by an Inspector of Public Charities. By 1883 similar asylums functioned at Parramatta and Liverpool; there was also the Erysipelas Hospital and Branch Asylum for the Infirm and Destitute at Parramatta. These asylums had surgeons, dispensers and matrons, suggesting that infirmity was the priority, although the infirm and the destitute homeless clearly overlapped.[12]

The other states adopted the public asylum system as the fundament of shelter for the sick and homeless. Some of the locational and administrative decisions seem peculiar to contemporary eyes. In Queensland, a Benevolent Asylum was established at Dunwich, an isolated community on Stradbroke Island. In South Australia a government office for the 'Destitute Poor' included a well-paid administrative board, a lying-in home, a girls' reformatory, an industrial school, a hulk for criminal and deserted children, and a series of auxiliary boards with 'clerks' in the principal country centres.

In Tasmania, a substantial framework of charitable institutions included general hospitals, lunacy asylums, the Brickfields Paupers Establishment, a Launceston Paupers Establishment for Males, a charitable establishment and a farm, and a well-staffed government branch for administering charitable grants. A Male Pauper Establishment, maintained by the government, was also described as a 'penal establishment'; it had a capacity for 148 paupers and an enviable take-up rate of 147. Although Victoria had a massive government machinery by the late nineteenth Century, only an Inspector of Public Charities was listed as an agent for helping vagrants and destitute. At least by the 1860s, however, a Benevolent Asylum and an Immigrants Home fully supported by the government were functioning in Melbourne. In Western Australia the official Poor House was administered by the Immigration Department and had only a small staff.

Besides asylums for the infirm and destitute, a formidable array of lunacy asylums emerged in the Australian colonies, and sheltered homeless people. For example, a descriptive note for one New South Wales mental asylum describes all occupants as 'residing within the building' and receiving rations, fuel, light and a uniform. The Tasmanian mental institutions were listed as charitable, rather than medical, institutions. In the larger states of Victoria, New South Wales and Queensland, the locational dispersal of mental asylums indicates that they provided some shelter for infirm and destitute homeless. Thus, mentally impaired people were sheltered in asylums for the destitute, and homeless destitute people admitted to lunatic asylums.

There are many fine literary depictions of the clientele and conduct of the asylums, the refuges of the destitute who could not afford even the sixpenny lodging houses. The most evocative, perhaps, is Marcus Clarke's vivid portrayal in the late 1860s of the Melbourne Immigrants Home, the only place in Melbourne where 'a man can obtain a supper and bed for nothing.[13] Excluding the criminal class, Clarke's 'Bohemia' comprised two types of homeless: the honest poor who 'won't work and won't steal', and the diseased, the crippled, the maimed, the halt and the blind 'who cannot work and who don't steal'. Both types resorted to a variety of improvised shelter:

> On the wharves, in gaspipes, behind sheds, near limekilns, in the parks and
> around the swamps . . . Some of them dine at the sixpenny eating houses, and

sleep at the sixpenny lodging houses; but all sooner or later sink to the common level of the [Immigrants] Home, and there we can see specimens of them all . . . this terrible Golgotha of ruined lives, this Immigrants Home, is close to the high road . . . and that at the moment I am writing these lines 'the applications for admittance and shelter are daily increasing in number and far exceed the means of accommodation.[14]

By the time Clarke wrote, the designation of Immigrants Home was largely a misnomer. It began in 1853 with the surge of goldrush immigrants, many lacking resources and distressed by the long, dangerous voyage. An Immigrants Aid Society raised private funds, with the state supplying a grant unconditional but variable. Although the buildings were decrepit and inadequate, it was regarded as clean, orderly and well-administered. The Immigrants Home comprised a straggling pile of buildings, with white entry gates and a burning lamp and bell providing access to clients, vigilantly monitored by the watchmen. The names of new entrants were entered into a book and they were fed. Notices for the conduct of visitors were posted on the wall, and the work test demanded of casual overnight guests was prominently displayed.

All able-bodied men were required to break not less than one-quarter of a cubic yard of road metal before breakfast or the time of leaving the home, as collateral for a night's shelter. Generally, this test was applied to previous inmates for more than two nights, or those who had been resident in Victoria for a year and had no immediate employment prospects. Failure to comply resulted in immediate expulsion and subsequent ineligibility for admission, unless suffering from sickness. Casuals staying overnight were differentiated from permanent occupants, who had comfortable beds in a sleeping place 'as clean and as sweet as a hospital ward'. The home admitted each night sixty more guests than there were beds, so the casuals slept on mattresses on the dining room floor. Many were classic vagrants: 'Next to us is H– –, who is a loafer pure and simple, and "lives about". His name is on the blacklist, for he has been given food and admitted eighty-nine times this year, and will not work; but as the night is cold and wet the authorities relent.'[15] Permanent occupants who could work were sent to 'the shed' to pick oakum or hair.

There were seventy-four women in the home, some young and supporting children whose illegitimacy prevented them from taking service in respectable homes. Others were also classic vagrants, in Clarke's eyes 'hideous, and repulsive, and dirty'. The women had a ward of their own, portrayed by Clarke as 'a sight worth seeing and not easy to forget'. Compared with the men, the women were regulated very strictly. Beds had to be made, children washed, and rooms cleaned by 10 a.m. Lights were extinguished at 8.30 p.m. Passes from the matron were needed for women to leave the home, and they had to return by 6 p.m. Women had to attend religious worship on Sunday and observe restricted meal hours. They were expected to work.

Generally, the regimen imposed on the men was more liberal, with a sort of modified club-like atmosphere pervading the sleeping quarters. The men

293

smoked and chatted, circulated newspapers, and could store books in their limited sleeping areas. Many of the permanents were incurables who could not work. It seems that the hospitals held some of these cases as long as they could but, inevitably, sent them to the Immigrants Home to die. Clarke described the institution in 1869 as in debt: private subscriptions were meagre and the government aid was wholly inadequate. He also praised its cleanliness, food and standards, much superior to the sixpenny lodging houses. The principal deficiency was the lack of good warm clothing.

The Immigrants Home was considered less desirable than the Benevolent Asylum, to which many of its permanents aspired: 'But it is full Sir, always full.' Indeed, the Melbourne Benevolent Asylum, accommodated in a 'truly magnificent building', was probably the pre-eminent institution for the homeless in the Australian colonies. Its charter was to relieve the aged, infirm, disabled and destitute of all creeds and nations, and to administer to them the comforts of religion. It was to receive and maintain in a suitable building those who would be most benefited by indoor relief. It also gave outdoor relief to families and individuals in temporary distress, provided medical assistance and medicine through its dispensary, and 'afforded facilities for religious instruction and consolation' to the inmates. In short, it was both a home for incurables and the closest approach to a traditional English poorhouse in Melbourne. Its vast dimensions comprising several large buildings, it was surrounded by tasteful pleasure grounds and, from an elevated and healthy site, it commanded a fine view of the city.

Those able to work were expected to contribute four hours of labour a day, part of it in production of clothing and household items for sale. Inevitably, many of the residents lacked even basic competencies for productive labour because of infirmities or 'previous habits'. The principal criticism made of the regimen by 'A Resident' who visited the asylum in the 1870s, was the lack of even rudimentary privacy in the sleeping wards. This caused the 'more respectable poor' to shrink from participating in the benefits of the asylum.[16] There were other smaller asylums in Melbourne, including the poorly regarded Sailors Home and the Old Colonists Home, whose eligibility covered arrivals dating back to 1851. Temporary relief was given to persons or families in distress by ladies' benevolent societies whose subscriptions were matched by state contributions. Unquestionably, however, the major burden of sheltering the numerous homeless, whether their situation was caused by poverty, infirmity, age, or unemployment, lay with the hospitals and asylums.

Because the Victorian system was probably the most generous of the Australian colonies—largely because of its gold-derived public wealth—there are dangers in generalising its qualities to the other states. Although there were variations, it seems that the fundamental model was essentially that of the commingling of charitable and public funding. The Victorian effort also seems to have been the most substantial relative to population. Figures quoted by Trollope from the early 1870s indicate that Victoria spent four times as much as New South Wales on hospitals and asylums (£135,945 to £33,224).[17]

In terms of overall relief, the commitment to the charitable institutions in late colonial Australia commands respect. Indeed, it may be questioned whether, relative to population and resources, subsequent public policy has done anywhere near as well in meeting the demands of the homeless. By the last quarter of the nineteenth century, however, the congealing of Australian social groups and patterns into more stable structures brought the accustomed charitable approach to shelter under increasing challenge. Although it was conceded that there was never any want of inmates for beds, 'investigations' had pronounced the number sheltered to be excessive, and calculated to encourage pauperism: 'therefore, it is probable that the Government support will shortly be withdrawn from those that are found to be superfluous'.[18] Familiar arguments!

The pages of the colonial press provide ample evidence of the prevalence of sleeping rough beyond the pale of the government asylums and the private societies. In Sydney, for example, where the climate was temperate for much of the year, and there was ready access to natural shelters around the harbour estuaries, coastlines and wooded hills, the risk of death by starvation or privation was still real enough. Death by exposure in the Sydney Domain was often used in a metaphorical sense in the colonial press of New South Wales to suggest the end-point of financial ruin or other colonial catastrophe. The columns of these journals also attest that, in a tangible sense, such a fate was common. More optimistically, much of this residue of homelessness was probably transferred to the boundless horizons and comparative licence of the Australian bush.

## Australia tramps

If Hoch's first category of 'vagrancy' as a conceptual basis for homelessness has to be refined somewhat by the Australian experience of destitution, his conception of 'tramping' is relevant if two major qualifications are made. First, tramping of the kind identified by Hoch was an earlier phenomenon in Australia than it was in America. Second, Australian tramps (or travellers), were motivated as much by the quest for a free, vagrant mode of living as they were by the search for work and permanency. Hoch's tramps were of a later vintage, and very much stimulated by the search for work and settlement:

> The rapid expansion of the national economy after the Civil War [1861–65] required a mobile work force of unsettled laborers. During the last quarter of the century hundreds of thousands of such transient workers called tramps, travelled across the United States, especially the western states. They mined, lumbered, herded, harvested, built, and otherwise labored to provide a crucial but overlooked economic contribution to national development.[19]

Most of these tramps included a substantial minority of foreign-born immigrants who, in their youth, travelled in search of work. The majority were white, law-abiding workers whose searches for work and shelter were given significant official tolerance. For example, transients were permitted access to police stations, where they endured cramped and often crowded quarters but were accommodated and fed. Poorhouses and mission refuges also sheltered tramps for little or no fee, although many transients found the religious imposition irksome. The lawlessness of jumping lifts on freight trains was often overlooked in the interests of keeping open the job-lines crisscrossing America.

In many ways, this was a high point in the relationship between law, society and a substantial vagrant class. There were, however, blemishes that eroded this tolerance and shortened its life. Hoch identifies a small element of social misfits known colloquially as 'bums'. It was hard to distinguish the *bums* in their poverty and homelessness from the *tramps* or *hobos* who resembled them but were genuine seekers of work. Furthermore, as labour markets coalesced in the great industrial centres and society stabilised, the population of the urban working class soared and the incursion of tramps became less welcome in communities where cheap housing was scarce and there were insufficient lodging houses to meet demand. It also became less acceptable for police to be diverted into controlling disease, poverty and homelessness at a time when crime rates were mounting. The heyday of tramping was over by the century's turn and increasingly the phenomenon of homelessness became tied to national business cycles.

In Australia, the phenomenon of 'tramping' emerged earlier and in a distinctly different guise. By the middle of the nineteenth century, the traveller was firmly installed in the social hierarchy of the Australian bush. This, of course, was largely due to mining, where the job-lines were defined by the latest Eldorados, and the pattern of movement was concentrated and predictable. Although based on 'tenting' and other transitory accommodation, and pervaded by rough outdoor living, 'homelessness' was not endemic in the years of the mining boom. Indeed, it generated eventual sites of settlement and housing development; witness Bathurst, Bendigo, Ballarat, Castlemaine. As the boom waned, the nomadic miners were diffused into more subtle forms of tramping.

Relatively, the job-lines of Australian tramping were much less crucial than American tramping networks. With employment opportunities outside the metropolitan areas overwhelmingly rural, patterns of movement, transportation and lodging were much simpler. In the Australian context, tramping has been dignified by numerous evocative labels: on the wallaby, waltzing Matilda, humping the bluey, swagmen, bagmen, illywhackers, bushwhackers, dossers. Historically, the most common usages were *travellers*, *loafers* and *swagmen*, referring to rural itinerants whose wanderings were directed as much to evading work as to locating it. In colonial Australia by the 1870s a firm tradition of support for the 'travellers' had emerged, a tradition underwritten, remarkably enough, in the often derogated persona of the Australian squatter. A contemporary account of life in colonial Victoria, published in 1876, refers to hordes of 'wanderers', some in search of work, others impelled by a 'wild, idle disposition'.[20] The stations of the squatters provided them with food and shelter, the calls for maintenance of 'travellers' forming a heavy charge on annual station revenue:

> As a class, the squatters have in this manner largely benefited the community, and have supplied from day to day with food and lodging numbers who, but for their liberality, must have perished, yet the services thus rendered have met with little recognition from the public, who coveted extensive leaseholds, and overlooked the heavy liabilities they entailed. The universal custom of receiving and feeding travellers led to the grossest abuse of hospitality. [21]

Marcus Clarke, who lived for some time in the Wimmera of Western Victoria described the region as the 'Feeding Track'. At one station in the Wimmera, three cooks were kept for the so-called 'Wallaby' season: one for the house, one for the men, and one for the travellers.

Trollope depicted the nomad tribe of Australian pastoral labourers in the 1870s as one of the strangest institutions ever known in a land.[22] In his eyes, it was more degrading and more injurious even than sheep stealing. Unfairly, Trollope lumped together as an exploitative class of travellers all men who 'professed' to be shepherds, boundary-riders, sheep-washers, shearers 'and the like'. The majority were *bona fide* workers providing essential labour to the squatters. Trollope had little gripe about the squatters entertaining in the station homestead 'travellers' of the superior class, presumably including himself. This was the exercise of a proverbial wide hospitality which had about it an Arcadian charm pleasing to the imagination. The charms of Arcady, however, were not to be wasted on the so-called workman with his swag. This, he said, enabled many men to follow a way of living enabling them to spend in rapid debauch the earnings from the labour of a few months and to exist in idleness for the remainder of the year:

297

> I heard of a squatter's establishment in Victoria at which £1,000 was expended in this involuntary entertainment of vagabond strangers. And the evil by no means ends here. A mode of life is afforded to recusant labourers which enables men to refuse work at fair terms, and to rebel against their masters when their work or their wages are not to their liking. They know that the squatters of the colonies do not dare to refuse them food and shelter.[23]

The squatters had some reason to fear reprisals. It was a relatively easy matter to leave open a gate or break down a fence so stock could stray, to kill an occasional beast, or burn grass, as Clarke recalled: 'I may mention as a strange coincidence that, was the requested hospitality refused by any chance, a bush-fire invariably occurred somewhere on the run within 12 hours.'[24]

Reprisals were a sombre reminder in a 'tramping' era often bathed in a retrospective nostalgic indulgence of the 'sundowners' who materialised out of the tree-line at sunset to claim their bed and rations without working for them.

The darker side, however, is typified not so much in the squatters' vulnerability to pay-backs as in the macabre end of many travellers who starved or died from serious injuries in the bush. Clarke dismissed one such story of a 'poor peripatetic' picked up near starvation in the bush: I take leave to remark that if a man dies of starvation on the Wimmera, he has no one to blame but himself.'

Other accounts confirm that perishing on the road or in the bush was not uncommon, despite the squatters' largesse:

> Painfully lingering deaths from want and exposure must have occurred far more frequently than could ever be ascertained among inexperienced travellers on the wide plains, or through the forest ranges. Occasionally remains of such were accidentally discovered, but many no doubt perished alone and unmissed, leading neither friend nor relative to regret them in a land of strangers.[25]

Implicit in this account of 'tramping' has been has been the notion of deviant homelessness, that temporary homelessness may become rejection of permanent shelter and its integuments. Many Australian travellers peregrinated on patterns of personal choice and satisfaction rather than sticking to the jobs and shelter of ordered job-lines. Edward Finn ('Garryowen') observed this phenomenon in the rural Victoria of the 1870s:

> I was much surprised to see two able-bodied men, who informed me that for 17 years they were swagging it from one place to another; indeed, they had travelled the colony and had no notion of now abandoning their nomadic way of life . . . They said they were not going to work for any master, and would eke out an existence for their remaining time in the world.[26]

The Australian variant of 'tramping' largely extinguished itself by innate drives towards settlement and permanency. The great era of the itinerant had ended by the turn of the century as the 'travellers' moved from vagrant freedoms subsidised by the land-holders to regular work and domicile. This domestication of the wandering Australian has yet to receive detailed study by historians, but Peter Carey's *Illywhacker*, who always contrived to build rudimentary shelter, illustrates the ends of rootlessness. The *Illywhacker* crafted dwellings with mud and wire netting, was a 'dab hand' at a slab hut, made houses from galvanised iron and the wooden crates that shipped the T-model Fords:

> I even spent one summer in the Mallee living in a hole in the ground. It was cool and comfortable in that hot climate and I would have got married but a poddy calf fell on top of us one night and broke the woman's arm. You can call that bad luck but it was my stupidity. I should have fenced it.[27]

The following checklist gives an impressionistic overview of historical homelessness as inherited from colonial Australia by the public policy and administration of a federated Australia. People who were likely to be homeless included:

- ageing ex-convicts, particularly those in poor health, disabled, or not skilled enough to find a place in the labour-market
- ex-convicts whose experiences in confinement had made them socially recalcitrant, incompetent or deviant
- free settlers who had arrived without sufficient means to establish themselves
- free settlers reduced in circumstances by financial or personal disasters
- recognised paupers, whether through formal bankruptcy and debt laws or by informal stigmatisation
- mentally impaired who evaded the net of the rather unpredictable lunacy laws of the time
- sane but eccentric persons unfairly caught by the lunacy laws
- itinerant workers seeking new opportunities
- travellers favouring a nomadic lifestyle beyond regular shelter and employment
- victims of emergencies and natural disasters
- women needing shelter for 'lying in' (childbirth)
- homeless children, often labelled delinquent or 'street arabs' in the colonial press and seemingly destined for reformatories.

## Deviant homelessness

According to Hoch's model of homelessness, in America the 'culture and autonomy' of the tramp had dwindled by the early twentieth century. Social controls were raised against a tramp-based homelessness that had previously been tolerated as part of 'melting pot' immigration and industrialisation, as traditional agriculture and mining in agriculture and minerals extraction declined. The evolution of radical politics helped incorporate working-class perceptions of homelessness and its causes into public policy. Increasingly, progressive reform acknowledged that unemployment sparked endemic homelessness. Substantial urbanisation meant that homelessness in America was perceived increasingly as a municipal phenomenon. Social theory moved its orientation from homelessness as a manifestation of personal vices and inadequacies to broader conceptions of social justice. In the academy, a major consequence was the conceptual growth of the sociological disciplines, linking with practical social work. Consequently, deviant homelessness was perceived as deriving more from insecurity than dependence.

Apart from a much greater emphasis on social case work, with the homeless family or individual treated as a client by professional social workers, two major innovations in public policy emerged. The first was the establishment of employment, or labour, exchanges to co-ordinate regional employment opportunities. Conjoined with this was the establishment of social insurance programs to counter the impact of sharp swings in the business cycle. Second, demands for shelter and support by deviant homeless were met by providing municipal, even neighbourhood, lodging houses. These had an element of environmental improvement, aiming to consolidate the deviant homeless by concentrating them in specific domains and containing Skid Row blight.

This deviant model expounded by Hoch provides for America a relatively coherent account of both the incidence of homelessness and remedial measures in the period roughly between the turn of the century and World War II (1900–40). There are superficial similarities here to the Australian experience during this period. The national insurance argument deriving from largely European social theory was extremely influential in the public policy debate. Non-Labor federal governments in the 1920s and 1930s sponsored extensive inquiry into national insurance schemes. Draft proposals for national insurance were presented in the late 1920s by the conservative Bruce–Page and Lyons–Page coalition governments in the late 1930s. Neither scheme was introduced. Strangely, no substantive proposal for national insurance was developed by the Australian Labor Party.

Universal entitlement principles, however, did have a crucial, although indirect, impact on homelessness as part of a spectrum of social policy issues. The severe depression in the colonial states during the 1890s stimulated the introduction of aged and invalid pensions, in New South Wales in 1900, and then by the federal government in 1908. Furthermore, the introduction of the living wage in Mr Justice Higgins's Harvester judgement of 1907 transformed the whole basis of social policy, as Dickey makes clear: 'No other single decision of the twentieth century in this field in Australia has done more than this creative judgement of Higgins to transform the lives of a whole sector of the community whose welfare in the nineteenth century had so often been a problem of selective charity.'[28]

Other aspects of Hoch's deviance model are relevant to Australia. The influence of social disciplines, particularly sociology and social work, gradually permeated social policy and practice but, in this period at least, did not match America in practical relevance. Some local government ventures provided co-operative and group housing for low-income earners, although not emergency shelter and deviant housing similar to American municipal lodging houses. The main source of change, however, was the displacement of charity-based assistance by universal entitlement to ameliorative assistance, including for homelessness and destitution.


## Victims and homelessness

From very early in the history of colonial Australia, the swings of the business cycle had influenced the supply of shelter and access to it. Although it is difficult to estimate precise cause and effect of economic dislocation in the early colonies, stringent economic recession was experienced in Sydney during the early 1840s. This was mirrored in the annual report of the Sydney Benevolent Society for 1843:

> Great as the number of persons is who have applied for and obtained relief during the past year, the committee fear that during the next, this number will be still greater. The general depression that prevails in every branch of business has begun now to bear with considerable weight upon the working classes . . . Many have been thrown out of employment, and many more, unless a great change for the better takes place, are likely to be in the same predicament.[29]

The cycle of homelessness induced by unemployment struck with much greater severity in the depression which afflicted all Australian colonies in the 1890s, perhaps most crushing in Victoria with the collapse of the land boom in Marvellous Melbourne. Overall, this depression lasted from the late 1880s until partial recovery in 1900. Although its incidence varied from state to state, it was comparable in extent, duration and peak intensity with the Great Depression of the 1930s. As noted earlier, one important consequence was legislation, first at colonial level and later through the federal government, seeking to stabilise the impact of economic recession by universal entitlement to pensions and other assistance. This marked the replacement of charitable relief with universal government programs. The depression posed difficult problems, particularly for relief of destitute families:

301

> The [1890s] depression was a heart-rending, confusing and exhausting phenomenon after so long a period of economic growth which had nurtured and reinforced, selective, moral notions of charity. The worst periods were in the winters of 1892 and 1893, particularly in Sydney and Melbourne.[30]

Swamped by an avalanche of applications from the destitute, the charitable institutions were forced to cut back assistance to the bare bones. This was also the era when evangelistic institutions such as city missions and the Salvation Army became entrenched as dominant providers of private social welfare assistance to the destitute and homeless in Australia. In varying degrees, even the most grudging colonial administrations were forced to assist the charitable institutions, although the Victorian and Tasmanian governments, in particular, expected private charity to bear the principal burden.

In the absence of social insurance, and with virtually no extension of entitlement to pensions and other social security support, particularly at the national level, Australia was ill-equipped to meet the Great Depression of the late 1920s and 1930s. Clearly, the application of basic wage standards was irrelevant in an era of mass unemployment. The federal government's inability to counter unemployment by an expansive fiscal policy and its adherence to orthodox budgetary management prevented any kind of effective New Deal in the Australian context. The dire consequence was an era of extreme homelessness far beyond the resources of an immature case-work approach. The response of state governments mostly reflected the impotence of federal government.

Although some attempt was made to provide emergency housing programs, these proved ineffectual. The law offered virtually no protection against foreclosure and repossession, and shanty towns of the dispossessed sprouted throughout the country. The tramping tradition of homelessness revived, this time without any semblance of idleness or exploitation. The 'tramps' of the 1930s overwhelmingly sought work, although their sustenance on the road also took some of the strain off hard-pressed families in urban areas. Unlike the 'tramping' of the late nineteenth century, the focus of work and sustenance was not the holdings of the squatters but the provincial and country towns, which bore a disproportionate part of the relief effort.

Furthermore, the great bulk of the population largely escaped the impact of the Depression, at least in terms of unemployment, homelessness and hunger. Unfortunately, this absence of fundamental deprivation was reflected often in an apathy, even hostility, towards mass relief and employment programs. In terms of housing stock forgone, the basis was established for later shortages of dwellings. Without the mobilisation of national resources to provide shelter programs, without social insurance for victims of a broken economy or substantial work relief projects, government agencies and private charities were swamped. Despite limited recovery in the late 1930s, economic recession did not abate until voluntary recruitment, and then conscription, combined with the high labour demands of a war economy to reduce economic hardship and hard-core homelessness. World War II also generated a high demand for housing in a market reflecting a cumulative shortage of dwelling stock that continued into the immediate postwar years.

This produced a quasi-homelessness which still vexes conceptual logic in assessing the impact of homelessness today. In short, are those who earn income and have the financial ability to pay for shelter to be considered as genuinely 'homeless' if, for structural reasons such as lack of housing stock, they double-up or share accommodation through necessity rather than choice? Were the returned soldiers and their baby-boom families who were forced to live with relatives victims of homelessness? Were those who had good incomes but little choice except to live in crammed dwelling space in any sense homeless? These were questions which re-emerged in the New Homelessness of the 1980s and 1990s, although reinforced by low incomes or subsistence on welfare payments. In the aftermath of World War II, this quasi-homelessness was rectified in part by special housing programs for ex-servicemen. Emergency housing was provided in new housing stock by state housing commissions and trusts established within the framework of the Commonwealth–State Housing Agreement. From the early 1950s, the private housing markets also mobilised in a great era of national development, which eventually eliminated remaining homelessness caused by lack of dwelling stock. Homelessness as a serious social problem did not re-emerge in Australia until the 1980s.

## The new homelessness

Conceptually, new forms of homelessness were first identified in America. Hoch concluded that the origins of New Homelessness lay with the conjunction in the early 1980s of the worst economic recession since the 1930s with unprecedented cutbacks in federally funded assistance programs by the Reagan administration. Generally, older segments of the workforce who had borne the brunt of the Great Depression were cushioned against housing deprivation by social insurance and security programs: 'The growing ranks of the underemployed and unemployed poor were not as fortunate . . . Middle-class families that ended up on the streets in the 1980s were the exception. Far more common were the unemployed male and female minority youths unable to find employment and a place to stay.'[31]

The New Homelessness in America also included the residual homeless from an era of relatively full employment and economic growth. These were generally deviants, mostly ageing men and women living in Skid-Row-type accommodation and resistant to social workers and case-study approaches.

A significant factor in the emergence of the New Homelessness was its essentially passive character. Unlike the earlier tramps of the late nineteenth century and the mass unemployed of the Great Depression, the New Homeless lacked the political and social clout to demand and obtain social reforms. Thus, they posed no serious threat to the integrity of the social fabric. New Homelessness was also coloured by a spirit of self-help, manifested in a modest corporatism receiving some municipal support but essentially private in its ethos and administration. Its public face was the mobilisation of homeless people to sell authorised journals on the streets, the sellers receiving part of the proceeds to provide them with shelter. This self-help, vendor approach was linked to more traditional relief and private fund-raising to ameliorate home-lessness. This phenomenon began in the major cities of America in the mid-1980s, spreading to Britain and other European countries in the early 1990s and, in relatively subdued form, to Australia in the mid-1990s. In some ways, it served as a yardstick for the relative intensity of homelessness, waxing and waning in harmony with economic cycles. Generally, these ventures into quasi-corporate organisation, as distinct from traditional co-operatives, were perceived favourably as a palatable alternative to conventional 'panhandling' (begging) on the streets.

In Australia, unemployment increased gradually from the mid-1970s, peaking around 10 per cent in the late 1980s and early 1990s, and stalling around 7–8 per cent in the late 1990s. High youth unemployment emerged as an intractable problem through the 1990s, a malaise largely impervious to economic recovery and responsive to the slightest economic slide. With home-lessness, the apparent inability of the markets to resolve intransigent youth unemployment was compounded by dwindling supply of suitable shelter. The classical model of urban housing markets assumes that the affluent classes

303

build new homes in undeveloped areas, leaving behind gradually deteriorating dwellings that become accessible to poorer people.[32] In Australia, this model has been eroded by redevelopment of old housing stock for high-density dwellings at higher unit prices. Thus, traditional low-income earners are cut out of the supply loop because the new stock provided is unaffordable. Further housing stress for the poor, invalid and elderly is caused by the gentrification and refurbishment of traditional single-room occupancies in hotels and residentials. The burden of change in traditional supply falls with particular intensity on the deviant homeless.

A chronic shortage of jobs is not the sole explanation for the youth homelessness phenomenon in Australia. Social changes in the pattern of youth movements in and out of the family home are also crucial factors. Briefly, the problem is twofold. Young people are moving out of home earlier, often before they finish schooling. The move is not to employment and independence in the accustomed mode, but to unemployment and, frequently, a dependence on crime for support. This is a manifestation of the traditional 'street arab' problem, but caused by social malaise rather than sheer poverty.

The homelessness of the very young has been perceived as malignant homelessness, in that it causes hardship, perhaps even permanent disadvantage. By contrast, benign homelessness causes relatively little hardship, lasting for a relatively short time, and recurring rarely. It may be argued that the return home of older youths, even young adults, is mostly benign in its incidence. There are signs, however, of recurrent and longer returns in the Australian experience, pointers to an increasingly malign homelessness. Returning home of the young unemployed also threatens the housing security of parents increasingly susceptible to downsizing and redundancy in the workforce. Thus, the New Homelessness in Australia should not be perceived as confined to unemployed youth and the traditional deviant.

In terms of public policy, little has been achieved by government to remedy or mitigate the impact of the New Homelessness. Formal channels of federal relations have failed repeatedly to establish responsibility for youth homelessness. Despite a plethora of reports, an effective co-ordinating framework for government and private relief for youth homelessness has yet to emerge. For example, an attempt in the early 1990s to establish protocols delineating responsibility for government assistance to youths up to seventeen years who were considered at risk ended in failure and confusion. Both public and private relief were ill-equipped to cope with what seemed an inevitable diversification of homelessness to include more young, more women, more rural people, more of the better educated, more members of family units, more members of minority groups, and more mentally ill. Demographically, the homeless in Australia are moving towards the norm: they are becoming more like the rest of us. These are the New Homeless in Australia, the product of evolutionary social and economic processes extending over almost two hundred years, a homelessness increasingly malignant and less benign.

1   Christopher Hill, *Liberty Against the Law: Some 17th Century Controversies* (London, 1996), p. 47.
2   'A Brief History of the Homeless Problem in the US', in Richard D. Bingham, Roy E. Green and Sammis B. White (eds), *The Homeless in Contemporary Society* (Newbury Park, 1987), p. 18.
3   *Ibid.*
4   *No Charity There: A History of Social Welfare in Australia* (Sydney, 1987), p. xvii.
5   *Ibid.*, p. 18.
6   Anthony Trollope, *Australia* (London, 1983) p. 709.
7   Dickey, *No Charity There*, p. 15.
8   Benevolent Society of NSW, *Annual Report for 1813* (Sydney, 1814), p. 4.
9   *Ibid.*, pp. 12–17.
10  *Ibid.*
11  Dickey, *No Charity There*, p. 16.
12  *The Official Almanac for Australia* (1883), p. 164.
13  L. T. Hergenthan (ed.), *A Colonial City: High and Low Life. Selected Journalism of Marcus Clarke* (1972), p. 173.
14  *Ibid.*, p. 134.
15  *Ibid.*, p. 137.
16  Marguerite Hancock (ed.), *Glimpses of Life in Victoria by 'A Resident'* (1996), p. 285.
17  *Australia*, pp. 709–10.
18  Hancock, *Glimpses of Life in Victoria*, p. 284.
19  Hoch, 'A Brief History of the Homeless Problem', p. 19.
20  Hancock, *Glimpses of Life in Victoria*, p. 163.
21  *Ibid.*
22  *Australia*, pp. 139ff.
23  *Ibid.*
24  Hergenthan (ed.), *A Colonial City*, p. 33.
25  Hancock, *Glimpses of Life in Victoria*, p. 166.
26  Margaret Weidenhofer (ed.), *Garryowen's Melbourne, 1835–1852* (Melbourne, 1967), p. 170.
27  *Macquarie Dictionary of Quotations* (1990), p. 200.
28  Dickey, *No Charity There*, p. 185.
29  Benevolent Society of NSW, *Annual Report for 1813*, p. 114.
30  Dickey, *No Charity There*, p. 75.
31  Hoch, 'A Brief History of the Homeless Problem', pp. 27–8.
32  Dickey, *No Charity There*, p. 101.

# Lowering the Standard

## Chapter 18

*Patrick Troy*

306      We saw in Chapter 2 that governments in the various colonies and states were slow to introduce building regulations covering structural safety and health aspects of housing. By early in the twentieth century all states had developed a set of regulations covering building. Although New South Wales had some regulations under the 1837 *Building Act*, it was the last state to introduce comprehensive building regulations, under the *Local Government Act 1919*. Victoria had been the first to do so in 1890. By the mid-twentieth century all states had extended their regulatory framework to cover land development. The evidence cited in this chapter is mostly drawn from New South Wales and Victoria, but the conclusions and generalities apply with equal force to the other States.

     Since Federation the formal responsibility for all aspects of urban regulation has lain with the states; the federal government displayed little interest in this area of policy or administration until World War II. The standard of housing, especially of low-income households, however, drew critical comment from social commentators and politicians, state and federal, throughout the period.

     Although each state's regulations were designed to address similar concerns, there was little uniformity between them. The regulations were often introduced in response to some specific incident: they followed some particularly disastrous episode or sequence of episodes in which people's lives were lost or injuries were sustained due to lack of fire prevention, structural weakness or unhealthy conditions. There was little translation of the experience in one colony or state to the next and, when there was, the differences in the political situations in other states led to different sets of regulations. For the most part, such regulations as were adopted were developed to meet the conditions in the inner city; scant concern was given to the housing in outer suburban or country areas.

## Uniform building regulations

When regulations were introduced in each state, local governments within them had a high degree of freedom in the standards they set. Consequently local governments varied widely in their standards. This was of no particular concern at the time; in fact, it was seen as a strength because it reflected the diversity of each community's attitudes and aspirations. For example, although Victoria had discussed the need for a uniform code of by-laws in the 1918 Royal Commission on the Housing Conditions of the People in the Metropolis and acknowledged the need to apply 'the laws of hygiene to the design of houses',[1] it was not convinced by the case for uniform regulations. The Victorian government did not introduce Uniform Building Regulations until 1945, and when they were introduced they were strongly opposed.[2] In Sydney in the 1870s there was little desire to introduce regulations for fear they would increase costs and discourage development (arguments which had accompanied the introduction of the original 1837 act); it was felt that regulations would be a tacit recognition that Sydney was not the paradise its proponents claimed, although a significant proportion of its housing was regarded as substandard.

The differing standards within each state, together with variable enforcement, increased the disparities in housing quality within and between the cities as they grew. The disparities between the standard of housing in the metropolis compared with that in rural towns also increased. Both Sydney and Melbourne had large amounts of poor-quality housing, to which attention was drawn by numerous inquiries and commissions. All the attempts to introduce building regulations were attempts to lift the standard of housing, especially that occupied by low-income households.

Owners (especially of rented accommodation), builders and architects were among the most vociferous opponents of the introduction of building regulations from the earliest initiatives in the nineteenth century.

Initially variations in building regulations within and between states were of little economic concern. By the mid-1960s, as states progressively introduced regulations, the large builders began to complain about the variation between local government areas in the regulations for the provision of urban services. Some of these were set in order to establish high standards for particular areas. In some cases local authorities sought to minimise future maintenance costs, in others to exclude low-income residents. Builders faced significantly different regulations in adjoining local government areas and, on occasion, found that adjoining local governments applied different regulations to developments that spread across boundaries. They pressed for uniformity.

Building suppliers found that the regulations governing the supply of fixtures and fittings varied in ways that were difficult to comprehend or justify. The laws of physics applied with equal force across the nation, yet the size of plumbing fittings varied from one jurisdiction to the next. Similar unjustifiable variations existed in relation to electrical fittings.

Not only did regulations governing the ventilation of buildings vary, but many were based on outmoded scientific notions and their administration had fallen into disrepute. In other cases local governments had been slow to revise their regulations to take account of technological advances and the development of new materials or construction processes. In New South Wales the regulations governing ventilation of buildings that had been in place since the 1880s were based on miasmatic theories of disease transmission. They were revised in 1973. Dwellings were no longer required to have external ventilators to every habitable room, and it was no longer necessary to separate bathrooms from laundries—although the great majority of new dwellings continued to have separate laundries.

## Commonwealth involvement

In creating the Commonwealth Housing Commission in 1943, the federal government began the process of engaging with the states in considering housing and development standards. The commission was charged with inquiring

into and reporting on 'the present housing position in Australia; and . . . the housing requirements of Australia during the post-war period'.[3] The commission interpreted this to mean it was to consider issues of supply as well as quality of housing and urban development, as it explained in the letter presenting its final report: 'We consider that a *dwelling of good standard and equipment is not only the need but the right of every citizen*—whether the dwelling is to be rented or purchased, no tenant or purchaser should be exploited by excessive profit. [emphasis in original].'[4] The commission clearly felt that it was making the case for improving housing standards. There was a sense that community standards rose over time and that it was bad policy to countenance the construction of low-standard housing which would be part of the urban fabric for a century or so.

The Commonwealth Housing Commission recommended the creation of the Experimental Building Station. Its establishment within the Department of Post-War Reconstruction in 1944 was the second step by the federal government to engage in housing standards issues. The station began operations in 1944. Its initial work was related entirely to housing and aimed to develop improved housing systems and materials in order to reduce housing costs and allow replacements for materials in short supply.

When a new Department of Works and Housing was created in 1946, the Experimental Building Station was transferred to it. An advisory committee was formed to ensure the full investigation of all technical matters and the establishment of a close relationship between the station and the practical requirements of the building industry generally. This committee was disbanded in 1948 when the CSIR (later CSIRO) and the Department of Works and Housing agreed on the need for co-ordination of research in building. From its inception the CSIR also carried out research on housing issues, such as its work on timber performance in house framing, which led to the adoption of new Australian standards.

The first attempt to introduce uniform national regulations came with the recommendation in the final report of the Commonwealth Housing Commission in 1944 that such a code should be framed.[5] This recommendation was not immediately acted on, but it became a call for more 'rational' regulations and probably spurred the states into developing uniform building regulations. The activities of the Experimental Building Station, the CSIRO and the Australian Standards Association all improved understanding of the issues involved in building construction and performance, and contributed to an increasing demand for the adoption of uniform standards.

The first meeting between the federal government and the states on housing issues was held early in 1945 so that federal officials could explain how the Commonwealth–State Housing Agreement would work. State officials and ministers soon found that they had sufficient reason to meet frequently to share information and experience and to develop a common response to the federal government. These meetings became a regular mechanism for the exchange of information over housing standards, and the federal government sought to send an official as an 'observer'. The meetings are now held regularly and chaired by the federal minister for housing. It can be argued that the Commonwealth–State Housing Agreement not only served to lift the standard of housing for low-income households but that by setting benchmarks it also forced a general improvement in housing quality.

The adoption and enforcement of building regulations led to increasing uniformity within each state, although substantial differences between them remained. With the evolution of building suppliers and builders which operated in several local government areas or in several states, criticism was raised about the lack of uniformity and the resulting inefficiencies.

Shared concerns over urban issues saw the state ministers for local government meet to pool their experience. Partly in response to this rising concern, the Local Government Ministers Conference in 1964 established the Interstate Standing Committee on Uniform Building Regulations.

By the late 1960s the general move for deregulation, coupled with the demand for standardisation of regulations, had created a climate in which federal politicians again began to see a role in sponsoring a national set of building regulations. The arguments were based on notions of 'administrative tidiness' as much as any other consideration, although the case for standardisation of electrical and plumbing fixtures seemed unassailable.

The Whitlam governments of 1972–75 set out to produce national standards governing urban development. Whitlam made much of the lack of standardisation and its consequences, with telling effect, drawing attention to the handicaps in fire-fighting when the size of fittings differed from one area to another. He also pointed out some of the difficulties in suburban development created by the different standards set by adjoining local government authorities. He used these examples as supplementary points in arguing the

309

case for federal involvement in urban development. Clearly there were inefficiencies that needed to be remedied and areas where the regulations had fallen into disuse and disrepute, but the federal government exaggerated the problems.

In the argument for standardisation, the case for regional variation and diversity was not strongly put. The tardiness of the states in reviewing and modernising building and development regulations provided the opportunity for the federal government to take initiatives, supported by the national organisations representing builders, land developers and building suppliers. Local government also became engaged in developing standardised regulations, in part because the initiative gave it an opportunity to become involved in negotiations at the national level—it was implicit acceptance of its important role and supported its claim for recognition as an independent level of government.

## Australian Model Uniform Building Code

310    The Interstate Standing Committee produced the Australian Model Uniform Building Code (AMUBC).

Most of the basic work leading to the regulations, especially relating to fire protection, was developed in the Experimental Building Station at Ryde, New South Wales. It was intended that the AMUBC would be based as far as practicable upon performance criteria together with deemed-to-comply provisions that satisfy the criteria. It was also intended that provisions would be developed to ensure that the standards required in building construction warranted the costs and would be an economical solution to meet the requirements of fire safety, structural safety, public health and consumer protection. In New South Wales this code was embodied in Ordinance 70 of the 1973 amendments to the *Local Government Act*.

In 1979 the Local Government Ministers Conference reviewed progress towards uniformity of approach through the AMUBC and in 1980 the Australian Uniform Building Regulations Coordinating Council was established. An inter-government agreement set out its role and function and included the basis of the arrangement between the parties to provide finance for research and development. The council consisted of state and territory administrators responsible for building control, with representatives of federal and local government. Its work was supported by the Department of Housing and Construction.

A major task of the Coordinating Council was the further development of the AMUBC as the technical basis for building control which could be adopted or adapted by all state and territory building control administrations and called up by reference in their legislation. The Coordinating Council devised the code, as far as practicable, on performance criteria together with 'deemed to comply' provisions which satisfied the criteria. The assumption was that provisions were to be developed to ensure that the standards required in building construction carried benefits commensurate with their cost and were economical solutions to meet the requirements of fire and structural safety, public health and consumer protection. The Coordinating Council produced a consolidated version of the AMUBC in April 1982.

The requirement for uniformity in the regulations meant that the standard had to be written for the lowest common denominator: states with higher standards had to reduce them. It was argued that the important thing was uniformity; later the standards could gradually be raised. In this argument regional and state variation were viewed as being of limited significance compared with the perceived benefits of uniformity. This argument was echoed later when, in order to gain the benefits thought to flow from globalisation of the economy, it was argued that Australia should reduce its regulatory framework.

## Australian Model Code for Residential Development

The process of producing uniform urban development regulations continued in the 1980s. In 1989 Edition 1 of the Australian Model Code for Residential Development (AMCORD) was released, with Edition 2 the following year. Both were prepared by the model code task force of the Green Street Joint Venture —an initiative by the government and housing industry, under which the federal government funded 'demonstration projects' to show that high-density housing could be of high quality. The initiative paid no attention to the history of similar projects that had been undertaken at different times. As with the earlier demonstrations, the private sector did not rush to build to the new standards, in spite of the claims that they would lower costs and increase returns. Those projects that were built or sponsored by the public sector tended to be for high-standard housing. Much of that built by the private sector and some built by the public sector at costs that low-income households could afford soon earned the epithet 'mean streets', rather than the Green Streets of the handsome brochures published to advertise the program and the building codes.

The pressure to pursue urban consolidation as a way of reducing demand for infrastructure investment continued and in 1991 the Special Premiers' Conference and the meeting of the Commonwealth State and Territories Housing Ministers' Conference called for the production of a code for higher-density housing. This code, AMCORD: Urban, was released for discussion in 1992.

In June 1991 the Victorian government produced the Victorian Code for Residential Development (VicCODE), based on AMCORD Edition 2 and its own initiatives of 1988. The purpose of this code was to give a 'wider range of housing choice' and to produce 'more cost-efficient use of infrastructure'. The accompanying publicity claimed that the existing codes had 'stifled innovation and increased costs'. It argued that escalating production costs resulting from the existing codes had put 'home ownership beyond the reach of a growing

311

number of Victorians', yet there was little evidence that home ownership rates had fallen. It made extreme claims, such as that the 'deposit for a median-priced home' had risen from 92 per cent of annual average income in 1983 to 277 per cent in 1990, but these seemed to be a political agenda to reduce housing standards rather than a sober analysis of the situation. The alleged dissatisfaction with the supply of housing was not reflected in household surveys, which suggested that the traditional free-standing house with its own garden was the preferred form of accommodation. Undeterred, the Green Street Task Force argued that, with appropriate campaigns, the public could learn to like the new smaller forms of accommodation.

In late 1993 Victoria introduced the Victorian Code for Residential Development: Multi Dwellings, based on AMCORD: Urban. It claimed that the code would 'give Victorians more chance of finding appropriate and affordable housing' by increasing density. None of the claims was based on rigorous research. The Victorian document was followed in 1994 by a similarly vague attempt at a national level, by an Urban Design Task Force appointed by the prime minister. The report of this Task Force rationalised the departure from setting minimum standards for housing and development, relying instead on a weakly defined commitment to high-quality design as a way of producing urban space of high amenity and efficiency. It was part of the campaign to reshape the attitudes of Australians to their cities and to get them to accept lower standards.

At the time of writing a consortium of private sector interests, together with some of the professional institutes, are engaged in an endeavour to 'reform' development controls on urban development, including subdivision and land use decisions. No attempt is being made to include the public or local government in the process; it is designed to establish a highly centralised system with the effect of reducing the rights of citizens and communities in responding to development proposals. In this initiative the private sector is trying to use a highly centralised institutional structure to achieve the deregulation of planning and development.

## Building Code of Australia

In 1990 the Australian Uniform Building Regulations Coordinating Council was transformed into the Australian Building Codes Board, which had the responsibility for producing and maintaining the Building Code of Australia (BCA90) published that year.

By 1996 when the revised Building Code of Australia (BCA96) was published, the circle was completed. Prescriptive regulations that had raised minimum standards of housing were replaced by 'performance-based' regulations. Theoretically these regulations allow flexibility in the design of buildings so that they meet the regulations appropriate to their use. The implication is that if buildings are operated in a manner which is inconsistent with their design and they therefore fail to meet their performance standard, owners may be required to cease the activities, make modifications or demolish them. The idea of performance-based building regulations was not new. Such an approach had been raised in some of the early research and was an important element in developing the AMUBC in the 1980s.

The states are progressively adopting the BCA and including it in their own legislation. New South Wales, for example amended its *Local Government Act* to adopt BCA96 in 1997.

## Performance-based regulations

The move from prescriptive to performance-based building regulations raises a number of concerns. It is claimed that performance-based regulations will streamline the approvals process—reduce waiting time and costs—and allow more flexibility in design and therefore more choice of housing types. The price for this convenience is reduced safety. The New South Wales legislation based on the BCA effectively deregulates the approval and development process. Performance-based codes are so loosely defined that they provide little control over developers' activities. The risk to public safety arises because these regulations are not legally binding: this opens the way for opportunistic developers to use cost-cutting practices that compromise the physical safety of buildings. Furthermore, the lack of prescriptive guidelines raises issues of accountability when things go wrong in the event of structural failure or fire: who is responsible? builder, building inspector, architect, municipal council, building owner, owner of business in the building, fire authorities? Another consequence of the departure from prescriptive regulations is that the interests and concerns of people with physical and sensory disabilities tend to be overlooked. Standards that specify the kinds of access which must be provided for disadvantaged people are more likely to enable participation than loosely defined performance standards such as the amount of open space, preservation of trees, aesthetic and amenity values.

Performance-based standards, allied with deemed-to-comply provisions, significantly reduce the opportunity for public participation in decision-making. This is a special concern in relation to site planning, subdivision and development because it can prevent the achievement of a variety of urban planning objectives.

Compounding these concerns is the possibility that approval of a proposal—determination of whether it meets the standards—could be 'outsourced' to private assessors. The assumption is that standards can be preset, thus eliminating discretionary aspects of the regulations: but in many, if not most, situations it is impossible to specify issues in advance in a standardised way. The engagement of private assessors in building approvals can reduce access by ratepayers to decision-making and open significant opportunities for corruption. It also raises questions about where liability lies following any structural or other failure of a building approved in such a way. In some states private assessors are required to insure themselves against the risk of litigation following some failure, but how long that responsibility can be maintained is in question. The new state regulations in New South Wales and Victoria also reduced the size of allotments, the minimum size of rooms and ceiling heights.

Although federal and state politicians spoke about the need for diversity and community participation, their respective governments adopted policies which had the effect of reducing it. The Victorian and New South Wales governments not only introduced population targets for local authorities, but also said that local authorities that did not achieve the targets would have their powers taken away and the state government would approve developments to ensure that the population targets were met.

The policy of consolidation has failed to produce savings in infrastructure costs, to reduce environmental stresses, or to increase housing choice. Moreover, it has led to greater polarisation and segregation.[6] Australian cities, which had been characterised by Hugh Stretton as being remarkably egalitarian in terms of the housing they offered,[7] are becoming unequal as a consequence of housing policies being forced on the population.

314 The history of the introduction of uniform building and development regulations provides us with insight into the workings of the political process. In the nineteenth century the lack of regulations or their low level of enforcement led to large numbers of dwellings (and other buildings) that were substandard. Chapter 2 pointed out that such standards as were applied in Australia were not even up to the contemporary standards in Britain at the time. It is clear that the progressive introduction of standards led to healthier, better housing for all, including low-income households. Nevertheless, at each stage in the development of regulations, builders and building owners opposed the measures.

The attempts by the federal government to enter the field provided an opportunity for the states to support the initiative. They acted as though national standards were a desirable end in themselves, without obviously appearing to their own constituency to be working for the reduction of housing quality. Appeals were made to 'national trends' in household size, dwelling size, alleged lack of housing choice, ill-defined but attractive ideas such as social and environmental sustainability, greater energy efficiency. None of these was buttressed by rigorous research, and some were clearly incorrect or wrongheaded. In some cases the connection with building standards was, at best, tenuous and usually contentious or problematic. The process of introducing national standards appears to be a cover for a deliberate lowering of standards. Government agencies spent such huge sums proselytising and making the case for the new codes that their efforts could be described as attempts to manipulate attitudes.

It is too early to be able to report on the effect of the new codes on building standards or housing choice. It is clear from the 1999 New South Wales and Victorian state government elections and the New South Wales local government elections that the community is strongly opposed to them. We have some evidence that the consolidation policy is increasing segregation and polarisation, but we do not have empirical evidence about the impact of the BCA on dwelling standards. The Swedish experience following the 1993 deregulation that removed prescriptive standards revealed a fall in the size of flats of 10 per cent in net floor area and, within them, a fall in bedroom size. There was some increase in housing choice, but at the expense of flexibility and usable space. The fear in Sweden is that the deregulation will lead to a loss of knowledge of buildings and how they are used, and the difference between good and bad quality housing will increase.[8] We cannot expect to replicate Swedish experience, but there is reason to believe that similar deregulation will produce similar falls in standards in Australia.

This chapter highlights a problem common to many areas of urban policy. The beneficiaries of many initiatives fall into two categories: those who stand to make direct, immediate and substantial gains, and those whose benefit is indirect, often delayed and frequently small. The former group is usually small and well-organised, the latter large and unorganised. Many in the latter group do not understand the connection between a policy, or changes proposed to it, and their own interest. This is especially the case in situations where the proposed changes do not seemingly affect the present situation of the population. Reductions in standards do not affect existing structures or developments; the problems resulting from low standards take some time to appear in sufficient magnitude to lead to public demands for the introduction of regulations to rectify them. The development of performance-based codes and the attendant deemed-to-comply provisions seriously limit the ability of governments, local and state, to protect the public interest.

The story of the introduction of building standards records responses to a set or series of incidents that threatened or occasioned sickness, injury and death and destruction of property; regulations were introduced to eliminate or minimise such dangers. The high standard of living attained by urban Australians results from the long, determined efforts by a host of activists and reformers leading political campaigns to improve living conditions for the low-income members of society. The flag they flew was one of progress and equity. The recent history of the introduction of national standard building codes is one of striking the colours, of lowering the standard. It is just as much a departure from the commitment to an egalitarian society as the capitulation to the demands of those who seek deregulation of the labour market and the introduction of market-led provision of educational and health services.

315

# Notes

1   Victorian Parliamentary Papers, Royal Commission on Housing Conditions of the People, *Second Progress Report* (Melbourne, 1918), p. 4.
2   *Victorian Year Book* (Melbourne, 1984), p. 239.
3   Commonwealth Housing Commission, *Final Report* (Canberra, 1944), p. 8.

4   *Ibid.*

5   *Ibid.*, p. 87, para. 632.

6   Patrick Troy, *The Perils of Urban Consolidation* (Annandale, NSW, 1996).

7   Hugh Stretton, *Housing and Government: Boyer Lectures* (Sydney, 1974).

8   U. Westerberg and J. Eriksson, personal communication, 1998; U. Westerberg and J. Eriksson, *Dwelling Habits and Values: Inertia and Change* (Stockholm, 1997).

319

321

323